EIGHTH EDITION

Mass Media and American Politics

Doris A. Graber
University of Illinois at Chicago

CQ PRESS

A Division of SAGE
Washington, D.C.

CQ Press
2300 N Street, NW, Suite 800
Washington, DC 20037

Phone: 202-729-1900; toll-free, 1-866-4CQ-PRESS (1-866-427-7737)

Web: www.cqpress.com

Cover design: Anne C. Kerns, Anne Likes Red, Inc.
Cover illustrations: Anne C. Kerns, Anne Likes Red, Inc.
Composition: C&M Digitals (P) Ltd.

♾ The paper used in this publication exceeds the requirements of the American National Standard for Information Sciences—Permanence of Paper for Printed Library Materials, ANSI Z39.48-1992.

Printed and bound in the United States of America

13   12   11   10   09   1   2   3   4   5

Library of Congress Cataloging-in-Publication Data

Graber, Doris A. (Doris Appel)
  Mass media and American politics / Doris A. Graber.—8th ed.
     p. cm.
  Includes bibliographical references and index.
     ISBN 978-1-60426-460-9 (pbk. : alk. paper) 1. Mass media—Social
aspects—United States. 2. Mass media—Political aspects—United States. I. Title.

HN90.M3G7 2009
302.230973—dc22

                                                                        2009024413

To

Tom, Susan, Lee, Jim, and Jack
—my very special students

CONTENTS

TABLES, FIGURES, BOXES, AND ILLUSTRATIONS

Tables

Figures

Boxes

Illustrations

PREFACE

News media are crucial in a democratic society because citizens need information about ongoing problems and policies. What happens to public life if established news-gathering institutions contract sharply because their main sources of income and their audiences are shriveling? What difference does it make if these debilitating shrinkages are mostly due to the explosive growth of new news channels? These are important questions at a time when established media institutions are wrestling with the challenges created by the Internet. The new technologies that are changing the news media scene require reinventing the media world. That reinvention was unfolding when this book went to press in summer 2009.

The reinvention represents a marriage of old and new technologies, fueled by mutual respect and tolerance for a great deal of diversity. As in previous periods of rapid technological change, the established media are surviving in familiar formats or in hybrid shapes, such as Web versions of traditional offerings. However, legacy media are hampered by radically reduced resources, and their control over news content is sharply diminished. The "new media" upstarts are filling some of the empty turf but largely rely on legacy media professionals for deciding what becomes news and then to gather and report it. The new media primarily provide commentary about the reported happenings. Most notably, much discussion on the Web is interactive, and Web-based communities of like-minded people have emerged. News transmission channels have become multidirectional paths, over which ordinary citizens and media elites engage in genuine conversations, rather than media elites preaching to silent flocks who lack opportunities for responding.

The most urgent problem looming over media development in the summer of 2009 was uncertainty about the means to pay for news creation and distribution. Clearly, advertising can no longer be the financial mainstay of established media, nor can it sustain the many new channels mushrooming on the Internet. What should take its place? What will take its place? There were numerous suggestions but no indication of the viability of any of these. It also remains unclear what choices various publics will make to assemble their individual news packages from the overabundance of available news sources on the Web. In this era of changing demographics and altered personal and business lifestyles, coupled with advancing technologies, who will determine the main thrust of political news in the second decade of the twenty-first century?

To make sense of what is currently happening one must understand the characteristics of the U.S. mass media system as well as the political, economic, and technological forces that are propelling the current transformations. The eighth edition of *Mass Media and American Politics* serves as a guide and interpreter.

It features up-to-date information about the structural and organizational characteristics of the current media system and the human factors and events that continually reshape its contours. The text focuses on news disseminated by over-the-air and cable television and by print or Web-format newspapers because they are still the chief sources of current political information for people in public and private life. But it also gives ample attention to the impact of the Internet on the information stream and on politics. The chapters highlight the many public policy issues that the new media have raised. Citizens must understand the implications of these issues so that they can voice their concerns when policies are still in the making.

The story told in this new edition draws on the rich array of current political communication studies, including my own research on television's impact on citizens' understanding of politics. The book's perspective is multi-disciplinary and objective, offering a variety of viewpoints about controversial issues. Readers can form their own opinions and evaluations from this evidence and from other studies of the news media reported in the ample, up-to-date citations. The text is written simply and clearly to serve the needs of novices in this area of knowledge without sacrificing the scholarly depth, documentation, and precision that more advanced readers require.

This new edition of *Mass Media and American Politics*, like prior editions, takes a broad approach to mass-mediated political communication. It covers the impact of media on all spheres and phases of political life, at all levels of government, in normal times and times of crisis. It does not limit itself to studying the relationships between media and politics during elections, which have been the prime focus of past news media studies.

Chapters 1 and 2 set the stage with descriptions of the mass media as institutions within the U.S. political system. The chapters explain how governmental structures and functions affect journalists and media institutions and how the media, in turn, influence politicians and the work of all branches of government. The discussion highlights the consequences of the proliferation of news outlets and the continuing debate about appropriate regulatory policies. Chapter 3 completes the analysis of the legal, political, and economic framework in which U.S. media operate. The discussion focuses on the legal rights of citizens, public officials, and journalists to gather and publish information and to seek protection from damaging publicity.

Chapter 4 deals with the many factors that affect the daily selection of news topics and the creation of stories about people and events. The chapter highlights reporters' backgrounds and orientations and details how they go about their work and the major challenges they face. It also appraises the quality of current news compared to that of the past. Chapter 5 describes how news patterns change during crises, such as natural disasters and wars. It clarifies the important role of news media in dealing with the difficulties facing people and their governments when normal life is disrupted. Chapter 6 deals with the ethical problems and political consequences of political activism by journalists. I define the barriers journalists face when they investigate corruption and other misbehaviors by public officials, business tycoons, or religious leaders. In chapter 7, I explore the wealth of new information that political communication scholars have accumulated to understand political learning and opinion formation. I also discuss the role of news in fostering pro-social and asocial behaviors, along with conflicting theories about the circumstances that increase or decrease media influence on political action.

The powerful role that news media play in a variety of political situations is the subject of chapters 8–11. These situations include media coverage of elections (chapter 8) and the interplay between the media and political institutions such as the presidency and Congress (chapter 9). In these chapters I pay particular attention to technological developments that are transforming the Internet into a political tool that can empower citizens, if they so choose. The media's role in the judicial system and at state and local levels is set forth in chapter 10. The discussion covers news about courts at the national and state levels and about the criminal justice system at state and local levels. The chapter explains the inadequacies of news about subnational political issues. Chapter 11 details the dwindling impact of American news media on global politics and even on the conduct of American foreign policy. I compare several theories about how the American press selects events abroad for coverage. The chapter also illustrates the difficult trade-offs when First Amendment freedoms must be balanced against national security concerns. *Mass Media and American Politics* concludes with an extensive discussion of developments and policy trends in the Web 2.0 era. I assess the significance of news making and distribution by citizens who lack journalism training and then examine the potential political consequences when netizens from all walks of life converse extensively via the Internet. The boxed vignette in chapter 12, about social network sites and cyberactivists, like vignettes in other chapters, casts a spotlight on an especially intriguing media innovation.

The changes in this new edition reflect the political and technological events that have transpired since publication of the previous edition, the rich crop of new mass media studies, and much-appreciated suggestions from colleagues and students who have adopted the book for their classes. I am indebted to my research assistants, especially Melanie Mierzejewski, who created new tables and figures and identified facts that needed updating. The editorial team at CQ Press and its freelance staff provided valuable assistance that greatly eased the many chores that are part of writing books. Assistant editor Allie McKay and production editor Sarah Fell did yeoman's service. As always, I am grateful to my family for cheering me on. Memories of my husband's loving support during all prior editions continue to inspire me; he was and is a source of strength in all I do.

Doris A. Graber

Media Power and Government Control

In December 2002, Sen. Trent Lott was on the verge of becoming majority leader of the U.S. Senate. News stories killed that dream. Lott's fall from political grace began with a story reported by a young reporter for ABC News, Ed O'Keefe. O'Keefe took offense at a toast that Lott made during a one-hundredth-birthday celebration for South Carolina's senator and onetime presidential candidate Strom Thurmond. O'Keefe considered Lott's toast high praise for the segregationist policies that Thurmond had embraced earlier in his career. ABC, after initially slighting the story, featured it when it exploded on the Web. When the embarrassing tale became widely known, Lott's colleagues in the Senate felt that they could not place him into this powerful position. Fear of further bad publicity led to his early retirement from the Senate in December 2007. News stories had undermined his career.[1]

News stories, which turned out to be false, also brought a major airline company—United Airlines—to the brink of bankruptcy just hours after they were widely publicized on September 8, 2008. The stories reported that the airline had filed for bankruptcy at a time when the economy was declining and nervous investors were keeping close watch on stock market reports. Investors panicked and dumped United Airlines stock, along with the stocks of other airlines. United Airlines stock, which had been worth about $12 a share, plunged to $3 in less than one hour, triggering a halt in trading. Airline stock prices recovered quickly, but not completely, when it was discovered that the bankruptcy story was based on events that had occurred six years earlier. Somehow, a story reporting a 2002 event had mistakenly resurfaced with a 2008 dateline.[2] Though false, it carried a devastating economic punch.

POLITICAL IMPORTANCE OF MASS MEDIA

The Trent Lott and United Airlines stories illustrate how mass media reports, in combination with other political factors, shape the views of political leaders and citizens about public policies and public officials.[3] News stories take millions of Americans, in all walks of life, to the political and military battlefields of the world. They give them ringside seats for presidential inaugurations or basketball championships. They allow the public to share political experiences, such as watching political debates or congressional investigations. These experiences then undergird public opinions and political actions.[4]

Print, audio, and audiovisual media often serve as attitude and behavior models. The images that media create suggest which views and behaviors are acceptable and even praiseworthy and which are outside the mainstream. Audiences can learn how to conduct themselves at home and at work, how to cope with crises, and how to evaluate social institutions such as the medical profession or grocery chains. The mass media also are powerful guardians of proper political behavior because Americans believe that the press should inform them about government wrongdoing. Media stories indicate what different groups deem important or unimportant, what conforms to prevailing standards of justice and morality, and how events are related to each other. In the process the media set forth cultural values that their audiences are likely to accept in whole or in part as typical of U.S. society. The media thus help to integrate and homogenize our society.

Media images are especially potent when they involve aspects of life that people experience only through the media. The personal and professional conduct of politicians, political events beyond hometown boundaries, frenzied trading at stock exchanges, medical breakthroughs, or corrupt corporate dealings are not generally experienced firsthand. Rather, popular perceptions of these aspects of life take shape largely in response to news and fictional stories in media. Like caricatures, media stories often create skewed impressions because they cannot report most stories in detail or full context. For example, thanks to a heavy focus on crime news and fiction stories, television exaggerates the likelihood of an individual becoming a victim of crime. Viewers therefore fear crime excessively, especially if they watch a lot of television.[5]

Attention to the mass media is pervasive among twenty-first-century Americans. The average high school graduate today has spent more time watching televised broadcasts than in school, particularly during his or her preschool and elementary school days. Even in school, media are the basis for much learning about current events. An average adult in the United States spends nearly half of her or his leisure time watching television, listening to the radio, reading newspapers and magazines, or surfing the Web. Averaged over an entire week, this amounts to more than seven hours of exposure per day to some form of mass media news or entertainment. Television, relayed over the air, via cable, through the Internet, or through a videotape recorder, occupies three-fourths of this time. Despite considerable dissatisfaction with the quality of television programs in all of these modalities, television remains the primary source of news and entertainment for the average American.[6]

Fifty-two percent of people responding to a national survey in late spring 2008 said that they had watched local television news the day before. Additionally, 34 percent claimed to have read a daily newspaper the day before, and 35 percent said that they had paid attention to radio news.[7] The ability to attract such vast audiences of ordinary people, as well as political elites, is a major ingredient in the power of the mass media and makes them extraordinarily important for the

TABLE 1-1 **News Consumption Patterns, 2004 and 2008 (in percentages)**			
Medium	2004	2008	Change
Local TV news	59	52	−7
Newspapers "read yesterday"	42	34	−8
Radio news "listened yesterday"	40	35	−5
Nightly network news	34	29	−5
Online news "three or more days"	29	37	+8
Fox News	25	23	−2
CNN	22	24	+2
Network morning shows	22	22	0
National Public Radio	16	11	−5
NewsHour with Jim Lehrer	5	5	0
C-SPAN	5	4	−1

Source: Adapted from the Pew Research Center for the People and the Press, "Audience Segments in a Changing News Environment," August 17, 2008, http://people-press.org.

Note: Telephone interviews conducted between April 30 and June 1, 2008, among a nationwide sample of 3,615 adults.

individuals and groups whose stories and causes are publicized. Although their percentages have been shrinking, as Table 1-1 shows, the traditional media retain their dominance, and the audiences for political Web sites are comparatively small. A 2007 survey reported that the total volume of traffic to political Web sites was "about the same as the typical audience for a single broadcast of *ABC World News Tonight*."[8] Moreover, most of the news content aired on Web sites is drawn from mainstream media reports.

Politically relevant information is often conveyed through stories that are not concerned explicitly with politics. In fact, because most people are exposed far more to nonpolitical information, make-believe media, such as movies and entertainment television, have become major suppliers of political images. In 2008, for example, Comedy Central's the *Daily Show* provided ample and steady coverage of the presidential election campaign in its "Indecision 2008" commentaries. NBC's *Saturday Night Live* election comedy sketches reached as many as 14 million viewers, more than most competing prime-time offerings. Young viewers in particular regularly cite *Late Show* with David Letterman and the *Tonight Show* with Jay Leno as their main sources of political information.[9]

Such entertainment shows portray social institutions, such as the police or the schools, in ways that either convey esteem or heap scorn. These shows also express social judgments about various types of people. For instance, television

BOX 1-1 **"Media" Is a Plural Noun**

It has become fashionable to talk about news media behavior and effects using the singular, as if the media were one giant, undifferentiated institution. Researchers strengthen that impression because they commonly generalize about media behavior and effects based on data drawn from a single news source—most often the *New York Times.* The resulting caricature hides the immense richness of the news media in topics and framing, in presentation forms and styles, and in the unique social and political environments that they reflect. Yes, indeed, "media" should be treated as a plural noun!

How does one medium differ from the next? Communications scholar Michael Schudson answers that question in the opening essay of a massive volume about the role of the news media in the contemporary United States. Schudson warns, "It is a mistake to identify American journalism exclusively with the dominant mainstream-television network news and high circulation metropolitan daily newspapers. This error is compounded...if attention is paid exclusively to leading hard-news reporting, and features, editorials, news analysis, opinion columns, and other elements of the journalistic mix are ignored."[1]

Schudson identifies four distinct types of journalism, which are often combined to please various audiences. There is traditional mainstream journalism, often called "hard" news, and there is "soft news" tabloid journalism. Both differ from advocacy journalism, which is devoted to pleading particular causes, and from entertainment journalism, which may offer news but only as a by-product. The stories produced in these styles also bear the imprint of the various types of venues that present them: newspapers and magazines of all shapes and sizes, radio and television broadcast stations, and Internet news sites and weblogs. These diverse venues brim with a veritable smorgasbord of news stories, told from different perspectives and framed to carry unique shades of meanings effectively.

Their impact varies, depending on audience characteristics. U.S. scholars tend to think that "hard" print news is and should be king, but both claims are debatable. Compared to print news, audiovisual news captures much bigger audiences, and evidence is growing that it may also be the public's most effective teacher. Some messages are primarily important because they reach huge audiences; others attract comparatively tiny ones but are enormously influential nonetheless because some audience members have access to the country's networks of power.

Finally, in the global world in which news now circulates, it is unduly parochial to think of U.S. media performing inside a national cocoon. "Media" is a plural noun in the truest sense because news media now have a global reach. Like the biblical tower of Babylon, they carry a multiplicity of voices, each reflecting different environments and perspectives. Fortunately, unlike biblical times, today the discordant voices, besides being heard, can be translated and considered. How they will be construed then becomes the paramount question.

1. Michael Schudson, "Orientations: The Press and Democracy in Time and Space," in *The Press,* ed. Geneva Overholser and Kathleen Hall Jamieson, 1–3 (New York: Oxford University Press, 2005).

in the past often depicted African Americans and women as politically naive and having limited abilities. This type of coverage conveys messages that audiences, including the misrepresented groups, may accept at face value, even when the portrayals distort real-world conditions. Audience members may also think that social conditions and judgments shown on television are widely accepted and therefore socially sanctioned.[10]

Not only are the media the chief source of most Americans' views of the world, but they also provide the fastest way to disperse information throughout society. Major political news broadcasts by twenty-four-hour services such as CNN or Fox News spread breaking stories throughout the country in minutes. People hear the stories directly from radio or television, secondhand from "new" media on the Internet, or from other people.

All of the mass media are politically important because of their potential to reach large audiences. However, the influence of each medium varies depending on its characteristics, the nature and quantity of the political messages it carries, and the size of the audience reached (see Box 1-1 for more on the various types of media and their audiences). Print media, including sites on the Internet that feature text, generally supply the largest quantities of factual political information and analysis. They need readers who are literate at appropriate levels. Electronic media, especially television broadcasts, provide a greater sense of reality, which explains why audiences find electronic media more credible than print media. Moreover, large segments of the U.S. population have limited reading skills and find it far easier to capture meanings from pictures and spoken language. Electronic media also convey physical images, including body language and facial expressions, much more effectively than print media. They are especially well suited to attract viewers' attention and arouse their emotions.[11]

FUNCTIONS OF MASS MEDIA

What major societal functions do the mass media perform? Political scientist Harold Lasswell, a pioneer in media studies, mentions three things: surveillance of the world to report ongoing events, interpretation of the meaning of events, and socialization of individuals into their cultural settings.[12] To these three, a fourth function must be added: deliberate manipulation of politics. The manner in which these four functions are performed affects the political fate of individuals, groups, and social organizations, as well as the course of domestic and international politics.

Surveillance

Surveillance involves two major tasks. When it serves the collective needs of the public, it constitutes "public surveillance," and when it serves the needs of individual citizens, we call it "private surveillance." Although private surveillance may lead to political activities, its primary functions are gratifying personal needs and quieting personal anxieties.

Public Surveillance. Newspeople determine what is news—that is, which political happenings will be reported and which will be ignored. Their choices are politically significant because they affect who and what will have a good chance to become the focus for political discussion and action.[13] News stories may force politicians to respond to situations on which their views would not have been aired otherwise. Without media attention the people and events covered by the news might have less influence on decision makers—or none at all. Conditions that might be tolerated in obscurity can become intolerable in the glare of publicity. Take Senator Lott's toast at Strom Thurmond's birthday party. Without the public airing of an essentially private situation, Lott's political downfall and its repercussions would not have happened. Politicians are keenly aware of the media's agenda-setting power. That is why they try mightily to time and structure events to yield as much favorable publicity as possible and to forestall damaging coverage.

The consequences of media surveillance can be good as well as bad. Misperceptions and scares created by media stories have undermined confidence in good policies and practices, good people, and good products on many occasions. The human and economic costs have been vast. For example, dubious stories that impugned the safety of bioengineered foods caused millions of dollars of losses in the affected industries.

If media stories overemphasize crime and corruption in the inner city, scared residents may move to the suburbs, leaving the inner city deserted and even less safe and deprived of tax revenues. Speculation that international conflicts or economic downturns are in the offing may scare investors and produce fluctuations in domestic and international stock markets and commodity exchanges. Serious economic (and hence political) consequences may ensue.

Fear of publicity can be as powerful a force in shaping action as actual exposure. Politicians and business leaders know what damage an unfavorable story can do and act accordingly, either to avoid or conceal censurable behaviors or to atone for them by public confessions. President Bill Clinton, whose eight-year term was pockmarked with scandals, tried valiantly to hide some of them by forceful denials of allegations. But whenever proof made the charges undeniable, he escaped much public wrath by publicly apologizing for his misbehavior.[14] There are no records to show how effective the threat of publicity has been in deterring presidential misbehavior.

The media can doom people and events to obscurity by inattention as well. When the media have more information than they can transmit, many important stories remain untold. That happens most dramatically when the news becomes focused on a single upheaval, such as a major natural or human-made disaster, an election outcome, or a scandal. The time and space used for the single event usurp the time and space of happenings that otherwise would be reported. The size of "news holes"—the time and space available for reporting the news—is fairly inelastic. Newspeople also ignore important events that do not seem "newsworthy" by accepted journalistic criteria or that fail to catch their attention. Conscious attempts to suppress information for ideological or political reasons are another, but far less frequent, reason for lack of coverage.

For many years left-wing social critics have faulted mainstream U.S. journalists for using their news selection power to strengthen white middle-class values and disparage socialist viewpoints. These critics claim that the media deliberately perpetuate capitalist exploitation of the masses, in line with the ideological preferences of media owners. Critics also claim that the media have intentionally suppressed the facts about dangerous products, such as alcohol and tobacco, and about the socially harmful activities of large corporations, which may be responsible for water and air pollution or unsafe consumer goods.[15] By the same token, right-wing critics complain that the media give undue attention to enemies of the established social and political order in hopes of undermining it. Each camp cites a long list of stories to support its contentions.[16]

Journalists reject these charges. They deny political motives in news selection and defend their choices on the basis of the general criteria of newsworthiness (treated more fully in chapter 4). They, too, can muster evidence from news stories to support their claims. At the heart of controversies over the ideological bias of the media lie two basic questions that cannot be answered conclusively. The first concerns people's motivations. How can one prove what motivates journalists to act in certain ways? Lacking proof, is it fair to ascribe motivations to them in the face of their denials? The second question relates to story effects. To what degree can media stories secure the goals that owners of print and electronic media and news professionals are allegedly seeking? If the desired effects are unattainable, the critics' concerns lack weight.

Besides calling attention to matters of potential public concern, the media also provide cues about the importance of an issue. Important stories are covered prominently—on the front page with big headlines and pictures or as major television or radio features. Less important matters are more likely to be buried in the back pages, be listed at the bottom of a Web page, or have brief exposure on television or radio. However, nearly all coverage, even when it is brief and comparatively inconspicuous, lends an aura of significance to publicized topics. Through the sheer fact of coverage the media can confer status on individuals and organizations. The media "function essentially as agencies of social legitimation—as forces, that is, which reaffirm those ultimate value standards and beliefs, which in turn uphold the social and political status quo."[17]

Television made African American civil rights leaders and their causes household names. Martin Luther King Jr. and Jesse Jackson became national figures in part because television showed them giving speeches and leading marches and protests. In King's case, television captured the riots following his assassination. An individual who wins a hearing on radio or television often becomes an instant celebrity, whether he or she is a political candidate, like 2008 vice presidential contender Sarah Palin, nominated as Republican presidential contender John McCain's running mate; or a social crusader, such as Ralph Nader, whose goals became front-page news; or a convicted mass murderer, such as John Wayne Gacy, accused of sadistic murders of thirty-three young men in the 1970s. Their unpublicized counterparts remain obscure. Because publicity is crucial for political success, actors on the political scene often deliberately create situations likely to receive media coverage. Daniel Boorstin has labeled events arranged primarily to stimulate media coverage "pseudo-events."[18] Such events range from news conferences called by public figures even when there is no news to announce to physical assaults on people and property by members of protest groups who want to dramatize grievances. Newspeople who must cover such events may feel manipulated and resentful, but they are loath to allow competing media to scoop them.

When events are exceptionally significant or have become widely known already, or when the story is reported by competing media, the journalism community loses control over the news flow. For example, journalistic standards demand the reporting of news about prominent political leaders and major domestic or international events.[19] Aside from such unavoidable situations, coverage is discretionary for a wide range of people and happenings.

The power of the media to set the agenda for politics is not subject to a system of formal checks and balances as is the power of the U.S. government. Media power does not undergo periodic review through the electoral process. If media emphases or claims are incorrect, remedies are few. Truth-in-advertising laws protect citizens from false advertising of consumer goods but not from false political claims or improper news selection or biases by media personnel. The courts have interpreted restrictions on the news media's power to choose freely what to report and how to frame it as impairing the constitutional rights to free speech and a free press. Media critic Jay Blumler expresses the dilemma well:

> Media power is not supposed to be shared: That's an infringement of editorial autonomy. It is not supposed to be controlled: That's censorship. It's not even supposed to be influenced: That's news management! But why should media personnel be exempt from Lord Acton's dictum that all power corrupts and absolute power corrupts absolutely? And if they are not exempt, who exactly is best fitted to guard the press guardians, as it were?[20]

Private Surveillance. Average citizens may not think much about the broader political impact of the news they read, hear, and watch. They use the media primarily to keep in touch with what they deem personally important. The media are their eyes and ears to the world, their means of surveillance. The media, as Marshall McLuhan, another pioneering media scholar, observed, are "sense extensions" for individuals who cannot directly witness most of the events of interest to them and their communities.[21] The media tell their audiences about weather, sports, jobs, fashions, economic conditions, social and cultural events, health and science, and the public and private lives of famous people.

The ability to stay informed makes people feel secure, whether or not they remember what they read or hear or see. Even though the news may be bad, at least people feel that there will be no startling surprises. News reassures us that the political system continues to operate despite constant crises and frequent mistakes. Reassurance is important for peace of mind. But it also tends to encourage political quiescence, because there is no need to act if political leaders seem to be doing their jobs. For good or ill, the public's quiescence helps maintain the political and economic status quo.[22]

Other significant private functions that the mass media fulfill for many people are entertainment, companionship, tension relief, and a way to pass the time with minimal physical or mental exertion. The mass media can satisfy these important personal needs conveniently and cheaply. People who otherwise might be frustrated and dissatisfied can participate vicariously in current political happenings, in sports and musical events, in the lives of famous people, and in the lives of families and communities featured in the news.[23]

Interpretation

Media not only survey the events of the day and bring them to public and private attention, they also interpret the events' meanings, put them into context, and speculate about their consequences. Most incidents lend themselves to a variety of interpretations, depending on the values and experiences of the interpreter. The kind of interpretation affects the political consequences of media reports. For example, since 1962 the way in which the media interpret the legal and social significance of abortions has changed considerably. Abortion almost universally used to be considered murder. The abortionist was the villain and the pregnant woman was an accomplice in a heinous crime. Now abortion is usually cast into the frame of women's rights to control their bodies and to protect their physical and mental health.

What spawned the switch in media interpretation and eased the change in public attitudes toward abortion was the experience of a beloved television personality. Sherri Finkbine, hostess of *Romper Room,* a popular children's show in the 1960s, had taken thalidomide during her pregnancy before the drug's deforming effects on the unborn were known. Once she learned that she was likely to give birth to a severely malformed baby, she had an abortion in 1962. Instead of reporting the action as murder, as had been the custom, news media throughout the country defended Finkbine's decision to terminate her pregnancy. To steer clear of the negative connotations of the word *abortion,* journalists used a new vocabulary. They talked of "surgery to prevent a malformed baby," of "avoiding the possibility of mothering a drug-deformed child," and of the necessity of inducing a miscarriage to spare a child from loathing "its own image and crying out against those who might have spared it this suffering."[24]

Numerous circumstances influenced the type of interpretation that the Finkbine story received. In the end, it hinged on journalists' decisions, made independently or in response to pressures, to frame the story in a specific way and to choose informants accordingly. Journalists' inclinations help decide how the news will be framed, which in turn determines its likely impact.

By suggesting the causes and relationships of events, the media may shape opinions without explicitly telling audiences which views seem right or wrong. For example, linking civil strife abroad during the Cold War to left-wing agitators ensured that the U.S. public would view violent protests with considerable alarm. Linking the protests to internal corruption and social oppression would have put the problems into a far less threatening light.

News presentations can predetermine people's conclusions in countless ways.

We [journalists] can attribute any social problem to official policies, the machinations of those who benefit from it, or the pathology of those who suffer from it. We can trace it back to class or racial inequalities, to ideologies such as nationalism or patriotism, or to resistance to the regime. We can root the problem in God, in its historic genesis, in the accidental or systematic conjuncture of events, in rationality, in irrationality, or in a combination of these or other origins. In choosing any such ultimate cause we are also depicting a setting, an appropriate course of action, and sets of virtuous and evil characters, and doing so in a way that will appeal to some part of the public that sees its own sentiments or interests reflected in that choice of a social scene.[25]

The items that media personnel select to illustrate a point or to characterize a political actor need not be intrinsically important to be influential in shaping opinions and evaluations. They do not even need exposure in respected media outlets. That is why House Speaker–designate Bob Livingston resigned from Congress in 1998, when he learned that the publisher of the pornographic *Hustler* magazine was about to publicize charges of adultery about him. Livingston had confessed extramarital liaisons to his colleagues in Congress but feared that an explosion of adverse media publicity would devastate his party and his career.

3. Socialization

The third function of major mass media that Lasswell mentions is political socialization (chapter 7). It involves learning basic values and orientations that prepare individuals to fit into their cultural milieu. Before the 1970s, studies largely ignored the mass media because parents and the schools were deemed the primary agents of socialization. Research in the 1970s finally established that the media play a crucial role in political socialization.[26] Most information that young people acquire about their political world comes directly or indirectly from the mass media either through news offerings or entertainment shows, or through social Web sites such as Facebook or MySpace. The media present specific facts as well as general values, teaching young people which elements produce desirable outcomes. Media also provide the young with behavior models. Because young people lack established attitudes and behaviors, they are receptive to using such information to develop their opinions.

Most of the new orientations and opinions that adults acquire during their lifetime also are based on information from the mass media. People do not necessarily adopt the precise attitudes and opinions that earn the media's praise; rather, mass media information provides the ingredients that people use to adjust their existing attitudes and opinions to keep pace with a changing world. The mass media deserve credit, therefore, for a sizable share of adult political socialization and resocialization. Examples of resocialization—the restructuring of established basic attitudes—are the shifts in sexual morality and racial attitudes that the American public has undergone since the middle of the last century and the changing views about relations with mainland China and with Russia.[27]

Manipulation

Journalists at prominent news venues periodically become major players in the game of politics; they do not just play their traditional role as chroniclers of information provided by others. The most common way for a journalist to break out of the role of political bystander is through an investigation. Many major print and electronic media enterprises have operated their own investigative units because investigative stories are very popular. They are also expensive to produce and tend to become scarce when media organizations are forced to economize.

The purpose of many investigations is to *muckrake.* Journalists who investigate corruption and wrongdoing to stimulate government to clean up the "dirt" they have exposed are called "muckrakers." The term comes from a rake designed to collect manure. President Theodore Roosevelt was the first to apply the term to journalism. Muckraking today may have several different goals.[28] The journalist's primary purpose may be to write stories that expose misconduct in government and produce reforms. Or the chief purpose may be to present sensational information that attracts large media audiences and enhances profits. Other manipulative stories may be designed to affect politics in line with the journalist's political preferences (chapter 6).

EFFECTS OF MASS MEDIA

The public believes that the media influence politics and public thinking. Politicians act on the basis of the same assumption. But many scholars are skeptical because many research studies fail to show substantial impact. Why is there such a discrepancy between social science appraisals of mass media effects and the general impression, reflected in public policies, that the mass media are extremely influential?

There are three major reasons. First, many studies, particularly those conducted during the 1950s and 1960s, took a narrow approach to media effects, looking for only a few specified effects rather than all effects. Second, theories about learning and how to test it have enhanced the belief because they use the accuracy of expressed memories as the prime indicator for learning. Accordingly, media are deemed to have minimal effects because people often fail to report specific facts mentioned in news stories. Third, social scientists have great

By permission of Steve Kelley and Creators Syndicate, Inc.

difficulty identifying media effects because they are embedded in a complex combination of social stimuli.

Early Studies

U.S. social scientists began to study the effects of the mass media primarily in one narrow area: vote change as a result of media coverage of presidential elections. Among these early studies, several are considered classics. *The People's Choice* by Paul Lazarsfeld, Bernard Berelson, and Hazel Gaudet, all of Columbia University, reported in 1944 how people made their voting choices in Erie County, Pennsylvania, in the 1940 presidential election. Sequels to the study followed in short order. The best known are *Voting: A Study of Opinion Formation in a Presidential Campaign, The Voter Decides,* and *The American Voter.*[29]

Focus on Vote Choices. The early studies were based on the assumption that a well-publicized campaign should change votes. If it did not, this proved that the media lacked influence. Subsequent studies have faulted that reasoning because there may be measurable media influences other than changes in vote choice. Besides, media effects vary depending on the social and political climate during various historical periods. At the time of the early voting studies, change of vote choice was rare because allegiance to parties was strong. Subsequently, party allegiance weakened among many voters, so that the opportunities for media influence on vote choice became far greater.

Had the investigators concentrated on other settings, such as judicial or nonpartisan elections (for which few voting cues aside from the media are available), they might also have discovered greater media-induced change in attitude. Substantial media influence might have been found even in presidential elections if changes in people's trust and affection or knowledge about the candidates and the election had been explored. Such changes constitute important media influences that are crucial components of a variety of political behaviors aside from voting.

The early voting studies focused almost exclusively on effects on individuals; they failed to trace effects on the social groups to which individuals belong and through which they influence political events. Gay men might not change their votes after hearing a candidate attack their lifestyle. But they might urge their association to testify against legislation favored by the candidate. They might even participate in violence in the wake of news stories reporting hate crimes against the gay community. In turn, these activities may have major political repercussions. Yet the early studies of media effects ignore such sequential impacts on the political system and its component parts.

The findings that media effects were minimal were so pervasive that social science research into mass media effects fell to a low ebb after an initial flurry in the 1940s and 1950s. Social scientists did not want to waste time studying inconsequential effects. Despite the seemingly solid evidence of media importance, they did not care to swim against the stream of established knowledge. As a consequence, study after study dealing with political socialization and learning ignored the mass media.

Learning Theories. The early findings were all the more believable because they tied in well with theories of persuasion. Mass media messages presumably miss their mark because they are impersonal. They are not tailored to address specific individuals, as are the messages of parents, teachers, and friends. They do not permit the mutual adjustment of messages that leads to consensus in interpersonal conversation. Furthermore, people are rarely compelled to listen to mass media messages and they need not answer. Hence it is easy to ignore media messages.

Although there is a lot of truth to these claims, they fail to consider that television can be a very personal medium. Audiences frequently interact with the television image as if what appears on screen were actually happening in front of them. They may look on television commentators and actors as personal friends. Viewers often imitate people and situations on television and identify with specific characters.

Further support for the minimal-effects findings comes from various cognitive consistency theories. They postulate that average individuals dislike being presented with information that is incompatible with cherished beliefs. Therefore they avoid information that might require changing established beliefs and take note only of messages that match their existing beliefs. Social scientists have evidence that people are indeed selective in their use of the media and search for confirming information. But, as will be discussed more fully in chapter 7, the phenomenon is limited.

Recent Research and Measurement Problems

When researchers resumed their investigations of mass media effects in the wake of persistent evidence of strong media impact, they cast their net more broadly. They began to look beyond effects on voting to other media effects during elections and in other types of political situations. Their research has confirmed media impact on factual learning, on opinion formation, and on citizens' political activities. Scholars also have looked beyond the individual, discovering significant media effects on political systems and subsystems in the United States and elsewhere.[30]

Aside from the strong scholarly findings, even if media stories lacked impact, they would nonetheless be influential because of the widespread belief that the media are powerful and deserve consideration in the world of politics. In sum, for multiple reasons, media coverage often has a strong impact on ongoing political developments, on the views and behaviors of political elites and other selected groups, and on the general public's perception of political life. As political journalist Theodore White put it, albeit with some exaggeration:

> The power of the press in America is a primordial one. It sets the agenda of public discussion; and this sweeping political power is unrestrained by any law. It determines what people will talk and think about—an authority that in other nations is reserved for tyrants, priests, parties, and mandarins.[31]

No major act of the U.S. Congress, no foreign adventure, no act of diplomacy, no great social reform can succeed in the United States unless the press prepares the public mind.[32] Although research of media effects has made great strides thanks to improvements in research designs and techniques, research into mass media effects remains hampered by serious measurement problems.

Measuring Complex Effects. Mass media effects are difficult to measure, both at the individual and societal levels, because the effects are highly complex and elusive. The most common measuring device at the individual level—self-assessment of media impact during interviews—is notoriously unreliable. Researchers lack tools to measure human thinking objectively, although advances in brain imaging hold promise for progress. Even when people engage in overt behavior, one cannot judge accurately what messages may have prompted the behavior. Opinion formation and actions spring from a variety of motivations, making it difficult to isolate the media's part.[33]

Assessing the impact of particular news stories is especially difficult because mass media audiences bring prior knowledge and attitudes to bear on new information. Because researchers rarely know precisely what those attitudes and knowledge are, or the rules by which they are combined with new information, they cannot pinpoint the exact contribution that particular mass media stories have made to an individual's cognitions, feelings, and actions. To complicate matters further, the impact of the mass media varies depending on the subject matter. For instance, media impact is greater on people's perceptions of unfamiliar issues than on their perceptions of familiar issues, especially when people have faced them personally.

Establishing effects at the societal level is even more difficult. A good example is the "CNN effect," which was widely credited as propelling President George H. W. Bush to dispatch U.S. troops to Somalia in 1992. The term refers to the belief that news media, such as the Cable News Network (CNN), inflame public opinion by showing gripping pictures of ongoing crises. The public's clamor for action then forces government to take action prematurely. Media coverage becomes the dog that wags the public policy tail. In the Somalia case, CNN and other television networks had aired reports and pictures of widespread starvation and devastation in the summer months of 1992. Those pictures presumably inflamed the public and aroused pressure groups, which forced members of the Bush administration, against their better judgment, to airlift relief supplies and later to dispatch U.S. troops to Somalia. The rescue effort ultimately failed, and U.S. lives were lost.[34]

Political scientists Steven Livingston and Todd Eachus reached a different conclusion about the respective roles of the news media and the Bush administration in determining U.S. policy in Somalia. After examining a variety of sources, including *New York Times* and *Washington Post* stories about U.S. humanitarian relief policies, and after interviewing key government decision makers and long-term relief personnel in Somalia, Livingston and Eachus concluded that plans for relief efforts had been under way for more than a year prior to CNN coverage of the tragedy. Government officials, including concerned members of Congress who had traveled to Somalia, rather than television news stories, had been the spur to action.

Despite persuasive evidence that extensive media coverage of the tragedy followed, rather than preceded, President Bush's announcement of the military airlift and other relief measures on August 14, 1992, many observers still argue that media mobilization of public opinion was an essential prerequisite for the Somalia intervention. They claim that the administration would have avoided the airlift in the absence of media coverage of the tragedy. Absolute proof, one way or the other, does not exist. Inability to prove the scope of mass media impact beyond a doubt has made social scientists shy away from assessing media influence on many important political events. Some social scientists even go to the other extreme and deny that effects exist simply because the effects defy precise measurement. This is unfortunate, because many important elusive effects can be readily observed in the field. Also, many news stories have significant consequences that are never measured or even acknowledged. For example, the stock market is highly sensitive to news reports that might have economic consequences. A brief story about one patient's "miracle cure" from an unusual disease may send drug company stocks soaring or nose-diving, even when the story was barely a blip on the audience's attention screen.

Statistical versus Political Significance. Social scientists often underestimate media impact because they falsely equate statistical significance with political significance. Media impact on a statistically insignificant number of individuals can still have major political consequences. For example, during an election, only 1 percent or 2 percent of the voters may change their votes because of media stories. That is a statistically negligible effect. From a political standpoint, however, the impact may be major, because many important elections, including several presidential elections, have been decided by a tiny margin of votes. The 2000 presidential race was decided by a fraction of less than 1 percent of the vote in Florida. Overall, more than 105 million votes were cast for president. An "insignificant" 1 percent of that total still represented more than one million people.

On a smaller scale, if a broadcast of details of a race riot attracts a few listeners to the riot site and stimulates some to participate, the situation may escalate beyond control. In the same way, the impact of a single news story may change the course of history if it induces one assassin to kill a world leader or convinces one world leader to go to war.

Influencing Elites. Another problem with social science research on mass media effects is that it has concentrated on measuring the effects on ordinary individuals rather than on political elites. The average individual, despite contrary democratic fictions, is fairly unimportant in the political process. Mass media impact on a handful of political decision makers usually is vastly more significant because it influences how they conduct political affairs. This is why governments everywhere, in authoritarian as well as democratic societies, try to control the flow of information produced by the media lest it thwart their political objectives.[35]

WHO SHOULD CONTROL NEWS MAKING?

Attempts by governments to control and manipulate the media are universal because public officials everywhere believe that media are important political forces. This belief is based on the assumption that institutions that control the public's information supply can shape public knowledge and behavior and thereby determine support for government or opposition to it. Although media control occurs in all societies, its extent, nature, and purposes vary for several reasons. Political ideology is an important one. In countries in which free expression of opinion is highly valued and in which dissent is respected, the media tend to be comparatively unrestrained. The right of the press to criticize governments also flourishes when the prevailing ideology grants that governments are fallible and often corrupt and that average citizens are capable of forming valuable opinions about the conduct of government. Finally, freedom of the press, even when it becomes a thorn in the side of the government, is more easily tolerated when governments are well established and politically and economically secure. In nations where governments are unstable and resources insufficient to meet the country's needs, it may be difficult to put up with press behavior that is apt to topple the government or retard its plans for economic development.

Nowhere are the media totally free from formal and informal government and social controls, even in times of peace. On the whole, authoritarian governments control more extensively and more rigidly than nonauthoritarian ones, but all control systems represent points on a continuum. There are also gradations of control within nations, depending on the current regime and political setting, regional and local variations, and the nature of news. The specifics of control systems vary from country to country, but the overall patterns are similar.[36]

Authoritarian Control Systems

Authoritarian control systems may be based on a totalitarian ideology and designed to control and use the media to support ideological goals, or they may be nonideological and simply represent the desire of the ruling elites to control media output tightly so that it does not interfere with their conduct of government. Examples of nonideological authoritarian control exist in states ruled by military governments or where constitutional guarantees have been suspended. Cuba and China are examples of control based on communist ideology.

In today's world, fully or partially authoritarian systems of media control prevail in the majority of countries, although many governments profess to want a less-controlled system and are struggling to move in that direction. Nonetheless, government attempts to control internal and external news flows are omnipresent because governments fear that unrestrained media will create serious political instability, whether through accurate messages or through unintentionally or deliberately false ones.

Authoritarian systems operate on the assumption that government must control the media because news stories are essential for engendering support for the government's mission (Table 1-2). The media may point out minor deficiencies or corruption of low-level officials and suggest adjustments in line with prevailing policies, but criticism of the basic system or its rulers is considered destructive.

Beyond that, the media are free to choose the stories they wish to publish, so long as government officials agree that the stories do not interfere with public policies. In totalitarian societies the likely political and social effects of a story—rather than its general significance, novelty, or audience appeal—determine what will be published and what will be buried in silence. For instance, news about accidents, disasters, and crimes is often suppressed because of fears that it may weaken the image of an all-powerful political system. Even entertainment programs, such as music and drama performances and cartoon shorts in movie theaters, must carry appropriate social messages or have historical significance. The government supports such entertainment financially because it serves the important public purpose of shaping people's minds in support of the political system.

Democratic Systems

In democracies, the public sees journalists as its eyes and ears. Journalists are expected to scrutinize government performance and report their findings. If media surveillance causes governments to fall and public officials to be ousted, democracy is well served.

TABLE 1-2 **Media Roles under Different Regime Types**	
Authoritarian regime assumptions	*Democratic regime assumptions*
Governments know and serve people's best interests.	Governments often fail to serve people's best interests.
Media should stress the government's virtues.	Media should confront the government when officials and policies seem flawed.
News should engender support for major policies.	News should stimulate critical thinking about major policies.
News and entertainment programs should be selected for their social values.	News and entertainment programs should be selected for audience appeal.

Source: Composed by the author.

Although this is the theory behind the role of media in democratic societies, the practice is less clear-cut. In the United States, for example, neither newspeople nor government officials are completely at ease with the media's watchdog role. The media limit their criticism to what they perceive as perversions of the public's basic social and political values or noteworthy examples of corruption and waste. They rarely question the widely accepted fundamentals of the political system, such as its orientation toward majority rule or private capitalism or individualism.

Because American journalists tend to choose established elites as their primary sources of news, their links to the existing power structures are strong. They may even share information with government agencies, including law enforcement bodies such as the Federal Bureau of Investigation and the Central Intelligence Agency. When disclosure might cause harm, reporters in a democratic society occasionally withhold important news at the request of the government. This has happened repeatedly when the lives of hostages were at stake or when military interventions were imminent. In an effort to keep their images untarnished by media attacks, government officials may try to control the media through regulatory legislation or through rewards and punishments (chapter 9).

The chief responsibility of the news media in democratic societies is to provide the general public with information and entertainment. According to the U.S. version of the libertarian philosophy, anything that happens that seems interesting or important for media audiences may become news. It should be reported quickly, accurately, and without any attempt to convey a particular point of view. Topics with the widest audience appeal should be pervasive, which explains the ample doses of sex and violence. Audience appeal is then expected to translate into good profits for media owners either through fees paid by audience members or through advertising revenues. Although audiences may learn important things from the media, libertarians believe that teaching is not the media's chief task. Nor is it their responsibility to question the truth, accuracy, or merits of the information supplied to them by their sources. Rather, it is left to the news audience to decide what to believe and what to doubt.

By contrast, adherents to the tenets of social responsibility believe that news and entertainment presented by the mass media should reflect societal concerns. Media personnel should be participants in the political process, not merely reporters of the passing scene. As guardians of the public welfare, they should foster political action when necessary by publicizing social evils such as rampant industrial pollution of air and water. In a similar vein, undesirable viewpoints and questionable accusations should be denied exposure, however sensational they may be. If reporters believe that the government is hiding information that the public needs to know, they should try to discover the facts and publicize them.

Social responsibility journalism and totalitarian journalism share some important features. Both approaches advocate using the media to support the basic ideals of their societies and to shape people into more perfect beings. Proponents of both schools of journalism are convinced that their goals are good and would not be achieved in a media system dominated by the whims of media owners, advertisers, or audiences. But the similarities should not be exaggerated. Social advocacy in democratic systems lacks the fervor, clout, and single-mindedness it has in their totalitarian counterparts. Social responsibility journalism rarely speaks with a single uncontested voice throughout society. Nevertheless, it frightens and antagonizes many news professionals and news audiences. If one agrees that the media should be used to influence social thought and behavior for "good" purposes, who should decide which purposes deserve to be included in that category? Critics of social responsibility journalism point out that journalists do not have a public mandate to act as arbiters of social values and policies in a society that has many disparate visions of truth and goodness. Newspeople lack the legitimacy that comes only from being elected by the public or appointed by duly elected officials.

Irrespective of the merits or faults of these arguments, today social responsibility journalism is popular with a sizable portion of the news profession.[37] Pulitzer prizes and other honors go to journalists who have successfully exposed questionable practices in the interest of social improvement. The most prominent "villains" targeted for exposure are usually big government and big business.[38]

MODELS OF NEWS MAKING

Beyond the basic concerns reflected in the philosophies of libertarians and social responsibility advocates, there are many other guiding principles for reporting events. For example, news making can be described in terms of five distinct models: the mirror model, the professional model, the organizational model, the political model, and the civic journalism model. Each represents judgments about the major forces behind news making that shape the nature of news and its political impact.

Underlying Theories

Proponents of the mirror model contend that news is and should be a reflection of reality. "We don't make the news, we just report it," is their slogan. The implication is that newspeople impartially report all significant happenings that come to their attention. Critics of the mirror model point out that this conception of news making is unrealistic. Millions of significant events take place daily, forcing journalists to determine their relative newsworthiness and decide which to report. Events that are publicized inevitably loom disproportionately large compared with unpublicized events. The way the story is framed in words and pictures further distorts reality.

In the professional model, news making is viewed as an endeavor of highly skilled professionals who put together a balanced and interesting collage of events selected for importance and attractiveness to specific media audiences. There is no pretense that the end product mirrors the world. For economic reasons, anticipated audience reaction is especially influential in determining which stories pass scrutiny and which are ignored.

The organizational model, sometimes called the "bargaining model," is based on organizational theory. Its proponents contend that the pressures inherent in organizational processes and goals determine which items will be published. Pressures spring from interpersonal relations among journalists and between them and their information sources, from professional norms within the news organization and from constraints arising from technical news production processes, cost-benefit considerations, and legal regulations.

The political model rests on the assumption that news everywhere reflects the ideological biases of individual newspeople as well as the pressures of the political environment in which the news organization operates. The media cover high-status people and approved institutions; people and events outside the dominant system or remote from the centers of power are generally ignored. Supporters of the prevailing system are pictured as good guys, opponents as bad guys.

In the 1990s public journalism, or civic journalism, became popular, spurred by widespread concern that average citizens shun participation in public affairs and distrust government and the news media. Proponents of the civic journalism model believe that the press can discover citizens' concerns and then write stories that help audiences play an active and successful role in public life.[39] Journalists must articulate and explain public policy choices in understandable language. They must facilitate a public dialogue that encourages and respects diverse views. After consensus has been reached among the clients of a particular news venue, the venue and its clients must vigorously champion appropriate public policies.

None of these models fully explains news making; rather, the process reflects all of them in varying degrees. Because the influences that shape news making fluctuate, one needs to examine individual news making situations carefully to account for the factors at work. Organizational pressures, for instance, depend on the interactions of people within the organization. Audience tastes change or are interpreted differently. Perceptions of "facts" differ, depending on reporters' dispositions. Moreover, the precise mix of factors that explains news making in any particular instance depends largely on chance and on the needs of a particular news medium.

Control Methods

Societies use legal, normative, structural, and economic means to control news media within their countries. All countries have laws to prevent common press misbehavior. For instance, laws may forbid publication of deliberate falsehoods. All societies also have social norms that the press generally heeds because it craves public approval or fears government or private sector retaliation. Hence media are unlikely to ridicule sacred concepts or widely accepted morality principles. The way media organizations are structured, operated, and financed also shapes their product. The Russian government closely regulates and controls media enterprises and finances them. Given these arrangements, Russian media dare not criticize the government's war against rebels in Chechnya. The few dissenters who did had their voices stilled in various ways. Journalists' behavior reflects the nature of their environments.[40] They are docile and obey rules strictly in countries where media control is heavy-handed, and they become far more daring and unconventional in liberal, individualistically oriented countries such as the United States and England.

The combination of methods by which governments control the media varies, and so do the major objectives of control. Governments can control media content by limiting entry into the media business. For example, the government may require licenses for entry and grant them only to people it deems desirable, as is common in authoritarian societies. By contrast, democratic regimes rarely make formal attempts to deny foes of the regime access to the media. However, because the capacity of the broadcast spectrum is limited, control through franchise is quite common for electronic media. Franchises often bestow monopoly control. In most democracies, newspapers rarely need licenses, and access to the Internet has remained equally unrestricted. In the United States, for instance, anyone with sufficient money can start a newspaper or newsletter or create a Web site or blog.

Media also may be controlled through the manipulation of access to news. Information may be put beyond the reach of media by declaring it to be "confidential" and by barring reporters from government archives. In addition to such formal control of potentially damaging news, informal restraints curb the actual flow of news. All government units, and often many of their subdivisions, have information control systems by which they determine which news to conceal or release and how to frame it (chapter 9). In 1993 President Clinton, who was annoyed with reporting about his presidency, took the unusual step of limiting reporters' easy access to the White House communication office by closing off a connecting hallway to the press room.[41]

Authoritarian governments often use censorship laws or regulations to control the flow of news. In some countries nothing may be printed or broadcast until the government censor has approved it. At times governments will direct papers or magazines to make deletions after their product has been prepared for printing or is already printed. This leaves tantalizing white spaces or missing pages. Government officials often write or edit television and radio scripts, and media outlets must broadcast these without editorial changes. In the past, totalitarian countries could frequently block all unapproved communications from abroad by jamming foreign broadcasts and prohibiting the import of foreign printed materials. In the Internet age, such controls have become well-nigh impossible. Democratic governments also often use legal and normative pressures to avert potentially damaging political news or news that violates widely cherished social norms. They commonly claim that concerns about press freedoms have motivated the restrictions on news. Publication controls increase markedly in periods of crisis and war.

All governments use treason and sedition laws to control media output. Treason and sedition can be defined broadly or narrowly. Anything that is critical of the government can be called treasonable or seditious, especially in times of war. In democratic societies, media and the government are in perennial disagreement about the tipping point. Governments lean toward protection; the media lean toward disclosure. People judged guilty of treason or sedition may be sentenced to prison or even executed. Given the social pressures to act patriotically and the severity of the penalty, treason is rare. Most journalists avoid difficulties with official censors and with treason and sedition laws by refraining from using material that is likely to be objectionable. Formal government censorship then becomes replaced largely by social pressures and self-censorship—which are the most potent forms of constraint on human behaviors.

The First Amendment to the U.S. Constitution, which provides that "Congress shall make no law…abridging the freedom of speech, or of the press," has given the media an exceptionally strong basis for resisting government controls in the United States. The courts have ruled, however, that the protection is not absolute. On occasion, it must give way to social rights that the courts consider to be superior. For example, media are forbidden from publicizing the names of CIA secret agents because that would endanger them and destroy their usefulness.

A limited number of controls, such as regulatory laws, court decisions, and informal social pressures, guard against excesses by the media. In the United States the courts have been loath to impose restraints prior to publication, such as granting injunctions that would stop publication of information on the grounds that it would cause irreparable harm. But informal social and political pressures and the fear of indictments after publication have restrained presentation of potentially disturbing stories. Besides guarding state survival through treason and sedition laws, government controls commonly shield sensitive governmental proceedings, protect individual reputations and privacy, and safeguard the prevailing moral standards of the community. Curbs on publication of government secrets—so-called classified information—often engender controversy because governments tend to be overzealous in controlling material that they deem potentially harmful to themselves. Finally, most governments also have laws protecting the reputations of individuals or groups and laws against obscenity (chapter 3).

Defining the limits of government control over information dissemination raises difficult questions for democratic societies. Does official censorship, however minimal, open the way for excessive curbs on free expression? What guidelines are available to determine how far censorship should go? What types of material, if any, can harm children? Or adults? Should ethnic and racial slurs be prohibited on the ground that they damage minorities' self-image? The answers are controversial and problematic.

The limitations on the freedom of publication in democratic societies raise questions about the actual differences in press freedom in democratic and authoritarian societies. Is there really a difference, for example, in the independence of government-operated television networks in France and in North Korea? The answer is a resounding "yes." The degree of restraint varies so sharply that the systems are fundamentally different. In authoritarian societies the main objective of controls is to support the regime in power. In democratic societies the media are usually free to oppose the regime, to weaken it, and even to topple it. Although the media rarely carry their power to the latter extreme, the potential is there. It is this potential that makes the media in democratic societies a genuine restraint on governmental abuses of power and a potent shaper of government action.

SUMMARY

The mass media are an important influence on politics because they regularly and rapidly present politically crucial information to huge audiences. These audiences include political elites and decision makers, as well as large numbers of average citizens whose political activities, however sporadic, are shaped by information from the mass media.

Decisions made by media personnel about what and whom to cover determine what information becomes available to media audiences and what remains unavailable. By putting stories into perspective and interpreting them, reporters assign meaning to the information and indicate the standards by which it ought to be judged. At times, reporters even generate political action directly through their own investigations or indirectly through their capacity to stimulate pseudo-events.

Although social scientists still find it difficult to pinpoint the scope of media impact on particular political events, politicians and their governments everywhere are keenly aware of the political importance of the media. Therefore, these governments have policies to shape the media's political role in their societies. Those policies have been buttressed by constitutional and legal rules as well as by a host of informal arrangements. In this chapter we have described briefly how the basic policies, constitutional arrangements, and legal provisions differ in authoritarian and democratic regimes.

NOTES

1. Jay Rosen, "The Legend of Trent Lott and the Weblogs," http://journalism.nyu.edu/pubzone/weblogs/pressthink/2004/03/15/lott_case.html.

2. David Greising, "Internet-Fueled Panic Rocks United Stock," *Chicago Tribune*, September 9, 2008.

3. For a brief overview of current knowledge about mass media effects, see W. Lance Bennett, *News: The Politics of Illusion*, 8th ed. (White Plains, N.Y.: Longman, 2009); and Leo W. Jeffres, *Mass Media Effects*, 2nd ed. (Prospect Heights, Ill.: Waveland Press, 1997).

4. Herbert J. Gans, *Deciding What's News: A Study of* CBS Evening News, NBC Nightly News, Newsweek, *and* Time (Evanston, Ill.: Northwestern University Press, 2004); Richard Campbell, Christopher R. Martin, and Bettina Fabos, *Media and Culture*, 7th ed. (Boston: Bedford/St. Martin's, 2009).

5. Daniel Romer, Kathleen Hall Jamieson, Sean Aday, "Television News and the Cultivation of Fear of Crime," *Journal of Communication* 53 (2003), no. 1: 88–104.

6. Pew Research Center for the People and the Press, "Audience Segments in a Changing News Environment," August 17, 2008, http://people-press.org.

7. Ibid.

8. Matthew A. Baum and Tim Groeling, "New Media and the Polarization of American Political Discourse," *Political Communication* 25 (2008), no. 4: 345–365.

9. Jody C. Baumgartner and Jonathan S. Morris, eds., *Laughing Matters: Humor and American Politics in the Media Age* (New York: Routledge, 2008); see also Bruce A. Williams and Michael X. Delli Carpini, *The End of Broadcast News*, forthcoming; Jeffrey P. Jones, *Entertaining Politics: New Political Television and Civic Culture* (Lanham, Md.: Rowman and Littlefield, 2004); Liesbet van Zoonen, *Entertaining the Citizen: When Politics and Popular Culture Converge* (Lanham, Md.: Rowman and Littlefield, 2004).

10. Robert M. Entman and Andrew Rojecki, *The Black Image in the White Mind: Media and Race in America* (Chicago: University of Chicago Press, 2000).

11. For a discussion of many aspects of visual presentations, see Gregory Stanczak, "Visual Research: Method and Representation," *American Behavioral Scientist* 47 (2004), no. 12: 1471–1642.

12. Harold D. Lasswell, "The Structure and Function of Communication in Society," in *Mass Communications*, ed. Wilbur Schramm (Urbana: University of Illinois Press, 1969), 103.

13. Chapter 4 gives a more detailed definition of news. Evidence that the media set the agenda for national issues is presented in David L. Protess and Maxwell McCombs, eds., *Agenda Setting: Readings on Media, Public Opinion, and Policymaking* (Hillsdale, N.J.: Erlbaum, 1991). For a more recent discussion of agenda setting for news consumers, see Maxwell McCombs, *Setting the Agenda: The Mass Media and Public Opinion* (Cambridge, UK: Polity, 2004).

14. Larry J. Sabato, Mark Stencel, and S. Robert Lichter, *Peep Show: Media and Politics in an Age of Scandal* (Lanham, Md.: Rowman and Littlefield, 2000). The authors discuss the appropriate ways to deal with scandal stories.

15. Examples of such criticism can be found in Bennett, *News: The Politics of Illusion;* Robert W. McChesney, *The Political Economy of Media: Enduring Issues, Emerging Dilemmas* (New York: Monthly Review Press, 2008); and Michael Parenti, *Inventing Reality: The Politics of the News Media*, 3rd ed. (New York: St. Martin's Press, 1993).

16. An example of a conservative Washington, D.C.–based media analysis group is Accuracy in Media, which publishes periodic reports of its media investigations. For claims that journalists in the elite media are ultraliberal, see S. Robert Lichter, Stanley Rothman, and Linda S. Lichter, *The Media Elite* (New York: Adler and Adler, 1986). Also see K. M. Schmitt, A. C. Gunther, and

J. L. Liebhart, "Why Partisans See Mass Media as Biased," *Communication Research* 31 (2004): 623–641.

17. Jay G. Blumler, "Purposes of Mass Communications Research: A Transatlantic Perspective," *Journalism Quarterly* 55 (Summer 1978): 226.

18. Daniel Boorstin, *The Image: A Guide to Pseudo-Events* (New York: Athenaeum, 1971).

19. Criteria of what constitutes *news* are discussed fully in a historical context in Kevin G. Barnhurst and John Nerone, *The Form of News* (New York: Guilford Press, 2001). Also see Samuel P. Winch, *Mapping the Cultural Space of Journalism* (Westport, Conn.: Praeger, 1997); and Herbert Gans, *Democracy and the News* (New York: Oxford University Press, 2003).

20. Blumler, "Purposes of Mass Communications Research," 228.

21. Marshall McLuhan, *Understanding Media: The Extensions of Man* (New York: McGraw-Hill, 1964).

22. The numbing effects of reassuring publicity are discussed by Murray Edelman, *The Symbolic Uses of Politics* (1964; reprint, Urbana: University of Illinois Press, 1985), 38–43.

23. Robert Kubey and Mihaly Csikszentmihalyi, *Television and the Quality of Life: How Viewing Shapes Everyday Experience* (Hillsdale, N.J.: Erlbaum, 1990), chap. 5, 7.

24. Marvin N. Olasky and Susan Northway Olasky, "The Crossover in Newspaper Coverage of Abortion from Murder to Liberation," *Journalism Quarterly* 63 (1986): 31–37.

25. W. Lance Bennett and Murray Edelman, "Toward a New Political Narrative," *Journal of Communication* 35 (1985): 156–171.

26. The early writings include David Easton and Jack Dennis, *Children in the Political System: Origins of Political Legitimacy* (New York: McGraw-Hill, 1969); Fred I. Greenstein, *Children and Politics* (New Haven: Yale University Press, 1965); Richard Dawson and Kenneth Prewitt, *Political Socialization* (Boston: Little, Brown, 1969); Robert D. Hess and Judith Torney, *The Development of Political Attitudes in Children* (Chicago: Aldine, 1967); Sidney Kraus and Dennis Davis, *The Effects of Mass Communication on Political Behavior* (University Park: Pennsylvania State University Press, 1976); Steven H. Chaffee, "Mass Communication in Political Socialization," in *Handbook of Political Socialization,* ed. Stanley Renshon (New York: Free Press, 1977).

27. For examples, see Benjamin I. Page and Robert Y. Shapiro, *The Rational Public: Fifty Years of Trends in Americans' Policy Preferences* (Chicago: University of Chicago Press, 1992); Benjamin I. Page, *Who Deliberates?* (Chicago: University of Chicago Press, 1996); Shanto Iyengar and Donald Kinder, *News That Matters: Television and American Opinion* (Chicago: University of Chicago Press, 1987); and John Zaller, "Monica Lewinsky and the Mainspring of American Politics," in *Mediated Politics: Communication in the Future of Democracy,* ed. W. Lance Bennett and Robert M. Entman (Cambridge, UK: Cambridge University Press, 2001).

28. David L. Protess, Jack C. Doppelt, James S. Ettema, Margaret T. Gordon, and Fay Lomax Cook, *The Journalism of Outrage: Investigative Reporting and Agenda Building in America* (New York: Guilford Press, 1991), 8–12. Also see Sabato, Stencel, and Lichter, *Peep Show.*

29. Paul Lazarsfeld, Bernard Berelson, and Hazel Gaudet, *The People's Choice* (New York: Columbia University Press, 1944); Bernard Berelson, Paul Lazarsfeld, and William McPhee, *Voting: A Study of Opinion Formation in a Presidential Campaign* (Chicago: University of Chicago Press, 1954); Angus Campbell, Gerald Gurin, and Warren E. Miller, *The Voter Decides* (Evanston, Ill.: Row, Peterson, 1954); and Angus Campbell, Philip E. Converse, Warren E. Miller, and Donald Stokes, *The American Voter* (New York: Wiley, 1960).

30. For examples, see the case studies presented in Frank Esser and Barbara Pfetsch, eds., *Comparing Political Communication: Theories, Cases, and Challenges* (Cambridge, UK: Cambridge University Press, 2004).

31. Theodore White, *The Making of the President, 1972* (New York: Bantam, 1973), 327.

32. Ibid.

33. For a discussion of the problem and examples, see Jan E. Leighley, *Mass Media and Politics: A Social Science Perspective* (Boston: Houghton Mifflin, 2004).

34. This account is based on Steven Livingston and Todd Eachus, "Humanitarian Crisis and U.S. Foreign Policy: Somalia and the CNN Effect Reconsidered," *Political Communication* 12 (1995): 413–429.

35. Jeffres, *Mass Media Effects*, presents an excellent overview of the media effects literature.

36. The discussion is modeled on Fred Siebert, Theodore Peterson, and Wilbur Schramm's foundational book, *Four Theories of the Press* (Urbana: University of Illinois Press, 1963). For a critique of the model, see Daniel C. Hallin and Paolo Mancini, *Comparing Media Systems: Three Models of Media and Politics* (Cambridge, UK: Cambridge University Press, 2004).

37. David H. Weaver and G. Cleveland Wilhoit, *The American Journalist in the 21st Century* (Mahwah, N.J.: Erlbaum, 2005). Public journalism embodies most of the principles of social responsibility journalism. See Edmund D. Lambeth, Philip E. Meyers, and Esther Thorson, eds., *Assessing Public Journalism* (Columbia: University of Missouri Press, 1998); and Theodore L. Glasser, ed., *The Idea of Public Journalism* (New York: Guilford Press, 1999).

38. See, for example, Dean Alger, *Megamedia: How Giant Corporations Dominate Mass Media, Distort Competition, and Endanger Democracy* (Lanham, Md.: Rowman and Littlefield, 1998). Also see the annual reports of "The Goldsmith Prize Investigative Reporting Finalists," issued by the Joan Shorenstein Center on the Press, Politics and Public Policy, Harvard University.

39. Lambeth, Meyers, and Thorson, *Assessing Public Journalism*.

40. Hallin and Mancini, *Comparing Media Systems*.

41. John Anthony Maltese, *Spin Control: The White House Office of Communication and the Management of Presidential News*, 2nd ed. (Chapel Hill: University of North Carolina Press, 1994), 232–233.

READINGS

Bennett, W. Lance. *News: The Politics of Illusion*. 8th ed. White Plains, N.Y.: Longman, 2008.

Bimber, Bruce. *Information and American Democracy: Technology and the Evolution of Political Power*. Cambridge, UK: Cambridge University Press, 2003.

Campbell, Richard, Christopher R. Martin, and Bettina Fabos. *Media and Culture: An Introduction to Mass Communication*, 7th ed. Boston: Bedford/St. Martin's, 2009.

Gans, Herbert. *Democracy and the News*. New York: Oxford University Press, 2003.

Graber, Doris A., ed. *Media Power in Politics*, 5th ed. Washington, D.C.: CQ Press, 2007.

Hamilton, James T. *All the News That's Fit to Sell: How the Market Transforms Information into News*. Princeton: Princeton University Press, 2004.

Jamieson, Kathleen Hall, and Paul Waldman. *The Press Effect: Politicians, Journalists, and the Stories That Shape the Political World*. New York: Oxford University Press, 2003.

Kline, David. *Blog! How the Newest Media Revolution Is Changing Politics, Business, and Culture*. New York: CDS Books, 2005.

Schudson, Michael. *The Sociology of News*. New York: Norton, 2003.

Willis, Jim. *The Media Effect: How the News Influences Politics and Government*. Westport, Conn.: Praeger, 2007.

Ownership, Regulation, and Guidance of Media

W hen the Soviet Union collapsed in 1989, Americans expected that the Soviets' Iron Curtain of information control would be lifted and a free press would emerge in Russia and its component states. And so it did, briefly. Soviet leaders pledged that the government would relinquish control over the nation's news media and would allow opposition voices to be heard. Twenty years later, however, nearly everything that was gained initially has been lost. Aside from the Baltic States and the Central European satellites, the press in Russia and most of the countries on its periphery is government owned and controlled and serves to perpetuate authoritarian governance. Aside from some access to the Internet, a new Iron Curtain has descended, barring the public from nearly all information beyond its own government's control. It is a brutally efficient, repressive media environment.[1]

The reversion to a captive press began in 2000 when Vladimir Putin, a former top-level official of the KGB secret police, became president of Russia and "cleansed" the media of all elements deemed hostile to the Putin regime. Most of the rulers of the Commonwealth of Independent States (CIS) followed suit. Putin's strenuous effort to regain control over all independent media enterprises is a typical, contemporary version of the battles fought by governments for control over their countries' information supply to ensure that it supports the reigning government and damages the opposition. Concern about who will wield media power has been a central issue in U.S. politics since colonial days. In this chapter we will weigh the pros and cons of various forms of government and private sector control of the mass media, as well as the implications of changing patterns. We will also assess the impact of various pressures on the mass media industry, such as economic constraints and lobbies. The policy issues involved in media control are so complex, so intertwined with political preferences, that no ownership and control system stands out clearly as "best." All have advantages and drawbacks. It is no wonder that attempts in the United States to legislate about media ownership and control have produced little agreement on what the laws should be.

CONTROL AND OWNERSHIP: PUBLIC AND SEMIPUBLIC

The different forms of control and ownership of the media affect not only media economics but also the substance of media output, in line with the old adage, "He who pays the piper calls the tune." People concerned about self-serving politicians are likely to oppose government ownership and operation of the media. They also are apt to be leery about extensive government regulation of privately owned and operated media. By contrast, people who believe that for-profit media enterprises cater to low-level mass tastes or who distrust the business ethics of corporations, especially huge ones, do not want a media system in which private ownership and control dominate.

The Crux of the Debate

Opponents of public ownership and control of news media fear that it leads to programming that uncritically supports government policies, even in democratic countries. The fear is well-founded. However, the programs that the British government's nonpartisan British Broadcasting Corporation offers show that governments can avoid direct political interference.[2]

Private control of television, if divided among many owners, is likely to bring more conflicting interests into play than government control. Even within large corporations, business interests are apt to be diverse and often incompatible, so that company leaders support diverse policies. Overall, when business enterprises control broadcasting, the prevailing political values reflected in the choice of programs are likely to be mainstream and middle class. Aside from the mainstream orientations of most owners, the pressures springing from profit considerations lead to offerings with mass appeal, rather than controversial social or cultural crusades. Advertisers generate the largest share of the media's income. They pay for the privilege of reaching large numbers of potential customers, particularly eighteen-to-forty-nine-year-olds, who are the most active shoppers. Government-owned and controlled media are free from commercial pressures because they can use tax money to finance whatever programs they believe to be in the public interest. They must consider intragovernment power struggles, but they do not need to consider the economic consequences of the size of their audience.

When most Americans distrust government more than business, private ownership and control of the mass media are the preferred option. Consequently, the bulk of news media fare, especially on television, is geared to simple, emotion-laden programming that attracts large, diverse audiences. Controversial or troublesome issues that may antagonize or deplete media audiences and diminish advertising revenues are largely shunned.

Popular, "lightweight" programming draws the wrath of many people, particularly intellectual elites who scorn the mass public's tastes even when they themselves flock to fluff programs. Some critics argue that people would choose highbrow, intellectual programs over lightweight entertainment if they had the chance, even though proof is plentiful that the public prefers shallow entertainment to more serious programs.[3] In 1998, for example, President, Bill Clinton's State of the Union message attracted 53 million viewers. Some months later, a broadcast in which he promised to discuss an inappropriate sexual relationship with a White House intern attracted 68 million. Later that year, the finale of the popular *Seinfeld* show on NBC drew 76 million viewers, topping the audience for the president's yearly report by more than 40 percent. In print news, magazines featuring sex or violence far outsell journals that treat political and social issues seriously. In fact, scholarly political journals frequently require subsidies to remain in print. Huge crowds are willing to pay heavily in time and money to see movies featuring heinous crimes and explicit sex. The most popular pay television channels show what is euphemistically called "adult entertainment," whereas channels devoted to highbrow culture languish and often perish. On the Internet, one-fourth of daily search engine requests and one-third of all downloads involve sexually explicit content.[4]

Related to concerns about news media domination by powerful public or private interests is the fear of undue influence if only a small number of organizations share media control. Diversity of media ownership presumably encourages the expression of diverse views, which to many Americans is the essence of democracy. The marketplace where ideas and opinions are debated must be wide open. But there is no agreement on exactly how many owners are required for sufficient diversity.[5] Americans appear to be more concerned about the concentration of media ownership in comparatively few hands than about control of the media by business. Social reformers, however, are more concerned about business control, claiming that it fosters tabloid journalism and suppresses discussion of pressing social problems.

How the Public and Semipublic System Works

In the United States outright government ownership and control over media has been limited. However, it is growing as more local governments own cable television systems or operate channels on privately owned systems. Government ownership raises serious unresolved questions about the limitations, if any, to be placed on the government's rights to use these outlets to further partisan political purposes.

The federal government is most heavily involved in broadcasting, with local governments in second place. The federal government controls broadcasts to U.S. military posts throughout the world through the American Forces Radio and Television Service in the Department of Defense. It also owns foreign propaganda outlets. In 2008 the Voice of America broadcast system (VOA), for example, broadcast more than 1,500 hours of programs weekly to a foreign audience of 134 million through radio, television, and the Internet. VOA has more than 1,200 affiliate stations and communicates in forty-five languages.[6]

Broadcasting by semipublic institutions is another control option. The public broadcasting system, created through the Public Broadcasting Act of 1967, represents a mixture of public and private financing and programming and public and private operation of radio and television stations. The public broadcasting system supports educational and public service television stations whose programs generally do not attract large audiences. Those stations need subsidies because they usually cannot find enough commercial sponsors to pay for their shows.

In 2009 members of the public broadcasting system included 356 noncommercial television stations, primarily operated by community organizations and colleges and universities, and more than 860 noncommercial radio stations linked together as the independently financed National Public Radio (NPR).[7] The administrative arrangements for the public broadcasting system have been complex. The Corporation for Public Broadcasting (CPB), staffed by political appointees, has handled the general administration, but it has been kept separate from the programming side of the operation to insulate public broadcasting from political pressures. A separate Public Broadcasting Service (PBS) has produced television programs, often in collaboration with state-supported foreign broadcast systems, such as Britain's BBC, or France 2, or Japan's NHK. The Independent Television Service, created by Congress in 1991, has awarded grants to independent producers for "programming that involves creative risks and addresses the needs of underserved audiences."[8]

The attempt to keep the CPB from influencing programming has failed. The corporation does not tell public television stations what programs they should feature. Instead, it has guided programming by paying for some types of programs and refusing to pay for others. This has constituted purse-string control of programming by government. The results have earned praise along with scorn. In radio, NPR was created to both produce and distribute programs. Because cost considerations made it impossible to include all noncommercial radio stations, only the largest, best-organized ones were included and are eligible for CPB funding grants and participation in NPR programs.

Private foundations and big business enterprises have subsidized 22 percent of the public broadcasting system income (Table 2-1). The Reagan administration authorized PBS to engage in some commercial broadcasting of economic news and to accept a limited amount of advertising. All of these changes have enhanced corporate influence over programming. The general public also has influenced public broadcasting through donations that constitute 27 percent of the income of public broadcasting systems and through community advisory boards. Nevertheless, securing adequate financing is an enduring problem. Dependence on federal funds, even when those funds constitute less than 20 percent of total funding, entails some subservience to federal control, despite barriers to direct government influence.

An emphasis on experimental programs—cultural offerings such as plays, classical music, and ballet—and a stress on high-quality news and public affairs programs distinguishes public television broadcasts from commercial television.[9] The nature and quality of programming vary widely because public television represents a decentralized bevy of local stations. The audience for public television, except for its children's programs, has been small, rarely more than 2 percent of television viewers. Even minority groups, to whom a number

TABLE 2-1 **Income Sources of the Public Broadcasting System, 2003 (includes nonbroadcast income)**

Income source	Millions of dollars	Percentage of budget
State/local government and colleges/universities	583	25
Subscribers and auction	620	27
Federal government	455	19
Business	351	15
Other	131	6
Foundations	155	7
Private colleges/universities	37	2
Total income	2,333	100

Source: Public Broadcasting Policy Base, "Public Broadcasting System Revenues, 1982–003," www.current.org/pbpb/statistics/totalrevs.html.

Note: The 2003 Public Broadcasting System included 700 Corporation for Public Broadcasting–qualified public radio stations and 350 public television stations.

of public broadcast programs are targeted, prefer commercial entertainment. Still, PBS serves nearly 65 million people weekly, and more than 26 million listen off and on to NPR programs. Because of the limited appeal of public broadcasting and the need to reduce public expenditures, there has been some pressure to disband the system completely and reallocate its frequencies to commercial channels. Some of its programs then might be shown on commercial cable stations, possibly with federal subsidies.[10]

Supporters of the system contend that it provides special services that commercial television neglects because they lack mass appeal. Innovations pioneered by public broadcasting have spread to commercial broadcasting, these supporters say. For example, public broadcasting played a leading role in developing captions for individuals with hearing impairments. At the turn of the century, it led in pioneering digital television, including interactive news and feature programs. Public radio and public television also were among the first to move to satellite distribution, which made it possible to deliver multiple national programs to communities. Nonetheless, the future of public broadcasting seems precarious.

PATTERNS OF PRIVATE OWNERSHIP

The overarching feature of media ownership in the United States is that it is predominantly in private hands. Arrangements vary from individual ownership, where one person owns a newspaper or radio or television station, to ownership by huge corporate conglomerates. Owners include small and large business enterprises, labor groups, religious and ethnic organizations, and many other types of interests in society. Explaining private media control patterns is relatively simple; agreeing on their consequences is not.

Business Configurations

"Independents"—individuals or corporations that run a single media venture and nothing else—are a vanishing breed in the media business. The most important exceptions are wire services, such as the Associated Press (AP). The organization supplies a huge share of the news stories printed and broadcast in the United States. Its roots go back to 1848, when six New York newspapers formed a cooperative association to share the cost of collecting foreign news. Out of this initial effort grew a handful of other wire service organizations, such as those operated by the *New York Times, Chicago Tribune,* and CNN to serve their own organizations along with an array of subscribers. Wire service companies employ reporters scattered throughout the world to collect and report news for sale to news distributing entities. Wire service news stories and bulletins are transmitted electronically to subscriber newspapers and radio and television stations. Service clients either rewrite wire news stories and bulletins or use them verbatim. The proportion of wire service stories used, directly or in rewritten form, may vary from less than 10 percent to 80 percent or more of all stories, depending on each media outlet's resources for carrying its own news. Wire service stories tend to predominate for foreign news, and even for national news for smaller papers and broadcast stations that cannot afford their own correspondents. This means that a small number of wire service companies dominate a large share of news production in the United States. It is the most concentrated form of control within the American media system.

Aside from developments on the Internet, various forms of multiple ownership have become the norm. Media chains are an example. In the chains, individuals or corporations own several media outlets—mostly radio or television stations or cable channels or newspapers. For example, in 2008 the Gannett Company published 85 daily newspapers in the United States, including the giant *USA Today* and nearly 900 nondaily publications. It also published 17 daily newspapers in the United Kingdom and roughly 300 weekly newspapers and magazines.[11] The predictable consequence of chain ownership has been a large degree of homogeneity in news offerings.[12]

National and regional chains control more than 80 percent of daily papers in the United States.[13] Like the Gannett Corporation, most of these newspaper groups also own papers published less frequently. The proportion of circulation controlled by chain-owned papers has been relatively stable, as Table 2-2 shows, using examples drawn from an array of circulation leaders. Although individual papers within chains generally enjoy editorial page autonomy, they tend to be more uniform in making political endorsements than is true for independently owned papers.[14]

In addition to newspaper chains, Gannett also owns chains of other media channels. The company operated 23 television stations in the United States in 2008, reaching more than 20 million households. Its on-line audience in the

TABLE 2-2 **U.S. Daily Newspaper Circulation: 2004, 2006, and 2008**

	2004	2006	2008	Change
USA Today[a]	2,192,098	2,272,815	2,284,219	+.042
Wall Street Journal	2,101,017	2,049,786	2,069,463	−.015
New York Times	1,133,763	1,142,464	1,077,256	−.049
Los Angeles Times	983,727	851,832	773,884	−.213
New York Daily News	747,053	708,477	703,137	−.059
New York Post	....	673,379	702,488	+.043
Washington Post	772,553	724,242	673,180	−.129
Chicago Tribune[b]	693,978	579,079	541,663	−.219
Houston Chronicle	549,300	513,387	494,131	−.10
Arizona Republic	466,926	438,722	413,332	−.115

Source: Audit Bureau of Circulation.

Note: Change based on difference in circulation from 2004 to 2008 except in the case of the *New York Post,* for which 2006 data were used.

[a] Numbers are based on best days only: Monday–Thursday.

[b] Numbers are based on best days only: Wednesday–Friday.

United States was estimated at 25.8 million unique visitors, which is almost 16 percent of the total Internet news audience. When media enterprises own different types of media, it is called "cross-media ownership." Although the arrangement carries the usual advantages of giant enterprises—ample resources for good performance and economies of scale—it is worrisome when one company controls all the news media in a market. It diminishes the chance for democratic dialog. Efforts to use the government's regulatory powers to curb cross-media ownership in the United States have been stymied by powerful lobbying by large media enterprises.[15] In fact, under a series of Republican presidents, the Federal Communications Commission (FCC) has favored loosening constraints on cross-media ownership, allowing this form of ownership to thrive. The FCC has actually encouraged mergers of multiple media platforms, even when they have involved the same market.

A market is the geographic area in which a medium attracts a substantial audience. For instance, each television station has a signal that can be received clearly by people living within a certain radius of the station. All of the people within that radius who can receive the signal are considered within the market. This means that they are exposed to the same programming and can be expected to respond to advertising for products and services provided by program sponsors. Large owners may supply news for more than a hundred markets. Advertisers who want to reach as many potential customers as possible favor owners with access to large markets and are willing to pay them premium fees.

A fourth type of ownership encompasses conglomerates—individuals or corporations that own media enterprises along with other types of businesses. CBS Corporation, General Electric, and the Walt Disney Company are examples. They own the CBS, NBC, and ABC networks. Along with Fox, these four major television networks supply most of the content broadcast by U.S. television stations. Conglomerate ownership raises fears that the companies' nonmedia business interests may color their news policies. If, for instance, there is a need to reduce the size of the military or to oppose construction of a missile system, the management of a conglomerate such as General Electric, which holds many defense contracts, may examine these questions from a biased perspective in the media outlets that it controls (see Figure 2-1).

In major urban centers most media fall into the multiple-owner, cross-media, and conglomerate classifications. For instance, the Tribune Company owns the *Chicago Tribune* as well as television and radio stations in Chicago and the Chicago Cubs baseball team. In 2008 Tribune media holdings included 12 daily newspapers throughout the country, 24 television stations in 19 markets, one radio station, and one national cable outlet, along with the Web sites associated with these enterprises. Its subsidiary Tribune Media Services operated as a major syndicator of news, features, and entertainment content sold to news outlets throughout the world.[16] All major television and radio stations in Chicago are owned by the national television networks and conglomerates or members of conglomerates.

Radio and television stations that remain under single ownership for the most part are small with comparatively weak signals. The number of media outlets controlled by various entrepreneurs ranges widely and fluctuates considerably, especially in an era of widespread consolidation. Since the turn of the century, many news media companies have added multiple Web sites to their holdings, as well as on-line versions of their newspapers and television programs and newspapers serving special groups such as Hispanics or young readers.

The Costs and Benefits of Big Business Control

Strong trends toward consolidation in the media industry have given a few very large organizations a great deal of control over the news that reaches the American public. Is it sound public policy to allow such consolidation? Does it bring undesirable uniformity and lead to neglect of local needs? Does it prevent diverse viewpoints from reaching the public? In short, what are the advantages and disadvantages of big business control over substantial portions of the public's news supply?

On the plus side of the ledger, producing television programs and gathering news worldwide are expensive. Only large, well-financed organizations able to spread their costs over many customers can provide the lavish media fare that attracts ample audiences. Compared to small, individually owned enterprises, large enterprises can more readily absorb the losses that are often incurred in producing expensive documentaries and public service programs.

FIGURE 2-1 The Diverse Holdings of the General Electric Company

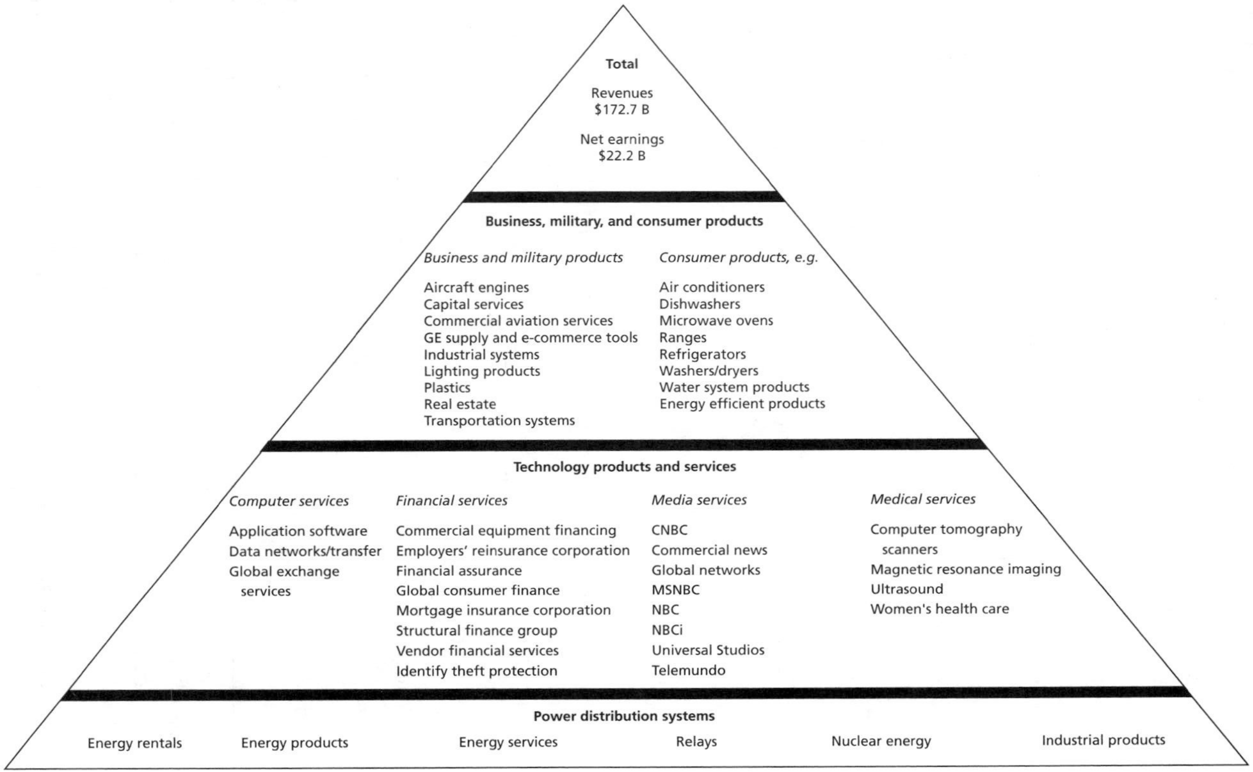

Total

Revenues
$172.7 B

Net earnings
$22.2 B

Business, military, and consumer products

Business and military products
Aircraft engines
Capital services
Commercial aviation services
GE supply and e-commerce tools
Industrial systems
Lighting products
Plastics
Real estate
Transportation systems

Consumer products, e.g.
Air conditioners
Dishwashers
Microwave ovens
Ranges
Refrigerators
Washers/dryers
Water system products
Energy efficient products

Technology products and services

Computer services
Application software
Data networks/transfer
Global exchange
services

Financial services
Commercial equipment financing
Employers' reinsurance corporation
Financial assurance
Global consumer finance
Mortgage insurance corporation
Structural finance group
Vendor financial services
Identify theft protection

Media services
CNBC
Commercial news
Global networks
MSNBC
NBC
NBCi
Universal Studios
Telemundo

Medical services
Computer tomography
scanners
Magnetic resonance imaging
Ultrasound
Women's health care

Power distribution systems

Energy rentals

Energy products

Energy services

Relays

Nuclear energy

Industrial products

Source: General Electric, *Annual Report*, 2008.

Large enterprises also can spend more money on talented people, research, investigations, and costly entertainment shows. Nonetheless, these advantages are bought at a high price. The brilliant, full spectrum of viewpoints that could be available has been contracted and grayed, and fresh new talents have far fewer opportunities to come to the fore.

Although there have been troubling incidents, many of the worst fears about the consequences of big business dominance have proved largely groundless. Media mergers have generated little change in the uniformity of news; the simultaneous multiplication of cable, satellite, and Internet television actually diversified the media marketplace to some extent everywhere.[17] Nor is there solid evidence that media giants squelch antibusiness news and routinely favor conservative political orientations.[18] In fact, there has been ample antibusiness news that has tarnished such business giants as Microsoft, Nike, Wal-Mart, Merck, and the major tobacco companies.[19] However, it is quite evident that serious news has been increasingly replaced by "infotainment" in the wake of mergers of news enterprises with entertainment giants, especially when the public prefers such shows to hard news offerings. "News you can use"—news relating to everyday needs such as food, medical care, and transportation—is on an upswing. Still, an ample supply of hard news remains available on cable stations, on news radio, and on the Internet.

Obviously, current policies designed to reduce media concentration and encourage local programming have failed to meet their objectives. The merits of these policies must be reconsidered, keeping in mind the media's mandate to serve the public interests of a democratic society. It has also become clear over many decades that most efforts to put broadcast media into a regulatory harness are doomed to fail because owners with major stakes in this business sector maintain close ties with high-level politicians, who need their support for winning public office and promoting policies.

The Impact of New Media on the Media Marketplace

The "new media" are having a marked impact on the structure and behavior of news media enterprises. The Project for Excellence in Journalism called the arrival of the Internet age "an epochal transformation, as momentous probably as the invention of the telegraph or television. Journalism...is becoming more complex. We are witnessing conflicting trends of fragmentation and convergence simultaneously, and they sometimes lead in opposite directions."[20] The term "new media" refers to the growing number of electronic forms of communication made possible through computer technologies. The term includes social networking Web sites such as MySpace and Facebook, which dabble in presenting news while fostering social networking.[21]

The most profound effect of the new media on the news media business springs from the multiplication of outlets that distribute news. In fact, in combination, there are far more providers of digital news than potential consumers of their services. This imbalance between supply and demand has created a chaotic marketplace where news suppliers compete for audiences and advertisers in

Reprinted by permission: Graham Roumieu

many novel ways. Most "old media" institutions have been weakened by the struggle, and some have succumbed. But there are many survivors, and some of them, such as cable television news, are thriving.

The vast majority of new media news providers produce very few, if any, original stories. They largely feed off news collected by the traditional media who use their shrinking corps of journalists to report ongoing events. New media news distributors elaborate stories gathered by old media, often interpreting them from unique perspectives. They have captured fragments of old media audiences. The three original networks—ABC, CBS, and NBC—which once supplied news to three-quarters of the nightly audience, now serve only 40 percent.[22] However, most digital news consumers continue to use old-style news sources alongside the new media.

As a consequence of sharpening competition in the news media marketplace, owning media enterprises has become less profitable and even unprofitable in many instances. To cope with tough economic conditions, some media empires have divested themselves of large chunks of their holdings, adding a movement toward deconcentration to the more common movement toward excessive concentration in the media business sector. Clear Channel, for example, has disgorged nearly 40 percent of its small-market radio stations, a total of 448 stations, as well as all of its local television stations. It retained an empire of more than 600 radio stations, demonstrating that even after massive divestments, concentration remains alive and well on the radio scene. Sixty percent of on-line news offerings come from providers owned by twenty media titans such as Time Warner and General Electric. Hundreds of smaller companies share the remainder.

Strained economic conditions have forced some old media into bankruptcy, and some have shut down operations in the face of impending financial collapse. Still others have sharply cut costs by sharing resources, trimming staffs and the scope of news gathering, and shutting down bureaus, especially abroad. The upshot has been a reduction in the scope and quality of coverage of serious news and an increase in trivial human interest stories that are cheap to produce.

The growth of the new media has thinned out old media, but only marginally. As in previous communications revolutions, newcomers—like the telephone, or radio, or television in earlier ages—have forced old-timers to adjust; they have not wiped them out.[23] In line with the old adage, "If you can't lick 'em, join 'em," the old-timers have adapted the new technologies to their own needs. Newspapers, for example, along with some television and cable stations, have created their own Web sites. The news collected for the traditional enterprise now does double duty by serving the needs of the Web site as well. In fact, much of the information collected by reporters that the traditional media could not publish in the past because of space and time constraints is now available on the Web. It enriches the old-style media because they can refer audience members to the expanded offerings. In addition, the ability to publish breaking news on the Web when it happens, rather than waiting for scheduled editions and broadcasts, restores the traditional media's scooping ability. They can once again be the first to break a story.

Privatization has been another major consequence of new media proliferation. When media properties are owned by publicly traded corporations, bottom-line concerns are paramount. If their published reports show that the media segments of the business are not as profitable as expected, management feels pressured to change the situation, often at the expense of the quality of media offerings. Such unwelcome pressures have produced a trend to privatize major media. The *Chicago Tribune* and the Clear Channel radio operations are examples. While privatized media ultimately need to be economically viable so that they can pay their operating costs, they are not forced to show the large profit margins to which media owners have been accustomed in the past. They also are less subject to public scrutiny, making media operations less transparent.

Further loosening of the economic constraints that currently hobble news media operations may be in the offing. Wealthy philanthropists have indicated their willingness to operate high-quality media on a break-even basis or to subsidize their operations. One subsidy example is *ProPublica*, a nonprofit investigative service that develops news stories and then offers them free to existing news organizations or assists news organizations in developing their own stories.[24] That is an exciting development because it points to a move away from news media as profit-making businesses to a system of media focused on public service that deserves support from private philanthropies. Yet we must remember that any major change in the system of media financing will not change the age-old fact that whoever pays the piper, controls the tune. We can only guess what the new tune would be.

Media Influence Variables: Prestige, Market Size, and Competition

One cannot judge the sweep of control exercised by any group of news media owners merely by looking at number of outlets. Three additional factors need to be considered: prestige of each media institution, market size, and competition within the market. The prestige a media enterprise enjoys is an important component of its political influence. Journalism has widely accepted standards of professionalism, just as does law, or medicine, or engineering. As part of this system of norms, certain members and products are accepted widely as models for the profession. Other news professionals watch what information the high-prestige news organizations present, how they present it, and what interpretations they give to it; they then adjust their own presentations accordingly. Critics derisively call this the "jackal syndrome" or "pack journalism." For political news, the *New York Times* is the lion whom the jackals follow. In television, major networks are models for the profession, strengthening the trend toward news uniformity. The many voices in the media marketplace sing in unison much of the time. Newcomers quickly join the chorus and hum the tunes orchestrated by the prestige leadership.

Media enterprises also gain influence based on the size of their market rather than the total number of markets accessible. The hundreds of newspaper and broadcast markets in the United States vary widely in audience size. In such major metropolitan areas as New York, Chicago, or Los Angeles, a market with a fifty-mile radius may have a population of several million. The same radius for a station in Wyoming might cover more cows than people.

Competition within most media markets used to be quite limited. A single newspaper and a handful of radio and television stations were the rule. That picture has changed dramatically in the wake of technology advances. Nonetheless, most Americans still get the bulk of their political news from one daily newspaper and over-the-air television. Ninety-eight percent of all U.S. cities have only one daily newspaper.[25] Suburban dailies, which flourish in a few major cities, do not alter the situation substantially because their coverage of major news stories usually is limited. However, even in one-newspaper towns, the news supply is not monopolized as long as there is competition from television, cable, and radio outlets.

Another factor to consider in gauging the influence of various media enterprises is the composition of their audiences in terms of age, education,

BOX 2-1 **Audiences under the Microscope**

Demographic differences matter hugely when it comes to audiences for various types of media. The maturing young—midtwenties to midthirties—are most prized by news organizations. That age group is likely to have a reasonably good income within various job categories and likely to spend a good portion of it on big-ticket purchases such as furniture, appliances, electronics, and cars. Garnering young families as audience members equates to attracting advertisers who are willing to pay high rates for the chance to reach as many young eyeballs and readily opened, ample wallets as possible.

Of course, not all media venues cater to the young. There are venues that cater to older audiences, to partisan audiences, to the prosperous, to the politically sophisticated, and many more. Given that human preferences for news vary along demographic lines, targeted offerings that cater to specific needs and likes are a good thing. It also makes it essential to be knowledgeable about the range of tastes for news among Americans.

The graph below is illustrative. It uses age and news venue choice as the distinguishing characteristics and displays the strikingly different responses when people are asked about their news consumption "yesterday."[1] Gaps are similarly wide when measured along education or income cleavages. They shrink when questions are measuring preferences for overview stories versus concentration on a specific topic, or when they are gauging the decline in use of traditional, off-line news sources.

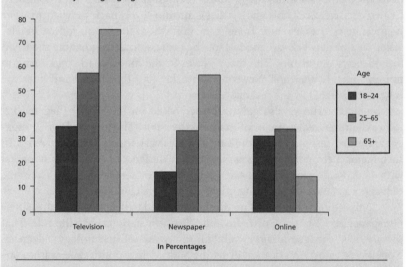

In Percentages

1. The data are adapted from the Pew Research Center for the People and the Press, "Key News Audiences Now Blend Online and Traditional Sources," August 17, 2008, http://people-press.org/report/?pageid=1352.

and income (see Box 2-1 for an examination of news audience demographics). However, numbers may be deceptive because the fragmentation of news channels and the multiplication of news content on entertainment programs make it hard to judge people's news sources. Evidence shows that most Americans watch the news when something exciting occurs, although that inclination has been declining.[26] In 2008, when asked about attention to news on the previous day, 52 percent of poll respondents had used television and 34 percent had read a newspaper. When asked to name their most important sources of news, people usually rank television first, followed by newspapers, radio, and the Internet.[27] Much of the Internet consumption is Web versions of mainstream newspapers and television.

THE REGULATION/DEREGULATION DEBATE

When the FCC compared the number of broadcast news outlets available to Americans living in communities of various sizes at the dawn of the twenty-first century, it found that, on average, the number of outlets had more than tripled since 1960. Congress had ordered the research to ascertain whether it was time to scrap rules restricting companies from owning multiple news enterprises in the same market. The rules were designed to ensure that the limited number of broadcast frequencies would represent a wide spectrum of interests. The conclusion of majorities in Congress, hotly disputed by the minority, was that a substantial loosening of restrictions was in order because advancing technology has multiplied available channels. Besides, companies eager to increase their holdings claimed that economies of scale would allow them to improve their offerings. They would also be better able to compete with unregulated cable and satellite television and the Internet.

Opponents of deregulation have pointed out that large conglomerates, such as the Tribune Company, Viacom, and News Corporation, already control the most popular stations and often share programs, contrary to the government's communication diversity goals. They also claim that loosening the existing restrictions encourages replacing local programming with bland, generic coverage suitable for large, diverse markets. The competition between giant corporations and smaller enterprises, like the fight between supermarkets and Ma and Pa grocery shops, invariably ends with the giants garnering most of the rights to exclusive stories and most of the advertising revenues while the dwarfs' economic base crumbles.

Opponents of deregulation point out that deregulation of radio in 1996 led to a frenzy of mergers that ended with a handful of giant corporations, led by Clear Channel and Infiniti Broadcasting Corporation, dominating the industry. Clear Channel grew from forty-three to more than 1,200 stations nationwide. Altogether, twenty-one companies had each acquired more than forty stations.[28] Some observers hailed this development as beneficial to consumers because larger companies have more resources to produce sophisticated programming. Others condemned it as a major disaster that shrank the diversity of offerings and reduced experimentation and creativity.

Despite the strong pressures for deregulation in the United States at the dawn of the twenty-first century, the federal government continues to regulate private electronic media to ensure that they "serve the public interest, convenience, and necessity" as mandated by the Communications Act of 1934 and its 1996 counterpart. The FCC, a bipartisan body appointed by the president and confirmed by the Senate, handles most regulation.[29] The FCC was a seven-member body until the summer of 1984 when, for financial reasons, Congress downsized it to five commissioners. In 1986 the appointment term was short-ened from seven to five years, ensuring faster turnover of commission personnel and greater control by the government. In theory, the commission is an indepen-dent regulatory body. In practice, congressional purse strings, public and indus-try pressures, and presidential control over appointment of new members, including naming the chair, have greatly curtailed the FCC's freedom of opera-tion. The commission's independence is weakened also because its rulings can be appealed to the courts, which frequently overturn them. Conflicting political pressures from outside the agency as well as internal political pressures further limit FCC policy making, so that it tends to be "a reactive rather than an innova-tive system sluggish to respond to change in its environment, particularly to technological change....Clearly there are problems with this kind of policy-making system."[30] On balance, the FCC's record of setting goals and enforcing its rules has earned it the reputation of being at best an ineffective watchdog over the public interest and at worst an industry-kept, pressure-group-dominated lapdog.

The FCC controls only over-the-air television. Cable television and the Internet have been excluded because they are considered "common carriers"—channels that carry information compiled by others rather than originating their own information. U.S. print media are also beyond the FCC's reach thanks to the press clause of the First Amendment. However, like cable and the Internet, they are subject to general laws such as those limiting monopolies and trusts. These regulations become operative when the eight largest firms in a particular type of business control more than half of the market and the twenty largest firms control three-quarters or more. Concentration in the news media business has remained substantially below these levels. The Justice Department does permit economically weak newspapers to combine their business and production facilities free from antitrust and monopoly restraints, as long as their news and editorial operations are kept separate.

FCC control takes four forms: rules limiting the number of stations owned or controlled by a single organization, examinations of the goals and performance of stations as part of periodic licensing, rules mandating public service and local interest programs, and rules to protect individuals from dam-age caused by unfair media coverage. Although none of these rules prescribes specific content, all of them were designed to increase the chances that content would be diverse and of civic importance.

In practice, none of the rules has been effective enough to overcome the pull of political and market forces, including the dawning of the Internet age. Despite the mushrooming of broadcast enterprises, the news diet that most Americans consume is surprisingly uniform, politically lightweight, and domi-nated by oligopolies. Licensing has become almost automatic with minimal quality controls. When processing licenses the FCC usually looks at the mix of programs, the proportion of public service offerings, and the inclusion of programs geared to selected minorities and interests. It does not scrutinize the subject matter of broadcasts in detail.

Compared with regulatory agencies in other countries, even in Western Europe, Canada, and Australia, the FCC controls the electronic media with a very light hand. The members of the FCC could, if they wished, rigorously define what constitutes "programming in the public interest." They could enforce FCC rulings more strictly and verify that stations are meeting their public service and local programming obligations before renewing their licenses. The threat of license withdrawal for rule violations could be used as a powerful deterrent to misbehavior and a strong guide to programming. That does not happen because political cross-pressures are strong, including the fear that FCC enforcement could impair press freedom. Besides, the FCC staff is much too small to cope with all their assigned duties. The FCC's performance in protecting individuals from unfair publicity has been somewhat stronger, as discussed in chapter 3.

PRESSURES BY MEDIA ASSOCIATIONS AND ADVERTISERS

Media lobbies are another means of controlling mass media policies. Radio and television interests, especially the networks and their affiliated stations, are active lobbyists. Most belong to the National Association of Broadcasters (NAB), a powerful Washington, D.C., lobby despite the diversity and often clashing interests of its members. A number of trade associations and publications, such as *Broadcasting* magazine, also lobby, often at cross-purposes. For newspapers the American Newspaper Publishers Association (ANPA), now merged with several other press associations, has been one of the most prominent groups. These organizations try to influence appointments to the FCC and to guide public policies affecting new technologies that may threaten established systems or practices. For instance, the network lobbies for many years tried to stifle cable television and to acquire control over domestic satellites. The National Cable Television Association and the National Association of Broadcasters have used members' stations to urge support for their policy recommendations. On other occasions, such as the passage of the Telecommunications Act of 1996, they have tried to downplay coverage that might arouse unwanted opposition.

To forestall regulation by outside bodies, the media industry has developed mechanisms for self-control. The NAB has had a radio code since 1929 and a television code since 1952 that set rules on program content and form. The NAB modernizes both codes periodically. Individual codes in major broadcast enterprises and codes adopted by the Council of Better Business Bureaus have supplemented or superseded industrywide codes. Print press self-policing has developed along similar lines. Scholars, too, have set forth codes of journalism ethics.

Most codes are quite vague, mandating honesty, fairness, independence, and concern for the public interest. Media outlets then decide what these principles mean in practice. Overall, the impact of industrywide codes has been limited. Typically they apply only to organization members that explicitly subscribe to them. Penalties for code violations have been minimal. The codes have been useful in blunting demands by pressure groups for government intervention to set and enforce standards. For instance, congressional leaders lifted a threat to pass laws limiting excessively violent and sexually explicit shows on programs available to children in return for industry promises to develop a rating system to guide parents.

In the 1970s advertisers began to influence program content by withdrawing their commercials from programs they considered obscene or excessively violent. Sears Roebuck was one of the earliest and largest advertisers to do so. McDonald's, American Express, and AT&T refused to place commercials on such shows. Other large advertisers, such as Procter and Gamble, retained consultants to seek out acceptable programs for their advertisements and avoid unacceptable ones. With advertisements on such top-rated shows as the Super Bowl yielding more than $3 million for a thirty-second spot, threats of withdrawal have had some impact on programming.[31]

While reductions in programs featuring sex and violence have been welcome, other changes have been problematic. There is deep concern that advertisers, spurred by pressure groups, may become unofficial censors. For instance, General Motors canceled its sponsorship of an Eastertime program on the life of Jesus because evangelical groups objected to the content. A CBS documentary on gun control, opposed by the gun control lobby, suffered crippling withdrawals of advertising. Fearing similar punishments from fundamentalist religious groups, the networks have refused advertising designed to instruct viewers about the use of condoms for protection against unwanted pregnancies and acquired immune deficiency syndrome (AIDS). Such unofficial censorship at the behest of advertisers impairs press freedom.

CITIZEN LOBBY CONTROL

Citizens' efforts to affect the quality of broadcasting began in earnest in 1966, when the Office of Communication of the United Church of Christ, a public interest lobby, challenged the license renewal of WLBT-TV in Jackson, Mississippi, accusing the station of discriminating against African American viewers.[32] At the time, 45 percent of Jackson's population was African American. The challenge failed, but it was the beginning of efforts by many other citizens groups to challenge license renewals.

Citizen groups won a major victory in 1975 when the FCC refused to renew the licenses of eight educational television stations in Alabama and denied a construction permit for a ninth because citizen lobbies had charged racial discrimination in employment at the stations. There also had been complaints that the stations unduly excluded programs dealing with affairs of the

African American community.[33] Since then numerous stations have yielded to pressure for increased minority employment and programming rather than face legal action. It is one of many examples that demonstrate that the threat of legal action is a powerful stimulant of social behavior.

During the 1980s many citizens groups formed to lobby for better programming and tighter government controls. They represented a broad array of ideological viewpoints as well as a variety of demographic groups. Despite the substantial impact of such groups on FCC rule-making and licensing procedures, citizen lobbying efforts at the national level declined in the 1980s and have never regained their original vigor. One reason has been the difficulty of sustaining citizen interest over time; others were lack of financial support and loss of leadership. The broadcast lobby defeated efforts to obtain public funding for citizens' lobby groups, and foundation support has dried up. Many groups also were discouraged when the appeals courts reversed substantial victories won in the lower courts and when the U.S. Supreme Court voided the 1996 Communications Decency Act.[34] Some citizens' groups have redirected their energy into local lobbying to ensure that cable systems in their locality serve the interests of various publics at reasonable prices to consumers.

In addition to the more than sixty organizations concerned exclusively with media reform, other organizations, such as the Parent Teacher Association (PTA), the National Organization for Women, and the American Medical Association, have lobbied on a variety of media issues. They have shown concern about stereotyping, access to media coverage and to media employment and ownership, advertising on children's programs, and enforcement of FCC program regulations. The groups' tactics include monitoring media content, publicizing their findings, and pressuring broadcasters, advertisers, media audiences, and government control agencies. PTA members have pressured advertisers, who in turn have succeeded in reducing the number of violent programs shown in the early evening. Legal maneuvers have ranged from challenges of license renewals to damage suits for the harmful effects of media content.

Assessing the precise influence of these organizations is difficult because many of their goals overlap with other forces that affect media policy. Some of the causes for which they have worked, such as measures fostering good programming for children, have prospered over the years, however, and part of the credit undoubtedly belongs to them. Yet these groups have a long road to travel before they can match the influence enjoyed by the broadcast lobby in protecting its interests even when they run counter to the concerns of many citizens.

SUMMARY

We have examined the most common types of ownership and control of the news media in this chapter. While most of the media establishment is in private sector hands, the federal government plays an important role as well. It owns and operates vast overseas radio and television enterprises as well as partially controlling a far-flung system of domestic public television and radio broadcasting that provides an alternative to commercial programming. For the average American, the government-controlled systems are peripheral and privately owned print and electronic media enterprises are the focus of concern.

The major political problems in the private sector are concentration of ownership of media in the hands of large business conglomerates and concentrated control over the production of news and entertainment programs. Scrutiny of the impact of the existing system on the quality of the news showed that business ownership has enhanced the focus on soft news and entertainment at the expense of serious political news that citizens need to perform their political roles. But it has not led to programming dominated by business perspectives, as many observers feared. Nor has coverage of local news withered in the wake of media mergers. Large enterprises, rather than small ones, have excelled in providing news and entertainment.

In this chapter we have also outlined the major changes in the news media system spawned by the mushrooming of novice news providers who populate and crowd the Internet. We found that as yet, the newcomers have remained a limited influence. The traditional media, thanks to creating their own Web sites, are retaining their market dominance. In addition, we examined the regulatory structures created by the federal government to ensure a diverse supply of information. We found that enforcement of regulations has been weak, primarily because it is a political football kept in play by multiple powerful stakeholders.

The multiplicity of influences at work in manufacturing news and entertainment programs makes it impossible to assess the precise impact of those influences on media content in general or even on a particular story. In the next chapter we will focus on major legal aspects of news production for additional clues to the mystery of what shapes the news.

NOTES

1. Christopher Walker, "Muzzling the Media: The Return of Censorship in the Commonwealth of Independent States," 2008, www.freedomhouse.org/uploads/specialreports/54pdf.

2. Daniel C. Hallin and Paolo Mancini, *Comparing Media Systems: Three Models of Media and Politics* (Cambridge, UK: Cambridge University Press, 2004). This book describes different government control styles in selected western democracies.

3. See www.nielsenmedia.com/nc/portal/site/Public/menuitem. Examples of the types of shows that attracted more than 12 million viewers in 2009 are *Desperate Housewives* (16,200,000); *Grey's Anatomy* (16,000,000); *House* (15,700,000); and *Lost* (13,400,000). In addition, there are the ever-popular sports events, such as *NBC Sunday Night Football* (14,847,000); competitions like *Wheel of Fortune* (12,379,000); and newsmagazine shows like *Sixty Minutes* (14,110,000).

4. See http://internet-filter-review.toptenreviews.com/internet-pornography-statistics.html#anchor4.

5. Ben H. Bagdikian, *The New Media Monopoly* (Boston: Beacon Press, 2004); Robert Picard, "The Challenges of Public Functions and Commercialized Media," in *The Politics of News, the News of Politics,* 2nd ed., ed. Doris Graber, Denis McQuail, and Pippa Norris (Washington,

D.C.: CQ Press, 2008). For a negative view of the "marketplace of ideas" concept, see Benjamin Ginsberg, *The Captive Public: How Mass Opinion Promotes State Power* (New York: Basic Books, 1986), 98–148.

6. See www.voanews.com/English/About/FastFacts.

7. See www.pbs.org 2009; www.npr.org 2009.

8. Ibid.

9. A content analysis of political discourse on PBS led to the conclusion that stories focused primarily on the strategic aspects of domestic politics and the economy and featured the views of political elites, especially insiders drawn from government and the business world. William Hoynes, "Political Discourse and the 'New PBS,'" *Press/Politics* 7, no. 4 (2002): 34–56.

10. For an impassioned analysis of the trials and tribulations of U.S. public television, see James Ledbetter, *Made Possible By…The Death of Public Broadcasting in the United States* (London: Verso, 1997).

11. See www.gannett.com/about/company_profile.com.

12. Project for Excellence in Journalism, "The State of the News Media 2008," www.stateofthenews media.org.

13. Ibid.

14. Media critic Dean Alger claims that quality deteriorates when papers are acquired by a chain. *Megamedia: How Giant Corporations Dominate Mass Media, Distort Competition, and Endanger Democracy* (Lanham, Md.: Rowman and Littlefield, 1998), 180–182.

15. Federal Communications Commission, www.fcc.gov. See also Jeff Chester, "Strict Scrutiny: Why Journalists Should Be Concerned about New Federal and Industry Deregulation Proposals," *Press/Politics* 7, no. 2 (2002): 105–115.

16. Tribune Company's Web site, 2008, www.tribune.com.

17. David Pearce Demers, *The Menace of the Corporate Newspaper: Fact or Fiction?* (Ames: Iowa State University Press, 1996); W. Lance Bennett and Timothy E. Cook, "Journalism Norms and News Construction: Rules for Representing Politics," *Political Communication,* special issue, Winter 1996. For contrary views, see Alger, *Megamedia,* 153–194; and Robert W. McChesney, *Rich Media, Poor Democracy* (New York: New Press, 1999).

18. Bennett and Cook, "Journalism Norms and News Construction."

19. Jarol B. Manheim, *The Death of a Thousand Cuts: Corporate Campaigns and the Attack on the Corporation* (Mahwah, N.J.: Erlbaum, 2001).

20. Project for Excellence in Journalism, "The State of the News Media 2008."

21. MySpace and Facebook had roughly 60 million active users by 2008; YouTube, the most popular video-sharing site, had 57.4 million users. Like the other Web sites, it was viewed as an attractive property, well supported by advertisers, and Google bought it in 2006. Project for Excellence in Journalism, "The State of the News Media 2008."

22. Ibid.

23. Bruce Bimber, *Information and American Democracy: Technology and the Evolution of Political Power* (Cambridge, UK: Cambridge University Press, 2003).

24. Project for Excellence in Journalism, "The State of the News Media 2008."

25. Alger, *Megamedia,* 31, 130–134.

26. Ibid.

27. Pew Research Center for the People and the Press, "Biennial Media Consumption Survey," 2008, http://people-press.org/.

28. Ibid.

29. 47 U.S.C.A. §307(a), 1934.

30. Erwin G. Krasnow, Lawrence D. Longley, and Herbert A. Terry, *The Politics of Broadcast Regulation,* 3rd ed. (New York: St. Martin's Press, 1982), 284.

31. "GM Won't Advertise during Super Bowl," MSNBC, September 22, 2008, www.msnbc.msn .com/id/26842347/.

32. *Office of Communication of the United Church of Christ v. FCC,* 359 F.2d 994 (D.C. Cir. 1966).

33. Krasnow, Longley, and Terry, *The Politics of Broadcast Regulation,* 54–62.

34. *Reno v. American Civil Liberties Union,* 521 U.S. 844 (1997).

READINGS

Aufderheide, Patricia. *Communications Policy and the Public Interest: The Telecommunications Act of 1996.* New York: Guilford Press, 1999.

Bagdikian, Ben H. *The New Media Monopoly.* Boston: Beacon Press, 2004.

Campbell, Richard, Christopher R. Martin, and Bettina Fabos. *Media and Culture: An Introduction to Mass Communication.* 7th ed. Boston: Bedford/St. Martin's, 2009.

Compaine, Benjamin, and Douglas Gomery. *Who Owns the Media: Competition and Concentration in the Media Industry.* 3rd ed. Mahwah, N.J.: Erlbaum, 2000.

Croteau, David, and William Hoynes. *The Business of Media: Corporate Media and the Public Interest.* 2nd ed. Thousand Oaks, Calif.: Pine Forge Press, 2006.

Einstein, Mara. *Media Diversity: Economics, Ownership, and the FCC.* Mahwah, N.J.: Erlbaum, 2004.

Graber, Doris, Denis McQuail, and Pippa Norris, eds. *The Politics of News, the News of Politics.* 2nd ed. Washington, D.C.: CQ Press, 2008.

Krasnow, Erwin G., Lawrence D. Longley, and Herbert A. Terry. *The Politics of Broadcast Regulation.* 3rd ed. New York: St. Martin's Press, 1982.

Price, Monroe E., and Stefaan G. Verhulst. *Self-regulation and the Internet.* The Hague: Kluwer Law International, 2005.

Zarkin, Kimberly, and Michael J. Larkin. *The Federal Communications Commission: Front Line in the Culture and Regulation Wars.* Westport, Conn.: Greenwood Press, 2006.

chapter 3

Press Freedom and the Law

H ow prevalent is press freedom? The disappointing answer is, "Not very," and the situation is deteriorating in a world gripped by fears of terrorism. Forty-two percent of the world's people, living in sixty-four countries, do not enjoy a free press at all, and another 40 percent, living in fifty countries, enjoy only partial press freedom. That leaves just 18 percent of the world's people in seventy-two countries benefiting from full press freedom.[1] These ratings are based on four sets of criteria: laws and regulations that influence media content, political pressures and controls over media content, economic influences over media content, and such repressive actions as censorship and physical violence, including the killing of journalists (Box 3-1).

The United States, along with most western democracies, ranks among the countries where, according to Freedom House's 2008 survey, print and broadcast media and the Internet are essentially free, though most fall considerably short of a perfect score. Why and how has the United States maintained its high press freedom rankings for more than sixty years? What does press freedom, guaranteed by the U.S. Constitution, mean in practice? How can the freedom of privately controlled institutions to choose, frame, and report all news be reconciled with protection of society from irresponsible news stories that damage public interests? How can an unfettered media establishment be kept responsive to the many voices that should be heard? In this chapter we will shed light on these puzzles by probing problems that arise when a free press claims the exclusive right to decide what to publish and, in the process, clashes with demands by citizen groups for different types of stories. We will then turn to barriers to information that the government claims is too sensitive to publish. Finally, we will examine restraints on publication that legislators and courts have imposed to safeguard private and public interests.

The First Amendment to the U.S. Constitution is the basis for press freedom. The amendment guarantees that "Congress shall make no law…abridging the freedom of speech or of the press." This makes the press the only private enterprise in the United States to which the Constitution grants a privileged status. The interpretations of the scope of this privilege, however, have fluctuated since the First Amendment was ratified in 1791, and federal and state courts have interpreted it in diverse ways.[2]

BOX 3-1 What Makes the Press Free?

Freedom House, a nonprofit, nonpartisan organization, reports annually about press freedom throughout the world. The organization rates each country's public information system as free, partially free, or not free. The criteria that Freedom House uses to gauge press freedom summarize the many ways in which governments around the world can and do curb the freedom of their news media. Three areas are crucial: the legal environment, the political environment, and the economic environment. Freedom House scores these areas based on surveys of local conditions. Restraints of press freedom receive penalty points.

Judging freedom in the legal environment entails screening potentially damaging laws and regulations and the government's inclination to use them. Additionally, it involves assessing the impact of security legislation, criminal statutes, and penalties for libel and defamation. Freedom House also weighs the positive impact of legal guarantees of freedom of expression including freedom of information laws. Institutional factors are important as well. They include the independence of the judiciary and of official media regulatory bodies, registration requirements for media outlets and journalists, and the freedom of journalists to organize to promote their concerns.

To appraise the political environment, Freedom House evaluates how free the media are to choose their content. That requires checking the editorial independence of government and privately owned media, as well as evaluating ease of access to information and ease of access to potential sources of information. Official censorship and self-censorship are appraised as well, as is the freedom of local and foreign reporters to cover the news without harassment by the state or other actors.

When judging the economic environment, Freedom House takes account of unfavorable economic conditions. It examines ownership issues such as excessive concentration, high start-up costs, high operating costs, and ease of obtaining financial subsidies or advertising. Corruption and bribery and insufficient transparency are also treated as threats to press freedom.

Judged by these criteria, the press freedom record for 2008 is wretched. Forty-two percent of the world's people live in countries where freedom of expression is severely constrained. Another 40 percent live in countries enjoying only limited opportunities for open discussion of controversial issues. A mere 18 percent of the world's people live in countries where the press is labeled "free," though never totally so. The leaders in press freedom are small European democracies: Finland, Iceland, Belgium, Denmark, Norway, Sweden, and Luxembourg. At the unfree end of the scale are small countries such as North Korea, Cuba, Burma, Turkmenistan, and Libya. The United States is rated as a free-press country but ranks only twenty-first among 195 countries on the Freedom House scale. That is a good record, but it leaves substantial room for improvement.

Source: Freedom House, "Freedom of the Press 2008," www.freedomhouse.org.

The nation's founders granted this special status to the press because they considered the right to express opinions and to collect and disseminate information free from government interference the bedrock of a free society.[3] If restraints are needed to protect society from pernicious publicity, they must not come through laws that forestall free expression through "prior restraint." Government can prevent publication only if it "will surely result in direct, immediate, and irreparable damage to our nation or its people."[4] The belief in the political importance of a free press has stood the test of time and remains a cornerstone of U.S. democracy.

ACCESS TO THE MEDIA

Ideally, government "by the people" means that the people have a right to express their political views. In practice, that requires that they must be able to use the mass media to publicize their views. The civil rights movement of the 1960s and the many environmental protection crusades that have swept the country, for example, never could have gathered widespread support without mass media publicity. Did the reformers have a *right* to news media publicity for their views and for their organizing activities? The answer is no. In fact, it is difficult for most people, other than journalists or major public figures, to gain access to the media.[5] Media personnel decide what stories to publicize and whose views to present, leaving many views without a public forum. There is simply not enough time and space available to accommodate all who want to be heard. Internet Web sites alleviate the problem, but much of the Internet is a wilderness that devours voices, leaving them bereft of listeners.

Uncontrolled Media

U.S. courts usually have held that the print media have a nearly absolute freedom to determine what they will or will not print and whose views they will present. Cable television and the Internet thus far enjoy the same freedom because, like the telephone, they are considered "common carriers" that merely transport other people's messages. However, this issue remains contested because many Americans favor restraints on press freedom. As it stands now, as long as unregulated media stay clear of deliberate libel and slander and do not publish top secret information, legal restraints do not hamper their publishing decisions.

The U.S. Supreme Court defined print press rights in the case of *Miami Herald Publishing Company v. Tornillo* (1974).[6] At issue was the constitutionality of a Florida statute that gave candidates for public office a right to immediate reply when they had been personally attacked by a newspaper. The rebuttal had to match the format of the original attack, and it had to be placed in an equally prominent spot in the newspaper. The law had been passed to deal with the problem of personal attacks published very late in a campaign, giving candidates little time to respond. The consequence might be loss of the election.

The case arose in 1972 when Patrick Tornillo Jr., leader of the Dade County Teachers Union, was running for the Florida state legislature. Just before the primary the *Miami Herald* published two editorials objecting to Tornillo's election because he had led a recent teachers' strike. Tornillo demanded that the paper print his replies to the editorials. The paper refused.

After Tornillo lost the primary decisively, he sued the paper. When the case reached the U.S. Supreme Court in 1974, the Court ruled unanimously that newspapers can print or refuse to print anything they like. No one, including a candidate whose reputation has been unfairly damaged, has the *right* to obtain space in a newspaper. Therefore, the Florida right-to-reply statute was unconstitutional. The decision reaffirmed what had been the thrust of the law all along. Private citizens may request that a story or response to a personal attack be printed and that request may be granted, but they have no right to demand publication.[7]

Controlled Media

The rules are different for the broadcast media because limited channel space makes them semi-monopolies. Entry into the broadcast media business requires a license from the government. In return for the privilege of broadcasting over the public airwaves, license holders must obey the many government regulations designed to keep the broadcast marketplace as open and fair as possible.

Technology advances have vastly expanded channel space, allowing entry to a huge chorus of new voices. In response, many members of Congress and many broadcasters and communication scholars have urged ending differential treatment of broadcast media based on the assumption of broadcast channel scarcity. Moreover, the distinctions between print and broadcast media are becoming increasingly blurred because many print media now broadcast their messages on Internet Web sites. Hence all media should be free from government interference in making publishing decisions.

Under current laws, broadcast media must air certain types of messages. Section 315 of the Communications Act of 1934 and its many subsequent amendments and interpretations identifies three categories: the equal time provision, the fairness doctrine, and the right of rebuttal. All of these rights arise only after a station has broadcast a particular type of information.

The Right to Equal Time. If a station gives or sells time during an election campaign to one candidate for a specific office, it must make the same opportunity available to all candidates for that office, including those with few backers. However, if the station refuses time to all candidates for the same office, none of them has a right to demand access under Section 315. The rules exclude coverage provided through regular news programs and specifically exempt talk shows.

Stations constrained by the *can be* all-or-none equal time rule often opt for "none," particularly for state and local offices and when many candidates are competing for the same office. This keeps many viable candidates off the air and has led to widespread dissatisfaction with the equal time rule and demands to abandon it. To make it possible to stage lengthy debates among mainline candidates for major offices without running afoul of the equal time provisions, the FCC exempted debates from equal time rules in 1983. The exemption allows radio and television broadcasters to stage political debates at all

"WELL IF YOU ASK ME, THE FIRST AMENDMENT SHOULD ONLY PROTECT UNCONTROVERSIAL EXPRESSION."

political levels among a limited array of candidates chosen in a nondiscriminatory way. Candidates who feel that they have been unfairly shut out may appeal to the FCC.[8]

The Right to Fair Treatment. The fairness doctrine has had a broader reach than the equal time provision because it is not limited to candidates for political office. It mandates free air time for the presentation of issues of public concern and the expression of opposing views whenever discussion of highly controversial public issues has been aired.

Like the equal time provision, the fairness doctrine (suspended in 2000) has had unintended consequences. It has impoverished public debate by suppressing controversy because broadcasters often shy away from programs dealing with controversial public issues to avoid demands to air opposing views, in place of regular revenue-producing programs. It also is difficult to decide who, among many claimants for airtime, has the right to reply to controversial programs.[9] Although the rule will likely never be reinstated, the pressures and litigation produced by the fairness rule have made the media more receptive to featuring opposing views. For example, it has become traditional to allow spokespersons for the opposition to offer rebuttals after presidential, gubernatorial, and mayoral speeches covering major policy issues. The temper of the times has thus fostered more open dialog, even without legal constraints.

Is there a right of reply to contentious statements made in business commercials? The oil industry, environmentalists, and the drug industry, among other groups, have used commercials to advocate controversial public policies. Commercial firms and public interest groups have petitioned for time to respond because press freedom rules do not apply automatically to commercial messages. In fact, free expression in commercial messages has been constrained severely through truth-in-advertising laws administered by the Federal Trade Commission. If courts order the media to make time available to respond to commercial messages, must the time be free of charge? The answer is unclear because the courts have spoken with forked tongues. Media willingness to allow rebuttals has been quite mixed.

The Right of Rebuttal. The 1969 landmark case *Red Lion Broadcasting Co. v. Federal Communications Commission* established a broad scope for the right of reply when individuals are assailed on radio or television in a way that damages their reputations.[10] The case arose because a book about a conservative senator was attacked on a program conducted and paid for by the ultraconservative Christian Crusade. Fred Cook, the book's author, asked for rebuttal time, free of charge. The station was willing to sell him reply time but refused free time, disclaiming responsibility for the content of programs prepared by clients who had bought air time.

The U.S. Supreme Court sided with Cook, who received the right of rebuttal, at station expense, on the grounds that maligned individuals deserve a right to reply and that the public has a right to hear opposing views. The decision proved to be a hollow victory for supporters of free access to the airways, however, because stations sharply curtailed air time available for controversial broadcasts, fearing rebuttal claims.

Besides illustrating that regulation efforts often boomerang, producing the very evil that they were intended to prevent, the *Red Lion* case is also noteworthy as an example of political manipulation of the regulatory process. The Democratic National Committee had paid for and orchestrated Cook's protest as part of an effort to generate an avalanche of demands for rebuttals that would force stations to cancel conservative radio and television programs to avoid the costs of free rebuttal time.[11] That did, indeed, happen. By 1975, 300 of 350 stations that carried the Christian Crusade had dropped it.

Problems of the Status Quo

Apart from the right to reply to a personal attack and the right of rival candidates to have equal broadcast time, individuals have no access rights to the traditional media that remain the most popular sources of news. However, one should not automatically equate the size of an audience with its influence. What matters most is what individual audience members do with the information that they receive. A few aroused audience members may be able to start a political avalanche, as happened in Illinois, where an initially small chorus of complainants led to the indictment of two successive governors on corruption charges.[12]

The denial of access goes beyond publicizing messages. The public also lacks any legal right to compel the publication of information that is readily available. An Alabama case makes that point. When public television in Alabama canceled the film *Death of a Princess,* in response to protests by Saudi Arabia's royal family and threats of economic boycott, a group of citizens charged unfair denial of their right of access to information. The federal district court disagreed.[13] The station, not the public, had the right to decide what to feature and what to reject.

Single networks or stations often secure exclusive broadcast rights to popular events, such as major sports competitions, barring other venues from covering them. Networks have negotiated exclusive contracts even for such public spectacles as the rededication of the Statue of Liberty during its centennial and the Olympic Games in Beijing, China, in 2008. Broadcast networks also have been very restrictive in airing programs by freelance reporters who are unaffiliated with the network. Similarly, professional organizations frequently restrain the flow of news to the general public until it has first appeared in a professional venue. Violators are punished by refusals to publish information that has first appeared elsewhere. That is why scientists kept silent for five months after discovering a treatment that could cut AIDS patients' pneumonia deaths by half. They wanted to ensure that the good news would be announced first by a bona fide medical journal, the renowned *New England Journal of Medicine*.[14]

Public officials who want access to the news media to explain their views face problems similar to those of private individuals. Although the media are likely to be more sympathetic to their requests, on many occasions coverage has been denied or granted only outside prime time. Several speeches by Presidents Ronald Reagan, Bill Clinton, and others were not broadcast at all because the media considered them partisan political statements or claimed that they contained nothing new. Some speeches were carried by only a few stations, sharply reducing the president's audience. Presidents prevent access problems by tailoring their requests for media time to the needs of the media. They particularly avoid schedule conflicts with major sports events.

The question of access rights to the airwaves also has been raised in connection with various interest groups. Requests have come from producers of children's programs and from African Americans, Hispanics, and lovers of classical music, to name a few. Occasional rulings have forced the electronic media to set aside time for broadcasts geared to such groups, whose needs might be ignored if the forces of the economic marketplace were allowed full rein. The FCC has further protected the interests of these groups by giving preference in license applications to stations whose programs are likely to serve neglected clienteles. In light of the growing number of cable, television, and radio outlets, making access easier for everyone, government protection of special interest groups declined. The U.S. Supreme Court formally freed the FCC from any obligation to weigh the effects of alternative program formats on different population groups when making licensing decisions. The Court's 1981 ruling arose from a series of cases in which radio stations had changed their format, for instance, from all news to all music.[15]

Other Approaches to Media Access

Attempts to gain access to the traditional news media through independently produced programs, individual requests for airtime, and FCC rulings that support fairness in access have been only moderately successful. Other routes to access, such as letters to the editor and op-ed essays, are even less satisfactory. Because of lack of space, most newspapers publish only a tiny portion of the letters and opinion pieces they receive. The *New York Times,* for example, receives more than a thousand letters daily and publishes fifteen or less, limiting length strictly. Even with these stringent controls, space devoted to letters equals the space allotted for editorials in the *Times.* Editors select the letters and op-ed essays to be published, using a variety of criteria that disadvantage average people. Unusual messages or those sent by someone well known are most likely to be printed.

Another avenue to access is through paid advertisements. Labor unions, business enterprises, lobby groups, and even foreign governments have placed advertisements on the air or in major newspapers to present their side of disputes and public policy issues. Usually only large companies can afford the steep purchase price, which may run into thousands of dollars for full-page advertisements and national broadcast exposure. Print and electronic media occasionally have refused to publish advertisements or sell airtime when messages about the energy crisis and the Arab–Israeli dispute, for example, seemed too controversial. The availability of the Internet has lessened public concern about the denial of advertising space. However, as mentioned, e-mail and Web site messages are less-effective means to reach the general public than the daily papers and major over-the-air broadcasts.

When people who are eager to publicize their views cannot afford paid messages, they may try to gain attention by creating a sensational event and inviting the media to witness it. For example, Cindy Sheehan, whose son Casey was killed in the Iraq War, staged a ten-day antiwar protest in 2005 near President George W. Bush's Texas ranch to catch the president's and sympathizers' attention worldwide. The protest received ample free publicity, reaching a global audience. Few publicity seekers meet with such success, and many fail miserably, as happened to a man who invited the media to a self-immolation to protest unemployment. Camera crews filmed the action and the story received nationwide coverage, but the emphasis was on the callousness of the film crew that did not stop the burning. The unemployment issue was well-nigh ignored.

As often happens, lobby group activities failed to change the rules of the game to ensure easier access by disadvantaged groups to traditional media. But publicity for their protests did make broadcasters more receptive to the demands of such groups. Still, even if broadcasters are willing to grant access, the problem of insufficient time to air every claimant's views persists. Irrespective of technological advancements, there will never be enough channels to publicize all important views to large audiences nor enough audiences willing and able to pay attention. The Internet may give everyone a public voice, but it does not guarantee that anyone will listen. Studies of cable television users have shown that regardless of the number of channels available and the important stories they feature, the average viewer rarely taps into more than six.

ACCESS TO INFORMATION SOURCES

Access to information sources involves two major issues: who shall have access and what information must be open for public scrutiny.

Special Access for the Media?

The right to publish without restraint means little if journalists are refused access to sources of information. Supreme Court decisions have denied that the media enjoy special rights in this regard. Neither ordinary citizens nor media personnel have a constitutional right to gather information.[16] In fact, "the First Amendment does not guarantee the press a constitutional right of special access to information not available to the public generally."[17] This even includes such mundane matters as the addresses of people who have been arrested.[18] The Court rejected the argument that the First Amendment entitles the press to special rights of access because of its obligation to scrutinize the political scene on behalf of the public.

Absent special access rights, journalists can be barred from many politically crucial events, thus depriving the public of important information. Closed White House and State Department meetings are examples. The media often are excluded from pretrial hearings and grand jury proceedings that determine whether evidence of wrongdoing justifies indictments. The press also has no right to attend conferences of the Supreme Court at which the justices explain why they decided to hear certain cases and declined to hear others. Media people may be barred from attending sessions of legislative bodies closed to the general public. Such sessions ordinarily deal with confidential information that may require protection or with matters that might prove embarrassing to legislators. Because such proceedings and sessions frequently involve high political stakes, participants may leak news about them to journalists.

Journalists have no right to be admitted to sites of crimes and disasters when the general public is excluded. Nor do they have the right to visit prisons or to interview and film inmates, even for the purpose of investigating prison conditions and confirming rumors of brutality. Supreme Court justices have stressed in several cases that reporters could get the needed information without special access privileges.[19] This suggests that the Court is willing to grant access in situations in which information about prison conditions is totally lacking. Many of the Supreme Court's decisions regarding access to information were controversial, as shown by five-to-four divisions among the nine justices. This clash of views has made media access rights an area of ongoing legal development.

In wartime, military officials have often barred news personnel from combat zones by denying transportation to these areas or by keeping invasion plans secret. Over time, the armed forces have realized that public support for wars is essential and that it is in the military's interest to communicate with the public. "Embedding" of reporters has been one strategy. It requires assigning journalists to a particular unit, which they accompany at all times to report its activities to the extent possible, considering safety concerns. Journalists have been reasonably happy with this type of front-line access. Critics claim that embedding amounts to being "in bed" with the troops, making their good image an overwhelming goal. Overall, the biggest hurdles for war reporting from Iraq and Afghanistan have been the inaccessibility of the terrain, language barriers that force journalists to rely on information gathered by local volunteers, and the substantial danger of being kidnapped, tortured, or killed by assassins or during combat. Casualties among journalists have been higher than ever before.

By custom, although not by law, newspeople often receive preferred treatment in gaining entry to public events. Press passes ensure media access to the best observation points for presidential inaugurations, Space Shuttle landings, and political conventions. The media often are admitted to the scene of events, such as accidents and crimes, from which the general public is excluded. Access, however, is purely at the discretion of the authorities in charge.[20]

Access to Government Documents

Government documents are other important sources of political information that are often off-limits to the public and media. The Freedom of Information Act (FOIA) was signed by President Lyndon B. Johnson on July 4, 1966, and has been expanded repeatedly since then, to make it more enforceable, while guarding sensitive national security information.[21] The Open Government Act of 2007, for example, added an Office of Government Information Services to mediate disputes between FOIA applicants and government agencies that are reluctant to release information.

Burdensome application requirements and the costs of duplicating information have limited FOIA's usefulness for news personnel. In recent years, the intricacies of scanning computerized records preserved in outdated formats have raised additional access hurdles. Nonetheless, the act has enabled important disclosures, such as CIA involvement in political upheavals in foreign countries, illegal financial dealings by members of Congress, and the government's failure to protect the public from chemical and biological hazards and ineffective drugs. Most reporters, however, prefer covering readily available current news to using the Freedom of Information Act to dig into government files to unearth past misdeeds.

Some serious abuses have marred the act's reputation as a bulwark of freedom. Organized crime and narcotics traffickers have used it to spot threats to their activities, and business firms have used it to spy on competitors. To cope with these and other abuses, Congress has amended the act repeatedly. Fees charged to businesses for information have been raised to cover the full costs of inquiries. Fees have been lowered for media enterprises to encourage their search for information. Although most of the changes have been praised because they attempted to resolve acute problems, most have also faced criticism as either an undue expansion of First Amendment rights or as an unsavory contraction.

General Rules. Many types of public documents remain unavailable to reporters despite the pervasiveness of freedom of information laws at all levels of government. Most laws provide for access to public records, but various political jurisdictions define *public records* differently. Laws obviously constitute a public record, but are citizens entitled to inspect the minutes of the meetings that preceded passage of a law, or tapes of the proceedings, or exhibits that a legislative committee considered before passing the law? In many states the term *public record* does not include any information about the genesis of laws and regulations.

The computerization of government records is raising many new access issues. The courts have acknowledged that information stored in government computers constitutes a public record, but they have yet to decide definitively what access rights exist. For example, it is unclear whether journalists have the right to ask for specific data within a database, or whether that entails the creation of a new "record" that public agencies are not required to supply. Must government agencies facilitate computer access by installing user-friendly programs? The *Congressional Record,* for example, could not be searched effectively until full text-searching facilities were developed. What about data stored in now obsolete files that current personnel cannot retrieve? It will take many years to find satisfactory answers to such questions, design appropriate computer programs, and develop reasonable policies.

People requesting information often must demonstrate a special need for it. They must specify precisely what information they want, which is difficult to do without knowing what exists. Administrators determine how specific the request must be and whether and how applicants must demonstrate that they truly need the information. A widely used rule of thumb about access to information is that disclosure must be in the public interest and must not do excessive harm. Access should be denied if the harm caused by opening records is greater than the likely benefit. Accordingly, a reporter's request for the records of welfare clients for a story on welfare cheating probably would be denied because it is embarrassing to many people to reveal that they need public assistance. Because there are no precise guidelines for determining what is in the public interest and what degree of harm is excessive, the judgments of public officials who control documents are supreme.

Many state legislatures are unwilling to leave access policies to the discretion of administrative officials. Therefore they construct detailed lists of the kinds of records that may and may not be disclosed. That approach is unsatisfactory, too, because legislators cannot possibly foresee all types of requests. Release of records may then be forestalled simply because the legislation does not specifically mention them.

Governments routinely bar certain types of documents from disclosure. For example, examination questions and answers for tests given by government agencies usually are placed beyond public scrutiny. If they did become public, the value of the examinations might be totally destroyed. However, if the fairness and appropriateness of examination questions for public jobs are in doubt, public scrutiny of questions and answers might be beneficial. Favoritism in grading exams of the protégés of the powerful is a common abuse that also is difficult to expose without access to graded exams.

Other data that governments frequently keep from media personnel are business records that could advantage competitors, such as bids for government contracts. Because corruption is common in awarding government contracts, reporters often are very interested in what companies have bid or what promises they made in return for contract awards. Without access to the records, investigative reporting of suspected fraud or corruption is impossible. However, secrecy is warranted because publicizing the details of a bid could give an unfair advantage to another firm to underbid the lowest bidder by a few dollars and clinch the contract.

Clearly, some restraints on access are essential to protect individuals and business enterprises, especially in the Internet age when access to computerized government information can make every citizen's life an open book. Yet restraints make betrayals of the public trust easier. The cloak of secrecy may conceal vast areas of corruption. Finding the right balance between protection of individuals and their business ventures and protection of the public interest through media access is extremely difficult and controversial.

Historical and National Security Documents. Access to the official and private records of major public officials is also limited. These records are usually unavailable to the media and the general public until twenty-five years after the public official's death. The lengthy limit was selected to spare possible embarrassment to people in the official's public and private network. When exceptions are made to the twenty-five-year rule, they are frequently contested in court, as happened when former president Richard Nixon unsuccessfully sued to recover control of many of his records about the Watergate affair that had been released to the media. The closure of the private records of public officials is part of the privacy protection afforded to all individuals, but it serves a public purpose as well. For uninhibited discussion in policy making, assurance of confidentiality is essential. Without it, officials will posture for an audience rather than freely address the issues under consideration. The danger of inhibiting free discussion also explains why deliberations prior to legislative or judicial decisions are generally closed to public scrutiny.

The news media ordinarily cannot publish documents concerning matters of national security. Examples are CIA intelligence data and information about prospective negotiations or sensitive past negotiations. Media may also be restricted in publishing news about weapons the United States has adopted or stories indicating that security devices are not operating properly. In some cases, however, such information does become available or can be pieced together from other published stories.

Overall the federal government annually classifies more than one million documents, which means that access to them requires special permission. Many more are beyond easy access because they contain information taken from previously classified documents. In addition, state and local officials withhold massive numbers of documents claiming that their release would harm public interests. Before the Nixon years, if a government agency decided that certain information needed to be kept from the media, the prevailing presumption, shared by the courts, was that the agencies charged with guarding national security are best qualified to assess such matters. That has changed. The Clinton administration eased the jams in information flow at the federal level by putting the burden on the government to show that secrecy was essential, rather than requiring applicants to prove otherwise. Still the problems of access to classified documents remain staggering.[22]

The most difficult aspect of security censorship is to determine which information is truly sensitive and must be protected and which information should remain open to media personnel and the public. Disputes about the safety of disclosing national security information are particularly difficult to settle because both the clamor of the media to obtain access and the government's contention that the information requires protection are often self-serving. What is dubbed "the public interest" may be simply reporters' interest in furthering their careers, or publishers' interest in making money, or the government's interest in shielding itself from embarrassment.

A graphic illustration of this perennial battle is the Pentagon Papers case. Daniel Ellsberg, a former aide to President Lyndon Johnson's National Security Council, claimed that foreign policy information in a Department of Defense study of the U.S. involvement in the Vietnam War had been classified improperly as top secret. He copied the information surreptitiously and gave it to prominent newspapers for publication. He hoped that its release would turn people against the war. The executive branch considered his actions a criminal breach of wartime security and sued Ellsberg and the media that printed the information.

In *New York Times Co. v. United States* (1971), the Supreme Court absolved the media, ruling that the government had been overcautious in classifying the information as top secret.[23] In the Court's view publication did not harm the country. Although the case cleared Ellsberg and the media of the charges, it left unchallenged the government's contention that officials may be prosecuted when they jeopardize national security by disclosing classified information to the press. That happened to Samuel Loring Morison, a naval intelligence analyst who was convicted in 1985 on espionage charges for providing a British military magazine with intelligence satellite photographs.[24]

The Supreme Court decision in the Pentagon Papers case and subsequent lower court rulings did not end the public controversy. Analysts still disagree about whether the disclosures from the Pentagon Papers damaged the national security of the United States. Concurrent opinion holders point out that much of the released information had been available already. Dissenters counter that the information had never been compiled in a single document and published in such prominent sources as the *New York Times* and the *Washington Post.* They also refer to the dismay expressed by many European leaders about publicizing events that they had deemed confidential.

At times security issues, such as information about hostage situations, are resolved through informal cooperation between the government and the media or through self-censorship. For instance, news organizations worldwide voluntarily withhold news about hostage incidents or kidnappings when news stories could jeopardize delicate negotiations to rescue the victims. These situations rarely attract attention because neither the government nor the media want to publicize their collaborative efforts to suppress news. Therefore, it was surprising when it became public knowledge in 2001 that the chief executives of the nation's major television networks had pledged to honor national security adviser Condoleezza Rice's request to abstain from broadcasting messages from Osama bin Laden, the alleged mastermind behind the 2001 terrorist assault on the United States. Rice contacted the executives shortly after the event, arguing that taped broadcasts by bin Laden might contain encoded messages encouraging further terrorism.[25]

Executive Privilege. The doctrine of executive privilege is deeply intertwined with the question of limits on secrecy. Chief executives have the right to conceal information that they consider sensitive. This privilege extends to all of their communications with their staffs. Prior to the Nixon years the courts usually upheld executive privilege, but decisions since then suggest that the scope of the privilege is shrinking. Efforts to make leaking information a crime have also mostly failed. However, it is a crime to leak the names of CIA agents. Vice President Dick Cheney's chief of staff, I. Lewis Libby, was sentenced to prison in 2007 for doing that, allegedly to discredit the agent's husband, who had challenged foreign policies of the Bush administration.[26]

Silence by various government departments and agencies also sharply restricts political news available to the media. Undisclosed information frequently concerns failures, incidents of malfeasance, malfunctions, or government waste. Agencies guard this type of news zealously because disclosure might harm the agency or its key personnel. Chief executives at all levels of government often issue directives restraining top officials from talking freely to journalists. President Reagan even ordered lie detector tests for officials to check compliance with disclosure rules but later rescinded the directive. Although not usually enforceable, directives that muzzle public officials tend to reduce the flow of information to the press and the public.

Except for the ever-present opportunity to get information through leaks by disgruntled insiders, reporters find it difficult to penetrate the walls of silence surrounding publicity-shy agencies. Instead, the media rely on an agency's press handouts or publicity releases or on secondary reports from agency personnel. These usually reflect the sources' sense of what is news, rather than the reporters'.[27] Occasionally, reporters on the trail of stories that would be highly embarrassing to government officials find themselves under strong pressure to stop their inquiries or suppress publication of the damaging news.[28]

Private Industry Documents

Although the problem of government withholding of information is formidable, it is small compared with the problem of access to news stories covering the private sector. Numerous enterprises whose operations affect the lives of millions of Americans as much or more than those of many government agencies shroud their operations in secrecy. If asbestos companies or major tobacco companies want to bar reporters from access to information about their business practices, they can do so with impunity. So can drug companies, repair shops, or housing contractors as long as the information has not surfaced in an official proceeding such as a court case or government report. Fear that a company might sue a media organization for millions of dollars is also a powerful deterrent to publicizing questionable business practices. Even *60 Minutes,* renowned for its fearless investigative reports, has occasionally caved in to such pressure. That happened in 1995 when the program temporarily shelved an interview with a tobacco industry whistle-blower because exceptionally high legal expenses loomed.[29]

The Freedom of Information Act does not cover unpublished records of private businesses, except for their reports to the government about sales or inventory figures or customer lists. As noted earlier, many of these reports are withheld from the public on the ground that business cannot thrive if its operational data are made available to its competitors. Moreover, the chances that withheld information will be disclosed through leaks are infinitely less in business than in government. Employees can be pledged to secrecy as a condition of employment and fired if they break their vow.

INDIVIDUAL RIGHTS VERSUS THE PUBLIC'S RIGHT TO KNOW

Thus far we have focused on barriers to the free flow of information imposed by the mass media to protect editorial freedom or by government or industry to shield sensitive information. But there are equally important barriers to circulation of information imposed by individuals or on behalf of individuals to protect the right to privacy, the right to an unprejudiced trial, the right to gather information freely, and the right to a good reputation.

Privacy Protection

How much may the media publish about the private affairs of people in public and private life without infringing on the constitutionally protected right of privacy? How much do privacy rights exclude from public scrutiny? The answers depend on the status of the people involved. Private individuals enjoy broad, though shrinking, protections from publicity; public officials and people who have become public figures because many people are interested in their lives do not enjoy such protections.

In general, state and federal courts have permitted the news media to cover details about the personal affairs of people when the information is based on public records. A Georgia case involving a young woman who had been raped and murdered epitomizes this trend. The family wanted to keep the victim's name out of stories discussing the crime. Nonetheless, the news media published the victim's name and gruesome details of the crime. The family sued for invasion of privacy, claiming that there was no need to disclose the name and that Georgia law prohibited releasing the names of rape victims. The U.S. Supreme Court disagreed and overturned the Georgia law. It held that crime was a matter of public record, making the facts surrounding it publishable despite protests by victims and their families.[30]

Circumstances may turn private individuals into public figures. That happened to Oliver Sipple, who attended a public rally featuring President Gerald Ford. Sipple prevented an assassination attempt on the president by grabbing the would-be assassin's gun. When newspeople checked his background they discovered that he was gay and included this information in subsequent stories. Sipple brought suit for invasion of privacy, but the courts denied his claim, saying that he had forfeited his right to privacy by seizing the gun. That action had made him an "involuntary public figure." Individuals also may lose their right to privacy when they grant interviews to reporters. Reporters are free to round the story out with "newsworthy" observations that were not part of the interview. Reporters are also free to publish facts that were told to them in confidence, though they usually honor their pledge of keeping an interviewee's name confidential.[31] If reporters, without malice, misrepresent some of the facts, this, too, is tolerated. The rationale is that the public is entitled to a full story, if it gets any story at all, and that fears of privacy invasion suits should not unduly inhibit reporting.

Many privacy invasion cases involve unauthorized photographs of people currently or previously in public life. When Jacqueline Kennedy Onassis, the widow of President John F. Kennedy, sued one particularly obnoxious photographer, the court ruled that even though she was no longer the first lady, she remained a public figure. Therefore, pictures could be taken and printed without her consent. The court, however, ordered the photographer to stop harassing her.[32] The courts have also permitted reporters to keep the homes of relatives of murder suspects under photographic surveillance and to film police officers during compromising sting operations. In fact, reporters are free to publish pictures taken in public settings without asking their subjects' permission.

To strengthen privacy protection, the courts in recent years have permitted subjects of unsolicited investigative reports to use trespass laws to stop the media. An example is the trespassing judgment against CBS won by the owners of a fashionable New York restaurant after reporters had entered the premises and filmed violations of the city's health code.[33] The courts also have been increasingly willing to protect people against willful inflictions of emotional pain by news media. However, the Supreme Court ruled unanimously in 1988 that the work of satirists and cartoonists enjoys full First Amendment protection.[34] It denied a plea by Rev. Jerry Falwell for privacy protection and for compensation for emotional injury inflicted by a salacious story about his family published by *Hustler* magazine.

Because relatively few cases of privacy invasion generate lawsuits, privacy protection rests primarily on the sensitivity of the news media. It is slim. Even mainstream newspapers feature columns devoted to celebrity gossip; tabloid papers and television shows revel in it. When former senator and presidential candidate John Edwards realized that stories were imminent about his extramarital affair with a business associate, he knew that efforts to protect his privacy would be futile. Therefore, like many other prospective victims of embarrassing publicity, he chose to announce the story himself during an interview on ABC television. In the current news climate it has become impossible to protect newsworthy individuals from the "feeding frenzy" of print and electronic tabloid journalists. Once the proverbial cat is out of the bag, all join the chase, including serious news professionals who do not want to ignore stories that draw large audiences.[35] Efforts by several states to prohibit privacy invasion when the news lacks "social value" are unlikely to succeed over objections that they violate the First Amendment.[36] The ready availability of the Internet for spreading messages has wiped out privacy rights, for the most part.

Fair Trial and the Gag Rule

The courts favor a broad scope of disclosure for most people in public life, but they insist on a limited scope of disclosure in their own bailiwick. The courts used to be zealous in guarding the right of accused persons to be protected against publicity that might influence judge and jury and harm their cases. This has been true even though scientific evidence that media publicity influences parties to a trial is scant and inconclusive.[37]

The stern posture of the courts in censoring pretrial publicity is weakening, however. In 1983 two Supreme Court justices refused to block a nationwide television broadcast about a sensational murder case scheduled for trial three weeks later. The trial involved seven white New Orleans police officers accused of the revenge slaying of four African American men suspected of participating in the murder of a white police officer. In the same vein, a federal court refused to prevent television stations from showing tapes of a cocaine transaction incriminating John DeLorean, a well-known automobile maker and jet-set celebrity. DeLorean's attorneys had argued that the pretrial publicity would make it impossible to find an impartial jury. In another case the courts ruled that incriminating tapes used in a corruption trial of several members of Congress could be shown publicly, even though some of the defendants had not been tried as yet and the convicted defendants were appealing the case.[38] When prominent national political figures have asked to have their trials moved out of Washington, D.C., because of prejudicial pretrial publicity, the courts have almost invariably refused their requests.[39] That did not happen in the case of Timothy McVeigh. His lawyers were able to have his 1997 trial moved away from Oklahoma City, the scene of his politically motivated bombing that killed 168 people and wounded 500 more.

Two murder cases, *Shepherd v. Florida* (1951) and *Sheppard v. Maxwell* (1966), brought the question of media coverage of court cases to wide public attention.[40] In these cases the U.S. Supreme Court held that the defendants, convicted of murder, had not had a fair trial because of widespread media publicity. As justices Robert H. Jackson and Felix Frankfurter stated in *Shepherd v. Florida*, "The trial was but a legal gesture to register a verdict already dictated by the press and the public opinion [it] generated."[41] The Court overturned the convictions.

Judges have the right to prohibit the mass media from covering some or all of a court case before and during a trial, even when the public is allowed to attend courtroom sessions. Gag orders interfere with the media's ability to report on the fairness of judicial proceedings. They also run counter to the general reluctance of U.S. courts to condone prior censorship. Nonetheless, the courts have upheld gag laws as a necessary protection for accused persons.

Judges may make rules restraining filmed coverage or may bar it completely without presenting evidence that the information covered by the gag order would impede a fair trial. Gag orders may extend even to judges' rulings that tell the media to refrain from covering a case. Thus the fact of judicial suppression of information may itself be hidden.

Numerous reporters have gone to jail and paid fines rather than obey gag rules because they felt that the courts were overly protective of the rights of criminal suspects and insufficiently concerned with the public's right to know. A 1976 decision, *Nebraska Press Association v. Stuart*, partly supports the reporters' views.[42] In that case the Supreme Court reversed a gag order in a murder trial. The Court declared that judicial maneuvers short of gag laws should forestall careless reporting that interferes with the rights of defendants. For example, trials can take place in different jurisdictions if there has been excessive local publicity. People can also bring suits against media enterprises or individual reporters who act irresponsibly by publicizing testimony from closed sessions of the courts, taking unauthorized pictures, or bribing court personnel to leak trial testimony.

The policy on gag laws is still unclear, however. Some lower courts have failed to comply with Supreme Court directives or have evaded the spirit of decisions. For example, instead of gagging the press, judges have placed gags on all the principals in a case, including the plaintiffs and defendants, their lawyers, and the jury, to prohibit them from talking about the case, particularly to members of the press. In an increasing number of cases, judges have barred access to information by closing courtrooms to all observers during pretrial proceedings as well as trials. However, this has not stopped legal personnel, including prosecutors, from leaking information to the press when that seemed advantageous.

During the 1980s the Supreme Court struck down several of these restrictions or limited their use by specifying the circumstances under which media access may be denied. In *Richmond Newspapers v. Virginia* (1980), the Court ruled that the public and the press had an almost absolute right to attend criminal trials.[43] In the same vein, the justices declared in 1984 that neither newspeople nor the public may be barred from observing jury selection, except in unusual circumstances.[44] The Supreme Court appears to be moving closer to the notion that the public's access to judicial proceedings is part of the First Amendment rights guaranteed by the Constitution. A change in direction seemed possible following adverse public reaction to televising the 1995 murder trial of O. J. Simpson as if it were a daily soap opera serial. However, people have complained little about this type of coverage in subsequent high-profile trials, such as Michael Jackson's trial for child molestation or Scott Peterson's trial for the murder of his pregnant wife. In fact, television programs like *America's Most Wanted*, which focuses on dramatic crimes, attract large audiences.

Shield Laws

Digging into the affairs of public officials and other prominent citizens or exposing the activities of criminals or dissidents often requires winning the confidence of informants with promises to conceal their identity. Newspeople contend that compulsion to reveal the identity of their sources or surrender unpublished bits of information could hamper their investigations. The sources are likely to dry up because they feel betrayed. That is why reporters want laws to shield them from subpoenas forcing them to break their pledge of confidentiality.

Unfortunately, failure to disclose information may allow criminals to go unpunished and innocent victims to be denied justice. Law enforcement agencies may find it difficult to penetrate dissident and terrorist groups that journalists have been able to use as sources. That is why media organizations at times agree to comply with subpoenas fully or partially. For instance, CBS agreed to surrender portions of unused filmed scenes from the hijacking of a TWA airliner to facilitate the prosecution of the hijackers.[45] When 400 news organizations were asked about subpoenas issued to their personnel, 36 percent of print media respondents and 77 percent of the broadcast media respondents reported receiving one or more subpoenas for disclosure of information that their organization had gathered on the job.[46] The Supreme Court has ruled that newspeople lack a common law right to protect their sources in the face of·a subpoena. Nor may they shield records or editorial deliberations from judicial scrutiny if these records are needed to prove libel, except when the needed information is available from unshielded sources.[47] However, more than half of the states have shield laws to protect reporters from forced testimony. Shield laws give journalists most of the rights enjoyed by lawyers, doctors, and clergy to keep relations with their clients confidential. Shield laws also may bar searches of news offices to discover leads to crimes.

Shield laws do not ensure absolute protection. For example, when the right of reporters to withhold the names of their sources clashes with the right of other individuals to conduct a lawsuit involving criminal offenses, state shield laws and common law protections must yield. In 2004 a federal judge ordered two reporters jailed for up to eighteen months for refusing to tell a grand jury the names of government officials suspected of leaking confidential government information.[48] Likewise, a television reporter was convicted in 2004 of criminal contempt for refusing to say who gave him an FBI videotape showing a politician taking a bribe.

Some journalists advocate a federal shield law to protect all newspeople throughout the country and to reduce the costs of litigation when they resist forced disclosure. Others, fearing that such a law would provide conditional shielding only, prefer to do without shield laws of any kind; they contend that the First Amendment is sufficient protection. Moreover, in the words of Supreme Court justice Byron R. White, "From the beginning of our country, the press has operated without constitutional protection for press informants, and the press has flourished." Hence the absence of shield laws has "not been a serious obstacle to either the development or retention of confidential news sources by the press."[49] These differences of opinion have taken steam out of the pressure for a federal shield law. Nonetheless, the House of Representatives passed a shield law—the Free Flow of Information Act of 2007—by a 398–21 vote. Senators also favored the bill but procedural issues derailed it.

The bill is likely to resurface. When it does, there will be spirited discussion about the extent to which laws currently affecting journalists should be extended to anonymous as well as identified bloggers. The basic issue underlying this discussion is whether training and experience or the nature of the publicized message should determine who deserves the designation "journalist." Court cases have varied on that score. Once judges have made a choice between these assumptions, more controversy will arise because there are sharp disagreements in the journalism community about the required experiences and training of journalists, and about the unique characteristics that make a message a "news story."[50]

Libel Laws

Libel laws provide redress when published information has unjustly tarnished a person's reputation. To win a libel suit, a plaintiff must prove that the defendant's negligence or recklessness led to publication of information that exposed the plaintiff to hatred, ridicule, or contempt. For years libel suits, even when lost in court, dampened investigative reporting. That changed substantially in 1964 for cases involving public officials. The police chief of Montgomery, Alabama, brought an action for libel because an advertisement in the *New York Times* had charged him with mishandling civil rights demonstrations. The Supreme Court absolved the paper, ruling in *New York Times v. Sullivan* that a public official who claims libel must be able to show that the libelous information was published "with knowledge that it was false or with reckless disregard of whether it was false or not."[51] The *Sullivan* rule has made it very difficult for public officials to bring suit for libelous statements made about them. Malicious intent and extraordinary carelessness are hard to prove, especially because the courts give the media the benefit of the doubt. By the same token, the *Sullivan* rule has made it much easier for media to publish adverse information about public officials without extensive checking of the accuracy of the information prior to publication.

Since the 1974 decision in *Gertz v. Robert Welch,* the Supreme Court has narrowed the "public figure" category.[52] In that case the Court held that a person who had not deliberately sought publicity would be deemed a public figure only in exceptional—as yet unspecified—circumstances. Therefore, a prominent lawyer whose name had been widely reported in the news was not a public figure and could sue for libel.[53] However, the best protection for public figures from unscrupulous exposure by the media comes from journalists' informal and formal codes of ethics. The increasing number of libel suits brought by public figures against media people also have become a damper on careless reporting because these suits are costly in time and money, even when the media are exonerated, which happens nearly half the time. The average initial awards in the ten to twenty cases that go to trial each year run to millions of dollars. These awards usually are sharply reduced if the case is appealed. Nonetheless, financially weak institutions cannot afford to risk multimillion-dollar judgments and staggering legal fees that might force them out of business.[54]

The emergence of the Internet has raised several new issues in libel law that need resolution. Most important, who bears responsibility for publishing libels?

Early decisions suggest that browsers, such as Netscape or Google, are not required to screen messages for libels and other illegal content such as foul language or obscenity. In fact, the Communications Decency Act of 1996 provides that "[n]o provider or user of an interactive computer service shall be treated as the publisher or speaker of any information provided by another information content provider."[55] The courts have quite consistently construed this provision to bestow immunity from libel suits on Internet information providers.[56]

Other Restrictions on Publication

As discussed in chapter 1, all governments prohibit the publication of information that, in their view, would harm the public interest. The United States is no exception. Censorship is most prevalent in matters of national security involving external dangers, national security involving internal dangers, and obscenity. In each category there is general agreement that certain types of information should not be publicized. There is very little agreement, however, about where the line ought to be drawn between permitted and prohibited types of material. We have already discussed the controversy surrounding the release of the Pentagon Papers. Additional examples involving external security will be presented in chapter 11.

Internal security news primarily entails investigations of allegedly subversive groups and reports on civil disturbances. The Patriot Act of 2001, passed in the wake of the terrorist attack on the United States in September of that year and renewed in 2006, vastly expanded the scope of government surveillance over messages potentially related to internal security. Many of its provisions have been challenged as violations of First Amendment rights.[57]

Irrespective of the outcome of those cases, the Democratic majorities elected to Congress in 2008 are likely to repeal the act partially or completely.

Constraints on internal news also involve media portrayal of asocial behavior that might lead to imitation. Attempts to limit the portrayals of crime and violence, either in general or on programs to which children have access, are examples (chapter 7). Closely related to restraints on the depiction of crime and violence are restraints on publication of indecent and obscene materials and broadcasts that include offensive language or that portray sexual matters or human excretion. Censorship advocates fear that such broadcasts may corrupt members of the audience, particularly children, and lead to imitation of undesirable behavior. They contend that publication of indecent and obscene materials, particularly in visual form, violates community standards and therefore should be prohibited by law. This argument rests on the notion that the public should have the right to prohibit the dissemination of material that offends most people's sense of propriety. Regulation of racy materials has often been quite heavy-handed. For example, the FCC has levied heavy fines on broadcasters for showing entertainer Janet Jackson's accidentally exposed breast during the 2004 Super Bowl, for the utterance of profanity by U2 lead singer Bono, and for showing scantily dressed actors during the 2004 Olympic Game opening ceremonies.

Despite the huge popularity of pornography, as shown by the millions of people who buy pornographic magazines, pay for pornographic movies and stage shows, rent pornographic videos, and visit pornography sites on the Internet, laws in many places bar free access to such information. FCC rules require scheduling indecent programming only between midnight and 6:00 a.m., when children are unlikely to be watching. Obscene programming is barred at all times. Indecent material has been defined by the FCC as "material that depicts or describes, in terms patently offensive by contemporary community standards for the broadcast medium, sexual or excretory activities or organs." Obscenity has been defined by the Supreme Court as "something that, taken as a whole, appeals to the prurient interest; that depicts or describes in a patently offensive way sexual conduct; and that lacks serious artistic, political, and scientific value."[58] Congress has repeatedly passed laws to make it difficult for children and adolescents to view pornography on the Internet. The 1996 Communications Decency Act and the 2000 Child Online Protection Act are examples. The Supreme Court has declared some of these measures unconstitutional.[59] But given the zeal of puritanical lobby groups, antipornography measures remain a lush crop on the American social scene.

Another example of protective censorship is the ban since 1971 on cigarette advertising on radio and television. It is designed to protect susceptible individuals from being lured into smoking by seductive advertisements. Pressures for additional areas of protective censorship have been considerable and range from pleas to stop liquor, sugared cereal, and casino gambling advertisements to requests to bar information dealing with abortion or drug addiction. Legislatures and courts have rejected most of them except when advertising on children's programs was involved.[60]

So-called hate broadcasters also remain a gray area in broadcast law, one that has achieved new prominence because hate messages abound on the Internet. Indeed, the Internet has thousands of racial hate Web sites and hate Web games have become popular.[61] When traditional broadcasts are involved, the FCC has been reluctant to withhold licenses from the offending parties because genuine freedom of expression includes "freedom for the thought we hate," as Supreme Court justice Oliver Wendell Holmes said long ago. Although formal restraints remain few, informal restraints have mushroomed. Television and radio stations have disciplined or dismissed reporters and commentators who made comments offensive to, among others, African Americans, Arabs, women, and homosexuals.

SUMMARY

In a democratic society, citizens have the right and civic duty to inform themselves and to express their views publicly. The press, as the eyes and voice of the public, must be free to gather information and disseminate it. In this chapter we have seen that despite the press freedom guarantees in the First Amendment to the Constitution and legislation such as the Freedom of Information Act, lots of information about government activities remains unpublished. It has been classified as secret for security reasons, or it has not been released to the public because it originated from a closed meeting or might embarrass government officials, or it has escaped media scrutiny simply because of the flood of information government generates.

People have challenged nearly all types of exclusions in the courts as unconstitutional restrictions on the right of access to information. The courts have ruled most of them compatible with constitutional guarantees of free speech and press. They also have ruled, for the most part, that news professionals enjoy neither greater rights of access to information than the general public nor, in the absence of shield laws, greater freedom to protect their access to information by refusal to disclose their sources.

Aside from use of the Internet, the right to publish information in mass media venues is also limited. Here the public is most seriously restricted because newspeople claim the exclusive right to determine what to publicize and what to omit. The power of print media to exclude stories is nearly absolute, except for social pressures to report issues that are vital to the public. Under current rules and regulations television must grant equal access to political candidates for the same office. The fairness rules requiring exposure of opposition views and the right of rebuttal are in limbo. Even when access to a media forum is ensured, the right to publish is not absolute. News has been suppressed because of public policy considerations, such as the need to safeguard external and internal security and the need to protect the moral standards of the community. The scope of permissible censorship has been the subject of countless inconclusive debates and conflicting court decisions, in a perennial contest between legislators eager to censor objectionable messages and judges equally eager to wave the banner of First Amendment rights.

The right to publish also conflicts on many occasions with the rights of individuals to enjoy their privacy, to be protected from disclosure of damaging information, and to be safe from publicity that might interfere with a fair trial. The courts have been the main forum for weighing these conflicting claims, and the scales have tipped erratically from case to case. Two trends stand out from the haze of legal battles: The right to a fair trial generally wins over the freedom to publish, and private individuals enjoy far greater protection from publicity than do people in public life. Shifting definitions of what turns a private person into a public person have blurred this distinction, however.

When one looks at the massive restraints on the rights of access to information, the rights of access to publication channels, and the right to publish information freely, one may feel deep concern about freedom of information. Is there cause for worry? Taking a bright view, Supreme Court justice Byron White commented that the press as watchdog has been chilled by legal restraints, but it has not been frozen into inaction. Unfortunately, many current political trends, including pressures by private organizations to enforce the norms of "political correctness," point toward greater restraints and greater public tolerance for restraints, especially when social and national security are involved. Self-censorship is on the rise as well. For example, on Veterans Day 2004 many stations skipped their traditional showing of the World War II classic movie *Saving Private Ryan*. They feared that the violence and harsh language in the film would subject them to FCC fines. Constant vigilance to deter curbs of First Amendment rights is the price of preserving America's heritage of freedom of thought and expression.

NOTES

1. Freedom House, "Freedom of the Press 2008," www.freedomhouse.org.
2. Robert F. Copple, "The Dynamics of Expression under the State Constitution," *Journalism Quarterly* 64 (Spring 1987): 106–113.
3. For an analysis of how well these rights have been used, see Doris A. Graber, "Press Freedom and the General Welfare," *Political Science Quarterly* 101 (Summer 1986): 257–275.
4. Justice Potter Stewart in *New York Times v. United States*, 403 U.S. 713 (1971).
5. Jerome Barron, *Freedom of the Press for Whom? The Right of Access to the Mass Media* (Bloomington: Indiana University Press, 1973).
6. *Miami Herald Publishing Company v. Tornillo*, 418 U.S. 241 (1974).
7. For a full discussion of the case, see Fred W. Friendly, *The Good Guys, the Bad Guys, and the First Amendment: Free Speech vs. Fairness in Broadcasting* (New York: Random House, 1977), 192–198.
8. *Arkansas Educational Television Commission v. Forbes*, 523 U.S. 666 (1998).
9. Stephen Labaton, "Court Rejects F.C.C. Mandate to Broadcast Political Replies," *New York Times*, October 12, 2000.
10. *Red Lion Broadcasting Co. v. Federal Communications Commission*, 395 U.S. 367 (1969).
11. Friendly, *The Good Guys*, 32–42.
12. Elizabeth Brackett, *Pay to Play: How Rod Blagojevich Turned Political Corruption into a National Sideshow* (Chicago: Ivan R. Dee, 2009).
13. *Muir v. Alabama Educational Television Commission*, 688 F.2d 1033 (5th Cir. 1982). First Amendment problems encountered when governments own media are discussed by William Hanks and Lemuel Schofield, "Limitations on the State as Editor in State-Owned Broadcast Stations," *Journalism Quarterly* 63 (Winter 1986): 797–801. Also see *League of Women Voters v. FCC*, 731 F.2d 995 (D.C. Cir. 1984).
14. "AIDS Panel Delayed News of Treatment," *New York Times*, November 14, 1990.
15. *FCC v. WNCN Listeners Guild*, 450 U.S. 582 (1981).
16. *Zemel v. Rusk*, 381 U.S. 1 (1965).
17. *Branzburg v. Hayes*, 408 U.S. 665 (1972).
18. *Los Angeles Police Department v. United Reporting Publishing Corporation*, 528 U.S. 32 (1999).
19. See, for instance, *Pell v. Procunier*, 417 U.S. 817 (1974); *Saxbe v. Washington Post Co.*, 417 U.S. 843 (1974); and *Houchins v. KQED*, 438 U.S. 1 (1978).
20. *Wilson v. Layne*, 526 U.S. 603 (1999).
21. The act was an amendment to the 1946 Administrative Procedure Act—5 U.S.C.A. 1002 (1946)—which provided that official records should be open to people who could demonstrate a "need to know" except for "information held confidential for good cause found" (Sec. 22). The 1966 amendment stated that disclosure should be the rule, not the exception, with the burden on government to justify the withholding of a document (5 U.S.C.A. Sec. 552 and Supp. 1, February 1975).
22. Douglas Jehl, "Clinton Revamps Policy on Secrecy of U.S. Documents," *New York Times*, April 18, 1995.
23. *New York Times Co. v. United States*, 403 U.S. 713 (1971).

24. *United States v. Morison,* 844 F.2d 1057 (4th Cir.), *cert. denied,* 488 U.S. 908 (1988).

25. Doris A. Graber, "Terrorism, Censorship, and the First Amendment: In Search of Policy Guidelines," in *Framing Terrorism: The News Media, the Government, and the Public,* ed. Pippa Norris, Montague Kern, and Marion Just (New York: Routledge, 2003), 27–42.

26. "The Libby Verdict," *Washington Post,* March 7, 2007, A16.

27. Doris A. Graber, *The Power of Communication: Managing Information in Public Sector Organizations* (Washington, D.C.: CQ Press, 2003), chap. 2.

28. Kristina Borjesson, ed., *Into the Buzzsaw: Leading Journalists Expose the Myth of a Free Press* (Amherst, N.Y.: Prometheus, 2002); W. Lance Bennett, Regina G. Lawrence, Steven Livingston, *When the Press Fails: Political Power and the News Media from Iraq to Katrina* (Chicago: University of Chicago Press, 2007).

29. William Glaberson, "'Sixty Minutes' Case Illustrates a Trend Born of Corporate Pressure, Some Analysts Say," *New York Times,* November 17, 1995.

30. *Cox Broadcasting Corp. v. Cohn,* 420 U.S. 469 (1975).

31. *Cohen v. Cowles Media Co.,* 501 U.S. 663 (1991).

32. *Gallella v. Onassis,* 487 F.2d 986 (2d Cir. 1973).

33. *Le Mistral Inc. v. Columbia Broadcasting System,* 402 N.Y.S.2d 815 (1978).

34. *Hustler v. Falwell,* 485 U.S. 46 (1988). See also Robert E. Drechsel, "Mass Media Liability for Intentionally Inflicted Emotional Distress," *Journalism Quarterly* 62 (Spring 1985): 95–99.

35. Larry J. Sabato, *Feeding Frenzy: Attack Journalism and American Politics* (New York: Free Press, 2000).

36. Linda Greenhouse, "National Enquirer Forces Trial on Invasion-of-Privacy Issue," *New York Times,* December 5, 1995.

37. Although judges often command jurors to strike improper information presented in court from their memory, they disclaim the ability to wipe out media information that jury members might have received outside the courtroom.

38. For examples of the Court's reasoning, see *U.S. v. Alexandro,* 459 U.S. 835 (1982); *U.S. v. Jannotti,* 457 U.S. 1106 (1982).

39. An example is Michael K. Deaver, a Reagan White House aide indicted for perjury. In his request for a change of venue, he presented the court with 471 hostile news clips from Washington, D.C., papers.

40. *Shepherd v. Florida,* 341 U.S. 50 (1951); *Sheppard v. Maxwell,* 384 U.S. 333 (1966).

41. *Shepherd v. Florida,* at 69.

42. *Nebraska Press Association v. Stuart,* 427 U.S. 539 (1976).

43. *Richmond Newspapers v. Virginia,* 448 U.S. 555 (1980).

44. *Press-Enterprise v. Riverside County Superior Court,* 464 U.S. 501 (1984). The controversy arose because the Riverside County, California, superior court closed jury selection in a rape and murder case. The Press-Enterprise Company of Riverside sued to gain access to the court proceeding and to the relevant transcripts.

45. Alex S. Jones, "CBS Compromises on Subpoena for Videotapes of Hostage Crisis," *New York Times,* July 27, 1985.

46. Reporters Committee for Freedom of the Press, "Agents of Discovery," 2001, www.rcfp.org/agents/.

47. *Anthony Herbert v. Barry Lando and the Columbia Broadcasting System Inc.,* 441 U.S. 153 (1979).

48. Adam Liptak, "Judges Skeptical of First Amendment Protection for Reporters in C.I.A. Leak Inquiry," *New York Times,* December 9, 2004; Loren Manly and Adam Liptak, "At Leak Inquiry's Center, a Circumspect Columnist," *New York Times,* December 31, 2004.

49. *Branzburg v. Hayes,* at 699.

50. Julie Hilden, "Can Bloggers Invoke the Journalist's Privilege to Protect Confidential Sources Who Leak Trade Secrets?" April 26, 2005, http://writ.news.findlaw.com/scripts.

51. *New York Times v. Sullivan*, 376 U.S. 254 (1964), at 279–280.

52. *Gertz v. Robert Welch*, 418 U.S. 323 (1974).

53. *Time Inc. v. Firestone*, 424 U.S. 448 (1976); *Hutchinson v. Proxmire*, 443 U.S. 111 (1979); *Wolston v. Reader's Digest*, 443 U.S. 157 (1979).

54. Libel Defense Resource Center, "Press Release, February 26, 2001," www.ldrc.com/damages01. html. The center has been renamed the "Media Law Resource Center."

55. Public Law No. 104-104 (Feb. 8, 1996), 110 Statutes at Large 56.

56. For example, see the California Supreme Court case *Barrett et al. v. Rosenthal*, 40 Cal. 4th 33 (Nov. 20, 2006).

57. Electronic Privacy Information Center, "The USA Patriot Act," www.epic.org/privacy/terrorism/usapatriot.

58. *Miller v. California*, 413 U.S. 5 (1973), at 15. Definition quoted in Tim Jones, "Broadcasters Get Long-Awaited Indecency Guidelines," *Chicago Tribune*, April 7, 2001.

59. See, for example, *Reno v. American Civil Liberties Union*, 521 U.S. 844 (1997). For an editorial opinion about such censorship laws see "Congress Quietly Censors the Web," *Chicago Tribune*, December 23, 2000. The fate of the Child Online Protection Act remains in limbo. See Linda Greenhouse, "Court, 5–4, Blocks a Law Regulating Internet Access," *New York Times*, June 30, 2004.

60. *Greater New Orleans Broadcasting Association v. U.S.*, 527 U.S. 173 (1999); *44 Liquormart, Inc. v. Rhode Island*, 517 U.S. 484 (1996).

61. Lisa Guernsey, "Mainstream Sites Serve as Portals to Hate," *New York Times*, November 30, 2000.

READINGS

Benjamin, Stuart Minor, Douglas Lichtman, and Howard A. Shelanski. *Telecommunications Law and Policy.* 2nd ed. Durham, N.C.: Carolina Academic Press, 2006.

Carter, T. Barton, Marc A. Franklin, and Jay B. Wright. *The First Amendment and the Fifth Estate: Regulation of Electronic Mass Media.* 7th ed. New York: Foundation Press, 2008.

Carter, T. Barton, Marc A. Franklin, and Jay B. Wright. *The First Amendment and the Fourth Estate: The Law of Mass Media.* 10th ed. New York: Foundation Press, 2008.

Dienes, C. Thomas, Lee Levine, Robert C. Lind. *Newsgathering and the Law.* 3rd ed. Newark: LexisNexis/Matthew Bender, 2005.

Heins, Marjorie. *Not in Front of the Children: Indecency, Censorship, and the Innocence of Youth.* New York: Hill and Wang, 2007.

Lewis, Anthony. *Freedom for the Thought That We Hate: A Biography of the First Amendment.* New York: Basic Books, 2007.

Sadler, Roger L. *Electronic Media Law.* Thousand Oaks, Calif.: Sage, 2005.

Singh, Tatindra. *Cyber Laws: A Guide to Cyber Laws, Information Technology, Computer Software, Intellectual Property Rights, E-Commerce, Taxation, Privacy, etc., along with Policies, Guidelines, and Agreements.* 3rd ed. New Delhi: University Law Publishing Co., 2007.

Sullivan, Kathleen M., and Gerald Gunther. *First Amendment Law.* 3rd ed. New York: Foundation Press, 2007.

Teeter, Dwight L., and Bill Loving. *Law of Mass Communications: Freedom and Control of Print and Broadcast Media.* 12th ed. New York: Foundation Press, 2008.

4

News Making and
News Reporting Routines

American journalists are worried about the direction in which their profession is moving. In a 2007 nationwide survey, 69 percent of national broadcast journalists thought that the direction was wrong. So did 56 percent of print journalists. Why? There are many reasons, and they differ substantially from the concerns that were expressed four years earlier. Worries about a decline in the quality of news have been supplanted by worries about the economic survival of traditional journalism and traditional venues in the Internet age. As Table 4-1 shows, 41 percent of national journalists named quality of coverage as the most important problem in spring 2004. That number plunged to 22 percent by December 2007, and business and financial conditions became the chief concern for 55 percent of the interviewees, up from 30 percent in 2004.

Journalists have realized that much of the action has moved to the Internet platform and have recalibrated their quality measurement scales accordingly. They are willing, even eager, to work in the Internet environment. But the nagging question that makes them uneasy is whether Web journalism can become profitable enough to sustain broad-gauge journalistic enterprises covering the news that today's citizens need to perform their civic duties. In this chapter we provide insights on these issues by focusing on reporters and their work under normal circumstances. In the next chapter we will address news making at times of crisis.

PROFILE SKETCH OF U.S. JOURNALISTS

How do journalists decide which information to report as news and how to shape it into news stories? The answers can be approached from three theoretical perspectives. Personality theory explains professional behavior in terms of personality and social background. Organization theory focuses on the impact of organizational goals and pressures on the behavior of members of news production organizations. Role theory maintains that stories will vary depending on the conceptions of their professional role that media personnel adopt. For instance, journalists who see themselves as impartial reporters of the news will behave differently from those who see themselves as partisan reformers.

TABLE 4-1 **The State of Journalism: Most Important Problems Facing Reporters in 2007 (in percentages; 2004 figures in parentheses)**

Problem	National	Local	Internet
Business/ financial pressures	55 (30)	52 (35)	48 (32)
Quality of coverage	22 (41)	21 (33)	25 (32)
Credibility	9 (28)	9 (23)	9 (19)
Media environment	20 (15)	18 (7)	18 (27)
Ethics	3 (5)	4 (6)	3 (4)

Source: Adapted from Pew Research Center for the People and the Press, 2008, http://people-press.org/report/?pageid=1269.

Note: Based on a survey of 585 national and local reporters, producers, editors, and executives. Respondents were drawn from national and local samples representing a cross-section of news organizations. The Internet component was drawn from online-only news organizations as well as from national and local news outlets with a significant Web presence. They were interviewed between September 17 and December 3, 2007. Percentages add to more than 100 percent because respondents were able to answer "yes" to more than one question.

Personality and Social Background Factors

What are some of the personality and background factors that influence the substance and shape of news? In terms of demographics, newspeople's profile resembles the profile of other professionals in the United States. At the start of the twenty-first century, four out of five American journalists were white, two-thirds were male, and nearly all had graduated from college, though many did not major in journalism. Education appears to be the single most important background characteristic that shapes newspeople's general philosophy of reporting. Like most people with a social science or humanities degree, journalists tend to be socially more liberal than the general population and to have a keener sense of social responsibility. [1]

Journalists are less likely than the general population to describe themselves as conservative. In 2007, 8 percent of national journalists (14 percent at the local level) professed to conservative leanings, compared to 36 percent of the general public. Roughly one-third claimed to be liberal and more than half called themselves moderate. The overall tone of stories selected is in tune with the political orientations of media personnel, albeit leaning a bit more toward the middle of the political spectrum. Economic and social liberalism prevails, especially in the most prominent media organizations. So does a preference for an internationalist foreign policy, caution about military intervention, and some suspicion about the ethics of established large institutions, particularly big business and big government. [2] However, despite perennial complaints about partisan bias in election campaign coverage, most studies show that media personnel attempt to treat the major parties fairly. Anticipation of scrutiny and criticism encourages evenhandedness. The extent to which biased reporting based on party preference is a problem in U.S. media is not fully known; scholars have rarely investigated media bias outside the election context.[3]

Minority journalists and women present a slightly different demographic profile. For example, African American, Hispanic, and Asian journalists are more likely to be women. Whereas the proportion of nonwhite journalists has risen, the proportion of women has remained steady at roughly one-third of the total. It is lowest in the wire services and television and highest in weekly newspapers and news magazines. By contrast, nonwhite males have their highest representation in radio and television and their lowest representation in weekly newspapers. Women and minority males are much more likely to call themselves Democrats than are male white journalists, and they are less likely to claim to be Independents.

Bloggers are a growing addition to the news-dispensing community, but their demographics, training, and biases remain something of a mystery. Estimates vary wildly because the majority of blogs are rarely active. Still, blog messages are posted on the Web every seven-and-a-half seconds, and estimates peg the Internet audience in the United States at more than 30 million viewers. In 2007 Technorati, a major blog tracking agency, estimated that there were 15.5 million English language blogs. Young women between fifteen and twenty years old were the largest blogger group and, like most bloggers, had minimal political impact because they reached tiny audiences. The story is different for the small number of blogs that enjoy popularity and influence because they reach more than 100,000 daily visitors. Intermittently they become influential news contributors because of the size of their audience and when they report original rather than recycled news that the mainstream media pick up and publish. The Trent Lott story told in chapter 1 is a good example.

Is it really important to know who the bloggers are? What effect do demographic characteristics have on the news product? The evidence is inconclusive, making it debatable whether adequate coverage of the nation's problems requires media organizations that are a microcosm of the larger society.[4] If demographically distinct groups are uniquely qualified to assess their own needs, then racial, ethnic, and gender underrepresentation in the media is harmful. Proponents of facsimile representation point out that most general media emphasize established white, middle-class groups and values, while neglecting the concerns of minorities and poor people. The media also stress urban rather than rural affairs and focus heavily on male-dominated sports. These patterns suggest that news output does reflect reporters' backgrounds and interests. But the patterns may also suggest that news is designed to cater to the tastes of the audiences that advertisers find most attractive, although most journalists deny that.[5]

Reporters' unique life experiences are also important in shaping their stories. In fact, idiosyncratic factors explain why newspeople who have similar backgrounds nonetheless focus on different stories or give a different emphasis to the same news story or entertainment plot. For instance, Washington, D.C.–based reporters routinely use friendships with well-connected government officials to get important scoops. As a result of close personal ties with these officials, the reporters are apt to become captives of their Beltway sources' perspectives on the world. In the end, personality factors and role demands intertwine with organizational factors to set the broad boundaries of what is acceptable news.

Organizational Factors

Colleagues and settings strongly influence newspeople. Every news organization has its own internal power structure that develops from the interaction of owners, journalists, news sources, audiences, advertisers, and government authorities. In most news organizations today, the ideology of working journalists is slightly to the left of middle America, quite similar to that of liberal Democrats. Left-wing extremism is rare. Most journalists support the basic tenets of the current political and social system.

By and large, print and broadcast journalists believe that many of the structural changes in the news business in the twenty-first century have harmed the quality of news. This includes the incorporation of media enterprises within large corporate entities (discussed in chapter 2), which has increased the emphasis on high profits and led to damaging cutbacks in staff and other resources for gathering news. The pressure to produce news around the clock, with diminished resources, accounts for bouts of sloppy, error-prone reporting. Not all organizational changes have been harmful, however. For example, most journalists say that the Internet has made journalism better because it is an excellent source of information that is easily available to anybody with a computer. Besides, knowing that news consumers can readily check the accuracy of news reports on the Web has forced reporters to be more circumspect in their reports.

Organizational pressures begin to operate even before the job starts. Most journalists join news organizations and remain with them only if they share the organization's basic philosophy. To win advancement, professional recognition, and approval from their colleagues, reporters learn quickly which types of stories are acceptable to their editors and colleagues. Relationships with colleagues are particularly important within large, prominent news enterprises in which newspeople receive their main social and professional support from coworkers rather than from the community at large.[6] The opposite holds true in small towns, where newspeople often interact freely with community leaders and receive their support.

Despite the substantial evidence of media influence on U.S. politics, most newspeople deny that they should be concerned about the real-life impact of their stories. They commonly argue that journalism is a craft and not a profession, even while claiming to subscribe to social responsibility journalism. Eschewing candor to protect their flanks, they allege that they simply mirror the news found in the marketplace—nothing more.

Role Models

Although editors and reporters throughout the country take cues about stories from the eastern media elite—the *New York Times, Wall Street Journal,* and

Washington Post—they shape their basic news policies according to their own views about the role that media should play in society. The effects of favoring a social responsibility role over other stances were discussed in chapter 1. News stories also vary depending on whether newspeople see themselves largely as objective observers, who must present facts and diverse views voiced by others, or as interpreters who must supply meanings and evaluations.

Reporters differ widely on that score in western democracies. Divisions are especially sharp among proponents of traditional journalism and advocates for civic or public journalism.[7] Civic journalism fans believe that reporters must tailor the news so that it not only informs citizens about important happenings but also helps them to take collective action to resolve problems.[8] Beyond turning reporters into interpreters of what the news means, this approach also makes them deliberate participants in the political process. That may be laudable in many instances, but it sacrifices journalists' role as neutral observers. When journalists are asked about the core values of their calling, most acknowledge neutrality as a core value that serves their audience's interests. Other highly rated values are acting as the public's watchdog over government, supplying news needed for citizenship duties, and analyzing complex problems to help the public understand them.[9] Over the past decade journalists have become less concerned about getting the news out quickly, serving all segments of the public, and entertaining the audience.

What do journalists identify as "news"?[10] Old-time journalists would say that it is news when a man bites a dog, but not when a dog bites a man. Why not? U.S. journalists see it as their role to cover exceptional events rather than ordinary ones. What seems exceptional depends on the conditions within a particular society at a particular point in time. It also depends on journalists' perception of which of the many extraordinary events that surround them is likely to interest their audiences and deserves and needs coverage. That is what makes news stories a human creation rather than a happening that journalists merely mirror. The fact that the decision of what is news hinges on multiple subjective judgments explains why there is much disagreement about what ought to be news on a given day. But it also explains the widespread uniformity of story types in U.S. print and electronic media.

GATEKEEPING

A small number of journalists have final control over story choices. These gatekeepers include wire service reporters, Web editors and other reporters who initially select stories, the editors who assign the reporters and accept or reject what they submit, disc jockeys at radio stations who present five-minute news breaks, and television program executives. In general, fewer than twenty-five people within a large newspaper or television organization are involved in the final decision of what news to use.

These few gatekeepers, particularly those who make news choices for nationwide audiences, wield an awesome amount of political power because

TABLE 4-2 **Sources of Front-Page News Stories (in percentages)**

Sources	Times/ Post staff stories	Tribune staff stories	Chronicle staff stories	Wire services staff stories	Total stories
Government officials	42	31	21	60	38
U.S.	26	16	10	51	23
State	5	6	3	—	5
Local	2	4	7	—	3
Foreign	9	5	1	8	7
Group-linked person[a]	35	40	51	35	38
Private person	13	28	26	—	16
Foreign person	4	—	—	5	3
Celebrity	4	>1	—	3	3
Other	2	>1	3	—	2

Source: Author's research. Based on content analysis of 131 news stories attributed to staff or wire service writers and published in the New York Times, Washington Post, Chicago Tribune, and San Francisco Chronicle. Data drawn from constructed week analysis from March 1, 2008, to November 30, 2008. Totals may not add up to 100 percent because of rounding.

[a] "Group-linked" persons are members of a group but are not necessarily official spokespersons for the group. This includes experts, medical staff, nonprofit organizations, and sources speaking on behalf of a private company.

their choices determine what will be widely available as news. This is why rankings of the political influence of U.S. institutions routinely place the news media among the top ten. When pollsters asked a national sample of Americans which telephone call the president should answer first if a top-notch editor, business leader, church figure, and educational leader called simultaneously, most chose the newspaper editor.[11] As discussed in chapter 1, news stories influence the issues that ordinary people, as well as political elites, think about. Of course, media gatekeepers are not entirely free in their story choices. Coverage of major events, such as wars, assassinations, and airline hijackings, is compelling. Other events can be included or omitted at will, within the limits set by news conventions. On an average evening, somewhat more than half of the stories on each major television network represent unique choices, ignored by the other networks. The figures are slightly lower for print media.

Gatekeepers also select the sources through whose eyes the public views the world. Government officials are the chief source of most political stories reported by the wire services, which are the main information source for the nation's news venues (Table 4-2). This gives public officials an excellent chance to influence the slant of the news. However, when highly controversial issues are at stake, gatekeepers usually turn to unofficial sources as well.[12] Basing the news on a narrow spectrum of sources can lead to biased reporting. Reporters may give the widest publicity to the views of "celebrity" authorities in tangentially related fields and ignore important specialists whose names are unfamiliar to the public.

A study of sources used for stories about welfare reform, consumer issues, the environment, and nuclear energy concluded that journalists favor sources that reflect their own inclinations.

> On welfare reform, liberal sources predominate over conservative ones. On consumer issues they look to Ralph Nader, the public interest movement, and liberal activist groups. On pollution and the environment, they select activist environmental groups and, once again, liberal leaders. On nuclear energy, antinuclear sources are the most popular. . . . Journalists by no means depend exclusively on liberal viewpoints. They cite a mixture of public and private, partisan and nonpartisan, liberal and conservative sources. But the liberal side consistently outweighs the conservative.[13]

Sources who have gained recognition as "experts" through media publicity tend to be used over and over again, while other, less-publicized sources are neglected.

When multiple media cover the same story, as happens routinely, they often use sources representing different elites. When that happens, the thrust of the story may vary widely even though the underlying facts are the same. For example, when researchers looked at 167 stories about a major stock market crash in 1987, they found that the causes and effects of the crash were assessed in quite diverse fashion by the *CBS Evening News, Newsweek,* the *New York Times,* and the *Wall Street Journal.* The three print media had relied most heavily on experts from the financial sector as primary sources, drawing 38 percent, 52 percent, and 65 percent of their sources, respectively, from that sector. Government sources and academics took second and third place but appeared far less frequently. For CBS, government sources came first, followed by sources from the business sector and the financial sector. CBS was also unique in drawing heavily (44 percent) on unnamed sources, a practice that journalism critics decry.[14]

The use of different sources led to disparate appraisals of the causes of the crash and hence different impressions about needed remedies. In *Newsweek* the national debt and presidential policies were the chief causes; in the *New York Times* it was the debt and computerized trading. *Wall Street Journal* sources emphasized computerized trading and the foreign trade deficit. On the *CBS Evening News,* the national debt was the chief villain, with twice the emphasis it had received in other sources. Presidential policies and partisan politics were other important causes. When it came to estimating the effects of the crash, all but the *Wall Street Journal* mentioned improved cooperation between president and Congress as a likely outcome. Beyond that, speculations about probable effects diverged widely, presenting media audiences with clashing images about the country's economic problems.

In the past, highly respected national newscasters also have been extraordinarily influential in putting their versions of news events on the political agenda. By singling out news events for positive or negative commentary, these media figures could sway public and official opinions. At the turn of the century, if anchors Peter Jennings, Tom Brokaw, or Dan Rather declared that pending health care legislation would lower the quality of medical care or that a U.S. military presence along the coast of China would risk war, popular support for these policies was likely to plunge.[15] The new crop of anchors that followed them has been far less influential. Nonetheless, a sixty-second verbal barrage on the evening news or a few embarrassing questions can still destroy programs, politicians, and the reputations of major organizations. During the 2008 presidential election, for example, Republican vice presidential nominee Sarah Palin's reputation for political savvy was seriously diminished by her frosty interview with CBS News anchor Katie Couric.

Because Americans like to view their media as effective guardians of the public interest, society usually focuses on the positive consequences of news story choices. Negative or questionable consequences should not be overlooked, however. For example, Peter Braestrup, chief of the Saigon bureau of the *Washington Post* during the Vietnam War, argued in his book *Big Story* that unwise story choices and interpretations about the conduct of the war misled the public and government officials.[16] Similarly, when it became clear in 2004 that reports about Iraq's possession of weapons of mass destruction had been false, the *New York Times* and *Washington Post* assumed some of the blame for the consequences. Better reporting, they argued, could have aborted the costly war against Iraq.[17]

General Factors in News Selection

As mentioned earlier, what becomes news depends in part on the demographics, training, personality, and professional socialization of news personnel. In the United States that means, by and large, upwardly mobile, well-educated white males whose political views are liberal and who subscribe in ever-larger numbers to the tenets of social responsibility journalism (discussed in chapter 2). News selection also hinges on norms within a news organization and how newspeople conceptualize their professional roles, plus pressure from internal and external competition.

Within each news organization, reporters and editors compete for time, space, and prominence of position for their stories. News organizations also compete with each other for audience attention, for advertisers, and in the case of the networks, for affiliates. If one station or network has a popular program, others often will copy the format and try to place an equally attractive program into a parallel time slot to capture their competitor's audiences and advertisers. Likewise, papers may feel compelled to carry stories simply because another medium in the same market has carried them.

News personnel operate within the broad political context of their societies in general and their circulation communities in particular. Most have internalized these contexts so that they become the frame of reference for the personnel. As media scholar George Gerbner observed long ago, there is "no fundamentally nonideological, apolitical, nonpartisan news gathering and reporting system." [18] For example, if a reporter's political context demands favorable images of religious leaders, news and entertainment will reflect this outlook. That used to be the case in the United States until the twenty-first century, when multiple stories unveiled sexual misconduct by priests. [19]

Political pressures also leave their mark. Media personnel depend on political leaders for information and are therefore vulnerable to manipulation by them. Powerful elites flood the media with self-serving stories that are often hard to resist. Intensive, frequent contacts between journalists and leaders and the desire to keep associations cordial may lead to cozy relationships that hamper critical detachment. Wooing reporters to elicit favorable media coverage is the mark of the astute politician. Reporters often succumb to the blandishments of politicians for fear of alienating powerful and important news sources.

Economic pressures are even more potent than political pressures in molding news and entertainment. Newspapers and magazines need to earn profits. Except for publications that are subsidized by individual or group sponsors, media enterprises must raise most of their income from subscriptions and advertisers. Therefore, media offerings must appeal to large numbers of subscribers or potential customers for the products that advertisers sell. That means that news organizations must direct their programs and stories either to general audiences in the prime consumption years of life (roughly ages twenty-five to forty-five) or to selected special audiences that are key targets for particular advertiser appeals. For example, toothpaste, laundry detergent, and breakfast cereals are best marketed to the huge nationwide audiences who watch the regular nighttime situation comedies or crime dramas. Expensive cameras, fancy foreign sports cars, and raft trips down the Amazon are most likely to find customers among a select few. Advertisers for such products are attracted to journals with well-to-do subscribers such as *National Geographic* or the *Wall Street Journal,* as well as to specialized cable channels and television documentaries.

Producers of broadcasts directed to nationwide audiences try to maintain a smooth flow of appealing programs throughout the prime evening hours to keep audiences from switching channels. As long as a program is unobjectionable, most audiences will remain with the station. Such considerations deter producers from mixing serious, audience-losing programs with light entertainment in prime time. The fear of losing the audience for an entire evening has also been a major reason for opposing the expansion of the nightly network news to a full hour.

The desire to keep audiences watching a particular station even affects the format of news and public service programs. Stations select newscasters for their physical attractiveness. The stations encourage informal banter, and nearly every newscast contains some fascinating bits of trivia or a touching yet inconsequential human-interest story. The news becomes "infotainment"—a marriage of information and entertainment values. Networks avoid complicated stories for fear of confusing audiences, just as they slight "dull" economic news irrespective of importance. However, journalists often underestimate the public's tastes for serious presentations, as shown by the popularity of the televised congressional debates about U.S. involvement in the Persian Gulf War in 1991 and by the massive audiences that Barack Obama's speeches attracted during his tenure as an Illinois senator and during his campaign for president.

Criteria for Choosing Specific Stories

In addition to deciding what is publishable news, gatekeepers must choose particular news items to include in their mix of offerings. The motto of the New York Times, "All the News That's Fit to Print," is an impossible myth; there is far more publishable news available than any daily news medium can possibly use. Gatekeepers also must decide how they want to frame each item so that it carries a particular message. For instance, when journalists cast stories about controversial policies such as health care reform as games of strategy, as they are wont to do, the policy issues blur and lose importance.[20] In 1993 and 1994, for example, when President Bill Clinton mounted a major campaign for health care reform, 67 percent of the health news coverage was framed as political gaming. Stories focused on who was winning and losing supporters for their favorite policy. Only 25 percent of the stories addressed substantive issues in health care reform. When political scientist Regina Lawrence studied use of the game frame in welfare reform debates, she discovered that frame choice hinged on the context. When the story was linked to elections or political battles in Washington, D.C., the game frame was prevalent. That was not the case when the story was linked to state policies or issues concerning implementation of reforms.[21]

The criteria newspeople use in story selection relate primarily to audience appeal rather than to the political significance of stories, their educational value, their broad social purposes, or the reporter's own political views. This holds true particularly for television, where viewer numbers, demographic characteristics, and viewer attitudes are constantly monitored by rating services, such as A. C. Nielsen and the American Research Bureau (ARB). For both radio and television, advertising rates rise and fall with audience size. An increase in audience size of just 1 percent can mean millions of dollars in additional advertising income. Newspaper advertising rates are also based on paid circulation, which is monitored by an independent agency, the Audit Bureau of Circulation. News outlets carefully check the popularity of individual programs but rarely ask audiences about major program changes that they might like. The fact that large numbers of people consume particular news products presumably proves that they like what they get.

The emphasis on audience appeal and the economic pressures that mandate it must be kept in mind when evaluating the totality of media output. These factors explain why the amounts and kinds of coverage of important issues often are not commensurate with their true significance at the time of publication. For instance, television news coverage of crime reached record highs in 1995 because journalists believed that the public wanted extensive coverage of the sensational O. J. Simpson murder trial. The combined story totals for health issues, the economy, and federal budget talks in 1995 fell substantially below crime story totals, leaving the impression that these stories mattered less than the crime sagas.[22] Stories like the Clinton sex scandals, the death of Britain's Princess Diana in a car crash, or the ups and downs of the careers of entertainers Britney Spears or Paris Hilton receive inordinate amounts of coverage at the expense of more significant events. News also projects distorted images when peaks in coverage of such events as urban riots or terrorist attacks do not match peaks in actual happenings. Peaks in news about street crime typically do not coincide with peaks in street crime as recorded by police.[23]

Discrepancies between the frequency of newsworthy events and their coverage are especially well illustrated by worldwide newspaper reporting about global warming (Figure 4-1).

Global warming has a major and growing impact on people everywhere. The problem is persistent, with no ups and downs. Yet, judged by global media coverage, the need to pay attention to the problem has dropped sharply since 2007. In South America and Africa the topic is scarcely covered. Elsewhere, the extent of coverage has fluctuated sharply from month to month, despite the constant urgency of the problem and the many newsworthy events available for reporting about the crisis.

Newspeople use five criteria for choosing news stories. First, stories must picture conditions that could have a *strong impact* on readers or listeners. Stories about health hazards, consumer fraud, or pensions for the elderly influence American audiences more than do unfamiliar happenings such as student riots in Greece or bank failures in China, with which they cannot identify. To make stories attractive, newspeople commonly present them as events that happened to ordinary people. Inflation news becomes the story of the housewife at the supermarket; foreign competition becomes the story of laid-off workers in a local textile plant. In the process of personalization, the broader political significance of the story is often lost, and the news is trivialized.[24]

Violence, conflict, disaster, or scandal is the second criterion of newsworthiness. Wars, murders, strikes, earthquakes, accidents, or sex scandals involving prominent people are the sorts of happenings that excite audiences. In fact, inexpensive mass newspapers became viable business ventures in the United States only after the publishers of the *New York Sun* discovered in 1833 that papers filled with breezy crime and sex stories far outsold their more staid competitors. Mass sales permitted sharp price reductions and led to the birth of the "penny press."

A third element of newsworthiness is *familiarity*. News is attractive if it pertains to well-known people or involves familiar situations of concern to many. That is why a story about a toddler rescued from a well became one of the best-remembered events of recent decades. Newspeople try to cast unfamiliar situations, such as mass famines in Africa, into more familiar stories of individual

FIGURE 4-1 The Real World/Media World Reality Gap: The Global Warming Example

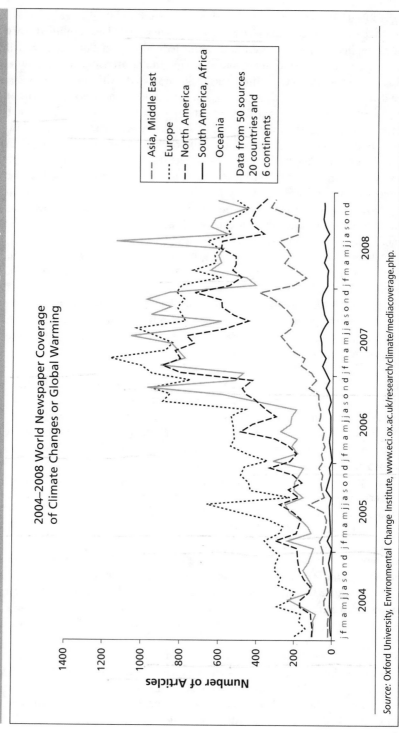

2004–2008 World Newspaper Coverage
of Climate Changes or Global Warming

Asia, Middle East
Europe
North America
South America, Africa
Oceania

Data from 50 sources
20 countries and
6 continents

Number of Articles

1400 1200 1000 800 600 400 200 0

j f m a m j j a s o n d j f m a m j j a s o n d j f m a m j j a s o n d j f m a m j j a s o n d j f m a m j j a s o n d

2004   2005   2006   2007   2008

Source: Oxford University, Environmental Change Institute, www.eci.ox.ac.uk/research/climate/mediacoverage.php.

babies dying from malnutrition. The amazing amount of detail that people can retain about the powerful and famous demonstrates that the public is keenly interested in celebrities. More than four decades after the assassination of President John F. Kennedy in 1963, many Americans still remember details of the funeral ceremony, as well as where they were when they heard about the murder. The sense of personal grief and loss has lingered, bridging the gap between the average person's private and public worlds. People value the feeling of personal intimacy that comes from knowing details of another person's life, especially if that person is beloved. People harbor somewhat similar feelings even toward the cast members of soap operas and reality dramas. People often adopt television stars as part of their families. They avidly follow the trials and tribulations of these people and may even try to model themselves after them.

Proximity is the fourth element of newsworthiness. Strong preference for local news signifies that people are most interested in what happens near them. Next to news about crime and health, people pay most attention to local news, far ahead of news about national and international affairs.[25] Local media flourish because they concentrate on events close to home; these outlets use roughly 75 percent of their space for local stories. Nonetheless, the public receives so much news from Washington, D.C., and a few major metropolitan areas that these cities and their newsmakers have become familiar to the nation. This, in a sense, makes such occurrences "local" in what media guru Marshall McLuhan called the "global village" created by television.[26]

The fifth element is that news should be *timely and novel*. It must be something that has just occurred and is out of the ordinary, either in the sense that it does not happen all the time—such as the regular departure of airplanes or the daily opening of grocery stores—or in the sense that it is not part of people's everyday lives. Stories about space exploration or the puzzling death of honeybee colonies, or reports about the latest weather conditions fall into that category.

Among these five basic criteria, conflict, proximity, and timeliness are most important, judging from analyses of actual news choices. A story's long-range significance is a lesser concern. It does play a part, however, when major events occur, such as national elections, the death of a well-known leader, or a calamitous natural disaster. Nevertheless, news makers select and frame most stories primarily to satisfy the five criteria.

Gathering the News

News organizations establish regular listening posts, or "beats," in places where events of interest to the public are most likely to occur. In the United States, government beats cover political executives, legislative bodies, court systems, and international organizations. Locations that record deviant behaviors, such as police stations or hospitals, are routinely monitored and publicized. So are fluctuations in economic trends, which can be checked easily at stock and commodity markets and at institutions designed to measure the pulse of the nation's business. Some beats, such as health or education, are functionally defined. Reporters assigned to them generally cover a wider array of institutions on a less-regular schedule than applies to the more usual beats. Stories emanating from the traditional national beats, such as the White House, Capitol, or Pentagon, have an excellent chance of publication because of their intrinsic significance, the prominence of their sources, or simply because they have been produced by beat reporters on the regular payroll. In the *New York Times* or *Washington Post*, for example, stories from regularly covered beats outnumber other stories two to one and capture the bulk of front-page headlines.[27]

All major traditional media monitor similar beats. Consequently, overall news patterns—the types of stories that are covered—are relatively uniform throughout the country and change in tandem. For instance, there has been a shift away from hard news, if one defines hard news as "breaking events involving top leaders, major issues, or significant disruptions in the routines of daily life, such as an earthquake or airline disasters."[28] The trend has been toward softer news and features. Figures vary depending on researchers' definition of "soft news," but there seems to be widespread agreement that more than half of print and broadcast news falls into the "soft" category.

Figure 4-2 shows the distribution of major news topics in 2007 in various types of news venues. There are major uniformities as well as major differences. All venues allocated substantial time and space to U.S. foreign affairs—mainly Iraq, Iran, and Pakistan—and to the presidential campaign. The venues were roughly equivalent in attention to government activities. On-line news devoted proportionately most attention to events happening beyond U.S. borders and to U.S. foreign affairs. Radio was the leader in election coverage, and cable television offered an above-average dose of crime. Newspapers were distinct in devoting more than 5 percent of their news hole—the space available for news stories, rather than advertising and announcements—to stories about business. Such diversity in emphasis indicates that average Americans can satisfy their preferences for various types of news by patronizing a particular media venue.

In practice, the choice is more complex because news hole sizes vary. For example, when a crime story fills 100 percent of the news hole of a radio show, the coverage may nonetheless be less ample than the corresponding newspaper coverage that fills 50 percent of that venue's news hole. Moreover, when one compares the public's preferences by measuring their attention to various stories against the extent of coverage that various media venues give the stories, one finds serious mismatches.[29] For instance, more than half of the responses to one poll indicated great interest in the rise of gasoline prices, but less than 5 percent of the news dwelled on that topic. Similarly, stories about weather disasters, the recall of imported Chinese toys, or living conditions inside Iraq were greatly underreported, as measured by public interest. Conversely, news allocations greatly exceeded the audience's expressed interest when it came to stories about the state of emergency declared in Pakistan, the nuclear weapons agreement concluded with North Korea, or various peace summits convened in the Middle East. In short, journalists' choices are out of tune with the topics publics would likely choose on their own. The Internet makes it possible for

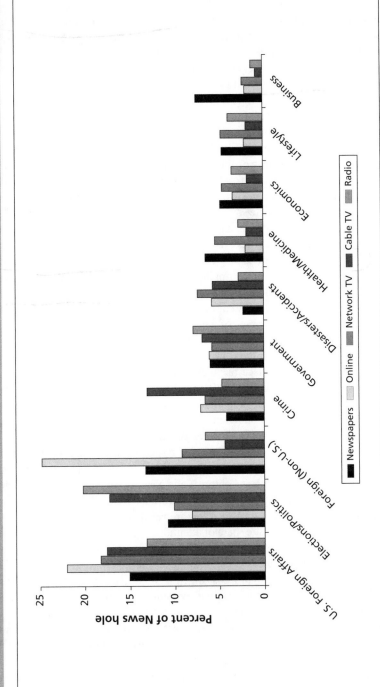

FIGURE 4-2 **Percentage of Space or Time Given to Major Topics by Various Media Sectors**

Percent of News hole

U.S. Foreign Affairs • Elections/Politics • Foreign (Non-U.S.) • Crime • Government • Disasters/Accidents • Health/Medicine • Economics • Lifestyle • Business

■ Newspapers ■ Online ■ Network TV ■ Cable TV ■ Radio

Source: Project for Excellence in Journalism, *A Year in the News, 2007,* www.stateofthenewsmedia.org/2008/narrative_overview_contentanalysis.php?cat=2&media=1. Based on analysis of more than 70,000 stories from 48 media outlets that were examined every weekday in 2007. For newspapers, Sundays were also included.

people to move into the news-choice driver's seat. Apparently, thus far, only a tiny minority has done so.

Thanks to more available space, newspapers carry more nonpolitical news. In fact, it is remarkable that they devote nearly half of the news hole to nonpolitical stories. Overall, readers of elite newspapers and viewers of evening television news on the networks, cable, or public television receive an ample supply of diverse hard political news. Readers of non-elite newspapers and viewers of the morning news do less well, and viewers of local news trail, with less than a third of offerings covering hard news topics. These infotainment-heavy venues attract the largest and youngest audiences.

News organizations, including the giants in the business, could never afford to have full teams of reporters and camera crews dispersed across the country to monitor important political happenings everywhere. Economic declines are forcing them to contract these slender bases drastically, especially abroad. Consequently, news coverage becomes even more sporadic and thin because reporters must cover a growing number of beats, time for investigation is shriveling, and news holes are shrinking.

Walter Lippmann once said that the press is like "the beam of a searchlight that moves restlessly about, bringing one episode and then another out of the darkness into vision. Men cannot do the work of the world by this light alone. They cannot govern society by episodes, incidents, and eruptions."[30] The extremely uneven, often sparse coverage of news about the American states is an example. Table 4-3 shows the percentage of network news stories devoted to individual U.S. states in broadcasts monitored from September 2007 to August 2008. The table also reports each state's electoral votes, which reflect the size of its population as a rough measure of its political significance. Eleven states were covered by fewer than twenty-five stories annually, and another eleven by no more than fifty. Such sparse coverage by network television denies these states a national audience. At the other end of the spectrum, events in six states were detailed in 151–483 stories. As is typical for presidential election years, states with special political significance—such as New Hampshire and Iowa, where the campaign starts in earnest, as well as the most populous states, such as California and New York—receive the lion's share of coverage. Overall, twenty-two states suffer from neglect, judged by the population metric used in Table 4-3, and six states are vastly over-covered; only twenty-two states receive an appropriate share of attention.

The distribution of picture coverage is also askew. Most pictures are taken in East Coast cities, such as Washington, D.C., and New York, with a sprinkling of pictures from Chicago and Los Angeles. Of course, reporters will cover special events anywhere in the country. Every network reports presidential election debates, wherever they are held, and routinely follows presidential travels, whether the destination is a secluded beach in Hawaii, Barack Obama's home state, or the Great Wall of China. States receive exceptional coverage when major news happens there. Newsworthy events in remote sites are most likely to be covered if they involve prominent people and are scheduled in advance, so that news venues can plan to have media crews available.

TABLE 4-3 **Network Coverage of State News, September 2007 to August 2008**				
Annual number of stories	States		Percentage of mentions	Percentage of electoral vote
1–24	Delaware Hawaii Idaho Maine Montana North Dakota	Rhode Island South Dakota Vermont Washington[a] Wyoming	3.3	8.4
25–50	Alabama Alaska Connecticut Kansas Minnesota Nebraska	Oklahoma Oregon Tennessee Utah West Virginia	8.8	13.9
51–100	Arkansas Arizona Colorado Georgia Indiana Kentucky Louisiana	Massachusetts Mississippi Missouri New Mexico South Carolina Wisconsin	20.1	22.3
101–150	Illinois Maryland Michigan Nevada New Jersey	North Carolina Ohio Pennsylvania Virginia Washington, D.C.[a]	25.9	26.0
151–483	California Florida Iowa	New Hampshire New York[a] Texas	41.8	29.3

Source: Data compiled from the Vanderbilt Television News Archive. Electoral vote percentage based on allocation for the 2008 presidential election.
N = 4,629 mentions in stories

[a]Search terms for New York and Washington, D.C., were adjusted to account for large percentage of datelines in the two cities. Two separate searches were carried out for New York, one using the search term "New York," and one using "New York City." The Washington, D.C., totals reflect only stories that referenced "Washington, D.C.," rather than "Washington," as is common in the dateline.

Prior planning is even important for more accessible events. News organizations need time to allocate reporters and camera crews and edit pictures and stories. The need to plan ahead leads to an emphasis on predictable events, such as formal visits by dignitaries, legislative hearings, or executive press conferences. Technology advances have eased this problem, providing one of hundreds of examples of the profound impact of technology on the content of news. "Spot news" can now be filmed and broadcast rapidly, using equipment that has been miniaturized in bulk while growing exponentially in complexity.

News Production Constraints Editors = #1 Constraint

Many news selection criteria reflect the pressure to edit and publish news rapidly. That is why pseudo-events—events created to generate press coverage—constitute more than half of all television news stories. Reporters attend events like bridge dedications or county fairs because these are quick and easy ways to get fresh story material. Politicians love such photo opportunities. When access to a newsworthy event is difficult, reporters resort to interviews with on-scene observers or ever-available "experts" anywhere in the country eager to discuss the situation. Since interviews are a comparatively cheap way to collect story material, they have become increasingly common in an era of strained resources.

Once stories reach media news offices, editors must make selections quickly. Ben Bagdikian, a former *Washington Post* editor, in a classic study of gatekeeping at eight newspapers, found that editors usually sift and choose stories on the spot.[31] They do not assemble and carefully balance them with an eye to the overall effects of a particular issue of the paper. The typical newspaper editor is able to scan and discard individual stories in seconds. At such speeds, there is no time to reflect or to weigh the merits or intrinsic importance of one story over another. If the editor has ideological preferences, they are served instinctively, if at all, rather than deliberately. Papers ordinarily will not save stories left over at the end of the day for the next day's news because newer stories will supersede them. A late-breaking story, therefore, unless it is very unusual or significant, has little chance for publication in the print edition of a newspaper—although it may make it onto the paper's Web site. The same holds true for afternoon events happening on the West Coast because much of the national news is produced on an East Coast schedule.

In Bagdikian's study, a distaste for the substance of the story or an objection to its ideological slant was reason for rejection less than 3 percent of the time. Twenty-six percent of stories were rejected because of space shortages. The chief reason for other rejections was lack of newsworthiness. The published newspaper usually contained the same proportions of different types of news as the original pool from which the stories were selected.[32]

Public relations experts and campaign managers know the deadlines of important publications, such as the *New York Times, Wall Street Journal, Time, and Newsweek,* and of the network television news. They schedule events and news releases to arrive in editors' offices precisely when needed and in easy-to-use formats. Public relations firms distribute thousands of releases annually. If these releases are attractively presented and meet newsworthiness criteria, journalists find it hard to resist using them. That is especially true for smaller news organizations that lack adequate resources to produce their own stories. They relish receiving such information subsidies.[33] Powerful elites in the public and private sector make ample use of these opportunities. Even though news organizations discard the bulk of public relations releases, they do use them in a substantial portion of news stories, usually without identifying the source. If publicists want to stifle publicity that is likely to harm their clients, they can announce news just past the deadlines, preferably on weekends when few newscasts air.

Publications with less-frequent deadlines, such as weekly newsmagazines, have a lot more time to decide which stories to publish. That makes it easier to separate the wheat from the chaff. Newsmagazine staffs also have more resources than most daily papers to explore background information and present events in a context that helps readers to evaluate them. Hence their reports are often far more measured and thought-provoking than corresponding stories in the daily press.

Television news staffs, especially those working for stations that broadcast around the clock, have even less time than newspaper staffs to investigate most stories. That is why background or investigative stories that appear on television frequently originate in the print media. The problem of insufficient time pertains not only to preparing stories but also to presenting them. The average news story on television and radio takes about a minute to deliver, just enough time to announce an event and present a fact or two. Newscasters may have to ignore complex stories if they cannot drastically condense them or broadcast them live, blow by blow, as they are happening.

Print media have space problems as well, but these are less severe than the time constraints that electronic media face. The average newspaper reserves 55 percent of its space for advertising. Straight news stories account for 27 percent of the remaining space, and features account for the rest. Some papers reserve a fixed amount of space for news; others expand or contract the news hole depending on the flow of news and advertising. But whether the paper is a slim, eight-page version or five to ten times that size, there is rarely enough space to cover stories as fully as reporters and editors would like.[34] The fact that many newspapers now publish online versions eases that situation. Off-line versions often refer readers to expanded versions of stories in the online editions, including links that can enrich the stories and access to the reporters who researched and wrote the stories.

Besides the need to capsule news stories, television reporters also seek stories with visual appeal. Events that lack good pictures may not make the cut. Racial violence in South Africa, for example, disappeared from television news worldwide after the government prohibited picture taking. Unfortunately, the most visually appealing aspects of a story may not be the most important. For instance, during political campaigns the motorcades, rallies, hecklers, and cheering crowds make good pictures, whereas candidates delivering speeches are visually dull. Television cameras therefore concentrate on the colorful scenes

Located in the heart of downtown Atlanta, the world famous CNN Center is the global headquarters of CNN and Turner Broadcasting. A bank of television monitors lines the center's twenty-four-hours-a-day newsroom.

Source: AP Photo/Ric Feld

rather than on the speeches. If interesting pictures are flashed on the screen in competition with a speech, they often distract attention from it.

A final constraint on news production is news staffing. For financial and personnel reasons, news outlets favor stories by their own staff. This saves the additional fees that must be paid to freelance journalists. News executives also have personal relationships with their own staff members and do not want to give scarce space and time to strangers in preference to their own employees.

EFFECTS OF GATEKEEPING

The gatekeeping influences discussed in this chapter give a distinctive character to U.S. news. There are many exceptions, of course, among individual programs or stories. There are also noticeable differences in emphases among the conservative rural press, more moderate papers in small and middle-sized towns, and the liberal press in major metropolitan centers. The unique conditions of Internet journalism have an even more profound impact on news presentation.[35] Unlike journalists in traditional media, who must rigorously prune the lush growth of incoming news stories because time or space is scarce, Internet journalists have abundant time and space and occasionally strain to fill it around the clock. Most newspapers and television operations use their Internet sites to expand stories covered in their traditional media, rather than enhancing the pool of news stories. The news organizations update these stories throughout the day and night, often scooping the printed and broadcast stories that they will later feature in their traditional venues. Most news Web sites also provide links to information that broadens and deepens the story by adding new data or refreshing previously published details. The upshot is more in-depth news at a much faster pace. And, of course, there are thousands of unaffiliated Web sites that graze on the news crop provided by traditional media and report it from fresh perspectives. Despite variations in the news story environment, four features of U.S. news are noteworthy. They fall under the headings of people in the news, action in the news, infotainment news, and support for the establishment.[36]

People in the News

Gatekeeping winnows the group of newsworthy people to a small cadre of familiar and unfamiliar figures. Most stories in newsmagazines and network television news feature familiar people, predominantly entertainers, athletes, and political figures. Fewer than fifty politicians are in the news regularly, and the most popular is the incumbent president. Other people may receive coverage primarily for unusual or remarkable activities, but incumbent presidents receive coverage regardless of what they do. News about leading presidential candidates ranks next; in presidential election years it often outnumbers stories about the president.[37]

A third well-covered group consists of major federal government officials, such as the leaders of the House and Senate, the heads of major congressional committees, and cabinet members in active departments. Major White House staff members are part of the circle. So are former officials such as secretaries of state and secretaries of defense when asked to comment on the current scene. The Supreme Court is in the news only intermittently, generally when it announces important decisions or during confirmation hearings for Supreme Court justices. Agency heads rarely make the news except when they announce new policies or feud with the president. Some people, however, are regularly in the news regardless of their current political status merely because their names are household words. Members of the Kennedy clan and a host of "experts," such as consumer activist Ralph Nader or civil rights activist Jesse Jackson, are prime examples.

Below the federal level, the activities of governors and mayors of large states and cities are newsworthy if they involve important public policy issues or if the incumbent is unusual because of race, gender, or prior newsworthy activities. Notorious individuals also receive frequent attention if their deeds have involved well-known people. Presidential assassins, mass murderers, or terrorists like Timothy McVeigh and Osama bin Laden fall into this category. Ample coverage also goes to targets of congressional investigations and politicians indicted for wrongdoing in office.

Among the many powerful people rarely covered in the news, except when they commit crimes, are economic leaders (such as the heads of large corporations), financiers, and leaders of organized business (such as the National Association of Manufacturers or the U.S. Chamber of Commerce). A few colorful labor leaders, such as George Meany, James Hoffa, and John J. Sweeney of the AFL/CIO have been news figures in the past, but probably more because of their personalities than their jobs. Important military leaders also remain obscure unless they conduct major military operations, for example, Gen. David Petraeus of Iraq War fame. Political party leaders surface during elections but remain in the shadows at other times. Political activists, such as civil rights leaders or the heads of minority parties, or pleaders of special causes, such as right-to-die activist Dr. Jack Kevorkian, come and go from the news scene, depending on the amount of controversy they are able to produce. The same holds true for the heads of voluntary associations, such as leaders of antiabortion groups or churches.

Most people never make the news because their activities are not unusual enough to command media attention, although coverage of average citizens has risen somewhat in recent years. Ordinary people have their best chance for publicity if they protest or riot or strike, particularly against the government. The next best chance goes to victims of disasters, personal tragedy, and crime and to the actors who brought about their plight. The grisly nature of crimes, disasters, or other human tragedies, rather than the identity of the people involved, determines their newsworthiness. Ordinary people also make the news if their lifestyles or social activities become outlandish or if their behavior diverges greatly from the norm for persons of their age, gender, and status. Finally, ordinary people make the news in large numbers as nameless members of groups whose statistical profile becomes news or whose opinions have been tapped through polls or elections.

Action in the News

The range of activities reported in the news is largely limited to conflicts and disagreements among government officials (particularly friction between the president and Congress about economic or foreign policies), violent and nonviolent protest (much of it in opposition to government activities), crime, scandals and investigations, and impending or actual disasters. When the nation is at war, the media report a large number of war stories but cut back on criticism of the government lest they seem disloyal.

Government policies involving health care reform, energy, or changes in tax rates also provide frequent story material. These stories often highlight the political maneuvers leading to policy decisions rather than the substance of the policy and its likely impact. Government personnel changes, including details about campaigns for office, are another news focus. Finally, two aspects of the ever-changing societal scene periodically receive substantial coverage: national events, such as inaugurations or space adventures, and important technological, social, or cultural developments, such as overhauls of the public school system or advances in the fight against cancer or AIDS.

Infotainment News

Newsworthiness criteria and news production constraints shape U.S. news and its impact, regardless of the particular subject under discussion. Among the constraints, economic pressures to generate large audiences are often paramount. Economist James T. Hamilton has amassed evidence that evening news broadcasts are pitched largely to fickle younger viewers who are likely to quit watching if the program does not please them. The upshot is a program mix that is short on hard news and long on infotainment.[38] Comparisons of news story topics show that the shift toward soft news has been dramatic. For example, between 1977 and 1997, soft news increased by an average of 25 percent in all news venues, at the expense of hard news.[39] Many critics inside and outside journalism deplore this turn, claiming that it diminishes citizens' concern about politics and hence weakens democracy. But there is also considerable evidence that the opposite may be true because infotainment news attracts audiences who would otherwise ignore the news altogether.[40]

Novelty and Excitement. When the goal is to attract young viewers, sensational and novel occurrences often drown out news of more significance that lacks excitement. For instance, a fairly typical newspaper such as the *Chicago Sun Times* devotes nearly twenty times more news to sports than to news about the state's government. Dramatic events, such as airline hijackings or serial murders, preempt more far-reaching consequential happenings. Preoccupation with a single striking event, such as the 2009 impeachment of Illinois governor Rod Blagojevich, can shortchange coverage of other news, such as a U.S. air strike against targets in Afghanistan.

The emphasis on excitement also leads to a stress on the more trivial aspects of serious stories. Inflation becomes a human-interest drama about John and Jane Doe, working-class homeowners who are struggling to pay their mortgage. Journalists are apt to ignore the larger issues involved in inflation unless they can be combined with human-interest aspects. In such cases, dramatization helps because personalized, dramatic stories are far more likely to catch audience attention than dry, learned discussions by economic experts. However, audiences are more likely to remember the drama than the underlying serious problem.

The orientation towards novelty and entertainment produces fragmented, discontinuous news that focuses on the present and ignores the past. When breaking news is published in a hurry, it often lacks background that places stories into context. Fragmentation makes it difficult for audiences to piece together a coherent narrative of events. Snippets of news may drive home an easily understandable theme, such as "Washington is in a mess" or "The inner city is decaying," thereby blurring individual news items. A few papers, such as the *Christian Science Monitor* in its heyday, and a few news programs, such as *The NewsHour with Jim Lehrer,* have covered fewer stories, allowing them to present more detail.[41]

Familiarity and Similarity. Young audiences like stories about familiar people and events close to home. That preference has circular effects. When familiar people and situations are covered in minute detail, they become even more familiar and therefore even more worthy of publicity. The reverse is also true. Journalists ignore unfamiliar people and events. Celebrities may become objects of prying curiosity. The details of their private lives may take up an inordinately large amount of time and space in the mass media. The sudden and unexpected death of a beloved entertainer, such as actor Heath Ledger, may command news and special feature coverage for days or weeks. Tabloids and serious media alike cover such stories at length.

The criteria of newsworthiness used in the United States lead to news that is very parochial compared with news in other countries. Coverage of news about foreign people and cultures is slim, leaving Americans ignorant about much of their world. When news outlets rarely cover events in distant countries, stories about them require a lot of background if they are to make sense to Americans. To avoid the need for lengthy introductions, U.S. media therefore prefer to cover people from western cultures whose policies are somewhat familiar, such as the people of western European countries. Foreign news concentrates on situations that are easy to report, which often means focusing on violent events like revolutions, major disasters, and the like. This type of coverage then conveys the faulty impression that most foreign countries are always in serious disarray.

Conflict and Violence. The heavy news emphasis on conflict and bad news, which is most prevalent in big city media, has three major consequences.[42] The first and perhaps most far-reaching is the dangerous distortion of reality. Crime coverage provides examples. Media stories rarely mention that many inner-city neighborhoods are relatively free of crime. Instead, they convey the impression that entire cities are dangerous jungles, and that may then turn into a self-fulfilling prophecy. Under the influence of such publicity, many people avoid the inner city. They even shun comparatively safe neighborhoods after a single, highly publicized crime. The empty streets then make crime more likely.

Studies of people's perceptions of the incidence of crime and the actual chances that they will be victimized indicate that their fears are geared to media realities. In the world of television drama, the average character has a 30 percent to 64 percent chance of being involved in violence; in the real world the average person's chance of becoming a crime victim is a small fraction of that.[43] In the same way, heavy media emphasis on air crashes and scant coverage of automobile accidents have left the public with distorted notions of the relative dangers of these modes of transportation.

A second consequence is that average people are left with the disquieting sense that conflict and turmoil reign nearly everywhere. This impression is likely to affect people's feelings toward society in general. They may contract "videomalaise," characterized by distrust, cynicism, and fear.[44] Such feelings undermine support for government, destroy faith in leaders, produce political apathy, and generally sap the vigor of the democratic process. The emphasis on conflict may also cause some people to believe that violence is an acceptable way to settle disputes. The popularity of violent stories has encouraged groups who seek media coverage to behave violently or sensationally to enhance their chances for publicity. The media usually dramatize and oversimplify conflict, picturing it as a confrontation between two clearly defined sides. The reality is murkier. Issues are rarely clear-cut, and viewpoints divide in multiple ways, rather than just two. On the positive side of the ledger, ample publicity may create enough pressure to bring about settlements that would have been impossible without it.[45]

A taste for conflict is not the same as a taste for controversy, however. Fear of offending members of the mass audience, or annoying prominent critics and business associates, may keep some topics—such as misconduct by clergy or high-level educators—out of the news, especially on network television. When news outlets do report such stories, the treatment is ordinarily bland, carefully hedged, and rarely provocative. In fact, the world that television presents to the viewer often lags behind the real world in its recognition of controversial social changes. The civil rights struggle, women's fight for equality, and changing sexual mores were widespread long before they received serious attention in the media. Compared with television, newspapers can afford to be more daring because normally there is no other daily paper in the same market to which annoyed readers can defect. Besides, because printed news has fewer stirring pictures than television, it is much easier for the audience to ignore distasteful stories.

Neglect of Major Societal Problems. Despite the ascendancy of social responsibility journalism, the constraints of news production still force the media to slight serious and persistent societal problems such as alcoholism, truancy, environmental pollution, and the care of preschool children, the elderly, and the disabled. The turn toward softer, human-interest oriented news that began in the 1970s has brought greater attention to such stories, but they rarely remain in the media limelight long enough to generate widespread public debate and political action. When trivial, sensational happenings dominate the news, matters of long-range significance become "old" news, which dooms them to oblivion.

Inadequate training of media staff is another reason for unsatisfactory coverage of major stories. Proper appraisal of the merits of health care plans, or prison systems, or pollution control programs requires technical knowledge. Only large news organizations have specialized reporters with expertise in such areas as urban affairs, science, or finance. Moreover, a science reporter can hardly be expected to be an expert in all fields of science. Nor can a reporter skilled in urban problems be expected simultaneously to master all the intricacies of a major city's budget, its transportation system, and its services to juveniles. Because most news organizations throughout the country lack the trained staffs needed to discuss major social and political problems constructively, politicians and all kinds of "experts" can easily challenge the merits of unpalatable media stories.

Support for the Establishment

Gatekeeping also yields news that supports political and social institutions in the United States. Although the media regularly expose the misbehavior and inefficiencies of government officials and routinely disparage politicians, they show respect and support for the political system and its high offices in general. Misconduct and poor policies are treated as deviations that implicitly reaffirm the merit of prevailing norms. News stories routinely embed assumptions that underscore the legitimacy of the current political system. For instance, when police protect a factory from violence by workers, reporters assume that the police are the legitimate guardians of public order who are acting appropriately. The possibility that workers, rather than capitalists, should own the factories is never raised. If it were, the story would be widely condemned as Communist propaganda or "socialism." Similarly, stories discussing the plight of homeless children tacitly assume that these young people ought to be living in conventional family units. Journalists rarely discuss the fact that other arrangements might be preferable.[46]

The media treat U.S. political symbols and rituals, such as the presidency, the courts, elections, and patriotic celebrations, with respect, enhancing their legitimacy. By contrast, news stories cast a negative light on antiestablishment behavior, such as protest demonstrations that disrupt normal activities, inflammatory speeches by militants, or looting during a riot.[47] Obscenity and profanity in public places generally are edited out of news events. When journalists do include them, they generate floods of complaints about poor taste and lack of regard for the sensibilities of young children.

Explicit and implicit support for the established system, as well as sugarcoating of political reality, sometimes helps and sometimes hurts the public interest. It hurts if faults in the established system and prevailing political ideologies are allowed to persist when publicity might lead to correction. The fear of publicity can also forestall inappropriate behavior by publicity-shy public figures. There are, however, situations in which shielding the shortcomings of the political system and even individual misconduct may be helpful. For instance, at times of national or international crises, when the nation's prestige is an important political asset, embarrassing stories can severely weaken the country. Similarly, the ability of elected leaders to govern effectively can suffer when stories focus disproportionately on failures and disregard successes and when stories dwell on irrelevant personal issues that diminish a leader's stature.

Generalized support for the establishment and the status quo is not unique to the media, of course.[48] Most institutions within any particular political system go along with it if they wish to prosper. People on government staffs have been socialized to believe in the merits of their political structures. People are socialized throughout their lives to support their country and its policies. They often resent exposés that undermine this comfortable sense of security. Media support for the establishment thus helps to maintain and perpetuate existing respect for it.[49] The media's heavy reliance on government sources and press releases further strengthens establishment support. Official viewpoints tend to dominate the news when story production requires government assistance for data collection or when reporters must preserve access to government beats.[50]

Reporters use government officials routinely to verify information, validating stories by attributing them to "official" sources; the higher the official's level and rank, the better. The assumption that government sources, such as police departments, Department of Agriculture spokespersons, or presidential press aides, are reliable information sources is, of course, debatable, especially because the particular thrust of a story may put agencies into a good or bad light. Many private groups have complained that the nearly exclusive reliance on government sources deprives them of the chance to publicize their own, in their view more accurate, versions of events and that the result is one-sided reporting tilted toward support of the establishment.

APPRAISING NEWS MAKING

Do newspeople do a good job in selecting the types of news and entertainment they cover? Do they allot appropriate time and space to each of these categories? Do they fill them with good individual stories? The answers depend on the standards that the analyst applies. If one contends that news can and should be a mirror of society, then news making leaves much to be desired. By emphasizing the exceptional rather than the ordinary, a few regular beats rather than a wide range of news sources, and conflict and bad news rather than the ups and downs of daily life, the media picture a world that is far from reality. Reality becomes further distorted because the process of shaping news events into interesting, coherent stories often gives those events new meanings and significance. That is why critics claim that the news creates reality rather than reporting it.[51]

If one shares the belief of many journalists and other elites that the media should serve as the eyes and ears of intelligent citizens who are hungry for news of major social and political significance, one will again find fault with news making (see Box 4-1 for an alternative perspective on this issue). The media devote much space and time to trivia and ignore many interesting developments or report them so briefly that their meaning is lost. Often the human-interest appeal of a story or its sensational aspects distract the audience from the story's real significance.[52]

Appraisal scores are far from perfect when one measures the media by their professed story formulas. An analysis of 352 average-length television news reports, selected from November 24 to December 23, 2008, yielded 271 routine stories and showed that only one of seven key story elements (who, what, where, when, why, how, and context) was nearly always covered. Most stories included major factual elements—what actually took place. Slightly fewer stories told who was involved and where and when it happened (Table 4-4). Coverage was less regular when it came to stating why the reported event took place, how it occurred, and in what context. The audience received the facts of what had happened but not the information that would help it grasp the meaning and implications of the facts.

BOX 4-1   **A Bird's-Eye View of News Coverage**

When critics appraise the quality of information that American citizens need to monitor their government and influence political action, they usually have individual citizens and their media in mind. Usually they deem coverage in American news media inadequate. Would that verdict change if audiences and media were considered in their totality? Are Americans as a whole served well or poorly by the combined news from all the readily available venues? A realistic answer requires acknowledging that the complexity of modern democracies demands divvying up citizenship duties. Individual citizens may attend to their special interests, but collectively, their interests should span the nation's major problems. It is also important that citizens bring a wide range of information to the collective judgment based on diverse news sources.

To assess the richness and quality of the citizenship-relevant information that reaches the U.S. public requires surveillance of all of the tributaries to the collective information stream. One recent study did just that. The researchers analyzed the content of daily news published in eight different types of venues in 2007. The venues included nationally and locally circulating newspapers and newscasts, cable newscasts, assorted liberal and conservative Internet blogs, and radio offerings such as National Public Radio (NPR) and all-news stations, along with popular syndicated radio talk programs like the *Rush Limbaugh Show*.

The table summarizes the findings. Every news source provided two to ten citizenship-relevant news items on an average day. These stories amounted to roughly 23 percent of the total political news offered. The proportion of citizenship-relevant news was highest for national television, at 35 percent of all political stories, and lowest for local television, at 13 percent. Individual citizens would find it difficult to cope with the wealth of citizenship-relevant information, but division of labor makes it manageable, with different citizens attending to different issues.

Furthermore, news venues vary sharply in their story choices. If one uses national newspapers as the prototype of what is news on a particular day, one finds that only 13 percent of the news stories appearing in a national newspaper such as the *New York Times* are published by other venues. Conversely, other venues carry citizenship-relevant news stories that are missing from the *Times*.

To find fault is easy; to suggest realistic remedies is far more difficult. Few critics agree on what is noteworthy enough to deserve publication. Gradations and ranks in significance depend on the observer's worldview and political orientation. One person's intellectual meat is another's poison. Conservatives would like to see more stories about the misdeeds of the country's enemies and about waste and abuse in social service programs. Liberals complain that the media legitimize big business and the military and neglect social reforms and radical perspectives.

When the media have featured controversial public policy issues, such as the dangers of nuclear energy generation or the merits of a new health care

Proportion of Citizenship News			
News Sources	No.	%	Overlap %
National paper	9	22	100
Local paper	6	17	23
24-7 cable	4	24	14
Local TV	2	13	0
National TV	3	35	9
Special host shows	4	25	17
Radio news	3	20	8
Blog: liberal	5	27	17
Blog: conservative	4	27	15

NOTES: No. = average daily number of citizenship-relevant news stories; % = percentage of total daily political news stories; overlap = percentage of stories shared with national newspaper.

In combination, the news venues covered twenty-three different topics each day, enabling citizens to monitor a broad range of topics. A core of important topics, including the Iraq War, the 2008 presidential campaign, and the emerging housing mortgage crisis, were covered by all venues. Collectively, they provided a wealth of detail and constituted a national political agenda available to all citizens. The persistence of a shared core of vital news in a splintered universe of news venues lessens the chance that Americans will isolate themselves in mutually exclusive communication ghettos.

The bird's-eye view of the news supply, judged in terms of satisfying citizenship needs in a democracy, provides a more reassuring vision than the analyses from other perspectives reported in chapter 4. Broadly viewed, the news media fill citizenship needs. Sadly, the content analysis also showed that all too often the totality of readily available information is too sketchy to fully judge the significance of situations, even considering that news stories are enriched by information stored in citizens' memories of past happenings. The news diet is thin, and junk food abounds. Still, it is rich enough to sustain democratic governance and, thanks to Internet search engines, substantially more nourishing than in the past.

system, or when they cover political campaigns or demonstrations, each side often charges that political bias dictated the choices about inclusion and exclusion of content and about the story's focus and tone. A number of content analyses of such stories definitely refute the charges of pervasive political bias, if bias is defined as deliberately lopsided coverage or intentional slanting of news. These analyses show instead that most newspeople try to cover a balanced array of issues in a neutral manner and do include at least a few contrasting viewpoints. But given the constraints on the number of sources that can be used and the desire to produce exciting stories that top the competition, the end product is rarely a balanced reflection of all elite viewpoints and all shades

TABLE 4-4 **Coverage of News Elements in National and Local Broadcasts (in percentages)**

News elements	Who	What	Where	When	Why	How	Context	Total no. of stories
Events abroad								
Mideast problems	88%	100%	88%	88%	38%	60%	25%	8
Asia politics	100	100	100	100	100	30	33	3
Europe politics	100	100	100	100	100	70	67	3
Other international issues	100	100	100	92	25	80	33	12
Natural events								
Weather/nature	73	91	100	91	73	90	64	11
Accidents/safety	100	100	100	95	52	90	24	21
Economic issues								
Economic conditions	88	100	74	77	81	70	84	43
Fiscal policies	100	100	59	94	88	80	35	17
Noneconomic issues								
Local/national government	94	100	88	97	73	80	36	33
Public officials	100	100	73	77	73	50	27	22
Crime/law enforcement	100	100	89	85	59	80	22	27
Other domestic issues	94	100	84	84	72	70	41	32
Private sector news								
Business news	92	100	77	81	69	70	38	26
Health/medical news	100	100	46	39	77	60	77	13
Average scores	94	100	82	84	69	70	44	271

Source: Author's research, based on analysis of 352 randomly selected television news stories aired November 24 to December 23, 2008. Feature stories and stories briefer than 20 seconds were omitted.

Note: Numbers represent the percentage of stories in each group that cover the question.

of public opinion.[53] Moreover, as mentioned, the prevailing political culture colors everything because it provides the standards by which events are judged and interpreted.

When coverage is unbalanced, as happens often, the reasons generally spring from the news-making process rather than from politically or ideologically motivated slanting. For instance, the media covered famine conditions in Somalia because that country was fairly accessible. They ignored similar conditions in Sudan because travel was too difficult there. Journalists report events happening in major cities more fully nationwide than similar events in smaller communities because the cities are better equipped for news collection and transmission. The New Hampshire presidential primary receives disproportionately heavy coverage because it happens to be the first one in a presidential election year.

Press output inevitably represents a small, unsystematic, and unrepresentative sample of the news of the day. In that sense, every issue of a newspaper or every television newscast is biased. Published stories often generate follow-up coverage, heightening the bias effect. Attempts to be evenhanded may lead to similar coverage for events of dissimilar importance, thereby introducing bias. For example, environmentalists have complained that the quest for balanced news has skewed the coverage of information about global warming. "By giving equal time to opposing views, these newspapers [*New York Times, Washington Post, Los Angeles Times, Wall Street Journal*] significantly downplayed scientific understanding of the role humans play in global warming. . . . [W]hen generally agreed-upon scientific findings are presented side-by-side with the viewpoints of a handful of skeptics, readers are poorly served."[54]

When news is evaluated from the standpoint of the audience's preference, rather than as a mirror image of society or as a reflection of socially and politically significant events, media gatekeepers appear to be doing well. People like the products of the mass media industry well enough to devote huge chunks of their leisure time to broadcasts and the Internet. Millions of viewers, by their own free choice, watch shows condemned as "trash" by social critics and often even by the viewers themselves. These same people ignore shows and newspaper stories with the critics' seal of approval. Most claim to enjoy broadcast news and to learn important information from it. Media critics may scoff at such accolades, but if an old saying is right that "the voice of the people is the voice of God," the people's voice deserves respect.[55]

SUMMARY

What is news depends on what a particular society deems socially significant or personally satisfying to media audiences. The prevailing political and social ideology therefore determines what type of information journalists will gather and the range of meanings they will give it. News collection is structured through the beat system to keep in touch with the most prolific sources of news.

Beyond the larger framework, which is rooted in the country's current political ideology, overt political considerations rarely play a major part in news selection. Instead, the profit motive and the technical constraints of news production are paramount selection criteria. These criteria impose more stringent constraints on television than on print media because television deals with larger, more heterogeneous audiences and requires pictures to match story texts. Unlike newspapers, which rarely have competition in the local market, television must compete for attention with multiple other electronic outlets as well as the mushrooming news sites on the Internet.

News making remains almost exclusively in the hands of the traditional news media. The majority of news consumers who rely on the Internet visit the news sites offered by major mainstream media, which mirror off-line news. The same holds true for other sites, such as the social networks or assorted blogs. The stories offered there mostly reflect the news gathered by traditional media, though they are often told from different, more critical perspectives.

The end products of the various constraints on news making are stories that generally support the U.S. political system but emphasize its shortcomings and conflicts because conflict is exciting and journalists see themselves as watchdogs of public honesty. News is geared primarily to attract and entertain rather than to educate the audience about politically significant events. The pressures to report news rapidly while it is happening often lead to disjointed fragments and disparate commentary. This leaves the audience with the impossible task of weaving the fragments into a meaningful tapestry of interrelated events.

Judged in terms of the information needs of the ideal citizen in the ideal democracy, news is plentiful but inadequate. This is especially true of broadcast news, which generally provides little more than a headline service for news and which mirrors the world about as much as the curved mirrors at the county fair. The news does reflect reality, but the picture is badly out of shape and proportion. It is no wonder then that distrust of the media is pervasive and growing, as are charges that the news media are politically biased and out of tune with the views of average Americans.[56]

Most Americans only faintly resemble the ideal citizen, and most look to the media for entertainment rather than enlightenment. From that perspective, a different appraisal suggests itself. By and large, U.S. mass media, old and new, serve the general public about as well as that public wants to be served in practice rather than in theory. News outlets intersperse entertainment with a smattering of serious information. They prefer breadth of coverage over narrow depth. In times of acute crisis, as we see in the next chapter, the media can and do follow a different pattern. Serious news displaces entertainment, and the broad sweep of events turns into a narrow, in-depth focus on the crisis. But short of acute crisis, kaleidoscopic, shallow storytelling prevails most of the time.

NOTES

1. Pew Research Center for the People and the Press, 2008, "The Web: Alarming, Appealing and a Challenge to Journalistic Values," www.stateofthenewsmedia.org/2008/Journalist%20 report%202008.pdf.

2. David H. Weaver, Randall A. Beam, Bonnie J. Brownlee, Paul S. Voakes, and G. Cleveland Wilhoit, *The American Journalist in the Twenty-first Century* (Mahwah, N.J.: Erlbaum, 2007).

3. Stuart Kallen, ed., *Media Bias* (San Diego: Greenhaven Press, 2004); Reginald Estoque Ecarma, *Beyond Ideology: A Case of Egalitarian Bias in the News* (Lanham, Md.: University Press of America, 2003); Si Sheppard, *The Partisan Press: A History of Media Bias in the United States* (Jefferson, N.C.: McFarland, 2008).

4. Wolfram Peiser, "Setting the Journalist Agenda: Influences from Journalists' Individual Characteristics and from Media Factors," *Journalism and Mass Communication Quarterly* 77 (Summer 2000): 243–257.

5. Pippa Norris, *A Virtuous Circle: Political Communications in Postindustrial Societies* (Cambridge, UK: Cambridge University Press, 2000); Kathleen Hall Jamieson and Paul Waldman, *The Press Effect: Politicians, Journalists, and the Stories That Shape the Political World* (New York: Oxford University Press, 2003); Matthew R. Kerbel, *If It Bleeds It Leads: An Anatomy of Television News* (Boulder: Westview Press, 2001).

6. Coverage patterns for prominent stories may set the mold for subsequent reporting, although this did not happen in the O.J. Simpson murder case. Kimberly A. Maxwell, John Huxford, Catherine Borum, and Robert Hornik, "Covering Domestic Violence: How the O.J. Simpson Case Shaped Reporting of Domestic Violence in the News Media," *Journalism and Mass Communication Quarterly* 77 (Summer 2000): 258–272.

7. Thomas E. Patterson, "Political Roles of the Journalist," in *The Politics of News, the News of Politics*, ed. Doris Graber, Denis McQuail, and Pippa Norris, 2nd ed. (Washington, D.C.: CQ Press, 2007). For comparisons of roles across international borders, see Daniel C. Hallin and Paolo Mancini, *Comparing Media Systems: Three Models of Media and Politics* (Cambridge, UK: Cambridge University Press, 2004).

8. Theodore L. Glasser, ed., *The Idea of Public Journalism* (New York: Guilford, 1999); Tanni Haas, *The Pursuit of Public Journalism: Theory, Practice, and Criticism* (New York: Routledge, 2007). Public journalism has been primarily a print news movement. But there are converts in television news as well, as discussed in David Kurpius, "Public Journalism and Commercial Local Television News: In Search of a Model," *Journalism and Mass Communication Quarterly* 77 (Summer 2000): 340–354.

9. Weaver et al., *The American Journalist.*

10. The question is explored briefly, but poignantly, by Michael Orestes, Tom Bettag, Mark Jurkowitz, and Rem Rieder in "What's News?" *Harvard International Journal of Press/Politics* 5 (Summer 2000): 102–113.

11. "Mr. President, Ben Bradlee Calling," *Public Opinion* 9 (September–October 1986): 40.

12. Jane Delano Brown, Carl R. Bybee, Stanley T. Wearden, and Dulcie Murdock Straughan, "Invisible Power: Newspaper News Sources and the Limits of Diversity," *Journalism Quarterly* 64 (Spring 1987): 45–54; Sharon Dunwoody and Steven Shields, "Accounting for Patterns of Selection of Topics in Statehouse Reporting," *Journalism Quarterly* 63 (Autumn 1986): 488–496. For complaints about news selection processes, see W. Lance Bennett, *News: The Politics of Illusion*, 8th ed. (New York: Pearson/Longman, 2009); and W. Lance Bennett, Regina G. Lawrence, and Steven Livingston, *When the Press Fails* (Chicago: University of Chicago Press, 2007).

13. S. Robert Lichter, Stanley Rothman, and Linda S. Lichter, *The Media Elite* (Bethesda, Md.: Adler and Adler, 1986), 62. The study is reported on pp. 54–71. Also see Hans Mathias Kepplinger,

"Artificial Horizons: How the Press Presented and How the Population Received Technology in Germany from 1965–1986," in *The Mass Media in Liberal Democratic Societies,* ed. Stanley Rothman (New York: Paragon, 1992), chap. 7.

14. Dominic L. Lasorsa and Stephen D. Reese, "News Source Use in the Crash of 1987: A Study of Four National Media," *Journalism Quarterly* 67 (Spring 1990): 60–63, and sources cited therein.

15. The impact of news stories attributed to highly credible sources is described in Benjamin I. Page, Robert Y. Shapiro, and Glenn R. Dempsey, "What Moves Public Opinion?" *American Journal of Political Science* 81 (March 1987): 23–43. For a negative reaction to the power of anchors, see James Fallows, *Breaking the News: How the Media Undermine American Democracy* (New York: Pantheon, 1996), chap. 1.

16. Peter Braestrup, *Big Story* (Garden City, N.Y.: Anchor Books, 1978).

17. Jacques Steinberg, "Washington Post Rethinks Its Coverage of War Debate," *New York Times,* August 13, 2004. Also see Bennett, Lawrence, and Livingston, *When the Press Fails,* chap. 1.

18. George Gerbner, "Ideological Perspective and Political Tendencies in News Reporting," *Journalism Quarterly* 41 (August 1964): 495–508.

19. For a discussion of the social systems framework for mass communications analysis, see James S. Ettema, "The Organizational Context of Creativity," in *Individuals in Mass Media Organizations: Creativity and Constraint,* ed. James S. Ettema and D. Charles Whitney (Beverly Hills, Calif.: Sage, 1982), 91–106.

20. Joseph N. Cappella and Kathleen Hall Jamieson, *Spiral of Cynicism: The Press and the Public Good* (New York: Oxford University Press, 1997).

21. Regina Lawrence, "Game-Framing the Issues: Tracking the Strategy Frame in Public Policy News," *Political Communication* 17 (2000): 93–114; also see Jim A. Kuypers, *Press Bias and Politics: How the Media Frame Controversial Issues* (Westport, Conn.: Praeger, 2002).

22. "1995 Year in Review," *Media Monitor* 10 (January–February 1996): 3. Also see Everett M. Rogers, James W. Dearing, and Soonbum Chang, "AIDS in the 1980s: The Agenda-Setting Process for a Public Issue," *Journalism Monographs* 126 (April 1991).

23. Chicago police crime reports and *Chicago Tribune* index, 2007.

24. Shanto Iyengar and Donald Kinder, *News That Matters* (Chicago: University of Chicago Press, 1987); Shanto Iyengar, *Is Anyone Responsible? How Television Frames Political Issues* (Chicago: University of Chicago Press, 1991).

25. Doris Graber, *Processing Politics* (Chicago: University of Chicago Press, 2001); Jarol B. Manheim, "The News Shapers: Strategic Communication as a Third Force in News Making," in *The Politics of News,* ed. Graber, McQuail, and Norris; see also Stephen Earl Bennett, Staci L. Rhine, and Richard S. Flickinger, "The Things They Cared About: Americans' Attention to Different News Stories, 1989–2002," *Press/Politics* 9 (1): 75–99; Project for Excellence in Journalism, *The State of the News Media 2008,* www.stateofthenewsmedia.org.

26. Marshall McLuhan, *Understanding Media: The Extensions of Man* (London: Sphere Books, 1967).

27. Leon V. Sigal, *Reporters and Officials: The Organization and Politics of Newsmaking* (Lexington, Mass.: Heath, 1973). Also see Leon V. Sigal, "Sources Make the News," in *Reading the News,* ed. Robert Karl Manoff and Michael Schudson (New York: Pantheon, 1987).

28. Thomas E. Patterson, "Doing Well and Doing Good: How Soft News and Critical Journalism Are Shrinking the News Audience and Weakening Democracy—And What News Outlets Can Do about It," John F. Kennedy School of Government Faculty Research Working Papers Series RWP01–001, December 2000.

29. Project for Excellence in Journalism, *The State of the News Media 2008.*

30. Walter Lippmann, *Public Opinion* (New York: Free Press, 1965), 229.

31. Ben Bagdikian, *The Information Machines* (New York: Harper and Row, 1971).

32. Ibid.; Dunwoody and Shields, "Accounting for Patterns of Selection of Topics."

33. Judy Van Slyke Turk, "Information Subsidies and Media Content: A Study of Public Relations Influence on the News," *Journalism Monographs* 100 (December 1986): 1–29. Also see Manheim, "The News Shapers," in *The Politics of News*, ed. Graber, McQuail, and Norris.

34. See Leo Bogart, "How U.S. Newspaper Content Is Changing," *Journal of Communication* 35 (Spring 1985): 82–91; Richard Campbell, Christopher R. Martin, and Bettina Fabos, *Media and Culture*, 7th ed. (Boston: Bedford/St. Martin's, 2009). Also see Bill Kovach and Tom Rosenstiel, *The Elements of Journalism: What Newspeople Should Know and the Public Should Expect*, 1st rev. ed. (New York: Three Rivers Press, 2007).

35. The content of Web sites sponsored by print and broadcast media mostly parallels their mainstream versions but covers the stories more extensively. For one snapshot of Web content on television Web sites, see Sylvia M. Chan-Olmsted and Jung Suk Park, "From On-Air to Online World: Examining the Content and Structures of Broadcast TV Stations' Web Sites," *Journalism and Mass Communication Quarterly* 77 (Summer 2000): 321–339.

36. The first two headings have been adapted from Herbert Gans's study of newsmagazine and network television news. See Gans, *Deciding What's News* (New York: Pantheon, 1979); see also Gaye Tuchman, *Making News: A Study in the Construction of Reality* (New York: Free Press, 1978); and Bennett, *News: The Politics of Illusion*.

37. Karen S. Johnson, "The Portrayal of Lame-Duck Presidents by the National Print Media," *Presidential Studies Quarterly* 16 (Winter 1986): 50–65. For a broad discussion of the coverage mix at the federal government level, see Stephen Hess, *The Washington Reporters* (Washington, D.C.: Brookings Institution Press, 1981).

38. James T. Hamilton, *All the News That's Fit to Sell: How the Market Transforms Information into News* (Princeton: Princeton University Press, 2004).

39. Graber, *Processing Politics*.

40. Patterson, "Doing Well and Doing Good," provides citations.

41. After a century of printing on weekdays, *The Christian Science Monitor* moved its operations on-line in the spring of 2009, printing only once a week.

42. Kerbel, *If It Bleeds, It Leads*.

43. George Gerbner, Larry Gross, Michael Morgan, and Nancy Signorielli, "Charting the Mainstream: Television's Contributions to Political Orientations," *Journal of Communication* 32 (Spring 1982): 106–107. Small-town newspapers are more apt to highlight the positive, telling what is good rather than what is bad, because conflict is less tolerable in social systems in which most of the leaders constantly rub elbows.

44. "Videomalaise" is Michael J. Robinson's term. See Robinson, "American Political Legitimacy in an Era of Electronic Journalism: Reflections on the Evening News," in *Television as a Social Force: New Approaches to TV Criticism*, ed. Richard Adler (New York: Praeger, 1975), 97–139.

45. Stephen E. Rada, "Manipulating the Media: A Case Study of a Chicano Strike in Texas," *Journalism Quarterly* 54 (Spring 1977): 109–113. Also see Gadi Wolfsfeld, "Symbiosis of Press and Protest: An Exchange Analysis," *Journalism Quarterly* 61 (Autumn 1984): 550–555.

46. Klaus Bruhn Jensen, "News as Ideology: Economics Statistics and Political Ritual in Television Network News," *Journal of Communication* 37 (Winter 1987): 8–27; Bennett, *News: The Politics of Illusion*.

47. Gadi Wolfsfeld, "Media, Protest, and Political Violence: A Transactional Analysis," *Journalism Monographs* 127 (June 1991): 1–61.

48. For a strong attack on status quo support, see Edward S. Herman and Noam Chomsky, *Manufacturing Consent: The Political Economy of the Mass Media* (New York: Pantheon, 2002).

49. There is resistance to change, even in entertainment program formats. See Jay G. Blumler and Carolynn Martin Spicer, "Prospects for Creativity in the New Television Marketplace: Evidence from Program-Makers," *Journal of Communication* 40 (Autumn 1990): 78–101.

50. A comparison of war movies made with and without Pentagon aid showed that aided movies depicted the military in a more favorable light. Russell E. Shain, "Effects of Pentagon Influence on War Movies, 1948–70," *Public Opinion Quarterly* 38 (Fall 1972): 641–647.

51. For a fuller exploration of this issue, see David L. Altheide, *Creating Reality: How TV News Distorts Events* (Beverly Hills, Calif.: Sage, 1976); Tuchman, *Making News*; Mark Fishman, *Manufacturing the News* (Austin: University of Texas Press, 1980); and Bennett, *News: The Politics of Illusion*.

52. But sensational news often contains a great deal of information. See C. Richard Hofstetter and David M. Dozier, "Useful News, Sensational News: Quality, Sensationalism, and Local TV News," *Journalism Quarterly* 63 (Winter 1986): 815–820; and Matthew A. Baum, *Soft News Goes to War: Public Opinion and American Foreign Policy in the New Media Age* (Princeton: Princeton University Press, 2003).

53. Frederick Fico and Stan Soffin, "Fairness and Balance of Selected Newspaper Coverage of Controversial National, State, and Local Issues," *Journalism and Mass Communication Quarterly* 72 (Autumn 1995): 621–633; Neil J. Kressel, "Biased Judgments of Media Bias: A Case Study of the Arab-Israeli Dispute," *Political Psychology* 8 (June 1987): 211–226; and Lichter, Rothman, and Lichter, *The Media Elite*, 293–301. The difficulties of defining "bias" are explained in Stephen Lacy, Frederick Fico, and Todd F. Simon, "Fairness and Balance in the Prestige Press," *Journalism Quarterly* 68 (Fall 1991): 363–370. Also see Todd F. Simon, Frederick Fico, and Stephen Lacy, "Covering Conflict and Controversy: Measuring Balance, Fairness, Defamation," *Journalism Quarterly* 62 (Summer 1989): 427–434.

54. Jennifer McNulty, "Top U.S. Newspapers' Focus on Balance Skewed Coverage of Global Warming, Analysis Reveals," *UC Santa Cruz Currents online*, September 6, 2004, http://cur rents.ucsc.edu/04-05/09-06/coverage.html.

55. Pew Research Center for the People and the Press, *Trends 2005*, http://peoplepress.org/commentary/pdf/05pdf.

56. Ibid.

READINGS

Callaghan, Karen, and Frauke Schnell, eds. *Framing American Politics*. Pittsburgh: University of Pittsburgh Press, 2005.

Emery, Michael, Edwin Emery, and Nancy L. Roberts. *The Press and America: An Interpretive History of the Mass Media*. 9th ed. Boston: Allyn and Bacon, 2000.

Glasser, Theodore L., ed. *The Idea of Public Journalism*. New York: Guilford, 1999.

Jamieson, Kathleen Hall, and Paul Waldman. *The Press Effect: Politicians, Journalists, and the Stories That Shape the Political World*. New York: Oxford University Press, 2003.

Kovach, Bill, and Tom Rosenstiel. *The Elements of Journalism: What Newspeople Should Know and the Public Should Expect*. 1st rev. ed. New York: Three Rivers Press, 2007.

McChesney, Robert W. *The Problem of the Media: U.S. Communication Politics in the Twenty-First Century*. New York: Monthly Review Press, 2004.

Overholser, Geneva, and Kathleen Hall Jamieson, eds. *Institutions of American Democracy: The Press*. New York: Oxford University Press, 2005.

Schudson, Michael. *Sociology of News*. New York: Norton, 2003.

Sheppard, Si. *The Partisan Press: A History of Media Bias in the United States*. Jefferson, N.C.: McFarland, 2008.

Van Zoonen, Lisbet. *Entertaining the Citizen: When Politics and Popular Culture Converge*. Lanham, Md.: Rowman and Littlefield, 2004.

Weaver, David H., Randall A. Beam, Bonnie J. Brownlee, Paul S. Voakes, and G. Cleveland Wilhoit. *The American Journalist in the Twenty-first Century*. Mahwah, N.J.: Erlbaum, 2007.

Reporting Extraordinary Events

Day of Terror! America's Darkest Hour! America's Nightmare! Hijacked Planes Destroy Trade Center! Terrorists Attack World Trade Center, Pentagon! Act of War! Those are some of the headlines that heralded the attack on the United States on September 11, 2001.[1] The assault began at 8:45 a.m. Eastern Standard Time when an American Airlines passenger jet crashed into one of the two 110-story towers at New York City's World Trade Center. Minutes later, another jetliner slammed into the second tower. By 9:16 a.m. one tower had collapsed; the second tower tumbled at 10:00 a.m. Nearly simultaneously, a plane crashed into the Pentagon in Washington, D.C., causing several floors to collapse. Initial news reports indicated that thousands had died and even more thousands were wounded, property had been destroyed, and people throughout the entire country were evacuating government sites.

What roles do media play when such extraordinary events occur, and how do they go about playing them? To answer these questions, we will take a close look at four types of crises: war situations, terrorism on U.S. soil, urban rioting fueled by racism, and a major natural disaster. After explaining how media cover such man-made and natural disasters, we will turn to several pseudo-crises. These are comparatively normal events that crisis-type coverage elevates to the status of extraordinary.

In times of crisis, the media, particularly radio and television, provide vital support for government agencies involved in crisis control. In addition to reporting news about the event, the media provide crisis workers quick access to the public by allowing them to use media channels personally or through media personnel. These messages keep endangered communities in touch with essential information and instructions. The messages also allow personnel on the scene, including government authorities, to form impressions about the nature and extent of the crisis, its causes, and appropriate remedies. The close collaboration between public officials and journalists raises major philosophical and policy questions. In times of crises, when citizens pay close attention to media messages, should public officials have unrestricted access to them to communicate with the public? Do journalists compromise their role as neutral observers when they become part of the crisis management team? Should the media concentrate their efforts almost entirely on serving crisis-related needs at the cost of keeping other stories out of the news? Does the widespread notion that criticism in times of crisis is unpatriotic stifle reporters at a time when the need for dispassionate analysis is greatest?

FOUR CRISES

To answer these questions, we will examine media coverage of four major crises: the war against Iraq that began in 2003; the terrorist strike on U.S. soil on September 11, 2001; race riots in Los Angeles that started on April 30, 1992; and the hurricane that devastated New Orleans and part of the Gulf Coast in 2005.

War against Iraq, 2003

On March 20, 2003, massive U.S. military forces invaded Iraq, supported by a coalition that included Britain, Australia, and Poland as well as Iraqi Kurdish militia. The invasion was preceded by an ultimatum demanding that Saddam Hussein, the country's president, and two of his sons leave the country or face immediate military attack. Allegedly they were a threat to the United States and its allies because they possessed weapons of mass destruction destined for use in wars on their enemies. Repeated requests by the United Nations to surrender these weapons had been denied.

After approximately three weeks of military operations, coalition forces overthrew Saddam's government and occupied the country. On May 1, 2003, President George W. Bush declared the war over. Fighting nonetheless continued beyond that date in many parts of the country. Subsequently investigators found no weapons of mass destruction, leading to charges that U.S. and British leaders had exaggerated the threat posed by Iraq to justify the invasion and depose the hated Saddam. Criticism of the war was widespread among world powers and grew steadily within the United States, when the initially low numbers of casualties increased sharply during the occupation period. The news media gave ample coverage to the war throughout, with a steady flow of blow-by-blow, daily reports.

Terrorism in 2001

On the morning of September 11, 2001, terrorists hijacked four U.S. passenger jets and crashed two into the World Trade Center in New York and one into the Pentagon in Washington, D.C. One plane's mission to attack the U.S. Capitol was aborted when it crashed in the Pennsylvania countryside. The hijacked planes were loaded with ample fuel for their scheduled flights from the East Coast to the West Coast, making them ideal weapons of destruction. Obviously the attacks were a well-planned, well-coordinated terrorist plot. Federal officials identified terrorists with links to the fugitive Osama bin Laden, believed to be in Afghanistan, as the likely perpetrators.

In the wake of the crashes, thousands of people were missing and presumed dead and many more were injured. The 110-story World Trade Center and its immediate surroundings lay in ruins and the Pentagon suffered substantial damage. The nation's domestic air traffic system shut down temporarily, as did many government and business operations. U.S. military forces at home and abroad went on the highest state of alert, and borders with Canada and Mexico were sealed. President Bush, in an address to the nation, denounced the hijackers and pledged that the United States would hunt down and punish all responsible parties and their supporters.[2]

Los Angeles Riots, 1992

On March 3, 1991, after a high-speed chase, several officers of the Los Angeles police stopped an African American motorist for traffic violations. An angry confrontation ensued that ended with the white officers severely beating the motorist. A resident of a nearby apartment building, alerted by the noise, videotaped the beating. Over the course of the next year, the shocking footage was broadcast thousands of times throughout the nation, creating widespread consensus among citizens of all races that the police had used excessive force. The repeated airing of the beating inflamed long-simmering public concerns about police brutality and racism.

When Americans heard in April 1992 that an all-white jury had exonerated all but one of the Los Angeles officers on the charges of brutality, protest demonstrations pockmarked the country. In Los Angeles the demonstrations turned into one of the ugliest urban riots in decades, complete with shootings, beatings, massive arson, and looting. Fifty-three people were killed, and more than 2,000 were injured. Rioters destroyed property worth millions of dollars, leaving sections of the city an economic wasteland that remains to be fully restored. In the aftermath of the rioting, the focus of the presidential campaign that year turned to the hitherto neglected problems of urban decay; the alienated, impoverished underclass; and deepening tension among races.[3]

Hurricane Katrina, 2005

Hurricane Katrina, one of the deadliest storms in U.S. history, smashed into the gulf coastal region in late August 2005. New Orleans took the brunt, suffering severe losses of life and property when levees broke and more than 80 percent of the city was flooded. In some areas, the water was more than 15 feet deep; it took weeks to dry them out and years to repair the damage to plant life, housing, and commercial establishments. Of the 480,000 residents, 90 percent were ultimately evacuated, many of them only after being stranded in the city for several days on rooftops or in severely overcrowded shelters, without adequate food and water. Those left behind in the city were predominantly elderly, infirm, and poor. Estimates of the disaster's toll put deaths near 2,000, injuries and diseases at thousands more, and property damage at around $80 billion.[4]

Immediately after the levees broke, the major roads connecting the city with the outside world were so severely damaged that it was difficult for emergency rescue services to operate. Airplane movements were also severely curtailed. Rescue delays became a major political issue when federal emergency

TABLE 5-1 **Principal Sources of News during Crises (in percentages)**

News source	Hurricane Katrina	War in Iraq	September 11 attacks
Television	89	89	90
Newspapers	35	24	11
Radio	17	19	14
Internet	21	11	5

Source: Adapted from Pew Research Center for the People and the Press, "Biggest Stories of 2008: Economy Tops Campaign," December 23, 2008, http://people-press.org/reports/pdf/479.pdf.

Note: Two answers were permitted. *N* = 1,489.

services were unduly slow to respond. Ultimately the sluggishness cost Michael Brown, the director of the Federal Emergency Management Agency (FEMA), his job. Destruction of much of the communications infrastructure made it almost impossible to coordinate individual rescue operations. Most landline and cell phones were inoperable because of power failures, destruction of base stations, and broken lines. Local television services were also disrupted as was access to the Internet. Amateur radio operators became the most reliable transmitters of information.

MEDIA RESPONSES AND ROLES

During crises, the public depends almost totally on the media for news and for vital messages from public and private authorities. The news media are the only institutions equipped to collect substantial amounts of information and disseminate it quickly to the general public. Therefore, when people become aware of a crisis, they monitor developments through their radios, television sets, or computers, often around the clock. Portable equipment that does not require connection to electricity sources is particularly important. Televised offerings, especially network and cable news, attract the largest audiences during crises because of their ability to report breaking stories quickly, while newspapers, with their slower publication cycles, lag behind (Table 5-1).[5]

The audience for crisis information is massive and loyal and generally pleased with the quality of coverage. After the 2001 terrorist attack, 74 percent of the U.S. public claimed to have watched news about the event very closely. The figures were 70 percent for the Los Angeles riots, 63 percent for the 2003 Iraq War, and 73 percent for Hurricane Katrina.[6] When one adds the numbers for people who said that they paid "fairly close" attention, they rise above the 90 percent mark for each crisis. During the 2003 Iraq War, cable news channels, which have become increasingly popular, tripled their audiences, averaging 7 million nightly viewers. Newspapers added roughly 15 percent to their audience during the later stages of the crisis when people were hungry for analysis in greater depth. Television nightly news, though yielding audience to the cable programs, still captured 28 million viewers, roughly ten times the figures that cable outlets could boast. In fact, those numbers topped prime-time entertainment shows such as *CSI: Crime Scene Investigation,* with an audience of 27 million, and *Friends,* with 22 million.[7]

Besides seeking information, the public looks to the media for interpretations of situations. Media personnel are often the first to try to fit breaking events into a coherent story. Official investigations and reports generally come much later. The media also guide the public's actions during a crisis. They direct people to shelters, announce which areas are unsafe to enter, describe purification processes for polluted food and water, and supply news of missing persons or schedules of schools and workplaces. News stories also report what immediate steps government authorities are taking to cope with the crisis.

Stages and Patterns of Coverage

Observers of crisis coverage have identified three stages that merge almost seamlessly and often overlap.

Stage One. During the first stage, the crisis or disaster is announced as impending or as having already struck. Reporters, officials, and onlookers rush to the scene. Radio and television stations interrupt regularly scheduled programs with uncoordinated bulletins announcing the extraordinary event. The stations may preempt the entire program for announcements about anticipated events or live reports from the scene.

Minutes after the start of the Los Angeles riots, television and radio reporters broadcast directly from the scene. They showed buildings on fire and beating and looting scenes, usually without a single police officer within camera range. Later these broadcasts were blamed for tipping off rioters about places where they might assault, burn, and loot with impunity. The same stories also helped police find locations where they were sorely needed. Media offices became information collection centers because people phoned them to report or receive information. At the start of a disaster messages are crucial when they direct people to places of safety, summon police and military units, and coordinate appeals for relief supplies, such as food, blankets, blood donations, and medical equipment.

During Stage One, news dissemination escalates and audience figures multiply, especially on twenty-four-hour news outlets. During all four events, crisis-related news and interviews replaced many regular programs. News bulletins were issued throughout the day on radio and television. Journalists interviewed a steady stream of eyewitnesses. With little new to report, media rehashed the same facts endlessly. During major catastrophes, the initial reports about the disaster reach many people by word of mouth through face-to-face or telephone conversations. The news of the attempted assassination of President Ronald Reagan in 1981 illustrates the speed of diffusion of crisis news. The story initially reached a large daytime audience that heard it on radio or television. Then, on average, each person told the news to three other people. More than 90 percent of the U.S. public—over 200 million people—received the news within ninety minutes after the shooting.[8] The rate of diffusion was equally swift for the 2001 terrorist strike because, like the assault on Reagan, it occurred during daytime on a working day, when most adults are in touch with their normal information networks.

The rapidity of news diffusion is the most striking characteristic of initial coverage of extraordinary events. Television, radio, and the Internet can focus the public's attention almost instantaneously on developing situations throughout the world. In many cases news about the extraordinary event replaces most other stories. On September 12, 2001, most major U.S. newspapers, as well as flagship papers around the world, devoted their entire front pages, along with many inside pages, to the terrorist attack on New York and Washington, D.C. Whatever else happens in the world during crisis periods, regardless of importance, may drop off the radar screen in the affected nations or even worldwide.

During Stage One of a crisis, the media are the major sources of information, even for public officials. Media reports help to coordinate public activities and calm the public. For example, during the New Orleans disaster, Mayor Ray Nagin used the news media to order evacuation of the city and to announce evacuation routes and pickup points for residents who needed public transportation. Reporters called Homeland Security secretary Michael Chertoff and FEMA director Michael Brown and suggested specific rescue measures based on their eye-witness experiences. They also told people about temporary housing, health care, emergency food supplies, and ways to deal with damage to their homes.

Next to reaching the disaster site, the chief problem for newspeople during the first stage is getting accurate information. Rumors abound. When the first plane crashed into the World Trade Center in 2001, the media first called it an aviation accident. Each subsequent piece of news sparked an explosion of rumors that turned out to be largely untrue or only partly correct. National Public Radio reported that a Palestinian group was claiming responsibility for the assault but warned listeners to bear in mind that government sources had "a history of disinformation and this information may not be correct."[9] Additionally, the number of dead and the extent of injuries are frequently inflated, although underestimates are also common. In reports about the Iraq War, death figures rarely included Iraqi casualties, which were vastly greater than American losses. Newspeople receive so many conflicting reports and official and unofficial guesstimates that they lack enough time to confirm accuracy.

The unrelenting pressure for fresh accounts often tempts media personnel to interview unreliable sources, who may lend a local touch but confuse the situation by reporting unverified or irrelevant information.[10] When reporters focus only on crisis events, as happened during the Los Angeles riots and the 9/11 terrorist strike, they may convey the wrong impression, for example, that the entire city has been left in ruins or that the affected areas have become a barren wasteland.[11] If highly technical matters, such as explosions, structural failures, and nuclear radiation disasters are involved, it may be impossible to present a coherent story, especially when government officials, eager to allay the public's fears and prevent panic, minimize dangers or obscure them by using impenetrable technical jargon.

The pressure for news encourages reporters and public officials alike to speculate about a disaster's causes. At times, these observers spin their own prejudices into a web of scenarios that puts blame for tragedies or their aftermath on socially outcast groups. For instance, the Los Angeles riots, which occurred during the 1992 presidential campaign, were blamed by Democrats on Republican inattention to urban blight and by Republicans on the welfare programs that had started during the liberal Democratic administration of Lyndon B. Johnson. "Outsiders" in a community (ethnic minorities or political deviants, for example) often become the hapless scapegoats. The racial riots of the 1960s were routinely attributed to "outside agitators" who were depicted as common criminals, bereft of moral scruples and social consciousness.

Stage Two. During the second stage of a crisis, the media try to correct past errors and put the situation into proper perspective. By that time, the chief dimensions of the crisis have usually emerged. For instance, in the Los Angeles riots, the 2001 terror strike, and the 2005 hurricane, the majority of victims and their injuries were known. Repairs and reconstruction plans were in place, and data rather than pure guesses informed damage estimates.

In general, the print media are able to do a more thorough job than radio and television in pulling together the various events and fitting them into a coherent story. Print media have larger staffs for investigation and more room to present background details that make the events understandable. For instance, in the months preceding the outbreak of the 2003 Iraq War and in the days following its start, major newspapers reviewed the reasons for the hostilities, the cost in human lives and property, and the damage done to America's foreign relations by policy disagreements with traditional allies. They drew much of their information from Web sites that, thanks to ample links, now rival and often surpass newspapers in completeness of coverage of breaking news. The Web also offers a huge pool of cell phone photographs posted by accidental eyewitnesses of an evolving event. As media scholar Al Tompkins said about the 2003 Iraq War: "If Vietnam was the 'living room war,' this was the 'real-time war.' . . . [W]e were actually seeing the story, not as it recently unfolded, but as it was unfolding."[12] The growing number of citizens who turn to cable television and the Internet for crisis news can sample an assortment of foreign news sources in addition to multiple U.S. venues. Widely available foreign sources include Arab news broadcast by Al Jazeera and Al Arabiya, the British Broadcasting Corporation (BBC), various European newspapers, and C-SPAN's nightly sampling of the world's television coverage.

During this second stage, governments and their critics may try to shape political fallout from the event in ways that support their policy preferences. Media sanitized coverage of the Iraq War, for example, by presenting it largely through the lens of military operations. Television showed a succession of successful military maneuvers recorded by reporters embedded in various units. Costly military failures were rarely shown. The political aspects of the war, including its drain on U.S. economic resources, were largely ignored. The torrent of specific information left journalists little time to interpret the significance of the events they were reporting. Military censorship prevented featuring casualties or showing the arrival of dead soldiers in body bags at Dover Air Force Base. During the terrorism disaster, political leaders, including the president, earned political plaudits for visiting the afflicted places and expressing sympathy and encouragement, as well as announcing emergency aid. By contrast, federal government officials received scathing blame for indifference and ineptitude in the New Orleans rescue operations during the second stage because aid was slow and paltry. Journalists were praised for effective assistance.[13]

Stage Three. The third stage overlaps with the first two. It involves attempts by media personnel to place the crisis into a larger, long-range perspective and to prepare people to cope with the aftermath. Following the Los Angeles riots, presidential candidates Bill Clinton and George H.W. Bush toured the damaged neighborhoods and announced plans for rebuilding. The media also reported about cleanup efforts and restored services, such as mail deliveries and bus transportation. Within days of the assault on the World Trade Center and Pentagon, news stories reported plans for restoring the New York skyline to renewed glory and resuming full operations at the Pentagon. To deal with long-range posttraumatic shock and to sustain morale during prolonged crises, the media describe how some of the hardest-hit victims are coping and give full coverage to healing ceremonies, such as memorial church services or fund-raising concerts and sports events.

Positive and Negative Effects of Coverage

Information about crises, even if it conveys bad news, relieves disquieting uncertainty and soothes people. The mere activity of watching or listening to familiar reporters and commentators reassures people and keeps them calm. It gives them a sense of vicarious participation, of "doing something." To maintain this quieting effect, media personnel may avoid showing gruesome details of the crisis. However, this was not true in Katrina coverage. Shocking, and even gruesome photographs of human and animal suffering and death, taken by thousands of amateur witnesses quickly flooded news channels thanks to cell phone cameras and the ease of computerized picture transmission. The tide of images generated an unprecedented outpouring of relief donations by people who were touched by the vivid disaster scenes.

After seeing the same pictures and listening to the same broadcasts, people find it easy to discuss the crisis with neighbors, friends, and co-workers and feel mutual support. Watching military briefings on television during the Iraq War, for example, made Americans feel that they were fully informed about the war's progress and that the authorities were in control of the situation. Similarly, scenes of collapsing buildings or city blocks put to the torch during a riot seem less frightening if the news shows that police, firefighters, ambulances, and medical personnel are on the scene. Watching the mayor or governor tour a disaster site provides further reassurance. Finally, directions conveyed by the media about appropriate behavior save lives and property and ensure that a stricken community continues to function.

Media coverage also can do harm during a crisis, raising serious questions about the responsibility of government and media personnel to consider the societal consequences of frankness. News messages may so disturb people that they panic, endangering themselves and others. For instance, a precipitous mass exodus of frightened people during an impending flood or storm calamity may clog roads and overcrowd shelters; it may lead to injuries and death for those caught beyond the safety of their homes and workplaces. Inflammatory accusations are more likely to be publicized in times of crisis because the exceptionally large demand for news and guidance reduces gatekeepers' vigilance. Pack journalism may run rampant when media pool their stories to provide as much coverage as possible. If news sources or reporters make mistakes, they are spread by all the media.

Pictures of violence often produce terrifying multiplication effects. Audiences tend to believe that the violent acts shown are merely a tiny sample. One house on fire or the sight of one victim's body may lead to visions of whole neighborhoods on fire and scores of victims killed. Overreaction may ensue. Police may be ordered to shoot lawbreakers on sight, and citizens may use excessive violence to protect themselves. When perpetrators of crimes are linked to an identifiable ethnic group, there may be a spate of hate crimes targeting members of that group, as happened when the 2001 terror strike was linked to Arab Americans.

Crisis and disaster news frequently attracts crowds of citizens and reporters to a site, impeding rescue and security operations. News coverage of physical disasters routinely draws looters to the scene. During the Los Angeles riots and Hurricane Katrina, police reported that the presence of television cameras seemed to escalate the violence. Rioters actually appeared to perform for the cameras. Sights of looters attracted other looters to the scene, particularly when the pictures revealed that no police officers were present. When violence pits government agents against antigovernment groups, as is often the case in terrorist incidents, ample coverage may incite retaliatory terrorism. Extensive media coverage has been called the lifeblood of terrorism because the perpetrators use their assaults to attract attention to their causes and gain sympathy and support. That usually turns out to be a false hope, however, because news coverage puts the spotlight on the deeds and neglects the underlying causes.[14] Wide publicity for terrorist acts and heinous crimes (such as airline hijackings, poisoning of food supplies, or serial mass murders) may lead to copycat crimes.

Economic crises, too, can escalate as a result of media images. When prices on the financial markets plunged precipitously on October 19, 1987, media accounts used highly alarming language. *Panic, carnage,* and *nightmare selling* were common descriptive terms. Moreover, the media frequently compared the crash to the 1929 stock market calamity and discussed the Great Depression that

Eyewitness accounts of the terror attacks in Mumbai spread quickly, propelled by Twitter and Flickr.
Source: REUTERS/Stringer (INDIA)

followed. Such gloomy news apparently fanned the growing panic and further weakened the markets.[15] The same scenario was reenacted during the severe economic crisis that began in the summer 2007. It, too, was compared to the Great Depression, though deemed a shade less severe. The president's plea to consumers to buttress the economy by continuing normal buying patterns fell on deaf ears, as daily horror stories about the collapse of financial institutions and key industries, unprecedented rates of home mortgage foreclosures, job losses, and a plunging stock market continued to break.

Planning Crisis Coverage

Because media play such a crucial role in keeping communities going during crises, most media organizations have plans to cope with the problems of crisis coverage. This is particularly true of electronic media in crisis-prone regions. For example, the *Times-Picayune*, New Orleans's only daily newspaper, has a portable newsroom for use when its regular headquarters become disabled. During hurricanes or floods, it can move to outlying bureaus or to a block of reserved hotel rooms in safe parts of the city, or it can use a newspaper delivery truck retrofitted with equipment for producing electronic versions of the newspaper.[16] Plans generally are more detailed for natural disasters than for civil disturbances because needs are more predictable and there is greater consensus about objectives. Nevertheless, much remains to be decided on the spur of the moment.[17] Confusion inevitably reigns at the start of a crisis. Contradictory messages are likely to abound until coordination can be arranged. In addition to media-sponsored plans, most stations are tied into the federal Emergency Broadcast System (EBS), a network for relaying news during emergencies.

Crisis coverage planning has two aspects: preparing for crisis routines and deciding how to present ongoing events. Aside from warning people about impending natural disasters and suggesting preparations, plans to forestall crises are rare, probably because the media focus on short-range happenings and because most crises cannot be accurately predicted. Nonetheless, viewers have often blamed the media for neglecting preventive coverage. The Kerner Commission in 1968 condemned media silence about the plight of African Americans in the United States for allowing frustrations to build and explode into race riots in the mid-1960s. In the same vein, the Los Angeles riots of 1992 were blamed in part on inattention by the media and other institutions to the plight of inner cities and their minority residents. When public approval of the 2003 Iraq War began to sag in reaction to mounting casualties and the failure to find the weapons of mass destruction that had been a major reason for going to war, the public criticized the media's gatekeeping decisions. Why had early opposition to the war received so little publicity? Why had news outlets relegated it to back pages of papers and tail ends of broadcasts while featuring the government's case in favor of war? Would media efforts to undermine the case for war have been a patriotic act or undue interference in the nation's foreign policy? The answer continues to be hotly debated.[18]

Plans for covering natural disasters are generally predicated on the assumption that people tend to panic and that coverage must forestall this. Unfortunately, stories that are graphic enough to arouse a lethargic population to prepare for a disaster may cause panic or denial. Denial seems rampant in Southern California, where most residents have not taken recommended precautions against earthquakes—such as fortifying buildings and storing emergency supplies—despite frequent warnings.[19] Similarly, when the Department of Homeland Security warns the nation that the danger of a terrorist attack has risen to a higher level, few citizens take suggested precautions. Government officials and newspeople often abstain from warning about an impending disaster because they fear citizens' anger if the danger does not materialize. Besides, the warning may lead to costly, unnecessary preventive measures. That happened in winter 1990, when warnings about a 50 percent chance of an earthquake in the New Madrid earthquake zone in the Midwest prompted residents to flee, public services to shut down, and numerous businesses to cancel events. A climatologist had made the predictions, and most people believed the story despite misgivings voiced by seismologists and geologists. Reporters by the hundreds gathered in the "danger zone" ready to report the event, which did not occur.

Reluctance to issue warnings is even greater when civil disorders threaten. Officials and their media mouthpieces assume that broadcasts about civil disturbances will produce panic and copycat effects among the public. Social scientists who study disasters deny that panic and contagion occur frequently.[20] Whether or not these scientists are correct, the important fact is that media personnel have been expecting these reactions and have shied away from warnings about impending civil strife. From the race riots of the 1960s media personnel learned to keep a low profile when violence occurs because the perpetrators are energized by the chance to have their actions publicized. Media personnel accordingly try to act unobtrusively. For example, they avoid bringing identified television trucks into areas where disturbances are taking place. However, such precautions are largely wasted when television reporters broadcast live coverage from the scene.

The media also try to avoid inflammatory details or language in news reports. Milder terms can replace such words as *carnage, holocaust, mob action,* or *massacre.* The general rule during crises is, "When in doubt, leave it out." Publicizing interviews with public officials and civic leaders who urge calm behavior and indicate that the situation is under control can soothe tempers. During the Los Angeles riots, mayor Tom Bradley and California governor Pete Wilson appeared repeatedly in the media to talk about progress in quieting the city. Rodney King, the victim of the police beating that sparked the disturbances, also made an impassioned appeal for ending the violence. Following the Twin Towers attack, President Bush and other public and private leaders throughout the country pleaded for ending hate crimes and discrimination against people presumed to have ties to Islamic countries. Many people failed to heed the appeals because people's emotions were continuously aroused by the barrage of news that displayed gruesome pictures over and over and by the mainstream media's extensive coverage of the activities of extremist groups after September 11.[21]

The Problem of News Suppression

In natural as well as human-failure crises, the suppression of news, either temporarily or permanently, raises major policy questions. How much coverage should the media present immediately, at the risk of telling an inaccurate story, spreading panic, and attracting bystanders and destructive participants to the scene? What facts should be withheld initially or permanently to forestall troublesome reactions? Should live coverage be banned, particularly in civil disturbances, lest it increase the intensity and duration of the crisis? Some news outlets routinely delay live coverage until officials have the situation under control. Others believe that suppression of live coverage will allow the spread of rumors that may be more inciting than judicious reporting of ongoing events. No one knows which of these views is most correct or how different circumstances affect reactions to media coverage of crises (Box 5-1).

Deciding whether to suppress coverage becomes particularly difficult when a crisis involves terrorists, prison rioters, assassins of political leaders, or maniacal mass murderers who crave publicity. Live coverage of the crime scene glamorizes their violent acts and may encourage further outrages. Making a killer a celebrity may encourage other malcontents to act out their murderous fantasies. As Rep. Edward Feighan, D-Ohio, pointed out after chairing congressional hearings on terrorism and the media, the television age poses new dilemmas for a responsible press. "Terrorism is a new form of symbolic warfare, and the television screen is the battlefield on which these wars will be fought in the future."[22] Even the print media face such dilemmas. The *New York Times* and the

Washington Post reluctantly agreed in 1995 to publish a lengthy tract by the "Unabomber." The terrorist had threatened to continue his spree of letter bombings if the media refused to publish his manifesto of complaints against society.

It is true that publicity spreads the terrorists' messages, raising sympathy for their causes. However, if mainstream media fail to cover the terrorist acts or subsequent court actions and penalties, including death sentences, they infringe on the public's right to know, even if the information is available elsewhere. They also miss out on publishing a dramatic event with wide audience appeal. If the press follows the government's official line in describing terrorists and their motives, it may become an inadvertent government propaganda tool.[23] If it dwells on either the human strengths or the frightful human frailties of the violent actors, it will be accused of making saints out of villains or villains out of hapless victims of society's malfunctions.

Decisions about news suppression are equally tough during international crises and in time of war. During the Iraq War, the military kept tight control over news stories by inviting journalists to join military units— "embedding" is the technical term—and report the news from an insider's perspective. Reporters' loyalty to their unit and a pledge to abstain from publishing sensitive information served to dull criticism of war activities. Some reporters resented such constraints and ventured forth on their own in defiance of official rules and at the risk of their personal safety. Although their fellow journalists generally approved, the majority of the public did not because it supported wartime censorship as a security measure.[24]

Muted coverage is problematic. It generally leads to presenting only the official story and suppressing unofficial views. The perspectives of civilian and military public security personnel then become paramount, so that security aspects are stressed, rather than the causes of violent behavior and the political and social changes, including new public policies, that might prevent future violence.[25] Consider the muted coverage of a tense racial incident that involved a murder in a New York City neighborhood. A review of the incident two years later revealed that the media had covered the facts adequately without further inflaming the tense public. But media had also omitted crucial details about mistakes made by former public officials in handling the crisis, largely because those officials had been their main information sources. The omissions delayed reforms and deepened the community's racial divisions.[26] In terrorist incidents or prison riots, failure to air the grievances of terrorists and prison inmates deprives them of a public forum for voicing their grievances. Their bottled-up anger may lead to more violent explosions. Wartime news suppression by government censorship or reporters' self-censorship out of a sense of patriotism may cover up misdeeds that need exposure followed by remedies.[27]

Some observers contend that muted reporting reduces the potential for arousing hatred and creating unbridgeable conflicts. Delayed coverage, these observers argue, can be more analytical and thus is more likely to produce reforms. Others contend that the drama of an ongoing crisis raises public consciousness much better and faster than anything else. People will act to

BOX 5-1 **Crisis Coverage Dilemmas in Mumbai**

During a crisis, everyone focuses on the main events. Many news organizations even have plans that systematize how these situations will be handled. There is little dispute about what the news should cover, right? Sadly, all of this happens to be wrong.

The terrorist strike on Mumbai, India's largest city, offers a perfect example of crisis coverage dilemmas. Between November 26 and November 29, 2008, terrorists attacked ten sites in the city, killing nearly 200 people and wounding more than 400. The terrorists belonged to the Lashkar-e-Taiba organization, which opposes India's military operations in Kashmir. Two luxury hotels, the Taj Mahal Palace and the Oberoi Trident, were among targets of bomb blasts and hostage-takings.

Indian press commentaries heavily criticized coverage of the events in U.S. and British news media for focusing on the luxury hotel locations and on the five Americans and one British citizen who were killed. Some critics thought that the news spotlight should have been on the train station that was the terrorists' first target, where most of the casualties occurred. As one commentator put it: "A lot of innocent commuters from middle and lower-income families were gunned down in cold blood, but I guess the news companies did not find it newsworthy enough when compared to the high profile Taj."[1]

Media outlets in Pakistan condemned the Indian media's coverage of the crisis for stressing that Lashkar-e-Taiba was based in, and controlled from, Pakistan. The Pakistani critics said that the stories implied that Pakistan's government bore some responsibility for the disaster.

Other media critics pointed out that many of the pictures that flooded the airwaves came from cell phones and camcorders, making it impossible to verify the accuracy of the visual record. Blogs and social networks, Twitter and Flickr in the lead, spread news about the attack within minutes of the initial strikes.

remedy injustice only if the situation is acute. If the crisis has already passed, action may seem pointless. A permanent news blackout will make reforms highly unlikely. Those opposed to muted coverage or news suppression are willing to risk paying a high price in lost lives, personal injuries, imprisonment, and property damage in the hope that immediate, complete coverage will shock the community into undertaking social reforms. Most American political leaders, as well as most newspeople, have hitherto opted for muting violent conflict rather than bringing it to a head.

Finally, there is the unresolved philosophical question about the wisdom and propriety of news suppression in a free society. The true test of genuine press freedom does not come in times of calm. It comes in times of crisis when the costs of freedom may be dear, tempting government and media alike to impose silence. Press freedom must be a paramount value in democratic societies! Therefore, the die must be cast in favor of unrestrained crisis coverage, moderated only by each journalist's sense of social responsibility.

All of this vividly demonstrates how control over news reporting has become shared between trained journalists and untrained members of the public. In fact, there is evidence that citizen journalists who report about familiar events enjoy greater trust, and are therefore more persuasive, than full-time, trained reporters.[2] That fact raises serious issues about control over news during crises.

Indian news media were accused of supporting the terrorists with vital information that they made available on the Internet and on television. The Mumbai police tried to stop them during the attack by imposing a news blackout, but the ban was abandoned when it became clear that it was doomed to fail. Subsequently, the Indian News Broadcasters Association proposed rules to prohibit publicizing specified types of information during a crisis. For instance, it would be forbidden to broadcast phone interviews with the terrorists or show live interviews with victims or security personnel. News about the identity, number, and status of hostages would be banned.

It seems doubtful that such prohibitions would be effective. Even if journalists abided by them during a crisis, it is unlikely that the rules would curb the behavior of citizen journalists eager to share their actual or vicarious experiences. If crisis broadcasting becomes an unrestrained jungle of news, which is quite possible, what will be the consequences for the victims of calamities throughout the world? It is a troubling, as yet unanswerable, question.

1. "CNN—Holiday Bad Time for Crisis Coverage," www.contactmusic.com/news.nsf/article/holiday%20bad%20time%20for%20crisis.
2. Claudine Beaumont, "Mumbai Attacks: Twitter and Flickr Used to Break News," *London Telegraph*, November 27, 2008, www.telegraph.co.uk/news/worldnews/asia/india/3530640/Mumbai-attacks-Twitter-and-Flickr-used-to-break-news-Bombay-India.html

COVERING PSEUDO-CRISES

Thus far we have discussed genuinely extraordinary events. But there are many other situations that the press treats like crises because that makes them interesting news stories. These pseudo-crises become front-page news for days on end, generating many hours of live television and radio coverage. In 2009 pseudo-events included exhaustive coverage about the life of Nadya Suleman, an unwed mother of six who, with the aid of a fertility clinic, had added octuplets to her economically distressed family. A pseudo-crisis heavily covered in 2008 was revelation of the elaborate scams by which banker Bernard Madoff defrauded a string of wealthy, big-name clients and well-known charities. Similarly, the news media dwelled at great length on the premature death of movie star Heath Ledger, who succumbed to an accidental drug overdose.

Excessive coverage of these real-world soap operas causes two serious problems: It exaggerates their significance and makes more significant happenings seem less significant. More important, it crowds out other situations that urgently need exposure. For example, the news media have largely ignored the problem of deaths from accidental drug overdoses, even though there were 24,000 such deaths in 2006, a 100 percent increase since 2000. Abuse of prescription painkillers is the main, preventable cause; the victims come from all segments and all ages of the population.[28] Similarly, despite huge problems that affect millions of Americans, news coverage of public education and public transportation has been extremely sparse. Had the media cut back on overblown coverage of pseudo-events, they could have filled their news hole with other dramatic but far more significant stories.[29]

SUMMARY

In U.S. political culture, the normal feuds of politics are put on ice when major emergencies happen. Although this unwritten rule has been mentioned most often in connection with foreign policy, where "politics stops at the water's edge," it applies as well to the types of domestic crises discussed in this chapter. When life and property are endangered, when sudden death and terror reign, when well-known leaders are assassinated, or when the nation goes to war, the media suspend normal coverage practices. Instead of playing their adversarial role, the media become teammates of officialdom in attempts to restore public order, safety, and tranquility.

The media perform indispensable functions during crises: they diffuse vital information to the public and officials, interpret events, and provide emotional support for troubled communities. Pocket-sized radios and cell phones are particularly helpful during disasters because their technical requirements are most adaptable to makeshift arrangements. They can broadcast without regular electric power, and they can reach isolated people in remote locations. Round-the-clock radio, television, and Internet news coverage and satellite transmissions from around the world make it possible to watch extraordinary events wherever and whenever they occur.

Because the media play such a huge role in crisis communication, public officials and the community at large are concerned about the quality of their performance. Common deficiencies such as information gaps, misinformation, and the dissemination of information that worsens the crisis have led to demands for control of the information flow. Many media institutions have formal plans that temporarily set aside the usual criteria for publishing exciting news in the interest of calming the public. The need to plan for crisis coverage is acute. Modern society faces crises of various sorts so frequently that policy makers in the media and in government are remiss when they fail to plan for emergencies. At the same time they must strive to avoid news distortion and overindulgence in pseudo-crisis coverage when titillating news becomes available.

Muted coverage, particularly during civil disturbances and incidents of political terrorism, may be unwise because it may drown out explicit and implicit messages about unmet societal needs and demands. Moreover, in the Internet age, it has become increasingly difficult to suppress information. As media scholar Robin Brown notes: "The ability of the global communications system to gather and disseminate information has vastly increased. . . . In such an environment it is no surprise that the sensitivity of governments to the media increases. . . . The effects of this will vary from case to case (and from country to country), but it can only increase the interpenetration of war, politics, and the media."[30]

NOTES

1. Newseum, "9/11 Terrorist Attacks Front Pages, September 12, 2001," www.newseum.org.

2. Michael Grunwald, "Terrorists Hijack 4 Airliners, Destroy World Trade Center, Hit Pentagon; Hundreds Dead," *Washington Post*, September 12, 2001; Matthew V. Storin, "While America Slept: Coverage of Terrorism from 1993 to September 11, 2001," in *Terrorism, War, and the Press*, ed. Nancy Palmer (Hollis, N.H.: Hollis Publishing Co., 2003), 1–26, analyzes terrorism coverage by the *New York Times* and *Washington Post* from 1993 through 2001.

3. For details of the Los Angeles riots, see "Rage in L.A.," *Chicago Tribune*, May 1, 1992; Erna Smith, *Transmitting Race: The Los Angeles Riot in Television News* (Cambridge, Mass.: Harvard University Press, 1994).

4. Carl Bialik, "Coming to Grips with a Grim Count," *Wall Street Journal*, September 7, 2005, http://online.wsj.com.

5. Pew Research Center for the People and the Press, "Biggest Stories of 2008: Economy Tops Campaign," December 23, 2008, http://people-press.org/reports/pdf/479.pdf.

6. Pew Research Center for the People and the Press, "Media Report, 1992–2003," http://people-press.org; Pew Research Center for the People and the Press, "What Was and Wasn't on the Public's Mind," http://people-press.org/commentary?analysisid=125.

7. Chris Jones, "This Living Room War," *Chicago Tribune*, April 20, 2003. Andrew Glass, "The War on Terrorism Goes Online," in Palmer, *Terrorism, War, and the Press*, 47–80, analyzes Internet coverage.

8. Walter Gantz, "The Diffusion of News about the Attempted Reagan Assassination," *Journal of Communication* 33 (Winter 1983): 56–65.

9. Whitecloud.com, "9/11/01 Events," www.whitecloud.com/events9-11-01.htm; also see Bialik, "Coming to Grips with a Grim Count."

10. T. Joseph Scanlon, "Media Coverage of Crises: Better than Reported, Worse than Necessary," *Journalism Quarterly* 55 (Spring 1978): 68–72. Crisis reporting is especially difficult when competing frames regarding causes of the disaster abound. See Frank D. Durham, "News Frames as Social Narratives: TWA Flight 800," *Journal of Communication* 48 (Autumn 1998): 110–114.

11. Dennis E. Wenger, "A Few Empirical Observations Concerning the Relationship between the Mass Media and Disaster Knowledge: A Research Report," in *Disasters and the Mass Media: Proceedings of the Committee on Disasters and the Mass Media Workshop* (Washington, D.C.: National Academy Press, 1980), 252–253; also see Morgen S. Johansen and Mark R. Joslyn, "Political Persuasion during Times of Crisis: The Effects of Education and News Media on Citizens' Factual Information about Iraq," *Journalism and Mass Communication Quarterly* 85, no. 3 (2008): 591–608.

12. Quoted in Allan Johnson, "Numbers Don't Lie," *Chicago Tribune*, April 20, 2003.

13. W. Lance Bennett, Regina G. Lawrence, and Steven Livingston, *When the Press Fails* (Chicago: University of Chicago Press, 2007).

14. See Storin, "While America Slept."

15. John Corry, "Network News Covers the Stock Market Frenzy," *New York Times*, October 21, 1987; and Mark Jurkowitz, "Obamanomics: No Deficit in Press," March 4, 2009, http://pewresearch.org/pubs/1139/media-budget-deficit-iraq-not-news.

16. Brian Stelter, "A Prophet of Katrina's Wrath Returns to His Storm Vigil," *New York Times*, September 1, 2008; also see Kris Axtman, "Big Relief Effort Meets Katrina," *Christian Science Monitor*, August 30, 2005, www.csmonitor.com/2005/0830/p01s02-ussc.html.

17. Private sector planning for dealing with media in crisis situations is discussed in detail in Kathleen Fearn-Banks, *Crisis Communications: A Casebook Approach*, 3rd ed. (Mahwah, N.J.: Erlbaum, 2007); also see the *Journal of Homeland Security*.

18. Many authors have wrestled with these questions. Their studies are reviewed in a book review essay by Christopher Hanson, "No Neutral Corner: The American News Media After 9/11," *Journalism and Mass Communication Quarterly* 80 (2003): 731–735.

19. Rodney M. Kueneman and Joseph E. Wright, "News Policies of Broadcast Stations for Civil Disturbances and Disasters," *Journalism Quarterly* 52 (Winter 1975): 671.

20. See the report on the work of the Disaster Research Center at Ohio State University in E.L. Quarantelli and Russell R. Dynes, eds., "Organizational and Group Behavior in Disasters," *American Behavioral Scientist* 13 (January 1970).

21. Barbie Zelizer and Stuart Allen, eds., *Journalism after September 11* (New York: Routledge, 2002); also Brigette L. Nacos, *Mass Mediated Terrorism* (Lanham, Md.: Rowman and Littlefield, 2002).

22. Edward F. Feighan, "After the Hostage Crisis, TV Focuses on Itself," *New York Times*, August 19, 1985.

23. Alex P. Schmid and Janny de Graaf, *Violence as Communication: Insurgent Terrorism and the Western News Media* (Beverly Hills, Calif.: Sage, 1982), 98. For an analysis of the symbiotic relationship of media and sources of crisis news, see Gadi Wolfsfeld, "Symbiosis of Press and Protest: An Exchange Analysis," *Journalism Quarterly* 61 (Autumn 1984): 550–555; Regina G. Lawrence, "Icons, Indexing, and Police Brutality: An Exploration of Journalistic Norms" (paper delivered at the annual meeting of the International Communication Association, 1995).

24. Pew Research Center for the People and the Press, "Terror Coverage Boosts News Media Images," November 18, 2001, http://people-press.org/reports/display.php3?PageID=143.

25. Douglas M. McLeod and Benjamin H. Detenter, "Framing Effects of Television News Coverage of Social Protest," *Journal of Communication* 49 (Summer 1999): 3–23.

26. William Glaberson, "Press Has Blind Spots, Too," *New York Times*, July 22, 1993.

27. For a fuller discussion, see Storin, "While America Slept."

28. Kathleen Doheny, "Drug Overdose Deaths on the Rise," WebMD, September 22, 2008, www.webmd.com.

29. Pew Research Center for the People and the Press, "The State of the News Media, 2008," www.stateofthenewsmedia.org/2008/Journalist%20report%202008.pdf.

30. Robin Brown, "Clausewitz in the Age of CNN: Rethinking the Military-Media Relationship," in *Framing Terrorism: The News Media, the Government, and the Public*, ed. Pippa Norris, Montague Kern, and Marion Just (New York: Routledge, 2003), 43–58.

READINGS

Allen, Stuart. *Online News: Journalism and the Internet*. Maidenhead, England: Open University Press, 2006.

Bennett, W. Lance, Regina G. Lawrence, and Steven Livingston. *When the Press Fails*. Chicago: University of Chicago Press, 2007.

Biel, Steven, ed. *American Disasters*. New York: New York University Press, 2001.

Fearn-Banks, Kathleen. *Crisis Communications: A Casebook Approach*. 3rd ed. Mahwah, N.J.: Erlbaum, 2007.

Hoskins, Andrew, and Ben O'Loughlin. *Television and Terror: Conflicting Times and the Crisis of News Discourse*. Basingstoke, UK: Palgrave Macmillan, 2007.

Lawrence, Regina G. *The Politics of Force: Media and the Construction of Police Brutality*. Berkeley: University of California Press, 2000.

Macek, Steve. *Urban Nightmares: The Media, the Right, and the Moral Panic over the City*. Minneapolis: University of Minnesota Press, 2006.

Nimmo, Dan, and James E. Combs. *Nightly Horrors: Crisis Coverage in Television Network News*. Knoxville: University of Tennessee Press, 1985.

Norris, Pippa, Montague Kern, and Marion Just, eds. *Framing Terrorism: The News Media, the Government, and the Public*. New York: Routledge, 2003.

Seeger, Matthew W., Timothy L. Sellnow, and Robert R. Ulmer. *Crisis Communication and the Public Health*. Cresskill, N.J.: Hampton Press, 2008.

The Media as Policy Makers

On July 23, 2006, the *Miami Herald* dropped a bombshell. The newspaper published the first article in a four-part, Pulitzer Prize–winning investigation that revealed corruption, misspending, and mismanagement at the Miami-Dade Housing Agency, the sixth-largest public housing agency in the nation. The story accused developers who had received millions of dollars from the agency of failing to build the homes they had promised. In some instances, not a single house had been built.

Following the paper's investigation and report of the scandal, Miami-Dade County mayor Carlos Alvarez ousted most of the Miami-Dade Housing Agency's top leadership and installed new executives. They were asked to clean up the mess and adopt new procedures to prevent future problems. All publicly financed low-income housing construction was put on hold. The U.S. Department of Housing and Urban Development intervened a few months later, in 2007, seizing control of the agency following serious management mistakes and arrests of dishonest contractors. Eighteen months later reforms were in place, dishonest contractors had been removed, and the agency was permitted to resume control over low-income housing projects, which are sorely needed by the many poor families who live in the county.[1]

Unfortunately, these types of scandals are all too common everywhere. That is why public exposés of evil and corruption in high places have been plentiful throughout recorded history. They rest on the assumption that exposure will shame the wrongdoers and lead to public condemnation of their deeds and possibly punishment. Reforms may ultimately ensue.[2] Exposés have always been, and always will be, an important feature of social responsibility journalism in America. They are a major part of the deliberate manipulation of the political process mentioned in chapter 1 as one of the media's important functions.

In this chapter we will examine muckraking—the exposure of political corruption and social injustice—to show how it really works, with particular attention to the role of public opinion. Agenda building is another media strategy for manipulating politics that merits examination in situations like leadership crises involving political scandal, the development of science and health policies, and the support of interest group goals. We will also assess the political impact of nationally broadcast factual and fictional documentaries. The chapter ends with reflections on journalists' responsibility to refrain from questionable methods in their zeal to reform society.

THE ETHICS OF MELDING POLITICAL ACTIVISM WITH JOURNALISM

Like other manifestations of the social responsibility orientation, manipulative journalism raises philosophical, ethical, and news policy questions. Does it create a witch-hunting climate that intimidates officeholders and deters capable people from careers in politics? Do journalists jeopardize important professional values, such as objectivity and neutrality, when they try to influence the events that they report? Do they lose credibility? Where can media audiences turn for a reasonably unbiased view of the complexities of political life if the media are partisans? Journalists' claims that their political activities reflect the wishes of their audiences are questionable because their data are purely impressionistic. In fact, public opinion polls show mixed rates of approval for many tactics of investigative journalism.[3]

Despite these concerns, the role of the journalist as political actor is popular. The rapid spread of civic journalism to newspapers, television, and radio stations in such cities as Chicago, Boston, Miami, Minneapolis, Charlotte, and Wichita is one example.[4] Practitioners of civic journalism explore the political concerns of their audiences by arranging town meetings, focus groups, and interviews. When the journalists have identified community problems, they try to find solutions. Journalists also become participants in politics when they write stories that support a specific politician's policy agenda. Collaboration may begin when politicians leak newsworthy information to journalists in hopes of enlisting them as partners in investigating troublesome situations. Similarly, citizens routinely contact the media with problems related to public affairs, hoping that publicity will spur government action. Just as the media have assumed many functions formerly performed by political parties during elections, so too have they taken on many of the ombudsman, reform, and law enforcement functions traditionally performed by other institutions in society. Whether this is the cause or consequence of the weakening of these other institutions is hotly debated.

MANIPULATIVE JOURNALISM IN PERSPECTIVE

Newspeople's efforts to participate in policy making have ebbed and flowed as philosophies of news making have changed. The turmoil of the 1960s, which raised the public's social consciousness; the Watergate scandal, which forced President Richard Nixon to resign in 1974; and the shift toward advocating a social responsibility ethic in journalism schools raised manipulative journalism from a position of disdain in the early 1900s to one of high esteem since

THREE BLIND MICE! SEE HOW THEY RUN!

THE "WHITE-WASHING COMMITTEE" INVITED BY
THE RING CONTROLLER TO INSPECT HIS BOOKS

Reprinted by permission: www.CartoonStock.com

the closing decades of the twentieth century. Activist journalism, while not unanimously approved, has been practiced and praised, especially by elite media. Reporters and media institutions whose investigations have led to important social and political reforms frequently win plaudits as well as prestigious prizes for high journalistic achievement.

Independent investigative organizations that collaborate with media sleuths have flourished as well. The nonprofit, foundation-subsidized Center for Investigative Reporting, established in San Francisco in 1977, is an example. The center uses freelance reporters who collectively conduct investigations and who can be hired by various media to undertake projects that cannot readily be handled internally. The Better Government Association in Chicago is one of many local institutions doing investigative work within a particular city or state. Investigative Reporters and Editors, a national organization, has been teaching its approaches to mainstream journalists. The Nieman Foundation for Journalism at Harvard University holds annual conferences to improve watchdog journalism.[5]

Collaboration between independent watchdog organizations and the media is mutually beneficial. When the Center for Investigative Reporting and National Public Radio (NPR) teamed up to track down who was financing vicious and scurrilous advertisements during the 2008 presidential campaign, publication of significant findings was assured. That increased the chances of mobilizing corrective actions.[6] Tapping into media resources also helps cover the costs of complex investigations, which can run into millions of dollars. This added financial support can be crucial. The media, in turn, gain collaborators who are skilled in investigating public issues and who often have excellent connections in government and in the community. The prestige and credibility of watchdog organizations enhance the credibility of jointly issued reports.

The substance and style of most investigative stories reflect three major media objectives. The first objective is to produce exciting stories that will appeal to audiences. The second is to gain praise from fellow journalists. In addition to these routine journalistic goals, the third goal is to trigger political action or be part of it. Even when political consequences are not initially envisioned, most reporters feel highly gratified when their stories lead to actions that accord with their political and social preferences.

The line between deliberate attempts to produce political changes and incidental sparking of reforms is often too fine to distinguish. For example, when the media follow up on a report of suspicious deaths in nursing homes and discover and report deplorable conditions that led to those deaths, is this a case of muckraking designed to instigate reform? Or does the idea that reform is needed arise naturally and purely incidentally from a routine news story? Was Lincoln Steffens, one of the early giants in investigative journalism, telling the truth when he claimed that he did not intend to be a muckraker?[7] Could he have specialized in writing sensational exposés of corruption in state and local government and in private business at the turn of the twentieth century for the sheer joy of delving into the muck, giving no thought to reforms that might follow in the wake of his stories?

From the standpoint of the political reformer, it may not matter whether reform was an intended or unintended consequence of investigative reporting. The distinction matters to newspeople, however, because it raises controversial issues about the proper role of journalism in U.S. society. Journalists, even when they favor social responsibility journalism in the abstract, do not like to admit that they wrote their stories intending to manipulate the social and political system. Moreover, they do not call attention to the fact that they often carefully select their sources to support their investigative goals.[8]

MUCKRAKING MODELS

Investigative journalism can lead to political action in three ways. Journalists may write stories about public policies in hopes of engendering a massive public reaction that will lead to widespread demands for political remedies.[9] They may write stories to arouse political elites who are officeholders or who have influence with officeholders. These elites, eager to forestall public criticism, may then attempt to resolve the problems, often even before a media report is published. Finally, action may ensue from direct collaboration between investigative journalists and public officeholders who coordinate news stories and supportive political activities.[10]

In each case, muckraking may follow one of three models: the simple muckraking model, the leaping impact model, and the truncated muckraking model. Social scientists Harvey Molotch, David Protess, and Margaret Gordon and their co-workers identified and tested these models in typical muckraking situations—sensational exposés of corruption usually involving high-status individuals.[11]

The simple muckraking model, presented schematically below, begins when journalists decide to investigate a problem situation and the investigation leads to the publication of news that stirs public opinion. An aroused public then mobilizes policy makers who solve the problem. The Florida housing scandal discussed at the beginning of the chapter is a good example. *Miami Herald* stories about corruption in building housing for low-income citizens angered the public. That prompted government authorities to act and ultimately led to complete revamping of the system.

| Journalistic investigation | → | Publication | → | Public opinion | → | Policy initiatives | → | Policy consequences |

When some elements in the model are skipped, it becomes a leaping impact model. For instance, following the investigation and publication of a story, officials may act without pressure from public opinion. Journalistic investigations may have policy consequences even when no reports about the investigation have surfaced because officials often act to forestall adverse publicity.

In the truncated muckraking model, the sequence is aborted at some point, so that reports about the investigation are not published or fail to lead to reforms. This happens when the evidence that journalists discover is weak or too risky to publish because it may lead to costly lawsuits or damaging retaliation by compromised individuals or organizations. Such considerations have come into play in investigations of major tobacco companies and racketeering operations. In many instances, published stories do not stir public opinion. If the public is aroused, public officials may still fail to act, or policy initiatives may not lead to any symbolic or substantive results.

Several examples of muckraking will illustrate these models. Most of the examples come from intensive studies of muckraking conducted by scholars who had arranged to be alerted to forthcoming media exposés. They were able to interview citizens and policy makers concerned with the issues under investigation, both before and after publication of the stories. The impact of the story could then be assessed far more accurately than is usually possible when stories come as a surprise, permitting assessment only after the fact. Scholars monitored changes in public policy for several months following the exposés and judged the journalists' motives and methods in conducting the investigations.[12]

Simple Muckraking

A story about the Chicago Police Department's shocking abuse of suspects to elicit confessions illustrates simple muckraking. John Conroy, a reporter for the weekly *Chicago Reader,* wrote graphic stories about the way police officers tortured three men who where then wrongly convicted and sentenced to death.

Illinois governor George Ryan was appalled by these stories and pardoned all death row prisoners in 2003. The men whose story Conroy had reported then sued the City of Chicago, which settled the case in 2007, granting a large payment to each of the former prisoners. In a thank-you note to John Conroy, one prisoner's mother wrote: "My son, Aaron Patterson, tortured by the Chicago Police Department, would not be alive today, I believe, without your articles about police torture in the City of Chicago. You documented and wrote the realization of police torture, of which we will never forget. You help save my son's life for which I thank you."[13]

Modest or long-delayed outcomes are typical in situations that reflect the simple muckraking model. Media-aroused public opinion rarely is a strong force for change. Why? Many Americans are complacent or cynical about the political status quo. That makes it difficult to spur them to take action on public problems, even when the problems directly affect them. For example, extensive efforts to arouse public concern about obesity and the need for avoiding fattening foods have proved largely futile.[14] Politicians accordingly may feel safe in ignoring swells in public opinion, believing that they involve relatively few people and that the issues will soon subside when new situations capture the public's fancy.

On the other end of the interest spectrum, investigative stories may be about an issue that is already of great concern to the public. Although the investigative story confirms that concern, it does not push the public across the barrier of reluctance to press for political action. For example, a five-part newspaper series in the *Chicago Sun-Times*—"Rape: Every Woman's Nightmare"— dealt with the incidence and consequences of rape in the Chicago area. Interviews conducted prior to the series had shown that the public was already greatly concerned about the problem. The series enhanced that concern but did little to spur new crime-fighting measures. However, it heightened reporters' sensitivity to the problem. The number of stories in the *Sun-Times* about rape more than doubled, and coverage became more insightful.[15] Such consequences are unexpected and, because they do not entail the government action specified in the model, are rarely recorded as muckraking triumphs.

Although it is difficult for the media to arouse public opinion, it does happen, as the police brutality case demonstrates. The elements that tend to arouse the public include an emotional issue—miscarriage of justice leading to an innocent person's death—a graphic report showing pictures of young prisoners and their mothers, and pictures of truncheon-wielding policemen. When such a story captures people's interest, and they have little prior knowledge about the situation, they may learn much and become highly concerned. Still, prompt action by government to correct the situation remains unlikely, especially if it involves high costs for which no funds are readily available.[16]

Leaping Impact Muckraking

A media exposé called "Arson for Profit" that ABC aired on its program *20/20* exemplifies the leaping impact model. The investigation indicated that a group of real estate owners were implicated in arson that caused extensive fire damage in Chicago's Uptown neighborhood. The group bought dilapidated buildings, insured them heavily, and then arranged to have them torched to collect the insurance. Following the exposé, community leaders voiced concern but failed to act. Nevertheless, the arson stopped because the perpetrators feared further public exposure. Fires declined by 27 percent in the afflicted neighborhood, the first decline in five years. Insurance payments for arson also dropped by more than 20 percent in the year following the arson stories. No other metropolitan area showed comparable drops. The Illinois legislature responded belatedly with very minor policy reforms. There were no criminal indictments of the parties implicated in the insurance fraud. This story illustrates the leaping impact model because publication of the story led directly to correction of the problem, even without elite action and the pressures of public opinion.

Leaping impact is most common when newspeople and public officials openly collaborate. Such coalition journalism may be initiated by media or government personnel, or it may develop by chance. Journalists are eager to involve government officials in investigative stories because the presence of these officials lends credibility and increases the chances of substantial policy consequences. Although working in coalition with government officials may jeopardize the media's zealous pursuit of the independent watchdog role, it gets results.

The events following an NBC *Newsmagazine* story, "The Home Health Hustle," which exposed fraud and abuse in home health care programs, provide a good example of coalition journalism. Public opinion polls showed that the broadcast aroused the concerns of many viewers who previously had been unaware of problems with these programs. But public opinion apparently was not instrumental in the decision of Congress to introduce appropriate reform legislation. In the fashion of the leaping impact model, legislative results seemed to flow directly from collaboration between investigative reporters and members of the U.S. Senate, which preceded the airing of the story by several months.

Journalists had met with officials of the Senate's Permanent Subcommittee on Investigations to plan hearings on home health care fraud and to coordinate their broadcasts with the Senate's activities. The hearings were then announced during the broadcast. Senators subsequently credited media personnel with major contributions to the investigation of home health care fraud. However, it is uncertain how much anticipation of embarrassing television coverage of the story spurred the senators to collaborate with the media. The combined investigative activities of the media and the Senate ultimately led to a number of proposals for corrective legislation. Still, in the end the bills failed to pass. Aside from the effects of increased vigilance by public officials and home health care consumers, no major changes could be directly linked to the investigative stories.[17]

In the same way, when the rape series appeared in the *Chicago Sun-Times* newspeople had already alerted policy makers about the issue. This permitted the policy makers to time announcements of previously planned measures, such as creation of a rape hotline, to coincide with the investigative series.

When a story about unnecessary and illegal abortions in state clinics was about to break in Illinois, the governor immediately associated himself with the media investigators prior to publication. That made it possible to make reform proposals part of the original story. It also enhanced the governor's image as an effective leader.

Truncated Muckraking

The Mirage investigation, conducted jointly by the *Chicago Sun-Times* and CBS's *60 Minutes,* illustrates the truncated muckraking model. With the help of Chicago's Better Government Association, a civic watchdog organization, the partners in the investigation opened a bar, appropriately named the Mirage, in the hope of demonstrating extensive graft in Chicago's regulatory agencies. The bar was wired to record transactions between its personnel and city officials. It took little time to gather ample evidence of bribery and fraud.[18]

Public opinion polls recorded that many citizens were outraged when they learned about the illegal transactions. But people did not pressure public officials for reforms to prevent similar graft in the future. The situation ended with the arousal of public opinion; the elite were not moved to action and there were no corrective measures. The failure to produce a correction does not necessarily mean that officials ignored the story, however. Symbolic responses in such circumstances are common. Politicians promise reforms or further studies of the problem, including public hearings, but no action follows. At other times, policy makers may punish individual offenders but do nothing to correct the underlying situation.[19]

The Minor Role of Public Opinion

These examples of muckraking suggest that the major influence attributed to public opinion in inspiring political action is greatly exaggerated. More often than not, news stories fail to arouse the public, even when investigative stories are excitingly presented. When stories do agitate the public and create political waves, the waters calm quickly. Politicians and journalists have learned that public anger is short-lived. It can be safely ignored, or it can be channeled to support reform movements that are already under way. Reforms are more likely when publicity-shy wrongdoers mend their ways, when the stories arouse elites, or when journalists and political elites have arranged to collaborate. It also helps when follow-ups on the story appear repeatedly in different media.

Even though publicity rarely causes a tidal surge of public opinion, fear that it might do so makes news media muckraking exceptionally influential.[20] Because public opinion is in fact largely irrelevant in generating political reforms, the media's claim that they are handmaidens to the democratic process becomes highly questionable. In fact, the media are using the façade of public opinion support to enhance their already powerful position as political movers and shakers.

BOX 6-1   **An Investigative Journalist Apologizes**

Watchdog journalism is a hallowed tradition in the United States that has helped to curb government and business excesses. But besides its triumphs, it also has a dark side. Nicholas D. Kristof, an op-ed columnist for the *New York Times*, unveils that facet in an engrossing story from his own life.

Kristof has been a lifelong crusading journalist, who travels to all parts of the globe to document the suffering of the world's poor and persecuted and bring it to world attention. He has won two Pulitzer Prizes for excellence in journalism. Yet this talented, experienced reporter felt compelled to apologize publicly to a scientist whom he had maligned in columns published in the *Times* in 2002. When Kristof wrote the stories, he believed that the FBI was bungling its investigation of the 2001 anthrax attack case, which had caused five deaths of people who handled letters containing deadly anthrax spores. Kristof's columns suggested that Dr. Steven Hatfill, a government scientist, should be investigated as the likely source of the poisonous letters. The accusations led to FBI raids of Hatfill's home, surveillance of his movements, and a flood tide of news media publicity. In the end, another scientist was identified as the sole culprit. Dr. Hatfill was officially exonerated.

Besides apologizing to Dr. Hatfill in his column, for erroneously suggesting that he might be the mass murderer, Kristof also outlined the dilemmas that investigative journalists face in targeting potential wrongdoers. In his view, it is often impossible to resolve the moral conflict between the public's need to know about important issues and the privacy of individuals thrust into the brilliant, merciless limelight of publicity. The column, written in 2008, ended on a defiant note. Given another chance, Kristof would again implicate Dr. Hatfill because "while the cost imposed on individuals can be huge, where crucial public interests are at stake, we in the press should be very wary of keeping what we know from the public."[1] In short, when the stakes are high, the interests of the collectivity must prevail. Despite the obstacles, costs, and moral dilemmas, investigative journalism must pursue its goals because a vigorous democracy needs articulate, widely heard voices that are positioned to "speak truth to power."

---

1.   Nicholas D. Kristof, "Media's Balancing Act," *New York Times*, August 28, 2008.

The Muddying of Public Figures

Stories about New York governor Eliot Spitzer's trysts with a prostitute, Alaska governor Sarah Palin's out-of-wedlock grandchild, or rumors of mental health problems that plagued Massachusetts governor Michael Dukakis's 1988 presidential campaign—all of these are part of the epidemic of mudslinging that mars the nation's political landscape.[21] In each case the media endlessly examined, interpreted, and judged incidents in the lives of the individuals, often regardless of the story's significance, truth, or private nature. It is true that these people are important political figures. Although the U.S. press is entitled to probe the lives and reputations of such public persons and the U.S. public has a right to know about matters that are politically relevant, there is widespread agreement that the press is often overzealous in such investigations and destroys reputations needlessly (see Box 6-1). Blogging has accelerated the pace. The Trent Lott story told in chapter 1, for instance, first appeared in the blogosphere and then gained notice from the mainline press, as now happens regularly.

Political scientist Larry Sabato, who refers to mudslinging episodes as "feeding frenzies," puts the blame on the increasingly stiff competition among media for attention and on the need for round-the-clock radio and television to fill long hours with emotional audience bait:

> In such situations any development is almost inevitably magnified and excessively scrutinized; the crush of cameras, microphones, and people combined with the pressure of instant deadlines and live broadcasts hype events and make it difficult to keep them in perspective. When a frenzy begins to gather, the intensity grows exponentially. Major newspapers assign teams of crack reporters and researchers to the frenzy's victims. . . . Television news time is virtually turned over to the subject of the frenzy.[22]

At times newspeople bully politicians and other public figures into action by threatening to publicize stories that these targets would prefer to conceal. Threats of unfavorable coverage can have major political consequences. Politicians often act or refrain from acting because they know that newspeople might publish damaging information. They especially dread adverse publicity from influential columnists.

Attack journalism raises a number of important ethical and political issues. From the perspective of the people whose reputations and careers are dragged through the mud and often ruined, attack journalism raises questions about the privacy rights of public figures and the ethics of journalists who publish such stories even when the subject matter has no relevance to current or future job performance. Some journalists justify focusing on such incidents by claiming that they illuminate the individual's character. But many others admit that they are merely jumping on the bandwagon of competition. If others exploit the story, they feel compelled to feature it as well. That is hardly the epitome of ethical behavior.

Beyond injury to individual public figures, there are broader consequences. The risk of having long past or more recent indiscretions exposed to public view or having offhand remarks elevated into major pronouncements sharply reduces the pool of people willing to make their careers in politics. Many talented people are likely to prefer the safety of private life over the merciless glare of unstoppable publicity in the public sector. "Gotcha" journalism also contributes to the public's growing cynicism about politics and politicians and erodes its respect for the news profession. Finally, the extraordinary amount of media time and space devoted to mudslinging frenzies comes at the expense of other, more worthwhile news that may never be published. The old Greek admonition "Everything in moderation" is relevant. Whenever attack journalism seems appropriate, the media should practice it. But there is never a need for feeding frenzies of journalists in sorry displays of pack journalism.

BEYOND MUCKRAKING: JOURNALISTS AS POLITICAL ACTORS

Direct media intervention in the government process may take a number of forms other than muckraking. Three types of situations are typical: media acting as surrogates for public officials, media acting as mouthpieces for government officials or interest groups, and media deliberately slanting stories to serve a political purpose.

Acting as Surrogates

News personnel occasionally act as surrogates for public officials by actively participating in an evolving situation, such as a prison riot or a diplomatic impasse. The outcome may then significantly shape government action. News anchor Walter Cronkite's influence on relations between Egypt and Israel in 1977, when he served as a go-between to get the parties to the peace table, is a legendary example of diplomacy conducted by a journalist. So were the efforts by CNN reporters stationed in Baghdad during the 1991 Persian Gulf War to broker an end to hostilities, and the activities of British and Irish media in 1994 to facilitate dialogue between their governments and the Irish Republican movements.[23] News stories about wrongful convictions of death-row prisoners incarcerated in Illinois helped to bring about the suspension of the state's death penalty in 2003. The stories rekindled the debate about banishing capital punishment worldwide.

Individual journalists, including media celebrities, are often instrumental in moving crises from obscurity to the political action agenda. Examples are genocide in Bosnia in 1995 and in Sudan's Darfur region in 2004.[24] More commonly, reporters spark investigations of illegal activities by alerting law enforcement officials. For example, a Chicago television station alerted city officials to the illegal storage of hazardous and flammable chemical waste on the campus of the University of Chicago. Hours later, city fire officials inspected the scene and cited the university for numerous fire code violations.[25]

To prevent impending tragedies and solve existing cases, journalists have also become involved in broadcasts about kidnapped children and in crime-stopper programs that feature accounts or reenactments of unsolved crimes. The programs use media stories, coupled with financial rewards, to elicit information from citizens that may help solve the crime. The programs are featured in thousands of communities in the United States and Canada and have helped to clear up thousands of felony cases.[26] Programs like the television series *America's Most Wanted* have facilitated the capture of more than 900 criminals on the FBI's most-wanted list.[27]

Acting as Mouthpieces

A far more common form of interaction occurs when the media become mouthpieces for government officials or interest groups, either because they believe in their causes or in return for attractive stories and other favors. This type of interaction often involves leaks. Government officials who are disgruntled with current policies or practices for personal, professional, or political reasons may leak information to sympathetic journalists to enlist their support. Journalists may cooperate and publish the allegations, or they may investigate the situation, often with the cooperation of the individuals who leaked the information.

When newspeople and officials collaborate, the boundary between ordinary reporting and manipulative journalism can blur. It is difficult to tell when journalists act as unbiased investigators and when they act as partisans who structure their stories to produce specific effects that further their political goals. In 2009, when the *Chicago Tribune* learned that emergency medical facilities at the University of Chicago were shifting Medicaid patients to nearby local clinics to free more space for insured private patients, the paper rushed to publicize the damage to the community's predominantly poor minority population. Was that impartial reporting, or journalism on the prowl to avenge social injustice, or merely pursuit of a dramatic, picture-rich story?[28] In other cases, the main objective in publicizing leaked information is mercenary. Newspeople put their services at the command of anyone who promises to be a fertile source for future news or who can provide an attractive, publishable story. Television networks are particularly eager for exciting scoops during "sweeps," when rating services check audience size to determine advertising pricing. Larger audiences mean higher prices.

Public officials and political interest groups often exploit the media's access to the public to attain their political objectives. The *New York Times* and the *Washington Post* agreed in 1995 to publish a terrorist's lengthy political ramblings to forestall further lethal bombings. The newspapers acted at the request of attorney general Janet Reno, who feared another terrorist attack by the crazed "Unabomber." Reno's office also hoped that someone would recognize the writing style or handwriting and identify the terrorist.[29] Similarly, the media were accused of playing the game of Miami's Cuban refugee community when they lavished coverage on six-year-old Elian Gonzalez, who had been rescued after a refugee boat was shipwrecked. The Cuban youngster's Miami relatives wanted the boy to remain in the United States rather than return to his father in communist Cuba.

Although the media are often quite willing to publish stories in compliance with government wishes when they believe that the story serves a good purpose, they are loath to become unwitting government tools. In 1986, for example, officials of the Reagan administration were suspected of spreading false information about Libya in an attempt to forestall terrorist attacks. When rumors about the administration's deception surfaced, news executives expressed outrage. The comment of Roone Arledge, president of ABC News, was typical of the general reaction when he called it "despicable to tinker with the credibility of one of our most sacred and basic institutions, the press, for whatever reason."[30] Yet in October 2001 the chief executives of all major television networks yielded to secretary of state Condoleezza Rice's request to forgo broadcasting messages sent by Osama bin Laden, the alleged mastermind of the terrorist assault on U.S. territory one month earlier.[31]

Acting as Chief Framers

Finally, the media can shape political action by "framing"—reporting the news from a particular perspective, so that some aspects of the situation come into

TABLE 6-1 **Framing Categories for Stem Cell Research (percentage of newspaper stories featuring the theme)**

Framing category	Major theme	Minor theme
Political strategy and/or conflict involving government and interest groups	29	16
New research findings and clinical trials	20	4
Regulatory framework for stem cell research; jurisdiction and oversight	16	27
Scientific and medical background of stem-cell-related research	15	29
Ethics or morality of stem-cell-related research, bioethicists' perspectives	15	27
Scientific and technical controversies about merits of various research plans	9	25
Market/economic aspects of stem cell research applications; competition	5	6
Anecdotes about specific, actual, or potential stem cell transplant patients	5	2
Patenting, property rights, ownership, and access to stem cell lines	2	6
Public opinion and public support; poll results	1	4
Reactions of average people outside research community and federal bureaucracy	1	1

Source: Adapted from Matthew C. Nisbet, Dominique Brossard, and Adrianne Kroepsch, "Framing Science: The Stem Cell Controversy in an Age of Press/Politics," *Press/Politics* 8, no. 2 (2003): 11–35.

Note: N = 841 articles from the *New York Times* and *Washington Post,* 1975–2001.

close focus and others fade into the background. How much control journalists have over framing varies widely, from merely reporting the frames chosen by regular beat sources or special pleaders, to choosing sources who share the frame preferences of journalists, to expressing their own frame choices in editorials and editorialized news. Journalists tend to exercise least control over the framing of uncontroversial news coming from official sources and most control over the framing of news about unexpected events or events unearthed by journalists through their own efforts.

Developments in an ongoing story also influence the evolution and choice of frames. Table 6-1 shows the types of frames used in 841 stories about stem cell research in the *New York Times* and *Washington Post* from 1975 through 2001. Frames describing new scientific developments were most prominent initially. Once the public learned that stem cells would come from human embryos, frames related to ethics and morality, and to strategies and conflict, leaped to the fore. For the entire period, the most widely used major frames,

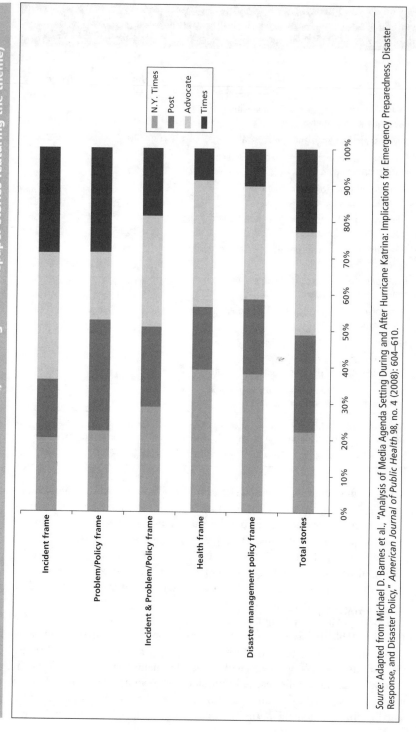

FIGURE 6-1 Framing Categories for Hurricane Katrina (percentage of newspaper stories featuring the theme)

Source: Adapted from Michael D. Barnes et al., "Analysis of Media Agenda Setting During and After Hurricane Katrina: Implications for Emergency Preparedness, Disaster Response, and Disaster Policy." *American Journal of Public Health* 98, no. 4 (2008): 604–610.

and hence the most likely to shape perceptions, were political strategies and conflict (29 percent), new research findings (20 percent), and regulation issues (16 percent). For minor themes, the top three were the scientific and medical background of the issue (29 percent), ethics and morality questions (27 percent), and again, regulation issues (27 percent).

When it comes to influencing debate and action on public policies, it is extraordinarily important whether journalists choose to frame issues in terms of the substance of the policy or in terms of the strategies used in battles about the policy. For example, as Figure 6-1 shows, reporting about the Hurricane Katrina disaster in the *New York Times,* the *Washington Post,* the *New Orleans Times-Picayune,* and the *Baton Rouge Advocate* stressed government failures in the relief process rather than the substance of essential reforms. Of 1,590 articles, 78 percent dealt with process issues. They appeared in the most prominent spots in the papers. Substance stories, dealing with the dimensions of the disaster and preventive measures, fared much less well. Scholars contend that the predominance of "process frames" in most public policy stories marginalizes the substance of political issues and prevents political leaders from explaining policy substance to the public prior to the adoption of laws. Lack of intelligent public dialogue about public policies is one of the damaging consequences of such framing. Public cynicism is another.[32]

AGENDA BUILDING

In many instances the media create the climate that shapes political action. This makes them important contributors to agenda building. The process goes beyond agenda setting. The media set the public agenda when news stories rivet attention on a problem and make it seem important to many people. The media build the public agenda when they create the political context that shapes public opinions. Agenda building often occurs around a precipitating event. Such was the case with the beating of African American motorist Rodney King by police officers in Los Angeles. The incident became an opening to dwell at length on the issues of police brutality and racism and turn them into a major focus of public policy.[33] The horrifying photos of tortured prisoners at Iraq's Abu Ghraib prison that appeared in major American media in 2004 are another example of agenda building. They created a political firestorm that brought major investigations, policy changes, and a heated nationwide dialog about torture.[34]

Constructing Political Climates

The breakup of the Soviet Union is another telling case of agenda building. In 1990, during the annual May Day parade, Soviet television covered the festivities for the nation, as was usual. Camera operators had been told to stop filming if protesters against the government appeared. Mikhail Gorbachev, the country's leader, did not wish scenes of unrest to be broadcast. He had given protest groups permission to march, to symbolize that he was a more liberal leader than his predecessors. But the television cameras kept filming when protesters came into view carrying banners that asked Gorbachev to resign, condemned the Communist Party and the Secret Service (KGB), proclaimed the end of the Red Empire, praised the secession of Lithuania, and carried images of Christ. The huge, nationwide audience watched—for the first time since the advent of communism—a vivid demonstration of opposition to the government. The broadcast demonstrated that the country was no longer united behind the leadership and that the voices of protest could make themselves heard. In the view of many observers, this televised humiliation built the agenda for the collapse of the Soviet empire.[35]

Newspeople have been criticized for rarely stirring up controversies when established elites agree on matters of public policy.[36] In the absence of conflicting reports, it may seem that no one opposes the policy even when that is not so. When an issue becomes controversial among political elites, the media frequently zero in on it. Thereby they "supply the context that . . . gives people reasons for taking sides and converts the problem into a serious political issue. In this sense the public agenda is not so much set by the media as built up through a cycle of media activity that transforms an elite issue into a public controversy."[37] The agenda-building role of the media in policy making is symbiotic. The media perform essential steps, but ultimate success hinges on the actions of other political actors as well.

Molotch, Protess, and Gordon make this clear in the conclusion of their study of investigative journalism in the Watergate scandal during the Nixon presidency. The resolution of the issue was not, as popularly believed, a triumph for unaided media power:

> We therefore disagree with those who would assign "credit" for the Nixon exposures to the media just as we would disagree with those who would assign it to the Congress. Nor should the credit go, in some acontextual, additive sense, to both of these sectors. Instead, the Watergate "correction" was the result of the ways in which news of the Nixon scandals fit the goals and strategic needs of important media and policy actors. All of these actors, each with some degree of "relative autonomy" . . . are part of an evolving "ecology of games," . . . part of a "dance" . . . in which actors have, by virtue of their differential skills and status positions, varying access to participate. Because they so continuously anticipate each other's moves, their activities are, as a matter of course, mutually constituted.[38]

Sociologists Gladys and Kurt Lang reached similar conclusions. Their study of the role of the media in Watergate traces the precise part played by the media in this "ecology of games" that creates political agendas. A look at the steps makes it clear that there is ample opportunity and often strong temptation for newspeople to guide agenda building deliberately.

Agenda building begins when newspeople decide to publish a particular story. In most instances this is a matter of free choice because few stories are so blatantly significant that omission is unthinkable. The second decision concerns the degree of attention to be given to the story. This is the point where ordinary agenda-setting activities can most readily turn into deliberate agenda building. If newspeople determine that a story should become prominent, they must feature it conspicuously and repeatedly to arouse the attention of the elite media, including national television, and the attention of political elites. The Watergate story, for instance, received extensive and sustained publicity in the *Washington Post*, serving the nation's capital, before it finally gained nationwide publicity.

Capturing attention throughout the United States usually requires several other media-controlled steps. Media must put issues into an interpretive frame that has nationwide appeal. For instance, as long as the Watergate story was framed as election campaign news, media audiences discounted it as just another partisan squabble. Once the story was depicted as a tale of pervasive corruption and dishonesty at the highest levels of government, it aroused widespread concern. Without this climate of apprehension, severe penalties for the Watergate offenders, including President Nixon, would never have been acceptable. In the course of putting issues into a conceptual framework, language becomes an important tool. When newspeople and politicians switched from writing and talking about the Watergate "caper" or the "bugging incident" and began to discuss the Watergate "scandal" and "tragedy," an incident initially viewed as trivial became a serious matter.

The particular sources that journalists choose to cite for their story are important. Skewing inevitably takes place when one human source, rather than another, provides information and interpretation. When major public policy issues are at stake, media audiences judge the merits of various options by the credibility of their proponents. The Watergate crisis justified drastic action, such as impeachment of the president, only after the media featured prominent Republicans and members of the judiciary who acknowledged the gravity of the issues and the need for a massive investigation.

Most agenda building does not concern momentous political events like the fall of the Soviet Union or Watergate. A more typical example occurred in 2004 when the *Chicago Sun-Times* published a brief story about four Chicago building inspectors accused of falsifying their work histories. Normally the city resolves such cases by levying small fines of $500 or less. But in the wake of the publicity, city authorities initiated a policy of vigorous prosecution of such offenses. The city filed lawsuits against the offenders and reinspected the buildings where they had worked. It also decided to investigate city hiring practices. The incumbent building commissioner had to institute significant reforms in hiring procedures to save his job. All these developments yielded ample news stories and kept alive interest in the story.[39]

Constructing Climates for Science Policies

Media agenda building is not limited to political scandals but includes many other issues. Building the climate for science and health policies is another example.

Government support and regulation of science operations became controversial U.S. public policy issues in the twentieth century.[40] Two environmental issues provide particularly interesting examples. The first one has been called "the great greenhouse debate," about the threat of global warming.[41] Researchers tracked media coverage of the global warming controversy over eight years, from 1985 to 1992, in television network evening newscasts and in the *New York Times,* the *Washington Post,* the *Wall Street Journal, Time, Newsweek,* and *U.S. News and World Report.* Coverage was minimal at first, totaling only twenty-five stories from 1985 through 1987 in all the media combined—not enough to arouse government and public concern. Coverage soared in 1989 and 1990, when the first Bush administration sought to defuse growing worldwide pressures for government action by expressing doubts about the seriousness of the situation. With the media taking their cues from the science community, the thrust of their coverage indicated otherwise. By a margin of nearly nine to one, news coverage suggested that global warming was indeed a major problem that required preventive government action throughout the world. News stories also focused the public's attention on specific remedies, such as controlling carbon dioxide emissions, halting or reversing deforestation, and conserving energy.

The media's efforts to create a climate favoring stricter control laws slowed down when the science community disagreed about the ability to keep global warming in check through various government regulation programs. As discussed in chapter 4, journalists also weakened their own efforts to promote climate cleanups by citing the views of naysayers in the name of "objective coverage."[42] That coupled with the strongly expressed resistance of the Bush administration—which the media could not ignore—caused the earlier pro-cleanup climate to become far less friendly. The climate improved rapidly when the Obama administration identified climate control as one of its major goals.

The second tale concerns cancer-causing agents in the environment which, unlike global warming, have been a topic of government attention for some time. The main issues related to identifying the most dangerous pollutants that required regulation. One would expect that experts in the field of environmentally caused cancers would be the dominant voices that the media would quote, but that is not always the case. When journalists select "expert" opinions to quote, they often find that frontline researchers are reluctant to sacrifice time for press interviews. When they do, their stories often lack punch because scientists hedge their claims, believing that no truth is absolute. That then drives reporters to less-qualified sources who are willing and able to express their views strongly and without caveats. Activists, such as spokespersons for environmental groups, make good storytellers. Reporters may also have their own views about environmental and other dangers and seek out spokespersons who share their views, especially if they think that most of their audience agrees or has no opinion. News opposing nuclear power plants is an example—it dominated because few journalists bothered to get stories that supported views that they themselves deemed undesirable.[43]

In the case of carcinogens in the environment, ABC, CBS, and NBC television, the three major newsmagazines, and the *New York Times,* the *Washington Post,* and the *Wall Street Journal* paid more attention to man-made chemicals than to any other cancer agent, including tobacco, in the twenty years from 1972 to 1992.[44] Judged by the number of stories devoted to each carcinogen, the dangers of tobacco were roughly on a par with those of such food additives as dyes, preservatives, and sweeteners and such reproductive hormones as birth control pills. By contrast, experts rated smoking, overexposure to sunlight, and diet as prime causes of cancer and downplayed the role of food additives and preservatives.

In fact, half or more of cancer experts believed that the media distorted the dangers of particular carcinogens in nine out of eleven areas (Figure 6-2). Media coverage got its best ratings—albeit only 60 percent or less approval—in rating the dangers of sunlight and tobacco. It got its worst ratings (less than 39 percent approval) on naturally occurring chemicals in food and food additives, nuclear plants, pollution, pesticides, household chemicals, and dietary choices. Chemicals in the workplace and radon received rankings of "fairly stated" by 42 percent and 50 percent of the scientists, respectively. Given that news stories, particularly stories in the key media examined for the study, provided the agenda-building context in which government actions and public opinion flourish, it is a worrisome finding that the media may stray widely from scientific opinions in matters of great public concern.

There is ample scholarly evidence that media coverage of scientific controversies influences public opinion. When the news media cover stories about controversial new technologies or medical treatments, public opposition to the highlighted developments is common. It diminishes when coverage abates. It seems that the public opts against scientific advances when news stories raise doubts about their safety. Political elites often are loath to challenge scientific findings that the media have labeled as "expert" opinion or to take actions that may alarm the public.[45] The media's choices mirror the interests of effective pressure groups. The media ignore many important science topics and thereby keep them off the public agenda. In fact, omissions may be a far more serious problem than the fact that most media reports contain minor and major errors of emphasis or fact because it is difficult to simplify highly technical matters.[46]

Nourishing Social Movements and Interest Groups

Just as the media regularly boost selected public policy issues, they can promote selected groups that are working for public causes. Whenever a group needs wide publicity to reach its goals, journalists' decisions to grant or withhold publicity become crucial for the group's success. Although journalists make most decisions about coverage without explicit political motivation to boost a movement or suppress it, many times the sympathies of newspeople for particular causes guide their choices of news content. This happened in the 1960s with Students for a Democratic Society (SDS), a "New Left" movement. The story is particularly interesting because it demonstrates that attention

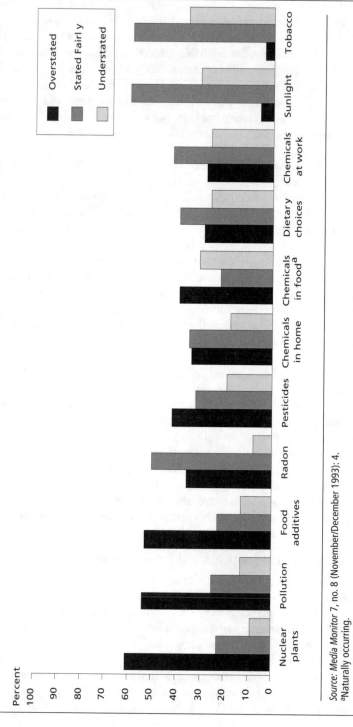

FIGURE 6-2 How Scientists Rate Media Portrayals of Cancer Risks

Source: Media Monitor 7, no. 8 (November/December 1993): 4.
[a]Naturally occurring.

from sympathetic newspeople may boomerang and produce unintended, destructive consequences.

SDS activities on U.S. campuses had received little media attention until *New York Times* reporter Fred Powledge wrote a long, supportive story in 1965, some five years after the movement's birth.[47] Coverage by a national news medium amounted to symbolic recognition that student radicalism had become an important political issue. When SDS sponsored a march on Washington, D.C., to protest the Vietnam War in spring 1965, the event received nationwide coverage. Although many newspeople sympathized with the left-liberal reforms SDS advocated, they focused their stories on the movement's most radical leaders and goals. The framing produced exciting news but misled media audiences, including SDS members, about the peaceful nature of the movement. The radicals that the media singled out as spokespersons for the organization became celebrities who attracted new Leninist and Maoist members, who then took over the organization and turned it away from its long-range reformist goals to short-range, violent antiwar activities.

Sociologist Todd Gitlin contends that the media's decision in 1965 to give wide publicity to SDS ultimately destroyed the movement and with it much of the power of the New Left. In his vivid metaphor, the media spotlight became a magnifying glass that burned everybody to a crisp. Powledge's efforts to bestow legitimacy on the movement through *New York Times* stories had done the opposite. As is often true in agenda building, political forces other than the media contributed to the turn of events. Radicalization of the SDS movement was also abetted by the Johnson administration's escalation of the Vietnam War and by the growing alienation from mainstream society that the war produced among many Americans.[48]

Of course many movements, interest groups, and lobbies have been helped by media coverage. Publicity has legitimized consumer organizations and environmentalist groups in the eyes of the public and the eyes of public officials.[49] The media also were instrumental in legitimizing the civil rights movement of the 1960s. The media framed civil rights protesters as victims of racism rather than as troublemakers and lawbreakers, as their opponents would have preferred. Sympathetic nationwide coverage of freedom marches and of battles fought for civil rights in Little Rock, Arkansas; Selma, Alabama; and Oxford, Mississippi, prepared lawmakers and the nation for passage of the Civil Rights Act in 1964 and the creation of public agencies to implement its mandates.

There seems to be a pattern in the role that the media play on behalf of successful social movements.[50] Legitimization of the incipient movement begins with favorable coverage by a few sympathetic journalists. Undisputed media praise then attracts support for the movement among segments of the public. In this favorable climate, the growing movement becomes strong and legitimate enough to make political demands and engage in protest activities. In response, opposing voices speak out in the hitherto silent mainstream media. They come too late, however, to stop the success of the movement in the legislative arena and among important groups within the public.

Protest groups are active partners in the agenda-building game. If they consider publicity essential to the success of their causes, as most of them do, they may initiate contacts with potentially sympathetic journalists and create newsworthy events to showcase their objectives. The environmental protection organization Greenpeace, for example, invites journalists to photo opportunities that it arranges to show the gruesome details of whale hunts. Attracting sustained media attention hinges on the perceived social and political legitimacy of groups, the newsworthiness of their story, and the consonance of their ideology with the journalists' inclinations.[51] Greenpeace has been highly successful on all of these scores. As exchange theory predicts, journalists exchange their ability to bestow publicity for a group's ability to supply newsworthy stories.

Low-status organizations whose goals encompass routine human concerns are least likely to attract helpful publicity. Political scientist Edie Goldenberg studied the attempts of four citizens groups in Massachusetts to attract newspaper coverage to the problems of welfare mothers, senior citizens, low-income tenants, and people treated unfairly by the courts. She found that these groups had little success and concluded, "There is bias in the system that consistently favors some and neglects others." The favored groups are "haves," those who possess the resources to make and maintain contact with the press and to arrange their operations so that they complement the needs of the press. The disfavored ones are those who are "most in need of press attention in order to be heard forcefully in the political arena" but are "least able to command attention and . . . least able to use effectively what few resources they do control in seeking and gaining press access." Goldenberg warns, "If intensely felt interests go unarticulated and therefore are unnoticed and unaffected by policy makers, one important aspect of rule of, for, and by the people is weakened."[52] In the eyes of social critics such as Goldenberg, a free press must use its agenda-building powers to benefit all segments of society.

DOCUMENTARIES AND DOCUDRAMAS

Newspeople are not limited to straight news and feature stories as means to influence public policy. Fictional productions, such as docudramas shown to millions of viewers on prime-time national television, are another tool. Docudramas are especially compelling because they reconstruct events in highly dramatic, emotional ways. The viewer cannot tell which part of the story is real and which part is dramatic frosting.[53]

The political motives leading to the production and broadcast of many documentaries and docudramas are obvious. As communications scholar Oscar Gandy has pointed out, "Too frequently to be mere coincidence, serial dramas, or the made-for-television movies we describe as docudramas, have been aired simultaneously with the discussion of related issues in Congress."[54] An example of a widely publicized docudrama that coincided with related political events was "The Day After," a two-hour ABC dramatization of a nuclear attack on Kansas City and its aftermath. It aired on Sunday, November

20, 1983, following an extensive pre-broadcast advertising campaign by the network that included an eight-page viewer's guide. Scenes of burned bodies, people rotting from radiation sickness, smoldering rubble, and survivors reduced to preying on each other were part of the episode.

At the time of broadcast, nuclear weapons policy was in the limelight. The Reagan administration was seeking support in the United States and in Europe for deploying U.S. missiles in European NATO countries. Antinuclear groups at home and abroad were working feverishly to stop the deployment. ABC aired the docudrama a few days before the West German legislature was to approve the decision to place the missiles. The station made excerpts of the docudrama available to German television. It denied that the timing had been politically motivated.

What was the political impact of "The Day After," which was viewed by more than 100 million people?[55] The broadcast energized antinuclear groups and aroused fears among pronuclear groups that the program might generate defeatist attitudes among Americans. Contrary to expectations, public opinion polls after the broadcast did not show massive shifts of public attitudes about nuclear missile policies. In Europe, the missiles were deployed without major obstacles. A number of analysts ascribed the lack of impact to flaws in the docudrama; others felt that the public had learned from the film but tended to distance itself psychologically from fictional disasters.

The apparent consequences of "The Day After" were less than expected, but other docudramas, as well as full-length motion picture versions of historical events, have been more compelling. *J.F.K.*, a 1991 movie docudrama, suggested that President John F. Kennedy's assassination sprang from a massive conspiracy that involved the White House, the CIA, and the FBI, among others. Polls subsequently showed that numerous viewers accepted the film's premises.[56] Docudramas like *Schindler's List*, about Jewish refugees escaping the Nazi holocaust; *Mississippi Burning*, which portrayed atrocities in the civil rights struggle; *Fahrenheit 9/11*, which condemned the 2003 invasion of Iraq as a nefarious plot of the Bush administration; and *The Road to Guantanamo*, which chronicled the incarceration of three British detainees at the Guantanamo Bay prison in Cuba, shape people's images of the nature and significance of events even when the producers disclaim historical accuracy. The potential impact and the associated media coverage and public discussion of such presentations obligate a responsible press to take great pains to present all sides of an issue and to be accurate in its depiction, even in fictional programs.[57]

METHODS: FAIR AND FOUL

The fairness and accuracy of news presentations and the appropriateness of news-gathering techniques become important issues when one considers that the media, in combination with other political actors, create the political reality that sets the context for political action.[58] It is a serious matter, therefore, when the media are accused of frequently resorting to improper methods.

Confirming Prejudgments

An incident during the 2004 presidential campaign illustrates concerns about the legitimacy of some media tactics.[59] CBS *Evening News* and *60 Minutes* broadcast a story about President George W. Bush's National Guard service in the early 1970s that suggested he did not fulfill his obligations. Purportedly he escaped penalties for his neglect of duty thanks to powerful political connections. His privileged status allegedly helped him get a lieutenant's commission in the National Guard. The report relied heavily on documents from the files of Bush's squadron commander. When the authenticity of the documents was questioned because they had been inadequately checked, all confirmation efforts failed.

When it became clear that the story drew on flawed sources, CBS appointed a panel of prestigious experts to investigate what had gone wrong. The panel's findings are a laundry list of major sins that journalists in high-quality media should never commit. The cardinal sin was failure to seek professional help to check the authenticity of the documents at the heart of the story. Misleading statements in the broadcast that suggested that the network had properly checked the story compounded this sin. In its haste to publish the story ahead of its competitors, CBS had failed to check the controversial background of the source who had supplied the documents, claiming that he received them from an unidentified person. The station made no effort to verify the identity of that person so that reliability could be established. Nor was evidence presented that the documents had actually come from the files of Bush's squadron commander, as claimed.[60]

The upshot of the Bush story was an apology by the network and anchor Dan Rather's announcement that he would resign his post within a few months. Several high-level CBS journalists resigned or were fired. It is difficult to tell whether the story damaged President Bush in the election. Had he lost, many would have speculated about the influence of the National Guard stories. The incident did show that there is little disagreement about the standards of fairness and accuracy that should be applied in broadcasts about important public issues. But—and this is the disturbing aspect—these standards continue to be breached all too often. Such breaches raise questions about the sense of responsibility of high-level media personnel when important public matters are at stake.

In many instances, inaccurate reports have permanent economic, professional, and social consequences for the individuals and institutions whose stories are told. The National Guard stories could have cost President Bush reelection. In a case involving the Kaiser Aluminum and Chemical Corporation, business losses could have run into millions of dollars. An investigative report had erroneously accused the company of knowingly selling dangerous household electrical wiring under false pretenses. Successful libel suits can recoup a portion of the damage, but they fall short of fully restoring damaged reputations. That is why careless or biased publicity has become a deep concern for civil libertarians. If networks permit rebuttals to misinformation in interpretive stories, the rebuttals are treated as opinion pieces rather than straight news and therefore are subject to editorial control.

Entrapment

Serious ethical issues arise also when newspeople undertake undercover operations or create bogus enterprises to entrap potential and actual wrongdoers. The story told earlier about the Mirage tavern, set up to elicit and record bribery by city officials, illustrates the practice. So does the preparation of NBC's program "Cataract Cowboys" in 1993. The NBC investigative team wanted to tell a story about unnecessary cataract surgeries.[61] When several Florida eye clinics turned down requests by healthy undercover reporters for eye surgery, the producers staged a partly successful entrapment. One "patient," whose requests for surgery had been denied initially, telephoned the clinic to schedule an appointment. The filmed report of her return to the clinic notes that she "was only a few tests and a half-hour away from surgery." The report neglected to mention that the pre-surgery tests might have forestalled the surgery and therefore did not constitute evidence of malpractice.

On a much bigger scale, NBC has frequently broadcast an episode called "To Catch a Predator" on its *Dateline NBC* program. For the "Predator" segment, the company uses a hidden camera program to attract sexual predators and bring them to justice. The men are lured by a person—often a volunteer from an activist group set up to catch child predators—who poses as an underage girl in a chat room. The "girl" sets up a date at a specified location. When the man goes to the site, a camera crew and television host confront him and film the segment. Later, there may be a police follow-up. The sting operation received wide publicity in 2007 when one of the trapped men committed suicide when it was obvious that he would be photographed. NBC aborted a lawsuit by the man's family when it settled by offering a large payment in 2007. The network has insisted that it did no wrong, even though a judge during the pretrial proceedings noted that a jury "could find that NBC crossed the line from responsible journalism to irresponsible and reckless intrusion into law enforcement."[62]

Sting operations like these raise serious civil liberties issues, even when regular law enforcement agencies conduct them under the watchful eyes of the courts. Concerns about protecting the rights of suspects are even greater when the sleuths are journalists acting without an official mandate and without supervision by a responsible public body.[63] Quite aside from civil liberties issues, sting operations raise fundamental questions about the proper functions of the press. Should its watchdog role be carried to the point where it becomes a quasi-police force, tracking down selected offenders whenever a good story promises to be the likely reward?

SUMMARY

In this chapter we examined direct involvement by journalists in the affairs of government. The chapter began with an analysis of muckraking, comparing reality to a series of models. The media's power to arouse public opinion with exposés of corruption turns out to be far less than is popularly believed. Even if the public becomes highly concerned, political action does not necessarily follow. It is a mistake to believe that exposés commonly produce reforms because an aroused public demands action.

The most promising road to reform is via direct liaison between newspeople and government officials. When officials provide story leads in areas in which they want to produce action, or when newspeople can interest officials in taking action on issues that have come to the media's attention, successful political activities are apt to occur. On rare occasions the media are also able to produce action by participating in political negotiations or by using the club of potential unwanted publicity to force officials to act.

The Watergate scandal illustrates how political action can emerge from the interplay of various political institutions. The media, through a series of agenda-building steps, created the climate that convinced President Nixon that he must resign. Agenda-building examples from science policy and from interest group politics demonstrate the media's impact on developments in these fields. The media serve as catalysts that precipitate the actions of other elements within the society. They enhance the influence of some political forces and weaken others, but the ultimate outcome is often beyond their control.

The media's public policy making roles influence U.S. politics in general as well as the lives of many individuals and institutions. How sensitively and accurately they are performed therefore becomes a matter of grave concern. News gathering and news production frequently are seriously flawed, even when media institutions profess to believe in high standards. How often the ethics and standards of the profession are violated, and what the costs are to people caught in the net of inaccurate publicity, are matters of conjecture.

At the heart of most instances that actively engage newspeople in politics lies the desire to produce exciting news stories. This is not surprising. Successful journalism requires telling stories that will attract audiences. That journalists are tempted to be good storytellers above all, even at the expense of other goals, should give pause to those who advocate that journalists should play the political game actively and regularly. One must ask whether journalists' professional standards equip them to guide politics wisely and well.[64] To put it another way: When issues are put on the crowded political agenda, should their newsworthiness be the controlling factor? If the answer is no, then widespread participation by the media in policy making may be quite troubling.

NOTES

1. Breanne Gilpatrick, "Miami-Dade Gets Back Its Housing Agency from HUD," *Miami Herald*, January 9, 2009.

2. See Larry J. Sabato, *Feeding Frenzy: How Attack Journalism Has Transformed American Politics* (New York: Free Press, 1991), chap. 2; David L. Protess, Fay Lomax Cook, Jack C. Doppelt, James S. Ettema. Margaret T. Gordon, Donna R. Leff, and Peter Miller, *The Journalism of Outrage: Investigative Reporting and Agenda Building* (New York: Guilford Press, 1991), chap. 2.

3. David Weaver and LeAnne Daniels, "Public Opinion on Investigative Reporting in the 1980s," *Journalism Quarterly* 69 (Spring 1992): 146–155. Ethical reporting guidelines for journalists are

laid out in Bruce J. Evenson, *The Responsible Reporter* (Northport, Ala.: Vision Press, 1995). Also see Louis A. Day, *Ethics in Media Communications,* 4th ed. (Belmont, Calif.: Wadsworth, 2003).

4. The pros and cons of public journalism as well as the relevant literature are examined in a collection edited by Theodore L. Glasser, *The Idea of Public Journalism* (New York: Guilford Press, 1999); and by John C. Merrill, Peter J. Gade, and Frederick R. Blevens, *Twilight of Press Freedom: The Rise of People's Journalism* (Mahwah, N.J.: Erlbaum, 2001).

5. David L. Protess, *Muckraking Matters: The Societal Impact of Investigative Reporting,* Institute for Modern Communications Research Monographs Series (Evanston: Northwestern University, 1987). The public's changing views about investigative journalism are traced in Lars Willnat and David Weaver, "Public Opinion on Investigative Reporting in the 1990s: Has Anything Changed Since the 1980s?" *Journalism and Mass Communication Quarterly* 75, no. 3 (1998): 449–463. The Nieman Watchdog conference reports are available on the foundation's Web site at www.nieman.harvard.edu. For an anthology of muckraking throughout U.S. history see Judith Serrin and William Serrin, *Muckraking! The Journalism that Changed America* (New York: New Press, 2002).

6. Will Evans and Peter Overby, "The Money behind the Anti-McCain Ad," truthdig: drilling beneath the headlines, March 6, 2008, www.truthdig.com/report/item/20080306_the_money_behind_the_anti_mccain_ad/.

7. Lincoln Steffens, *The Autobiography of Lincoln Steffens* (New York: Harcourt Brace, 1931), 357.

8. Protess and others, *Journalism of Outrage,* 214–227.

9. Matthew C. Ehrlich, "The Journalism of Outrageousness: Tabloid Television News vs. Investigative News," *Journalism and Mass Communication Monographs* 155 (February 1996) describes how investigative stories differ from other forms of journalism. Also see the annual reports about Pulitzer and Goldsmith awards for the best investigative stories of the previous year.

10. Eytan Gilboa, "Media Diplomacy: Conceptual Divergence and Application," *Harvard International Journal of Press/Politics* 3, no. 3 (1998): 56–76, makes a similar distinction.

11. Harvey L. Molotch, David L. Protess, and Margaret T. Gordon, "The Media-Policy Connection: Ecologies of News," in *Political Communication Research: Approaches, Studies, Assessments,* ed. David L. Paletz (Norwood, N.J.: Ablex, 1987), 26–48. The process was modeled somewhat differently later in *Journalism of Outrage.* But the earlier version is more explicit.

12. Protess and others, *Journalism of Outrage,* chaps. 3–6, details six investigations. For more recent investigations, consult the Center for Investigative Journalism's blog, http://centerforinvestigative reporting.org/.

13. David Carr, "The Media Equation: Muckraking Pays, Just Not in Profit," *New York Times,* December 10, 2007.

14. Regina G. Lawrence, "Framing Obesity: The Evolution of News Discourse on a Public Health Issue," *Press/Politics* 9, no. 3 (2004): 56–75 discusses how the issue has been presented to the public.

15. Protess and others, *Journalism of Outrage,* chap. 4.

16. Often the chief point of a program is simply to alert the public to a problem; immediate action may not be expected.

17. Protess and others, *Journalism of Outrage,* chap. 3.

18. The full story is told in Zay N. Smith and Pamela Zekman, *The Mirage* (New York: Random House, 1979).

19. Protess and others, *Journalism of Outrage,* 240–244.

20. Experiments that test media framing influence are discussed by Leslie A. Rill and Corey B. Davis, "Testing the Second Level of Agenda Setting: Effects of News Frames on Reader-Assigned Attributes of Hezbollah and Israel in the 2006 War in Lebanon," *Journalism and Mass Communication Quarterly* 85, no. 3 (2008): 609–624.

21. Larry J. Sabato, Mark Stencel, and S. Robert Lichter, *Peepshow: Media and Politics in an Age of Scandal* (Lanham, Md.: Rowman and Littlefield, 2000) discusses many cases of scandal reporting along with guidelines that media should follow in publishing or ignoring such incidents.

22. Sabato, *Feeding Frenzy,* 53.

23. Philip Seib, *Headline Diplomacy: How News Coverage Affects Foreign Policy* (Westport, Conn.: Praeger, 1997), 108–111; Kirsten Sparre, "Megaphone Diplomacy in the Northern Irish Peace Process," *Press/Politics* 6, no. 1 (2001): 88–104.

24. Yaeli Bloch and Sam Lehman-Wilzig, "An Exploratory Model of Media-Government Relations in International Crises: U.S. Involvement in Bosnia 1992–1995," in *Media and Conflict: Framing Issues, Making Policy, Shaping Opinion,* ed. Eytan Gilboa (Ardsley, N.Y.: Transnational Publishers, 2002), 153–174; Piers Robinson, "Global Television and Conflict Resolution: Defining the Limits of the CNN Effect," in *Media and Conflict,* ed. Gilboa, 175–192.

25. Protess and others, *Journalism of Outrage,* 134–135.

26. Greg Cima, "Fighting Crime: Crime Stoppers Program Connects Police with Community, Media," February 13, 2005, www.pantagraph.com; Stefan Lovgren, "'CSI Effect' is Mixed Blessing for Real Crime Labs," National Geographic News, September 23, 2004, http://news.nationalgeographic.com.

27. John Walsh, "America's Most Wanted," www.amw.com/index.cfm.

28. Bruce Japsen, "Doctors Group to U. of C.: Practices Close to 'Patient Dumping,'" *Chicago Tribune,* February 19, 2009.

29. Tim Jones and Gary Marx, "Unabomber Has Media in a Bind," *Chicago Tribune,* September 20, 1995.

30. Robert D. McFadden, "News Executives Express Outrage," *New York Times,* October 3, 1986.

31. Doris Graber, "Terrorism, Censorship and the First Amendment: In Search of Policy Guidelines," in *Framing Terrorism: The News Media, the Government, and the Public,* ed. Pippa Norris, Montague Kern, and Marion Just (New York: Routledge, 2003), 27–42.

32. Regina G. Lawrence, "Game-Framing the Issues: Tracking the Strategy Frame in Public Policy News," *Political Communication* 17, no. 2 (2000): 93–114; and Joseph N. Cappella and Kathleen Hall Jamieson, *Spiral of Cynicism* (New York: Oxford University Press, 1997), chaps. 3, 8.

33. Regina G. Lawrence, *The Politics of Force: Media and the Construction of Police Brutality* (Berkeley: University of California Press, 2000).

34. W. Lance Bennett, Regina G. Lawrence, and Steven Livingston, *When the Press Fails* (Chicago: University of Chicago Press, 2007).

35. Ellen Mickiewicz, *Opening Channels* (New York: Oxford University Press, 1996).

36. Bennett, Lawrence, and Livingston, *When the Press Fails.*

37. Gladys Engel Lang and Kurt Lang, *The Battle for Public Opinion: The President, the Press, and the Polls during Watergate* (New York: Columbia University Press, 1983), 58.

38. Molotch, Protess, and Gordon, "The Media-Policy Connection," 45, citing Peter Dreier, "The Position of the Press in the U.S. Power Structure," *Social Problems* 29 (February 1982): 298–310; also see Gadi Wolfsfeld, "Media Protest and Political Violence: A Transactional Analysis," *Journalism Monographs* 127 (June 1991); William A. Gamson, *The Strategy of Social Protest,* 2nd ed. (Belmont, Calif.: Wadsworth, 1990); and Clarice N. Olien, Phillip J. Tichenor, and George A. Donahue, "Media Coverage and Social Movements," in *Information Campaigns: Balancing Social Values and Social Change,* ed. Charles T. Salmon (Beverly Hills, Calif.: Sage, 1989), 139–163.

39. Fran Spielman, "Fired Inspectors Face City Lawsuits," *Chicago Sun Times,* January 8, 2005.

40. Oscar H. Gandy, *Beyond Agenda Setting: Information Subsidies and Public Policy* (Norwood, N.J.: Ablex, 1982), 149–162; also see Matthew C. Nisbet, Dominique Brossard, and Adrianne Kroepsch, "Framing Science, the Stem Cell Controversy in an Age of Press/Politics," *Press/Politics* 8, no. 2

(2003): 11–35; Debra E. Blakely, "Social Construction of Three Influenza Pandemics in the *New York Times*," *Journalism and Mass Communication Quarterly* 80 (2003): 884–902.

41. The title and the information that follows come from "The Great Greenhouse Debate," *Media Monitor* 6, no. 10 (December 1992): 1–6.

42. Jennifer McNulty, "Top U.S. Newspapers' Focus on Balance Skewed Coverage of Global Warming, Analysis Reveals," *UC Santa Cruz Currents Online*, September 6, 2004, http://currents.ucsc.edu/04-05/09-06/coverage.html.

43. Stanley Rothman and S. Robert Lichter, "Elite Ideology and Risk Perception in Nuclear Energy Policy," *American Political Science Review* 81 (June 1987): 383–404. For a more general discussion of the problem of sources of science information, see Hans Mathias Kepplinger, "Artificial Horizons: How the Press Presented and How the Population Received Technology in Germany from 1965–1986," in *The Mass Media in Liberal Democratic Societies,* ed. Stanley Rothman (New York: Paragon House, 1992), 147–176.

44. The information about this case comes from "Is Cancer News a Health Hazard? Media Coverage vs. 'Scientific' Opinion on Environmental Cancer," *Media Monitor* 7, no. 8 (November–December 1993): 1–5. Also see the Kaiser Family Foundation and the Pew Research Center, *Health News Coverage in the U.S. Media: January 2007–June 2008* (Washington, D.C.: Project for Excellence in Journalism, 2008).

45. Patrick Leahy and Alan Mazur, "The Rise and Fall of Public Opposition in Specific Social Movements," *Social Studies of Science* 10 (1980): 191–205; and Alan Mazur, "Media Coverage and Public Opinion on Scientific Controversies," *Journal of Communication* 31 (Spring 1981): 106–115. Also see Jill A. Edy and Patrick Meirick, "Wanted Dead or Alive: Media Frames, Frame Adoption, and Support for the War in Afghanistan," *Journal of Communication* 57 (2007): 119–141, and other articles in the same issue.

46. Renate G. Bader, "How Science News Sections Influence Newspaper Science Coverage: A Case Study," *Journalism Quarterly* 67 (Spring 1990): 88–96; Eleanor Singer, "A Question of Accuracy: How Journalists and Scientists Report Research on Hazards," *Journalism Quarterly* 40 (Fall 1990): 102–116.

47. Todd Gitlin, *The Whole World Is Watching: Media in the Making and Unmaking of the New Left* (Berkeley: University of California Press, 1980), 25–26.

48. For models of the roles played by the media in fostering social movements, see Kevin M. Carragee, "News and Ideology," *Journalism Monographs* 128 (August 1991); Wolfsfeld, "Media Protest and Political Violence"; and Gamson, *The Strategy of Social Protest.*

49. Laura R. Woliver, *From Outrage to Action: The Politics of Grass-Roots Dissent* (Urbana: University of Illinois Press, 1993).

50. Hans Mathias Kepplinger and Michael Hachenberg, "Media and Conscientious Objection in the Federal Republic of Germany," in Paletz, *Political Communication Research,* 108–128. Also see Fay Lomax Cook and Wesley G. Skogan, "Convergent and Divergent Voice Models of the Rise and Fall of Policy Issues," in *Agenda Setting: Readings on Media, Public Opinion, and Policymaking,* ed. David L. Protess and Maxwell McCombs (Hillsdale, N.J.: Erlbaum, 1991), 189–206.

51. Wolfsfeld, "Media Protest and Political Violence."

52. Edie Goldenberg, *Making the Papers* (Lexington, Mass.: Heath, 1975), 146–148.

53. The potential impact of docudramas is discussed by William C. Adams, Allison Salzman, William Vantine, Leslie Suelter, Anne Baker, Lucille Bonvouloir, Barbara Brenner, Margaret Ely, Jean Feldman, and Ron Ziegel, "The Power of *The Right Stuff:* A Quasi-Experimental Field Test of the Docudrama Hypothesis," *Public Opinion Quarterly* 49 (Fall 1985): 330–339. Also see Alan Rosenthal, ed., *Why Docudrama? Fact-Fiction on Film and TV* (Carbondale: Southern Illinois University Press, 1999).

54. Gandy, *Beyond Agenda Setting,* 88.

55. Sally Bedell Smith, "Film on a Nuclear War Already Causing Wide Fallout of Partisan Activity," *New York Times,* November 23, 1983.

56. Bernard Weinraub, "Hollywood Wonders if Warner Brothers Let 'J.F.K.' Go Too Far," *New York Times,* December 24, 1991; Jack R. Payton, "'J.F.K.' Premise Is Full of Holes—But So Was Warren Report," *Chicago Tribune,* December 24, 1991.

57. For a discussion of the subtle yet significant consequences that are often missed, see Stanley Feldman and Lee Sigelman, "The Political Impact of Prime-Time Television: 'The Day After,'" *Journal of Politics* 47 (May 1985): 556–578.

58. For a full discussion of the role of the media as political actors, see Timothy E. Cook, *Governing with the News: The News Media as Political Institutions* (Chicago: University of Chicago Press, 1998); and Maxwell McCombs, *Setting the Agenda: The Mass Media and Public Opinion* (Cambridge, UK: Polity Press, 2004).

59. The account is based primarily on Bill Carter, "Post-Mortem of a Flawed Broadcast," *New York Times,* January 11, 2005.

60. Jarrett Murphy, "CBS Ousts 4 for Bush Guard Story," *CBS News,* January 10, 2005, www.cbsnews.com/stories/2005/01/10/national/main665727.shtml.

61. Walter Goodman, "What's News Worthy Is in the Eye of the Beholder," *New York Times,* August 30, 1993.

62. Brian Stelter, "NBC Settles with Family That Blamed a TV Investigation for a Man's Suicide," *New York Times,* January 26, 2008.

63. Louis A. Day, *Ethics in Media Communications,* 5th ed. (Belmont, Calif.: Wadsworth, 2007), chaps. 4, 9.

64. Thomas Patterson, *Out of Order* (New York: Knopf, 1993).

READINGS

Bausum, Ann. *Muckrakers: How Ida Tarbell, Upton Sinclair, and Lincoln Steffens Helped Expose Scandal, Inspire Reform, and Invent Investigative Journalism.* Washington, D.C.: National Geographic, 2007.

Day, Louis A. *Ethics in Media Communications.* 5th ed. Belmont, Calif.: Wadsworth, 2006.

Fitzpatrick, Ellen F., Jacqueline Jones Royster, Jane Addams, Victoria Brown, and Victoria Bissell. *Muckraking + Southern Horrors and Other Writings.* New York: Bedford/St. Martins, 2008.

Lang, Gladys Engel, and Kurt Lang. *The Battle for Public Opinion: The President, the Press, and the Polls during Watergate.* New York: Columbia University Press, 1983.

Miljan, Lydia, and Barry Cooper. *Hidden Agendas: How Journalists Influence the News.* Vancouver, B.C.: UBC Press, 2003.

Robinson, Piers. *The CNN Effect: The Myth of News, Foreign Policy, and Intervention.* New York: Routledge, 2002.

Sabato, Larry J., Mark Stencel, and S. Robert Lichter. *Peepshow: Media and Politics in an Age of Scandal.* Lanham, Md.: Rowman and Littlefield, 2000.

Seib, Philip M. *The Al Jazeera Effect: How the New Global Media are Reshaping World Politics.* Washington, D.C.: Potomac Books, 2008.

Serrin, Judith, and William Serrin. *Muckraking! The Journalism that Changed America.* New York: New Press, 2002.

Smith, Rebecca, and John R. Emshwiller. *24 Days: How Two Wall Street Journal Reporters Uncovered the Lies That Destroyed Faith in Corporate America.* New York: HarperBusiness, 2003.

Streitmatter, Rodger. *Mightier than the Sword: How the News Media Have Shaped American History.* Boulder: Westview Press, 2008.

chapter 7

Media Influence on Attitudes and Behavior

D o adults learn from media exposure? Research shows that they do and that entertainment programs, along with news, are potent knowledge transmitters. A study of the impact of health messages embedded in a prime-time medical drama is a good illustration.[1] Health knowledge surveys had shown that a mere 15 percent of viewers of *Grey's Anatomy* knew that simple treatments can prevent mother-to-child transmission of HIV. When this message was embedded in one episode of the show, 61 percent of the viewers learned the information. A follow-up survey six weeks later showed that 45 percent of the audience still remembered the information. That is an astoundingly high number considering that few viewers were likely to be affected by the problem and that many were multitasking while watching the show.

How representative is that example? Do media stories really shape the thinking and behavior patterns of countless Americans? Are people's values and attitudes about social and political issues influenced substantially by what they read, hear, and see? Do desirable and undesirable behaviors in television fiction and news programs produce imitations in real life? How much do people learn from the media, and what, precisely, do they learn?

We will examine these questions, beginning with the shaping of attitudes that occurs as an unintended by-product of media exposure. Aside from programs directed at children, journalists usually do not see themselves as the audience's teachers, nor do audiences regard themselves as pupils. Rather, exposure to individual, dramatic events or to the incremental impact of the total flow of information over prolonged periods leads to "incidental" learning about the political world. We also will consider the ways in which people choose the media to which they pay attention and the sorts of things they learn. Finally, we will address the question posed at the start: To what degree does exposure to the mass media influence behavior in politically and socially significant ways?

DIFFERENTIAL EFFECTS OF PRINT AND AUDIOVISUAL NEWS

Most Americans are exposed to the combined effects of print and broadcast media either directly or indirectly through contact with people who tell them what they have heard or seen or read. We may know that President Barack Obama selected his political rival, Hillary Clinton, as his secretary of state. We may feel reassured or disturbed by the appointment and may believe that it is either good or bad to have Mrs. Clinton in that position. But which of these thoughts and feelings come from television, newspapers, conversations, or a combination of media? It is nearly impossible to disentangle such strands of information.[2]

Each medium, however, does make unique contributions to learning. For example, television, because of its visuals, is especially powerful in transmitting realism and emotional appeal. Print media excel in conveying factual details. Because most tests of learning from the media focus on the kinds of facts that print media emphasize, they are generally credited with conveying more knowledge than audiovisual media do.[3] Television bashing is popular when social critics search for a scapegoat for the ills of society.[4] The critics downplay the learning opportunities provided by seeing events unfold on the television screen. Media scholar Neil Postman, for example, warns that massive use of television will turn the United States into a nation of dilettantes who avoid serious thinking because television trivializes the problems of the world.[5] Rod Hart calls it a "seductive" medium that turns people into passive watchers of the political scene, rather than active participants.[6]

The claim that audiences who are print—rather than audiovisual—reliant are better informed and that this proves the superiority of print news must be put into the appropriate context. As a group, print-reliant people differ from those who depend mostly on televised media. These differences make factual learning easier. Print aficionados generally enjoy higher socioeconomic status and better formal education. Their mid- and upper-level jobs provide above-average incentives for learning the factual details by which social scientists judge citizens' knowledge. Attitudes toward the media matter as well. Most people who view print media as primary information sources think of electronic media largely as sources of entertainment. These differences, rather than the nature of each medium, may explain some of the disparities in the effects of various types of media.[7] Television emerges as the most instructive medium if one tests for information that is best conveyed audiovisually, such as impressions of people and dramatic events.[8] Television is also the most readily comprehensible medium for millions of people with limited education. That includes the 32 million U.S. adults who are functionally illiterate and, therefore, almost entirely beyond the reach of print media.[9] What the poorly educated learn about politics from audiovisuals may be fragmentary and hazy, but it represents a quantum leap over the knowledge available to pre–television age generations.

Television's greatest political impact, compared with nonvisual media, springs from its ability to reach millions of people simultaneously with the same images. Although the traditional networks lost more than half of their nightly news viewers in the closing decade of the twentieth century, they remain kings of the information market by a wide margin.[10] Televised events still are experiences shared nationwide. Millions of Americans saw the September 11, 2001, terrorist attack and its aftermath on television. They watched U.S. troops fight in Iraq and Afghanistan and joined in vicarious visits to the Vatican during the papal transition in 2005. They witnessed the amazing

2008 presidential campaign that broke through the dikes of race and gender prejudice by featuring, for the very first time, a white woman and a black man as the major parties' standard-bearers. U.S. print media have never equaled the reach of television and the power that flows from it, including the power to shape collective memories.[11]

In short, the research on the differential effects of media reveals that different types present stimuli that vary substantially in nature and content. It would be surprising, therefore, if their impact were identical, even when they deal with the same subjects. However, "there is no evidence of *consistent* significant differences in the ability of different media to persuade, inform, or even to instill an emotional response in audience members."[12] Because current research does not provide adequate answers about the precise effects of these stimulus variations and about the processes by which individuals mesh a variety of media stimuli, we will focus on the end product—the combined influence of all print and electronic media stimuli on mass audiences, irrespective of the means of delivery.

THE ROLE OF MEDIA IN POLITICAL SOCIALIZATION

Political socialization—learning about political life and internalizing its customs and rules—affects the quality of interactions between citizens and their government. To operate smoothly, political systems need the support of most of their citizens, who must be willing to abide by the laws and to sustain government through performing duties such as voting, paying taxes, or serving in the military. Citizens are more likely to support their government if they are convinced of its legitimacy and capability and if they feel strong emotional ties to it.

Childhood Socialization

Political socialization starts in childhood. Children usually learn basic attitudes toward authority, property, decision making, and veneration of political symbols from their early childhood caretakers. When they enter school, teaching about political values becomes quite systematic. At school, children also learn new facts about their political and social world, much of it based on information from mass media.[13]

Children's direct contacts with the media are equally abundant.[14] Millions of babies watch television. In the winter, young children in the United States spend an average of thirty-one hours a week in front of the television set—more time than in school. Between the ages of twelve and seventeen, weekly television and digital media consumption can run up to forty-eight hours.[15] Eighty percent of the content that children see is intended for adults and shows incidents that differ substantially from those in the child's immediate environment. Children watch military combat, funerals, rocket launchings, courtships, seductions, and childbirth. If they can understand the message, the impact is potentially powerful because children's brains are primed for learning and are apt to take such presentations at face value.

When asked the sources of information on which they base their attitudes about the economy or race, or about war and patriotism, high school students mention the mass media far more often than they mention their families, friends, teachers, or personal experiences.[16] Youngsters who are frequent media users gain substantial information from the media. Compared with infrequent users, they show greater understanding of and support for basic American values, such as the importance of free speech and the right to equal and fair treatment.[17]

The finding that mass media strongly influence socialization runs counter to earlier socialization studies that showed parents and teachers as the chief socializers. Several reasons account for the change. The first is the pervasiveness of television, which exposes even the youngest children to a wealth of images depicting their world. The second reason involves deficiencies in measurement. Much of the early research discounted all media influence unless it came through direct contact between the child and the media. That excluded indirect media influence, such as contacts with parents and teachers who conveyed media information to the child. Finally, research designs have become more sophisticated. In the early studies, children were asked to make their own general appraisal of learning sources. A typical question might be, "From whom do you learn the most: your parents, your school, or newspapers and television?" The questions used in recent studies have been more specific, inquiring first what children know about particular subjects, such as immigration or nuclear energy, and then asking about the sources of their information. In nearly every case the mass media are named as the chief sources of information and evaluations.

What children learn from the mass media and how they evaluate what they learn depends on their stage of mental development. According to child psychologist Jean Piaget, children between two and seven years of age do not detect the connections among various phenomena or draw general conclusions from specific instances. Many of the lessons presumably taught by media stories therefore elude young children. Complex reasoning skills develop fully only at the teenage level. Children's interest in certain types of stories also changes sharply with age, as do their attention and information retention spans.[18] Most children strongly support the political system during their early years but often become disillusioned about authority figures during their teenage years. Their skepticism diminishes as they finish their education and enter the workforce. What role the media play in this transformation is unclear.[19] Knowledge is also slim about children's and adolescents' imitation of behavior that media stories depict, about the duration of memories, and about the persistence of media effects on learning, behavior, and social relationships.[20]

Adult Socialization

The pattern of heavy reliance on media exposure for political news continues into adulthood, though it has been declining sharply in recent decades. For instance, 70 percent of senior citizens read a newspaper regularly in 1991. The figure dropped to 55 percent in 2008. In 2008 only 24 percent of adults younger than 34 were regular readers. The average American adult spends 30 minutes daily watching television news, 14 minutes listening to radio news, 13 minutes reading a newspaper, and 9 minutes getting news on-line. Of course, the total time spent watching and listening to non-news offerings is much greater, although it has been slipping as well.[21] All of that exposure to news and to the political information embedded in entertainment programs contributes to the lifelong process of political socialization and learning.[22] The mass media form

> the mainstream of the common symbolic environment that cultivates the most widely shared conceptions of reality. We live in terms of the stories we tell, stories about what things exist, stories about how things work, and stories about what to do....Increasingly, media-cultivated facts and values become standards by which we judge.[23]

Once people have formed their basic attitudes toward the political system, their attitudes usually stabilize, so that later learning largely supplements and refines earlier notions. The need to cope with information about new events and shifting cultural orientations force the average person into continuous learning and gradual readjustments, although people's basic value structures generally remain intact, even when attitudes are modified.[24] However, major personal or societal upheavals may lead to more-or-less complete resocialization and revised political ideas.

People learn about political norms, rules, values, events, and behaviors largely from fictional and factual mass media stories. Personal experiences are severely limited compared with the range of experiences the media offer to us explicitly or implicitly about the social order and political activities. An accident report, for example, besides telling what happened, may suggest that police and fire forces respond too slowly and that emergency facilities in the local hospital are inadequate. When societal problems such as poverty or pollution are framed as discrete events and reflect just one family's starvation or a particular oil spill, attention is likely to be focused on individual solutions, obscuring the larger societal problems.[25] TV soap operas may persuade audiences that most politicians are corruptible—after all, the majority of those shown on television are.[26] In fact, fictional stories are the most widely used sources for political information. Surveys show that only one-half to two-thirds of the adult television audience regularly exposes itself to explicitly political news.[27]

People's opinions, feelings, and evaluations about the political system may spring from their own thinking about facts supplied by the media; from attitudes, opinions, and feelings explicitly expressed in news or entertainment programming; or from a combination of the two.[28] When audiences have direct or vicarious experiences to guide them, and particularly when they have already formed opinions grounded firmly in their personal values, they are least likely to be swayed by the media. Many people who use the media for information and as a point of departure for formulating their own appraisals nonetheless reject or ignore attitudes and evaluations that media stories supply

---

BOX 7-1 From Individual Learning to Informed Public Opinion: Is the Whole Greater than Its Parts?

E *Pluribus Unum*—Out of many, one—is a hallowed motto in the United States. Among other meanings, it symbolizes that individual voices become truly powerful only when they blend and become the public's opinion. Does individual learning about politics aggregate into informed, collective public opinion that shapes public policies in the U.S.?

The answer is "yes." One example will have to suffice, but it represents a pool of seven studies of learning about policy areas such as civil liberties concerns, public education issues, and global warming concerns.[1] In each policy area, the results were the same: Public opinions fluctuated by ten or more percentage points in reaction to ongoing political happenings, suggesting that, collectively, publics were learning from the news and expressing rational reactions.

Assessment of the quality of the Bush administration's energy policies is one example. As the table below shows, "Good job" public opinion scores dropped thirteen percentage points between 2003 and 2007, and "Poor job" scores rose by eighteen percentage points. During the same time span, the percentage of voters who had not yet formed opinions dropped by half, from 9 percent to 4 percent, illustrating that political ignorance about publicized topics tends to decrease over time.

The nationwide polls asked: Do you think George W. Bush is doing a good job or a poor job in…improving the nation's energy policy?

Poll Date	Good Job %	Poor Job %	Fair/Mixed %	Unsure %
Mar. 11–14, 2007	26	63	7	4
Mar. 13–16, 2006	25	63	7	5
Mar. 7–10, 2005	32	54	7	7
Mar. 8–11, 2004	34	51	8	7
Mar. 3–5, 2003	39	45	7	9

Source: Adapted from Gallup polls; www.gallup.com/poll/2167/Energy.aspx.

The changes in poll scores displayed in the table tally well with various widely reported events that indicated that the president was mishandling diverse energy problems. The first shock came in August 2003, when massive blackouts engulfed the American East Coast and upper Midwest. It was the most widespread electrical blackout in history and affected an estimated 45 million people in eight U.S. states

---

explicitly or implicitly (see Box 7-1).[29] For example, the public gave little credence to the widely publicized predictions by media pundits that proof of President Bill Clinton's affair with White House intern Monica Lewinsky would end the Clinton presidency.

People are prone to accept newspeople's views about national and international issues absent personal experience or guidance from social contacts. Even when people think they are forming their own opinions about familiar issues,

and 10 million more in Ontario, Canada. The blackout initiated a blame game between Democrats and Republicans about who had neglected energy safety.

Then in 2004, the price of gasoline and heating oil rose sharply, threatening people's living standards. News reports claimed that the steep increases in gas prices were unjustified. The increases were blamed mainly on the government's failure to rein in greedy speculators. More bad news about energy surfaced in 2005 during acrimonious congressional debates about oil exploration in Alaska's Arctic National Wildlife Refuge. Television news pictures dwelled on the beautiful, pristine environment, including herds of caribou and other wildlife that would be put at risk by oil diggings. Environmental groups mounted colorful demonstrations against the administration's proposals. The country's energy supplies were also severely disrupted in 2005 by hurricanes Katrina and Rita, which destroyed oil refineries along the Gulf Coast. The flow of bad energy news finally abated in 2006, and public opinion stabilized until it was aroused again two years later by a precipitous rise in gas prices.

From the swings in public opinion about the president's energy policies, as well as in the six cases covering other policy areas, it seems fair to infer that the public pays attention to widely publicized important problems, that it processes the information rationally, and that it forms sound collective opinions. Well-reasoned opinions are a sign of an attentive, intelligent public that learns from the most readily available sources of current information. As Benjamin Page and Robert Shapiro concluded nearly two decades ago in *The Rational Public*, when the opinions of individual Americans meld into collective public opinions, they constitute reasonable responses to current information and changing circumstances; they also reflect the American public's basic values and beliefs.[2] That finding bodes well for the future of democratic governance. U.S. democracy may be muddling through, as democracies are wont to do. But it is adequately supported by the combined learning of citizens who join their voices into a multitonal public opinion chorus.

1. Doris A. Graber, assisted by Catherine Griffiths, Melanie G. Mierzejewski, and James M. Smith, "Re-Measuring the Civic IQ: Decline, Stability, or Advance?" (paper prepared for presentation at the annual meeting of the American Political Science Association, Boston, August 28–31, 2008).

2. Benjamin I. Page and Robert Y. Shapiro, *The Rational Public: Fifty Years of Trends in Americans' Policy Preferences* (Chicago: University of Chicago Press, 1992).

they often depend on the media more than they realize. Extensive television exposure has been shown to lead to "mainstreaming," making people's outlook on political life "congruent with television's portrayal of life and society."[30]

The media's persuasiveness does not mean that exposure is tantamount to learning and mind changing. Far from it. Multiple studies show that two-thirds of newspaper readers generally do not know their paper's preferred position on specific economic, social, and foreign policy issues.[31] Most media stories are promptly forgotten. Stories that become part of an individual's fund of knowledge tend to reinforce existing beliefs and feelings. Acquisition of new knowledge or changes in attitude are the exception rather than the rule. Still, they occur often enough to be significant.

PATTERNS IN SOCIALIZATION

Race, ethnicity, gender, age, income, education, region, and city size generate differences in habits of newspaper reading, radio listening, and television viewing. For instance, blacks and Hispanics rely more on television than whites, and women are the primary audience for daytime television. Age has a bearing on newspaper reading, with older people reading more than younger ones. Southerners listen to much less radio than northerners. Program preferences vary as well. Women aged fifty and older are the heaviest viewers of television news, followed by men fifty and older. Twelve-to-seventeen-year-olds are the lightest news watchers. Men far exceed women in following sports coverage, whereas women spend more time watching television dramas.

Differences in patterns of media use are particularly pronounced among income levels, in part because the most meaty news media cater primarily to the interests of the wealthier segments of the public. High-income families, who usually are better educated than poor families, use print media more and television less than the rest of the population. Upper-income people also use a greater variety of media than lower-income groups. Being better informed helps the information-rich maintain and increase their influence and power in U.S. society.[32]

Although different media exposure and use patterns partly explain differences in knowledge and attitudes, the notion of vastly different communications environments for various population groups should not be carried too far. The bulk of media entertainment and information is similar throughout the country and is shared by all types of audiences. In chapter 4 we saw that the news media cover basically the same categories of stories in the same proportions. Specific stories vary, of course, depending on regional and local interests. Newspapers on the West Coast are more likely to devote their foreign affairs coverage to Asian affairs than are newspapers on the East Coast, which concentrate on Europe and the Middle East. Tabloids put more stress on sensational crime and sex stories than elite papers like the staid *New York Times*. Nevertheless, news sources everywhere provide a large common core of information and interpretation that imbues their audiences with a shared structure of knowledge and basic values. Although audience predispositions, such as party affiliation or religious orientation, produce wide disparities of views on many issues despite shared news, a broad consensus remains on the basic principles that undergird U.S. democracy.[33]

CHOOSING MEDIA STORIES

General patterns of media use do not reveal *why* people pay attention to specific stories, but a number of theories suggest reasons.

Uses and Gratifications Theories

One of the most widely accepted news-choice theories is the "uses and gratifications" approach. Put simply, proponents of this approach contend that individuals ignore personally irrelevant and unattractively presented messages. They pay attention to the kinds of things that they find useful and intellectually or emotionally gratifying if time and effort constraints permit it.[34]

Media scholar Lance Bennett groups uses and gratifications into three broad categories: curiosity and surveillance, entertainment and escape, and social and psychological adjustment.[35] For instance, people pay attention to stories that help them decide how to vote or whether to participate in protest demonstrations. They use the media to gain a sense of security and social adequacy from knowing what is happening in their political environment. People feel gratified if the media reinforce what they already know and believe. They also use the media to while away time, reduce loneliness, participate vicariously in exciting ventures, and escape the frustrations of everyday life.[36] People from all walks of life are most likely to view prime-time programs that are action filled, humorous, and relaxing. They are least likely to choose educational programs, particularly when the presentations involve complex political analysis.[37]

Of course, there is no guarantee that people will attain the gratifications they seek. In fact, news stories may produce anxieties, fears, hatred, or alienation. When a long strike in Israel shut down radio and television in 1987, the public reacted with relief rather than dismay. Israeli philosopher David Hartman gave this explanation:

> When television and radio become the prisms through which you look at reality, you come away saying, "What an ugly place this is." But when you take away those prisms and people's perceptions of reality are derived exclusively from their own daily experiences, which are for the most part prosaic, they inevitably become more relaxed and stable.[38]

Table 7-1, based on interviews with a national sample of adult Americans, indicates how many news consumers claim that they regularly pay a lot of attention to various categories of news about which they were questioned. The topics that attract attention from the largest numbers of people presumably supply the broadest array of gratifications. The rank order of responses varies slightly depending on the type of news medium that the respondent uses most often, but the differences are relatively small in all categories, rarely exceeding ten percentage points. National television was the most-used medium in six of the thirteen news categories that receive the surveyed audience's closest attention. However, national data tend to mask the fact that special subcultural needs may lead to significant variation in gratification patterns. For instance, a Jewish person may be particularly eager to receive news from the Middle East and other places that concern Israel. A person of Polish ancestry may look for news about political developments in Poland. Women who favor increased job opportunities for women are apt to notice stories about women's expanding presence in the business world.

TABLE 7-1 **Bull's-Eye News Topics: 2004, 2006, and 2008**			
Topics audiences watch "very closely"	2004 %	2006 %	2008 %
Crime	32	29	28
Community	28	26	22
Public figures/events in D.C.	24	17	21
Health	26	24	20
Sports	25	23	20
Local government	22	20	20
Religion	20	16	17
International	24	17	16
Business/finance	14	14	16
Science/technology	16	15	13
Consumer news	13	12	13
Entertainment	15	12	10
Culture and the arts	10	9	11

Source: Adapted from Pew Research Center for the People and the Press, "Audience Segments in a Changing News Environment," August 17, 2008, http://people-press.org.

What people actually select depends very much on their lifestyle and the context in which they are exposed to information. What is useful and gratifying in one setting may be less so in another. When people change their lifestyle, for example, when they retire from full-time employment or move from a desk job to one that requires travel, their media patterns may change drastically to bring them into closer accord with the people they encounter in the new setting.[39]

Besides knowing the kind of news that attracts various audiences, it is also important to know why people ignore much of the news that is available. Table 7-2 reports journalists' appraisals of why the public now finds news less useful and less gratifying than in prior decades. Their views shed light on some of the reasons for the sharp and continuing decline in news consumption that has raised concern about the status of civic knowledge and the health of the journalistic enterprise. The table suggests that the problem can be summed under three headings: The news is not geared well enough to people's major concerns; it is not enjoyably presented; and there is a rapidly growing crop of other news venues that are more useful and gratifying.

Other Selective Exposure Theories

Failure to pay attention to news may also spring from psychological factors. Cognitive balance theories postulate that people avoid information that disturbs their peace of mind, offends their political and social tastes, or conflicts with information, attitudes, and feelings that they already hold. People are uncomfortable when exposed to ideas that differ from their own or that question the validity of their ideas. To avoid discomfort, people ignore

	National journalists	Local journalists	Internet journalists
Reason for audience loss			
Growing range of news options	81	84	82
Growing range of specialized news sites	57	55	53
Americans are too busy	47	51	44
Overdose of scandal news	42	34	39
Americans disdain serious news	35	24	31
Stories lack meaning for average people	33	41	36
Boring, static news formats	18	25	19

TABLE 7-2 Why Attention to News Stories Is Sagging: Journalists' Appraisals, 2008 (in percentages)

Source: Adapted from Pew Research Center for the People and the Press, "The Web: Alarming, Appealing and a Challenge to Journalistic Values," March 17, 2008, http://people-press.org.

Note: Based on a survey of 585 journalists, including local reporters, editors, producers, and executives. Respondents were drawn from national and local media samples. They represent a cross-section of news organizations and their personnel. Interviews were conducted Sept. 17–Dec. 3, 2007, by the Pew Research Center for the People and the Press and the Project for Excellence in Journalism.

discordant information. Selective exposure reduces the already slim chance that learning about different views will alter an individual's established beliefs, attitudes, and feelings. Selectivity helps to explain the considerable stability in basic political orientations, such as party allegiance or foreign policy preferences.

Selective exposure occurs less often, however, than was thought initially. Many people find it too bothersome to avoid news they dislike, particularly when watching broadcasts. When television news programs carry stories that viewers find objectionable, it is difficult to screen out the undesired stories without skipping other parts of the program. Many people are actually curious about discrepant information or pride themselves on being open-minded and receptive to all points of view. Some actually enjoy hearing news that contradicts their own ideas so that they can refute what they hear. Apparently exposure to discrepant information is less painful than previously thought. Besides, people often fail to notice that stories diverge in major ways from their own views.[40]

Much of the evidence for selective exposure comes from settings in which available media supported the preferences of the audience; selection was de facto rather than deliberate. For example, unionized workers with friends and associates who are also in unions may encounter a lot of pro-union information at home and at work. Anti-union information may be unavailable. Genuine rather than de facto selective exposure does occur, of course, but it operates more like a preference for congenial news rather than a total exclusion of displeasing information.

Agenda-Setting Theories

If personal needs and pleasures entirely determined choices of news items, news selection patterns would show infinite variations. This is not the case. Similarities in the political environment of average Americans and social pressures produce common patterns in news selection, although polarization along ideological lines is on the rise. For example, conservatives have been flocking to Fox News, while liberals choose CNN. Where the political orientations of these two cable channels differ, their audiences' opinions reflect the cleavages.[41] As previously mentioned, gatekeeping practices largely account for the similarity in news supply. That means that the American public continues to rely on a shared base of information, which is a powerful force for keeping the nation united. Media also tell people in fairly uniform fashion which individual issues and activities are most significant and deserve to be ranked highly on the public's agenda of political concerns.[42] Importance is indicated through cues such as banner headlines, front-page placement in newspapers, or first-story placement on television. Frequent and ample coverage also implies significance.

Many people readily adopt the media's judgment of importance, often inadvertently, rather than selecting or rejecting news on the basis of personal likes and dislikes. When we look at the front page of the newspaper or the top of a news Web page, we expect to find the most important stories there. We may watch the opening minutes of a telecast eagerly to catch the "big" stories and then allow our attention to slacken. As a result, agenda setting by the media leads to uniformities in exposure, as well as in significance ratings of news items. When the media make events seem important, the general public as well as politicians discuss them and form opinions. This enhances the perceived importance of the events and ensures even more public attention and possibly political action.

Numerous studies confirm the agenda-setting influence of the media.[43] When people are asked which issues are most important to them personally or to their community, their lists tend to correspond to cues in the news sources that they use. However, agenda setting varies in potency. Audiences follow media guidance but not slavishly. Past and current experiences, conversations with others, and independent reasoning provide alternatives to media guidance.[44] Comparisons of media agendas with public opinion polls and reports about political and social conditions show that media guidance is most important for new issues that have not been widely discussed and for issues beyond the realm of personal experience.[45] The need for raw material for conversations with friends and associates is a particularly strong force when people select stories. Prominent media coverage ensures that an issue will be noticed, but it does not guarantee that the audience will assign it the same relative importance that media have indicated. Likewise, people will note information that is useful or gratifying to them, even if it is on the back pages, receives minuscule headlines, or is briefly reported at the tail end of a newscast.[46]

HOW PEOPLE LEARN

How do audiences interpret the stories that they have selected? The early models that depicted a straight stimulus–response relationship have been disproved. There is no "hypodermic effect": the media do not inject information unaltered into the minds of audiences. Rather, the images that media convey stimulate perceptions in audience members that meld the media stimuli with each individual's perceptual state at the time he or she receives the message.

Blending New and Old Information

From childhood on, people develop ideas and feelings about how the world operates. When those ideas relate to politics, they are usually grounded in information drawn from the mass media. Cognitive psychologists call these mental configurations by various names, including *schemas* and *scripts*.[47] They serve as organizing devices that help people assimilate new information. As the journalist Walter Lippmann explained it,

> For the most part we do not first see, and then define, we define first and then see. In the great blooming, buzzing confusion of the outer world, we pick out what our culture has already defined for us, and we tend to perceive that which we have picked out in the form stereotyped for us by our culture.[48]

For example, media crime stories and statistics have conditioned most Americans to consider African Americans as more likely perpetrators of violent crimes. Numerous experiments accordingly show that Caucasians who have seen a white person wielding a murder weapon later on mistakenly identify a black person as the assailant.[49] Their image is "perceiver determined," meaning that it is shaped by what they already believe, rather than "stimulus determined," meaning that the image reflects the actual stimulus that their senses have absorbed.

Research shows that images of political candidates are largely perceiver determined for those aspects for which the audience already has developed complex schemas. For instance, people assume that Democratic presidential candidates will pursue policies typically associated with Democrats. They read or view the news in that vein, picking up bits of information that fit while rejecting, ignoring, or reinterpreting those that do not fit. The same is likely to hold true for information about big business or labor unions, the pope, or England's queen. Average Americans are likely to interpret big business and big labor news negatively. Similarly, if reports about the pope or Queen Elizabeth permit a choice between favorable and unfavorable interpretations, the favorable image is apt to prevail.

Information about aspects of events or people not widely known or stereotyped leads to stimulus-determined images. How the media frame these political issues and depict the people largely determine what the audience perceives. Perceptions about the personalities of newcomers to the political scene, assessments of their capabilities, and appraisals of the people with whom they surround themselves, for example, usually are stimulus determined.[50] Likewise, when the media describe present-day China, when they cast doubt on the safety of nuclear energy production, or when they praise the merits of a newly developed drug, they create images that are apt to dominate people's schemas.

Numerous studies show that political elites and other well-informed people have developed exceptionally large arrays of schemas that allow them to absorb many stories that are beyond the reach of the poorly informed.[51] They even are more physically stimulated by new information and therefore are more likely to remember it.[52] The knowledge gap between the privileged and underprivileged widens as a result. Those with the least political knowledge are likely to remain politically unsophisticated and impotent. The knowledge gap between the information rich and the information poor also makes mutual understanding of political views more difficult.

Transient Influences

Many transitory factors impinge on news processing. People are intermittently attentive or inattentive and inclined or disinclined to learn. Up to half of television viewers eat dinner, wash dishes, read, or talk on the telephone while watching television. Examination time at school, illness in the family, or the year-end rush at work may preempt time normally devoted to media. Researchers cannot predict the effect of media messages without knowing the group context in which the exposure or conversation took place. For instance, if one watches or talks about a presidential inauguration with friends who are making fun of the way the president talks and acts, the occasion loses its solemnity and becomes banal. How a person interacts with information also depends on the format of that information. If news reports present conflicting facts or opinions; if they are too long or too short; if they are repetitious, dull, or offensive; their effect is apt to be diminished. Moreover, the total communications matrix affects the influence of its parts, so that the impact of print news may be blunted by prior or subsequent presentations on television and radio or by interpersonal conversations.[53]

Source credibility and appeal are also significant factors in news processing. People find television news more believable than comparable print news because viewers tend to trust news anchors; seeing them on their living room television screens makes them familiar and trustworthy. Partisanship, too, plays an important role in source appraisal. It may cast a rosy glow over fellow partisans and a pall over the opposition.

LEARNING EFFECTS: KNOWLEDGE AND ATTITUDES

What kinds of politically relevant knowledge, attitudes, feelings, and actions spring from people's contacts with the media? Because of the limitations of measuring instruments, the answer to that question is difficult. In chapter 1 we pointed out the impossibility of isolating media influence when it is one of many factors in a complex environment. For example, a sample of citizens who were asked during the Reagan years why their worries about nuclear war had increased cited the following mixture of reasons: increased media coverage (52 percent); Reagan administration policies (19 percent); new weapons/new technology/proliferation (19 percent); unrest in developing countries (13 percent); East–West tensions (11 percent); Soviet belligerence (4 percent); children/ grandchildren's lives (4 percent); other reasons (2 percent); don't know/no answer/can't explain (5 percent).[54] Although these answers tell us which factors played a role, and how many audience members mentioned them, they do not indicate the precise impact of each factor. Until researchers can trace an individual's mental processes and isolate and appraise the significance of each of the components that interact and combine to form mental images, media's influence on knowledge and attitudes cannot be fully assessed. Nor can researchers understand completely just what is learned from media.

Measurement Problems

Research up to now has focused on very small facets of learning, such as testing what specific facts individuals learn about political candidates or about a few public policies. Even within such narrow areas, testing has been severely limited. It has zeroed in on memorizing of factual details from stories rather than on total knowledge gains. For instance, election coverage of a presidential candidate teaches more than facts about the candidate. It may also inform the audience about the role played by White House correspondents in campaign coverage and about living conditions in other cities. Such knowledge gains often are far more valuable for the news consumer than the story details, but they are usually overlooked. Much learning occurs at the subconscious level. People are unaware that they have learned something new and therefore fail to mention it when asked what they have learned. At times people may temporarily forget new information, only to have it reenter consciousness a short while later.[55]

Many assumptions about learning that seem intuitively correct remain untested; nonetheless, they are widely accepted as true. For example, news reports and dramatic television programs presumably teach audiences how lawyers or police officers or hospitals conduct their business. Media researcher Joshua Meyrowitz argues that television has radically changed social roles so that women working in the home, who were previously isolated, have learned about the attractive roles open only to males in U.S. society. News stories have motivated them to compete for those jobs. Omnipresent television and increased Internet access allow children to experience the adult world long before they are physically and emotionally prepared to cope with these experiences. The probing eye of news cameras has transformed political heroes into ordinary mortals. The mystery of social distance has been pierced and destroyed.[56]

We believe that adults as well as children often model their behavior after characters they encounter in the media. We assume that unfavorable stereotypes will hurt the self-esteem of the groups so characterized. Therefore, we urge newspeople to present traditionally adversely stereotyped groups—people with disabilities, gays and lesbians, or people of color—in a better light. Although there is every reason to believe that such effects are quite common, most of them remain unmeasured.

An important exception has been the Cultural Indicators project conducted since the mid-1960s at the University of Pennsylvania's Annenberg School for Communications. Using "cultivation analysis," the investigators have studied trends in the dramatic content of network television and the conceptions of social reality produced in viewers. Their findings confirm that people who watch television for more than four hours daily see the world as television paints it and react to that world rather than to reality more than do their demographic counterparts who watch much less television. For instance, heavy viewers exaggerate the danger of becoming a crime victim.[57] They fear crime more and are more distrustful and suspicious than are light viewers. They also are generally more pessimistic and tend to gravitate toward the middle-of-the-road, mainstream politics depicted on television.

Like most research on mass media effects, these findings have been challenged on the ground that factors other than mass media exposure account for the results. The characteristics of viewers, rather than their exposure to television, may be responsible for their images of the world and their addiction to television. The technical aspects of the Cultural Indicators project have also been challenged. Such scientific controversies indicate that research on mass media effects still needs much refinement.

This holds true, too, for a number of experimental studies that have found, for example, that television news coverage of specific events "primes" audiences to appraise politicians in light of these events. Viewers' political perspectives narrow, so that a single phenomenon deflects attention from the broader context.[58] For example, it is not surprising that experiments indicate that a president's popularity ratings fare better when the audience has been primed with questions about his political successes rather than his failures.[59] But thus far, experiments have failed to tell us how long the priming effects persist in natural situations and their likely political impact. Further testing in natural settings is required to judge under what conditions and for what length of time priming persists.

Forgetting remains a neglected research sphere. Much learning gleaned from news stories is evanescent. When China is rocked by a devastating earthquake or the governor of New York resigns in the middle of a sex scandal, the salient names and facts are on many lips. But after the events have passed, the knowledge evaporates rapidly. How rapidly seems to depend on several factors, most importantly people's ability to store and retrieve information. After three months of inattention, ordinary stories are hard to recall, even for people with good memories. If media periodically revive stories with follow-ups or with closely related stories, memory becomes deepened and prolonged. In fact, the media have rehearsed a few crucial incidents so often that they have become permanent memories. The Great Depression, World War II, the assassination of President John F. Kennedy, and the horrors of the 2001 collapse of the World Trade Center towers are examples.[60]

Factual Learning

Given these limitations on initial learning and on remembering, what can be said about the extent of political learning from the mass media? Average people are aware of an impressive array of politically important topics that the media have covered. However, they do not master many details. They recognize information if it is mentioned to them but fail to recall it without such assistance.[61] When John Robinson and Dennis Davis tested recall of specific facts mentioned in thirteen television news stories within hours of viewing, accuracy scores hovered around 40 percent, with only minor differences among age groups. Education and prior information levels produced the largest variations in scores, with the best informed scoring 13.8 percentage points higher than the poorly informed; 11.2 percentage points separated the scores of college graduates and the scores of people who ended their education in grade school.[62]

Many people are shocked by low recall scores because they believe that stories cannot be fully understood without memorizing factual details. For example, political scientists Scott Keeter and Cliff Zukin titled their study of voter knowledge gains during the 1976 and 1980 presidential elections *Uninformed Choice* because recall scores were low. Keeter and Zukin argued that most citizens are too uninformed to make intelligent political choices.[63] Such judgments may be unduly harsh, because these studies gauge knowledge solely by a citizen's ability to recall facts like the names of prominent office-holders and figures about the length of their terms of office or the growth rate of budget deficits. Such factual information tests are inadequate for judging political knowledge and competence. What really matters is that citizens understand what is at stake in major political issues and what policy options are available for coping with problems. An extensive repertoire of factual detail is not essential for that. As media scholar Michael Schudson puts it: "There's a difference between the 'informational citizen,' saturated with bits and bytes of information, and the informed citizen, the person who has not only information but a point of view and preferences with which to make sense of it."[64]

Are people aware of major political issues and their significance? Are they able to place them in the general context of current politics? When researchers ask these genuinely important questions, the picture of the public's political competence brightens considerably. People may not remember the content of political speeches very well, but as already mentioned, they are aware of a wide range of current issues. Moreover, when interviewers probe for understanding, rather than for knowledge of specific facts, they often discover considerable political insight. For instance, people who cannot define either *price deregulation* or *affirmative action* may still have fairly sophisticated notions about these matters. They know about government price controls on some goods and services and fully understand the burdens that minorities face in finding a job.[65]

Learning General Orientations

Some media stories leave the audience with politically significant feelings that persist long after facts have faded from memory. Although many details of the

2001 terrorist strike have faded in memory, Americans still retain vivid feelings of horror, sympathy, and grief. News may leave people with generalized feelings of trust or distrust, even when it etches few facts into their memories. For instance, prominently featured stories of serious corruption in government may lower the public's esteem for the integrity of government. People who read newspapers that are severely critical of government actions express significantly less trust in government than do those exposed to favorable views. People who have not gone beyond grade school seem to be particularly susceptible to erosion of trust in the wake of mass media criticism.[66] Cynical people, in turn, tend to participate less than others in such civic activities as voting and lobbying.[67]

As political scientist Murray Edelman has pointed out, news stories may make people quiescent because they become fearful of interfering with crucial government actions or because they become complacent about the need for public vigilance. Fear that dissension weakens the government may decrease tolerance for dissidents. Edelman also warns that political quiescence has significant downsides. It may lead to acceptance of faulty public policies, poor laws, and ineffective administrative practices.[68]

On a more personal level, millions of people use the media to keep in touch with their communities. Their contacts help to counter feelings of loneliness and alienation because information becomes a bond among individuals who share it.[69] The models of life that the media depict create wants and expectations as well as dissatisfactions and frustrations. These feelings may become powerful stimulants for social change for the society at large or for selected individuals within it. Alternatively, the feelings may bolster support for the political status quo and generate strong resistance to change. Whether media-induced orientations and actions are considered positive, negative, or a mixture of both depends, of course, on one's sociopolitical preferences.

Deterrents to Learning

Lack of interest in politics and distaste for media offerings, as well as deficiencies in the supply of information, deter many people from keeping up with politics. Rather than discussing politics, which they see as a sensitive topic, they prefer to talk about sports, or the weather, or local gossip. In fact, as the level of abstract, issue-oriented content in political news rises, the attentive audience shrivels. People scan the news for major crises without trying to remember specific facts. Political interest and learning perk up quickly and often dramatically whenever people sense that events will greatly affect their lives, or when they need information for their jobs or for social or political activities.[70] For example, media coverage of the disputed outcome of the 2000 presidential election fired up public interest that had smoldered during the campaign. The postelection events received more public attention in five weeks than the entire primary campaign had received during a five-month span.[71] A similar sharp rise in public attention to news followed the 2001 terrorist attack, the 2004 tsunami in Asia, and Hurricane Katrina in 2005.[72]

Widespread public interest in most political crises flares up like a straw fire and then dies quickly. Attention spans for news are erratic and brief, even though most Americans believe that, as good citizens, they ought to be well informed about political news. They feel guilty, or at least apologetic, if they are not. The alienation of many population groups from the media further inhibits learning. Members of many white ethnic groups, such as Polish Americans or Italian Americans, as well as police and union members, for instance, consider most mass media hostile. They often believe that the media lie and distort, casting police as trigger-happy oppressors of the disadvantaged or unions as corrupt and a barrier to economic progress. Public opinion polls in recent decades show considerable erosion of public confidence in the trustworthiness of the media in general. The media now rank near the bottom of trustworthiness, along with Congress and the legal profession.[73]

How the media present information also affects learning. The media bombard the public daily with more news than it can handle, given the pressures of daily living. Most of the news is touted as significant, even though much is trivial. The constant crisis atmosphere numbs excitement and produces boredom. Audiences are not likely to try hard to learn a wealth of factual information that is of no immediate use and provides little gratification. Moreover, "happy talk" television news formats and exciting film footage encourage the feeling that news is a lighthearted diversion.

The presentation of stories in disconnected television snippets complicates the task of making sense out of news stories and integrating them with existing knowledge. This is especially true when stories are complex, as are most reports about controversial public policies. People who feel that they cannot understand what is happening are discouraged from spending time reading or listening. Learning also suffers when media present conflicting stories and interpretations without giving guidance to the audience. Journalists hesitate to take sides in controversies, fearing accusations of unacceptable editorializing. If people watch several newscasts, hoping for an enriched news diet, they find that roughly half the material is repetitive. Even within a single newscast a large proportion of every story is rehashed background information that puts the story into perspective for viewers who are seeing it for the first time.

The internal structure of television newscasts also impedes learning. Most news stories (74 percent) take up less than two-and-a-half minutes, yet they are crammed with information that people cannot possibly absorb in that time (see Table 7-3). Fully 30 percent of the stories exhibit more than ten pictures in addition to the verbal text, which usually offers additional information that is not in sync with the pictures. The pictures tend to remain on the screen too briefly to extract the full range of their messages. Two-thirds flash by in ten seconds or less. Furthermore, most news programs tightly package disparate items without the pauses that are essential for viewers to absorb information. Hence, it is not surprising that half the audience after the lapse of a few hours cannot recall a single item from a television newscast. Distracting activities that viewers combine with watching television aggravate the problem.

TABLE 7-3 **Television News Characteristics**	
Story characteristic	Percentage of total stories
Length (seconds)	
Less than 60	53
61–150	21
151–200	12
200+	16
Average picture exposure (seconds)	
0–5	34
6–10	28
11–19	20
20+	18
Number of pictures	
0–5	58
6–10	13
11–19	18
20+	12

Source: Author's research based on a sample of 154 news stories from newscasts on NBC, PBS, and MSNBC, March 24–April 2, 2009.

Note: Percentages may add to more than 100 percent because of rounding.

Despite all of the deterrents to learning, Americans still learn much about politics from their many thousands of hours of news consumption over a lifetime. During childhood and adolescence, much news exposure is indirect, conveyed by caregivers and teachers. It usually does a good job of socializing youths into the U.S. system. As adults, they may be disappointed and cynical about particular leaders or policies, but relatively few individuals question the legitimacy of the government, object to its basic philosophies, or reject its claims to their support. The dire predictions about television-induced deterioration of political life and rampant political alienation among citizens have not materialized.[74] In fact, if the media improve political reporting, and political leaders arouse the public's interest, knowledge levels could rise sharply.

LEARNING EFFECTS: BEHAVIOR

Because the media shape people's knowledge, attitudes, and feelings, they obviously can influence behavior. Two areas that have long been of great political concern illustrate the extent of behavioral effects: imitation of violence and crime, particularly among adolescents, and stimulation of economic and political development in underdeveloped regions. In addition, in chapter 8 we will discuss the effects of media coverage on voting behavior, and in chapter 11 the effect of the media on the conduct of foreign affairs.

Jeff Stahler: © Columbus Dispatch/Dist. by Newspaper Enterprise Association, Inc.

Crime and Violent Behavior in Children

Many social scientists believe that portrayals of violence and crime in the media, particularly on television, lead to imitation, especially by children and young adults. Researchers have thoroughly investigated the possible link between television exposure and deviant behavior. The Surgeon General's Office has produced a bookshelf of information on the topic since the 1970s.[75] Congressional committees have spent countless hours listening to conflicting testimony by social scientists about the impact of television violence, and it has been an issue in recent election campaigns. Meanwhile, the amount of violent content, particularly in fictional programs, has escalated, though numbers vary widely depending on the definition of "violence." A 1996 study that defined "violence" broadly as "any overt depiction of the use of physical force or the credible threat of such force intended to physically harm an animate being or group of beings" found most violence on premium cable channels. On HBO and Showtime, 85 percent of programming contained violence. The rate was 59 percent for basic cable channels and 44 percent for broadcast television.[76]

The Parents Television Council, a nonprofit watchdog group, surveyed 180 hours of early-evening prime-time broadcasts on ABC, CBS, Fox, NBC, CW, and My Network TV in 2007 and found more than twelve instances of violent, profane, and sexual content per television hour. Only 11 percent of the 208 episodes included in the study were free of violent or sexual content or foul language. Three out of four programs contained foul language. Furthermore, reruns shown on television during the hours when children are likely to be present increasingly include graphic and explicit shows that originally aired in later time slots. Since 2000–2001, violent content during the prime-time evening hours has increased by 52 percent, and sexual content has grown by 22 percent. The escalation of crime and violence incidents on television is a matter of widespread public concern, as demonstrated by a March 2007 Zogby Poll. Seventy-nine percent of the respondents agreed that there is too much sex, violence, and coarse language on television.[77]

What have studies of the impact of television violence revealed? Despite the strong inclination of many of the researchers to find that crime fiction causes asocial behavior, the evidence is inconclusive because many other factors influence behavior and cannot be ruled out. Some children do copy violent behavior, especially when they have watched aggression that was left unpunished or was rewarded and when countervailing influences from their parents and their teachers are lacking.[78] But aside from imitating television examples when tempted to do so, very few children become violent after exposure to violence in the mass media. Most children lack the predisposition and usually the opportunity for violence, and most do not live in an environment that encourages asocial behavior.[79] A number of studies have tracked the behavior of children exposed to a great deal of violence on television during their early years. As adults, these individuals display a higher incidence of asocial behaviors. Still, that does not point definitively to television as the cause, given the complexity of the environments that mold children and young adults.[80]

Age-linked comprehension differences further confound the situation. Younger children may not be able to comprehend many of the events presented by the media in the same way that adolescents do. The complex social reasoning that adults often ascribe to even young children does not develop until youngsters reach their teenage years. Several studies of children in preschool and early grade school suggest that much of what adults consider to be violent does not seem so to children. Cartoon violence is an example.[81] Therefore, many of the programs that adults consider glorifications of violence may actually suggest more benign behavior to children.

The proportion of preadolescents and adolescents in the United States who are prone to imitate crime is unknown. However, the wide dispersion of television throughout U.S. homes makes it almost certain that the majority of children susceptible to imitating violence will be exposed. Even if the actual number of highly susceptible preadolescents and adolescents is tiny and statistically insignificant, the social consequences can be profound. Such considerations prompted Congress to mandate in the Telecommunications Act of 1996 that television sets should include a "V-chip" to enable adults to block violent television programs from transmission to their homes. The device has not been used extensively, and probably least often in the kinds of homes where the most vulnerable youngsters are likely to live, considering the correlation between child delinquency and flawed home environments. Likewise, in 2000 Congress passed the Children's Internet Protection Act (CIPA), which mandated that schools and libraries install technology to protect children from obscene and violent content on the Internet, but some local systems have chosen to forgo federal funds and leave their computers unfiltered.

Behavior Change in Adults

What about imitation of socially undesirable behavior by adults? The same considerations apply. Imitation depends on the setting at the time of media exposure and on the personality and attitudes that viewers bring to a situation. Widespread societal norms seem to be particularly important. For instance, the 1986 report of the Attorney General's Commission on Pornography noted that exposure to aberrant sexual behavior led to comparatively little imitation. In fact, there was some evidence that greater availability of obscene and pornographic materials reduced sex crimes and misdemeanors because vicarious experiences substituted for actual ones.[82] There was a great deal more evidence that exposure to criminal behavior encourages imitation. The difference may be more apparent than real, however, because crime is more likely to be reported, whereas sexual perversions usually remain hidden.

In sum, the precise link between exposure to media images and corresponding behavior remains uncertain. Attempts by government bodies to regulate media offerings that might stimulate undesirable behavior therefore lack a firm scientific basis. Even if that hurdle can be overcome, it is questionable whether a democratic society should attempt to manipulate the minds of its citizens to protect them from temptations to violate social norms. It seems best to leave control of the content of entertainment programs to widely based informal social pressures. The question of whether social pressures should be allowed to interfere with reporting real-world violence poses even more difficult dilemmas. The possibly adverse effects on behavior must be balanced against the public's need to keep informed about the real world.

Socioeconomic and Political Modernization

The potential of the media to guide people's behavior has led to great efforts to use them as tools for social and political development. The results have been mixed; there have been some successes and many failures.

Psychic Mobility. Hope that using the media could bring about industrialization, improved social services, and democratization ran very high in the decades following World War II. A personality characteristic that political scientist Daniel Lerner labeled "empathic capacity" was called the key to human and material development. The idea behind this theory was that when the media present new objects, ideas, and behaviors, audiences presumably empathize with what is happening in the story and try to imitate it. For instance, when the media show how slum dwellers have built new housing, or how flood victims have purified their polluted water supply, audience members apply the information to their own lives.

Crediting the media with a major role in modernization and democratization rests on three assumptions: (1) that the mass media can create interest and empathy for unfamiliar experiences; (2) that the mass media can provide graphic audiovisual examples of new practices, which audiences can readily understand and imitate; and (3) that development, once started, encourages people to increase their knowledge and skills. Where formal education is not readily available, the media provide information and enhance the capacity to learn. Progress in industrialization, living standards, and political advancement that has followed the spread of media to many formerly information-deficient regions is cited as proof that the assumptions are correct.[83]

Psychological Barriers to Modernization. Although many technologically and politically underdeveloped regions have shown measurable progress, with the media apparently serving as catalysts, social and political change has been far slower and more sporadic than development theorists expected. Many psychological and physical obstacles have stood in the way, including the hostility of individuals or communities to change and unwillingness to alter long-established patterns. Mass media may actually become a negative reference point when people condemn the lifestyles that the media depict. In fact, various fundamentalist groups around the world have mobilized to bar mass media offerings in their communities and stop social and political innovations.

People who are not overtly hostile to change still may be uninterested in altering their lifestyles. To persuade them to adopt innovations may require the intervention of a trusted person, such as a priest, a health care provider, or a family member. The influence of the mass media then becomes a "two-step flow," moving from the media to opinion leaders and then to their followers.

Adoption of Changes. Although it is difficult to use the mass media to change people's basic attitudes and ingrained behaviors, many mass media campaigns have succeeded. Five steps are important. First people must become aware of the possibility for change. Here the media are especially helpful. Radio can inform people about new energy-saving devices or new child-rearing methods. Television and movies can demonstrate new behaviors and new technologies. The Internet offers many previously unavailable, inexpensive opportunities for political participation. Second is understanding how to accomplish the suggested changes. For example, people may be aware that public assistance is available, but they may not know how to apply for it. Mass media usually fail to supply detailed information, although the Internet increasingly fills this information gap. On average, only one-third of all stories that might inspire action, such as environmental protection or energy conservation, contain information about implementation.[84] Unless this gap is filled, the chain leading to the adoption of innovations is broken.

Third is evaluation. People assess the merits of an innovation and decide whether they want to adopt it. Innovations often fail to take root because prospective users reject them as bad, inappropriate, too risky, or too difficult. Media messages alone may not be persuasive enough. It may also be crucial to have a trusted person urge or demonstrate adoption of the innovation. Fourth is trial.

The effect of the media in getting people to try innovations is limited. Factors beyond media control are more important, such as social and financial costs of the change as well as the audience's willingness to change. In general, young men are most receptive to innovations; older people are most skeptical and cautious. Fifth is adoption. The media contribute most to this phase by encouraging people to stick with the changes that they have made part of their life and work styles. For example, the adoption of birth control practices is useless unless they are kept up. The same holds true for many health and sanitation measures or improved work habits. To ensure persistence, mass media must cover a topic regularly, stressing long-range goals and reporting progress.

It is difficult to predict which media campaigns designed to reform behavior will succeed and which will fail.[85] Douglas S. Solomon, who studied health campaigns conducted by private and public institutions, believes that four factors account for success or failure. To succeed, campaigns must set well-specified, realistic goals that are tailored to the needs of the target groups. They must carefully select appropriate media and media formats and present their message at key times and intervals. Messages must be properly designed for greatest persuasiveness. Successful campaigns also must include continuous evaluation and appropriate readjustments.[86]

Above all, the success of the mass media in bringing about change hinges on receptivity to reforms. Ongoing efforts to use the media to modernize developing areas, to turn former communists into democratic citizens, or to bring socially helpful information to individuals who are poor, elderly, and handicapped must concentrate on identifying the specific circumstances most likely to bring success. Responding to requests initiated locally, rather than designing information campaigns from the outside, and integrating local traditions into new approaches seem to hold the most promise.[87]

SUMMARY

The mass media play a major role in political socialization and in learning and accepting the beliefs, norms, and rules that govern political life. Contrary to earlier findings that indicated limited impact, the media are very influential in this process. Consequently, they represent a tremendously powerful political force.

However, the impact of the media on political socialization and other aspects of political learning varies, depending on people's lifestyles and circumstances. Psychological, demographic, and situational factors influence perceptions, as do the manner of news presentation and framing. Although many factors contribute to diversity in socialization and learning, there are powerful unifying forces as well. Most Americans are exposed to similar political information and develop roughly similar outlooks on what it means (and ought to mean) to be an American both politically and socially.

Various theories explain why and how individuals select their information sources, process the available information, and commit facts and opinions to memory. Overall, memory for specific facts that the media present is spotty because most people forget the details after they have drawn conclusions from them. Through repeated exposure to news over time, many people become aware of significant political problems and appreciate their basic significance. Equally important, exposure to the media can produce a range of politically relevant moods, like apathy, cynicism, fear, trust, acquiescence, or support. These moods condition participation in the political process, which may range from no participation at all to efforts to overthrow the government by force.

The media may also produce or retard behavior that affects the quality of public life. We assessed the role of the media in fostering socially undesirable behaviors, especially crime and violence. We also explored the ways in which the media influence the political and social development of various population groups. The media are most successful in informing people and creating initial attitudes. They are least effective in changing established attitudes and ingrained behaviors.

Given the many largely uncontrollable variables that determine media influence, efforts to manipulate media content to foster societal goals are risky at best. They could set dangerous precedents for inhibiting the free flow of controversial ideas or for using the media as channels for government propaganda.

NOTES

1. "'Grey's Anatomy' Lesson? TV Ups Awareness," *Healthbeat,* September 17, 2008, http://abclocal.go.com/wls/story?section=news/health&id=6396541. The impact of learning about politics from straight news stories is detailed in Jason Barabas and Jennifer Jerit, "Estimating the Causal Effects of Media Coverage on Policy-Specific Knowledge," *American Journal of Political Science* 53, no. 1 (January 2009): 73–89.

2. Impact differences between print and electronic media are discussed in W. Russell Neuman, Marion R. Just, and Ann N. Crigler, *Common Knowledge: News and the Construction of Political Meaning* (Chicago: University of Chicago Press, 1992); the political impact of conversations is addressed in Katherine Cramer Walsh, *Talking about Politics: Informal Groups and Social Identity in American Life* (Chicago: University of Chicago Press, 2004). For the view that differences in media modality are very important, see Patricia Moy and Michael Pfau, *With Malice Toward All? The Media and Public Confidence in Democratic Institutions* (Westport, Conn.: Praeger, 2000).

3. Michael X. Delli Carpini and Scott Keeter, *What Americans Know about Politics and Why It Matters* (New Haven: Yale University Press, 1996).

4. Robert D. Putnam, *Bowling Alone: The Collapse and Revival of American Community* (New York: Simon and Schuster, 2000); Pippa Norris, "Does Television Erode Social Capital? A Reply to Putnam," *PS: Political Science and Politics* 29 (1996): 474–480; Pippa Norris, *Digital Divide: Civic Engagement, Information Poverty, and the Internet Worldwide* (Cambridge, UK: Cambridge University Press, 2001).

5. Neil Postman, *Amusing Ourselves to Death: Public Discourse in the Age of Show Business* (New York: Viking Penguin, 1985); Roderick P. Hart, *Seducing America: How Television Charms the Modern Voter* (New York: Oxford University Press, 1994). For a good discussion of the differences between the effects of print and television news on people's behavior, see Joshua Meyrowitz, *No Sense of Place: The Impact of Electronic Media on Social Behavior* (New York: Oxford University Press, 1985), 94–106.

6. For a succinct discussion of the controversy about the scope of learning from television, see Jan E. Leighley, *Mass Media and Politics: A Social Science Perspective* (Boston: Houghton Mifflin, 2004), chap. 6; also see Sally Sugarman, *If Kids Could Vote: Children, Democracy, and the Media* (Lanham, Md.: Lexington Books, 2007).

7. The advantages of learning from audiovisuals are detailed in Doris A. Graber, *Processing Politics: Learning from Television in the Internet Age* (Chicago: University of Chicago Press, 2001).

8. Ibid., chap. 3.

9. Robert Roy Britt, "14 Percent of U.S. Adults Can't Read," *Live Science*, January 10, 2009, www. livescience.com/culture/090110-illiterate-adults.html.

10. Pew Research Center for the People and the Press, "The State of the News Media, 2008," www. stateofthenewsmedia.org/2008.

11. The importance of collective memories is spelled out in Jill A. Edy, *Troubled Pasts: News and the Collective Memory of Social Unrest* (Philadelphia: Temple University Press, 2006); Yoram Peri, "The Media and Collective Memory of Yitzhak Rabin's Remembrance," *Journal of Communication* 49, no. 3 (Summer 1999): 106–124.

12. W. Russell Neuman, *The Future of the Mass Audience* (New York: Cambridge University Press, 1991), 99 (emphasis added); Zhongdang Pan, Ronald E. Ostman, Patricia Moy, and Paula Reynolds, "News Media Exposure and Its Learning Effects during the Persian Gulf War," *Journalism Quarterly* 71, no. 1 (Spring 1994): 7–19; Raymond W. Preiss, ed., *Mass Media Effects Research: Advances through Meta-Analysis* (Mahwah, N.J.: Erlbaum, 2007).

13. Dhavan V. Shah, "Civic Engagement, Interpersonal Trust, and Television Use: An Individual-Level Assessment of Social Capital," *Political Psychology* 19 (1998): 469–496; Eric M. Uslaner, "Social Capital, Television, and the 'Mean World': Trust, Optimism, and Civic Participation," *Political Psychology* 19 (1998): 441–467; Dafna Lemish, *Children and Television : A Global Perspective* (Malden, Mass.: Blackwell, 2007).

14. Bruce Watkins, "Television Viewing as a Dominant Activity of Childhood: A Developmental Theory of Television Effects," *Critical Studies in Mass Communication* 2 (1985): 323–337. Average high school graduates have spent 15,000 hours watching television and 11,000 hours in the classroom. They have seen 350,000 commercials. For an excellent discussion of various aspects of youth socialization, see Jack M. McLeod and Dhavan V. Shah, guest eds., "Special Issue: Communication and Political Socialization," *Political Communication* 26, no. 1 (January–March 2009), esp. 65–117.

15. "Connected to the Future: A Report on Children's Internet Use from the Corporation for Public Broadcasting," 2003, www.cpb.org/stations/reports/connected/connected_report.pdf.

16. David O. Sears and Nicholas Valentino, "Politics Matters: Political Events as Catalysts for Pre-Adult Socialization," *American Political Science Review* 91 (1997): 45–65; David O. Sears and Carolyn L. Funk, "Evidence of the Long-Term Persistence of Adults' Political Predispositions," *Journal of Politics* 61 (1999): 1–28; and Marco Calavita, *Apprehending Politics: News Media and Individual Political Development* (Albany: State University of New York Press, 2005).

17. Suzanne Pingree, "Children's Cognitive Processes in Constructing Social Reality," *Journalism Quarterly* 60 (Fall 1983): 415–422; also see Jack Demaine, ed., *Citizenship and Political Education Today* (New York: Palgrave Macmillan, 2005); and Sugarman, *If Kids Could Vote*.

18. Jean Piaget, *The Language and Thought of the Child*, 3rd ed. (New York: Harcourt Brace, 1962); see also Pamela Johnston Conover, "Political Socialization: Where's the Politics?" in *Political Science: Looking to the Future; Political Behavior*, vol. 3, ed. William Crotty (Evanston: Northwestern University Press, 1991), 125–152.

19. A study of prime-time values on television showed that fewer than 4 percent featured citizenship values, such as patriotism or citizen duties. Gary W. Selnow, "Values in Prime-Time Television," *Journal of Communication* 40 (Summer 1990): 69.

20. Robert Kubey, "Media Implications for the Quality of Family Life," in *Media, Children, and the Family*, ed. Dolf Zillmann, Jennings Bryant, and Aletha C. Huston (Hillsdale, N.J.: Erlbaum, 1994); George A. Comstock and Erica Scharrer, *Media and the American Child* (Amsterdam: Elsevier, 2007).

21. Pew Center for the People and the Press, "Key News Audiences Now Blend Online and Traditional Sources: Audience Segments in a Changing News Environment," August 17, 2008, http://people-press.org/report/444/news-media.

22. Matthew A. Baum, *Soft News Goes to War: Public Opinion and American Foreign Policy in the New Media Age* (Princeton: Princeton University Press, 2003) explains the important role played by soft news in informing the public. See also Pew Center for the People and the Press, "Key News Audiences Now Blend Online and Traditional Sources."

23. George Gerbner, Larry Gross, Marilyn Jackson Beeck, Suzanne Jeffries Fox, and Nancy Signorielli, "Cultural Indicators: Violence Profile No. 9," *Journal of Communication* 28 (Summer 1978): 178, 193; see also George Gerbner, Larry Gross, Michael Morgan, and Nancy Signorielli, "Political Correlates of Television Viewing," *Public Opinion Quarterly* 48 (Summer 1984): 283–300. Also see Markus Prior and Arthur Lupia, "Money, Time, and Political Knowledge: Distinguishing Quick Recall and Political Learning Skills," *American Journal of Political Science* 52, no. 1 (2008): 169–183; J. Celeste Lay, "Learning about Politics in Low-Income Communities: Poverty and Political Knowledge," *American Politics Research* 34, no.3 (2006): 319–340.

24. The importance of preadult political learning for subsequent political orientations is discussed in Kent Jennings and Laura Stoker, "Of Time and the Development of Partisan Polarization," *American Journal of Political Science* 52 (July 2008): 619–635; and Kent Jennings, "Political Participation as Viewed through the Lens of the Political Socialization Project," in *Advances in Political Psychology*, ed. Margaret Herman (Oxford: Elsevier, 2004), 1–18. Also see Doris A. Graber, *Processing the News: How People Tame the Information Tide*, 2nd ed. (Lanham, Md.: University Press of America, 1993); and Graber, *Processing Politics*, chap. 2.

25. Shanto Iyengar, *Is Anyone Responsible? How Television Frames Political Issues* (Chicago: University of Chicago Press, 1991), 136–143.

26. Stanley Rothman, S. Robert Lichter, and Linda Lichter, "Television's America," in *The Mass Media in Liberal Democratic Societies*, ed. Stanley Rothman (New York: Paragon House, 1992), 221–266.

27. Paula M. Poindexter, "Non-News Viewers," *Journal of Communication* 30 (Fall 1980): 58–65; and Michael X. Delli Carpini and Bruce A. Williams, "Constructing Public Opinion: The Uses of Fictional and Nonfictional Television in Conversations about the Environment," in *The Psychology of Political Communication*, ed. Ann N. Crigler (Ann Arbor: University of Michigan Press, 1996), 149–175.

28. For examples of various types of general and specific information supplied by entertainment programming, see " 'Grey's Anatomy' Lesson?"; G. Ray Funkhouser and Eugene F. Shaw, "How Synthetic Experience Shapes Social Reality," *Journal of Communication* 40 (Summer 1990): 75–87; and W. James Potter and William Ware, "The Frequency and Context of Prosocial Acts on Primetime TV," *Journalism Quarterly* 66 (Summer 1989): 359–366.

29. Graber, *Processing the News*, 90–93.

30. Gerbner and others, "Political Correlates," 286.

31. Donald L. Jordan, "Newspaper Effects on Policy Preferences," *Public Opinion Quarterly* 57 (1993): 191–204; and William Schneider and A.I. Lewis, "Views on the News," *Public Opinion* 8 (August–September 1985): 5–11, 58–59.

32. However, the benefits derived from the use of a particular medium vary for demographic groups. For example, while use of local news media coincides with civic participation for most

audiences, this does not hold true for African Americans. Their civic participation is encouraged more by interpersonal networks. Teresa Mastin, "Media Use and Civic Participation in the African-American Population: Exploring Participation among Professionals and Nonprofessionals," *Journalism and Mass Communication Quarterly* 77, no. 1 (2000): 115–127.

33. Doris A. Graber, "Do the News Media Starve the Civic IQ? Squaring Impressions and Facts," *Hedgehog Review* 10, no.2 (Summer 2008): 36–48.

34. Robert LaRose and Matthew S. Eastin, "A Social Cognitive Theory of Internet Uses and Gratifications: Toward a New Model of Media Attendance," *Journal of Broadcasting and Electronic Media* 48, no. 3 (2004): 358–377; Kathryn Greene and Marina Krcmar, "Predicting Exposure to and Liking of Media Violence: A Uses and Gratifications Approach," *Communication Studies* 56, no. 1 (2005): 71–93; John Raacke and Jennifer Bonds-Raacke, "MySpace and Facebook: Applying the Uses and Gratifications Theory to Exploring Friend-Networking Sites," *CyberPsychology and Behavior* 11, no. 2 (2008): 169–174.

35. W. Lance Bennett, *News: The Politics of Illusion*, 8th ed. (New York: Longman, 2009), chap. 3; and Charles Atkin, "Information Utility and Selective Exposure to Entertainment Media," in *Selective Exposure to Communication,* ed. Dolf Zillman and Jennings Bryant (Hillsdale, N.J.: Erlbaum, 1985), 63–92.

36. Michael Morgan, "Heavy Television Viewing and Perceived Quality of Life," *Journalism Quarterly* 61 (Fall 1984): 499–504; Philip Palmgreen, Lawrence A. Wenner, and J.D. Rayburn II, "Relations between Gratifications Sought and Obtained: A Study of Television News," *Communication Research* 7 (April 1980): 161–192; Robert W. Kubey, "Television Use in Everyday Life: Coping with Unstructured Time," *Journal of Communication* 36 (Summer 1986): 108–123.

37. Neuman, *The Future of the Mass Audience,* 122.

38. In Thomas L. Friedman, "No TV? Israel Is Savoring the Silence," *New York Times,* November 6, 1987.

39. Graber, *Processing the News*; see also Stuart H. Schwartz, "A General Psychographic Analysis of Newspaper Use and Life Style," *Journalism Quarterly* 57 (Fall 1980): 392–401; also see Gil A. Frisbie, "Demarketing Energy: Does Psychographic Research Hold the Answer?" *Journal of the Academy of Marketing Science* 8, no. 3 (June 1980): 196–211.

40. The literature is reviewed in Zillman and Bryant, *Selective Exposure to Communication.*

41. Pew Research Center for the People and the Press, "The State of the News Media, 2008."

42. For a discussion of replacement of older issues by newer ones, see Hans-Bernd Brosius and Hans Mathias Kepplinger, "Killer and Victim Issues: Issue Competition in the Agenda-Setting Process of German Television," *International Journal of Public Opinion Research* 7, no. 3 (1995): 211–231.

43. Maxwell E. McCombs, *Setting the Agenda: The Mass Media and Public Opinion* (Cambridge, UK: Polity Press, 2004); Shanto Iyengar and Donald R. Kinder, *News That Matters: TV and American Opinion* (Chicago: University of Chicago Press, 1987); Benjamin I. Page and Robert Y. Shapiro, *The Rational Public: Fifty Years of Trends in Americans' Policy Preferences* (Chicago: University of Chicago Press, 1991); Wayne Wanta, *The Public and the National Agenda* (Mahwah, N.J.: Erlbaum, 1997); Spiro Kiousis, Michael McDevitt, and Xu Wu, "The Genesis of Civic Awareness: Agenda Setting in Political Socialization," *Journal of Communication* 55, no. 4 (2005): 756–774.

44. Diana Mutz, *Impersonal Influence: How Perceptions of Mass Collectives Affect Political Attitudes* (Cambridge, UK: Cambridge University Press, 1998); Jason Barabas and Jennifer Jerit, "Estimating the Causal Effects of Media Coverage on Policy-Specific Knowledge," *American Journal of Political Science* 53, no. 1 (January 2009): 73–89; Stephen C. Craig, James G. Kane, and Jason Gainous, "Issue-Related Learning in a Gubernatorial Campaign: A Panel Study,"

Political Communication 22 (October–December 2005): 483–503; Doris A. Graber, "Mediated Politics and Citizenship in the Twenty-First Century," *Annual Review of Psychology* 55 (January 2004): 545–571.

45. James N. Druckman, "Does Political Information Matter?" *Political Communication* 22 (October–December 2005): 515–519; Brian Gaines, James H. Kuklinski, Paul J. Quirk, Buddy Peyton, and Jay Verkuilen, "Same Facts, Different Interpretations: Partisan Motivation and Opinion on Iraq," *Journal of Politics* 69 (November 2007): 957–974; Markus Prior, *Post-Broadcast Democracy: How Media Choice Increases Inequality in Political Involvement and Polarizes Elections* (New York: Cambridge University Press, 2007).

46. The importance of personal and contextual factors in news selection and evaluation is discussed in Lutz Erbring, Edie Goldenberg, and Arthur Miller, "Front-Page News and Real World Cues: Another Look at Agenda-Setting by the Media," *American Journal of Political Science* 24 (February 1980): 16–49; and David B. Hill, "Viewer Characteristics and Agenda Setting by Television News," *Public Opinion Quarterly* 49 (Fall 1985): 340–350. Also see Walsh, *Talking about Politics*.

47. Graber, *Processing the News*, 27–31, and for details on learning processes, chaps. 7–9. Also see Robert H. Wicks, "Schema Theory and Measurement in Mass Communication Research: Theoretical and Methodological Issues in News Information Processing," *Communication Yearbook* 15 (Newbury Park, Calif.: Sage, 1991): 115–154. An excellent discussion of processing of audiovisual information research, including a lengthy bibliography, is presented by Annie Lang, "The Limited Capacity Model of Mediated Message Processing," *Journal of Communication* 50, no. 1 (2000): 46–70. How learning goals affect processing is reported by Li-Ning Huang, "Examining Candidate Information Search Processes: The Impact of Processing Goals and Sophistication," *Journal of Communication* 50, no. 1 (2000): 93–114.

48. Walter Lippmann, *Public Opinion* (New York: Harcourt Brace, 1922), 31.

49. See, for example, Mary Beth Oliver, "Caucasian Viewers' Memory of Black and White Criminal Suspects in the News," *Journal of Communication* 49, no. 3 (1997): 46–60, and references cited there; and Robert M. Entman and Andrew Rojecki, *The Black Image in the White Mind: Media and Race in America* (Chicago: University of Chicago Press, 2001).

50. Shanto Iyengar, "Television News and Citizens' Explanations of National Affairs," *American Political Science Review* 81 (September 1987): 815–831. The impact of stereotyped beliefs on public policy is discussed in detail in Martin Gilens, *Why Americans Hate Welfare: Race, Media, and the Politics of Antipoverty Policy* (Chicago: University of Chicago Press, 1999).

51. Vincent Price and John Zaller, "Who Gets the News? Alternative Measures of News Reception and Their Implications for Research," *Public Opinion Quarterly* 57, no. 1 (1993): 133–164; and Cecilie Gaziano, "Forecast 2000: Widening Knowledge Gaps," *Journalism and Mass Communication Quarterly* 74, no. 2 (1997): 237–264. For evidence of shared reactions to television programs, irrespective of educational level, see W. Russell Neuman, "Television and American Culture: The Mass Medium and the Pluralist Audience," *Public Opinion Quarterly* 46 (Winter 1982): 471–487.

52. Maria Elizabeth Grabe, Annie Lang, Shuhua Zhou, and Paul David Bolls, "Cognitive Access to Negatively Arousing News: An Experimental Investigation of the Knowledge Gap," *Communication Research* 27, no. 1 (2000): 3–26.

53. Larry L. Burriss, "How Anchors, Reporters, and Newsmakers Affect Recall and Evaluation of Stories," *Journalism Quarterly* 64 (Summer/Fall 1987): 514–519. The impact of framing on the perception of the legitimacy of social protest is discussed in Douglas M. McLeod and Benjamin H. Detenber, "Framing Effects of Television News Coverage of Social Protest," *Journal of Communication* 49, no. 3 (1999): 3–23; also see Annie Lang, "The Limited Capacity Model of Mediated Message Processing"; William L. Buscemi, "Numbers? Borrinnnggg!!!"

PS: Political Science and Politics 30, no. 4 (1997): 737–742; and Patti M. Valkenburg, Holli Semetko, and Claes H. de Vreese, "The Effects of News Frames on Readers' Thoughts and Recall," *Communication Research* 26, no. 5 (1999): 550–569.

54. Michael A. Milburn, Paul Y. Watanabe, and Bernard M. Kramer, "The Nature and Sources of Attitudes toward a Nuclear Freeze," *Political Psychology* 7 (December 1986): 672; also see Jonathan Renshon, "Stability and Change in Belief Systems," *Journal of Conflict Resolution* 52, no. 6: 820–849; and Constantinos Hadjichristidis, Simon J. Handley, Steven A Sloman, Jonathan St. B. T. Evans, David E. Over, and Rosemary J. Stevenson, "Iffy Beliefs: Conditional Thinking and Belief Change," *Memory and Cognition* 35, no. 8 (2007): 2052.

55. An overview of hypermnesia research is presented in Robert H. Wicks, "Remembering the News: Effects and Message Discrepancy on News Recall over Time," *Journalism and Mass Communication Quarterly* 72, no. 3 (Fall 1995): 666–682.

56. Meyrowitz, *No Sense of Place.*

57. The chances of becoming a crime victim are small in real life, but in television life they are 30 percent–64 percent. See Gerbner and others, "Cultural Indicators," 106–107; and Nancy Signorielli, *Violence in the Media: A Reference Handbook* (Santa Barbara, Calif.: ABC-CLIO, 2005). For a critique of the work of Gerbner and his associates, see W. James Potter, "Cultivation Theory and Research: A Methodological Critique," *Journalism Monograph* 147 (October 1994). James Shanahan and Michael Morgan, *Television and Its Viewers: Cultivation Theory and Research* (Cambridge, UK: Cambridge University Press, 1999) lays out the pro and con arguments of the cultivation research program. Exposure to news about actual crime predicts salience of crime better than does personal exposure to crime.

58. Iyengar, *Is Anyone Responsible?*; Iyengar and Kinder, *News That Matters.*

59. An example of corroborative research is Jon A. Krosnick and Donald R. Kinder, "Altering the Foundations of Support for the President through Priming," *American Political Science Review* 84 (June 1990): 497–512.

60. John Stauffer, Richard Frost, and William Rybolt, "The Attention Factor in Recalling Network Television News," *Journal of Communication* 33 (Winter 1983): 29–37. Also see Graber, *Processing Politics.*

61. Ibid., chap. 2; Teun A. Van Dijk, *News as Discourse* (Hillsdale, N.J.: Erlbaum, 1988); and John P. Robinson and Mark R. Levy, *The Main Source: Learning from Television News* (Beverly Hills, Calif.: Sage, 1986); also see Samuel Popkin and Michael A. Dimock, "Political Knowledge and Citizen Competence," in *Citizen Competence and Democratic Institutions,* ed. Stephen L. Elkin and Karol Edward Soltan (University Park: Pennsylvania State University Press, 1999), 117–146.

62. John P. Robinson and Dennis Davis, "Television News and the Informed Public: An Information-Processing Approach," *Journal of Communication* 40, no. 3 (Summer 1990): 106–119; also see John P. Robinson and Dennis Davis, "News Flow and Democratic Society in an Age of Electronic Media," *Public Communication and Behavior,* vol. 2 (New York: Academic Press, 1989), 60–102.

63. Scott Keeter and Cliff Zukin, *Uninformed Choice: The Failure of the New Presidential Nominating System* (New York: Praeger, 1983). But see Arthur Lupia and Mathew D. McCubbins, *The Democratic Dilemma: Can Citizens Learn What They Need to Know?* (New York: Cambridge University Press, 1998); also see Delli Carpini and Keeter, *What Americans Know about Politics and Why It Matters.*

64. Michael Schudson, *The Power of News* (Cambridge, Mass.: Harvard University Press, 1995), 27.

65. V. O. Key, with the assistance of Milton C. Cummings Jr., reached the same conclusion in *The Responsible Electorate* (Cambridge, Mass.: Harvard University Press, 1965), 7. Also see Page and Shapiro, *The Rational Public,* 383–390, regarding the wisdom inherent in public opinion,

and Daniel R. Anderson, "Educational Television Is Not an Oxymoron," *Annals of the American Academy of Political and Social Science* 557 (May 1998): 24–38.

66. Arthur H. Miller, Edie N. Goldenberg, and Lutz Erbring, "Type-Set Politics: Impact of Newspapers on Public Confidence," *American Political Science Review* 73 (March 1979): 67–84.

67. Joseph N. Cappella and Kathleen Hall Jamieson, *The Spiral of Cynicism: The Press and the Public Good* (New York: Oxford University Press, 1997).

68. Murray Edelman, *Politics as Symbolic Action* (New York: Academic Press, 1976); and Murray Edelman, *Constructing the Political Spectacle* (Chicago: University of Chicago Press, 1988).

69. Susan Hearold, "A Synthesis of 1043 Effects of Television on Social Behavior," in *Public Communication and Behavior,* vol. 1, ed. George A. Comstock (New York: Academic Press, 1986), 66–133. Also see George E. Marcus, W. Russell Neuman, and Michael MacKuen, *Affective Intelligence and Political Judgment* (Chicago: University of Chicago Press, 2000); and Antonio R. Damasio, *Descartes' Error: Emotion, Reason, and the Human Brain* (New York: Grosset/Putnam, 1994).

70. The desire to be politically informed varies widely. News selection criteria are discussed in Graber, *Processing the News,* chap. 4.

71. Center for Media and Public Affairs, "Florida Trouble Triples TV Attention," www.cmpa.com-pressrel/electpr13.htm.

72. Check chapter 5 for sources for these events; for Hurricane Katrina see Pew Research Center for the People and the Press, September 19–22, 2008 News Interest Index, Omnibus Survey, Topline, http://people-press.org/reports/questionnaires/454.pdf.

73. Harold W. Stanley and Richard G. Niemi, *Vital Statistics on American Politics, 2007–2008* (Washington, D.C.: CQ Press, 2008); published every two years. Also see Pew Center for the People and the Press, "The State of the News Media, 2009," www.stateofthenewsmedia.org/2009.

74. For dire predictions see Jarol B. Manheim, *All of the People All the Time: Strategic Communication and American Politics* (Armonk, N.Y.: M.E. Sharpe, 1991); Robert Entman, *Democracy without Citizens: Media and the Decay of American Politics* (New York: Oxford University Press, 1990), chap. 7. For a more positive view see Graber, "Mediated Politics and Citizenship in the Twenty-First Century"; Doris A. Graber, "Framing Politics for Mass Consumption: Can American News Media Meet the Challenge?" in *Advances in Political Psychology,* vol. 1, ed. Margaret G. Hermann (Amsterdam: Elsevier, 2004), 19–39; and Page and Shapiro, *The Rational Public,* 383–390.

75. None of these studies focuses on the effects of exposure to nonfictional violence in the media. The series began with a report by the surgeon general on television violence effects; see *Television and Growing Up: The Impact of Televised Violence,* www.surgeongeneral.gov/library/youthviolence/chapter4/appendix4bsec2.html. For a critical review of one of the follow-up reports, see Thomas D. Cook, Deborah A. Kendzierski, and Stephen V. Thomas, "The Implicit Assumptions of Television Research: An Analysis of the 1982 NIMH Report on 'Television and Behavior,'" *Public Opinion Quarterly* 47 (Spring 1983): 161–201.

76. "Violence Dominates on TV, Study Says," *Chicago Tribune,* February 7, 1996.

77. Parents Television Council, "The Alarming Family Hour…No Place for Children," 2009, www.parentstv.org/ptc/publications/reports/familyhour/exsummary.asp.

78. Russell G. Geen, "Television and Aggression: Recent Developments and Theory," in *Media, Children, and the Family,* ed. Zillmann, Bryant, and Huston, 151–162; Jerome L. Singer, Dorothy G. Singer, and Wanda S. Rapaczynski, "Family Patterns and Television Viewing as Predictors of Children's Beliefs and Aggression," *Journal of Communication* 34 (Summer 1984): 73–89. The politics of research on the effects of television violence are discussed by Willard D. Rowland Jr., *The Politics of TV Violence: Policy Uses of Communication Research* (Beverly Hills, Calif.: Sage, 1983).

79. James M. Carlson, *Prime Time Law Enforcement: Crime Show Viewing and Attitudes toward the Criminal Justice System* (New York: Praeger, 1985); Marjorie Heins, "Blaming the Media: Would Regulation of Expression Prevent Another Columbine?" *Media Studies Journal* 14, no. 3 (2000): 14–23; Marjorie Heins, *Not in Front of the Children: Indecency, Censorship and the Innocence of Youth* (New York: Hill and Wang, 2001).

80. James T. Hamilton, ed., *Television Violence and Public Policy* (Ann Arbor: University of Michigan Press, 1998); George Comstock and Haejung Paik, "The Effects of Television Violence on Antisocial Behavior: A Meta-Analysis," *Communication Research* 21 (1994): 516–539; David Gauntlett, *Moving Experiences: Media Effects and Beyond*, 2nd ed. (London: J. Libbey, 2005).

81. Robert P. Snow, "How Children Interpret TV Violence in Play Context," *Journalism Quarterly* 51 (Spring 1974): 13–21.

82. *Attorney General's Commission on Pornography: Final Report* (Washington, D.C.: Government Printing Office, 1986); see also Richard A. Dienstbier, "Sex and Violence: Can Research Have It Both Ways?" *Journal of Communication* 27 (Summer 1977): 176–188; Presidential Commission on Obscenity and Pornography, *Report of the Commission on Obscenity and Pornography* (New York: Bantam Books, 1970); Patricia M. Greenfield, "Inadvertent Exposure to Pornography on the Internet: Implications of Peer-to-Peer File-Sharing Networks for Child Development and Families," *Applied Developmental Psychology* 25 (2004): 741–750, www.center-school.org/pko/documents/Inadvertentexposure.pdf.

83. David O. Edeani, "Critical Predictors of Orientation to Change in a Developed Society," *Journalism Quarterly* 58 (Spring 1981): 56–64. The carefully measured impact of the introduction of television into a Canadian community is presented in *The Impact of Television: A Natural Experiment in Three Communities*, ed. Tannis MacBeth Williams (Orlando: Academic Press, 1985).

84. Janet A. Weiss and Mary Tschirhart, "Public Information Campaigns as Policy Instruments," *Journal of Policy Analysis and Management* 13, no. 1 (Winter 1994): 82–119, www.jstor.org.proxy.cc.uic.edu/stable/pdfplus/3325092.pdf; James B. Lemert, Barry N. Mitzman, Michael A. Seither, Roxana H. Cook, and Regina Hackett, "Journalists and Mobilizing Information," *Journalism Quarterly* 54 (Winter 1977): 721–726.

85. Ronald E. Rice and Charles K. Atkin, eds., *Public Communication Campaigns*, 3rd ed. (Thousand Oaks, Calif.: Sage, 2001). Also see Sina Odugbemi and Thomas Jacobson, eds., *Government Reform Under Real-World Conditions: Citizens, Stakeholders and Voice* (Washington, D.C.: World Bank, 2008).

86. Thomas E Backer, Everett M Rogers, and Pradeep Sopory, *Designing Health Communication Campaigns: What Works?* (Newbury Park, Calif.: Sage, 1992).

87. John L. Crompton and Charles W. Lamb Jr., *Marketing Government and Social Services* (New York: Wiley, 1986); Marc L. Lame, "Communicating in the Innovation Process: Issues and Guidelines," in *Handbook of Administrative Communication*, ed. James L. Garnett and Alexander Kouzmin (New York: Marcel Dekker, 1997), 187–201.

READINGS

Calavita, Marco. *Apprehending Politics: News Media and Individual Political Development*. Albany: State University of New York Press, 2005.

Comstock, George A., Erica Scharrer, and George A. Comstock. *Media and the American Child*. Amsterdam: Elsevier, 2007.

Entman, Robert M., and Andrew Rojecki. *The Black Image in the White Mind: Media and Race in America*. Chicago: University of Chicago Press, 2000.

Grabe, Maria Elizabeth, and Erik Page Bucy. *Image Bite Politics: News and the Visual Framing of Elections.* New York: Oxford University Press, 2009.

Graber, Doris A. *Processing Politics: Learning from Television in the Internet Age.* Chicago: University of Chicago Press, 2001.

Kubey, Robert, and Mihaly Csikszentmihalyi. *Television and the Quality of Life: How Viewing Shapes Everyday Experience.* Hillsdale, N.J.: Erlbaum, 1990.

Lupia, Arthur, and Mathew D. McCubbins. *The Democratic Dilemma: Can Citizens Learn What They Need to Know?* New York: Cambridge University Press, 1998.

Neuman, W. Russell, Marion R. Just, and Ann N. Crigler. *Common Knowledge: News and the Construction of Political Meaning.* Chicago: University of Chicago Press, 1992.

Preiss, Raymond W., ed. *Mass Media Effects Research: Advances through Meta-Analysis.* Mahwah, N.J.: Erlbaum, 2007.

Strasburger, Victor C., Barbara J. Wilson, Amy B. Jordan. *Children, Adolescents, and the Media.* 2nd ed. Los Angeles: Sage, 2009.

Elections in the Internet Age

"**I**t is hard to imagine two campaigns more fully epitomizing the historical juncture crossed in the 2008 election. The McCain campaign was prototypical campaign past. The Obama campaign heralded campaigns to come."[1] That is how political science Professor G.R. Boynton characterized the 2008 presidential election campaign. What were the main features of the campaigns of the past? And what has replaced them?

Starting in 1952, television became the main battlefield for presidential contests. Republicans excelled in producing clever television advertisements that created images of attractive rags-to-riches Horatio Alger candidates. Their rise up the social status ladder readied them to be president and snatch the nation from the jaws of impending disaster. Dwight Eisenhower, for example, came from tiny Abilene, Kansas, earned a West Point diploma, and ultimately rose to become commander in chief of the Allied forces that defeated Hitler's armies in World War II. Ronald Reagan, another Republican contender, was born and raised in rural Illinois in a low-income household. He began his career as a lowly radio reporter and worked his way up, serving two terms as governor of California before winning the presidency. The rags-to-riches Republican candidate in 2008 was Sen. John McCain of Arizona. Born into a navy family, McCain advanced through the ranks of the navy, then retired, and subsequently won election to Congress. The toughest hurdle in his life was enduring five-and-a-half years as a prisoner of war in North Vietnam, where he was severely tortured by his captors. In a steely display of courage and character, he had refused a release offered to him as a special privilege, choosing to stay instead with his imprisoned compatriots.

Presidential candidate John McCain was marketed in a typical Republican television campaign that relied heavily on brief television advertisements. Even though some were broadcast on "new media" channels and were supplemented by social networking contacts, the campaign relied most heavily on traditional thirty-second ads. The ads were filled largely with negative messages because McCain faced an extremely hostile environment. His party affiliation linked him to a very unpopular Republican incumbent who was blamed for a costly, unsuccessful war and economic disaster. In addition, McCain's claim early in the campaign that "the fundamentals of our economy are strong" harmed him severely; it led many voters to believe that a McCain administration would do little to revive the economy.

In this Democrat-friendly environment, Barack Obama launched the most sophisticated "new media" campaign in history and won the presidency, although he, too, had to overcome great political hurdles. The odds were against him because of his race and past experiences—a black man in a white-dominated society, a left-leaning former community organizer easily linked to Chicago's culture of political corruption, a relative newcomer to the national political scene, and on top of all that, a silver-tongued, Harvard-trained egg-head, who had been a University of Chicago law professor. How could such a vulnerable candidate possibly win?

Aside from his opponent's weaknesses, a substantial part of the answer is that candidate Obama used an array of new, incredibly speedy and cheap Internet tools—e-mail, social networks, Twitter, and the like—to run a grassroots campaign that contacted individual voters in seemingly personalized encounters, often on a daily basis. He did it imaginatively and wisely, assisted by a vastly talented group of paid advisers and unpaid volunteers. Among his impressive achievements, possible only via new Internet channels, was using hip messages to communicate with a huge audience of predominantly young citizens on social Web sites. By the end of the campaign, Obama had more than two million "friends" on Facebook, compared to 600,000 for McCain. Obama even bought advertising space that put him on the front page of individuals' Facebook accounts and made him the top sponsored link on many Google search queries. He targeted young males in swing states with showy advertisements on video games, hoping to stimulate turnout among that politically passive group. Even on YouTube, Obama stole the thunder, beating McCain four to one. His supporters uploaded more than 1,800 videos onto the BarackObama.com channel, which counted about 115,000 subscribers. Only 330 videos were uploaded to McCain's YouTube channel; they attracted just over 28,000 subscribers. The disparities were similar on many other venues, like old-hat e-mail and newcomers like Twitter, Flickr, Digg, BlackPlanet, and on and on. Moreover, the potential audience for the Internet campaign had grown substantially by 2008. Nearly half of the public (46 percent) was using e-mail, texting, or the Web. The Obama campaign sent them more than a billion messages. Considering such explosive numbers, it was inevitable that Internet use soared ahead of newspapers as a source of campaign news for the first time, as Table 8-1 shows.

Through his direct contacts with supporters, Obama was able to brand himself as the candidate of badly needed change away from current distressed conditions and a champion of the neglected needs of younger voters. Possibly more important, he was also able to brand his Republican opponent, John McCain, as a clone of the unpopular incumbent president. The clone image made it easy to blame McCain as an accomplice in starting the failing Iraq War, and facilitating the disastrous collapse of the country's economy. The clone image put McCain on the defensive through much of the campaign. Obama's vigorous Internet campaigning recruited millions of volunteer workers and raised a record $745 million, mostly from small contributions by three million donors. The average donation was $86. Obama's style and charisma mesmerized the press. Although there were some negative stories, the overall

TABLE 8-1 **Voters' Main Sources of Campaign News, 2000, 2004, and 2008 (in percentages)**			
News source	*2000*	*2004*	*2008*
Television	70	76	72
Cable	36	42	46
Network	22	33	24
Local	21	12	13
Newspapers	39	46	29
Radio	15	22	21
Internet	11	21	33
Magazines	4	6	3

Source: Pew Research Center for the People and the Press, "Internet Now Major Source of Campaign News," http://people-press.org. Based on combined surveys of 2,011 voters conducted October 17–20 and October 24–27, 2008.

Note: Figures add up to more than 100 percent because multiple answers were allowed.

impression voiced in comments about the campaign was that the press treated Obama like a rock star. His picture and his messages appeared over and over in headlines, on magazine covers, and on television.

But what was really so new about the campaign blitzkrieg that culminated in a victory for the Democrats? They won just under 53 percent of the popular vote, a solid win but short of a landslide, except in the electoral votes. The campaign was guided by the familiar principles that candidates must communicate with their base as well as attract new voters who have weak or no ties to the opposition party or who are likely to stay away from the polls. The Internet, particularly its Web 2.0 manifestations, provided a range of new, inexpensive channels that candidates could use to distribute messages of their choice to audiences around the clock, around the country, and around the world. The target audiences, as before, were potential voters, who were a bit easier to pinpoint because of channel diversity. Here essentially was old wine in new bottles, much of it branded more heavily than before by the candidates rather than the thinning ranks of professional journalists. Presidential candidates had more money than ever before, unless they opted to receive federal money in return for a pledge to abide by campaign finance limitations. The new media did not crowd out the familiar old-timers; they supplemented them. Therefore, the key question addressed in this chapter is the collective influence of all media platforms on various aspects of nationwide elections.

THE CONSEQUENCES OF MEDIA-DOMINATED POLITICS

The ready availability of television in nearly every home, the pervasiveness of public opinion polling, and easy access to the World Wide Web, where election-related sites abound, guarantee that the news media will play a major role in presidential elections. What exactly does that role entail? We will consider three main facets: the power of journalists to influence the selection of candidates, the requirement for candidates to "televise well," and the explosive growth and diversification of made-for-media campaigns.

Media as Kingmakers

Before television, voters had little chance to assess the candidates on their own. The political parties controlled nominations and voters made their choices based largely on party labels. Party affiliation remains important at the state and local levels, where media information about candidates is scant, particularly on television. The exceptions were nonpartisan local elections, when candidates run without party designation and endorsement, or primary elections, in which candidates of the same party compete against each other. In the television age, journalists became the chief influence in the selection of candidates and the key issues of the campaign. Television brought candidates, especially presidential contenders, directly into the nation's living rooms, giving voters information for making choices based on the media's menu. Candidates, like actors, depend for their success as much on the roles into which they are cast as on their acting ability. In the television age, media people did most of the casting for presidential hopefuls, whose performance was then judged according to the assigned role. The new media have changed the power balance moderately, giving candidates more control over shaping their image. Barack Obama is an example of a candidate with substantial control over his image. Republican vice presidential candidate Sarah Palin, who was ridiculed by powerful media voices, is an example of the opposite, namely major news media clout in branding candidates.

Casting occurs early in the primaries when newspeople, on the basis of as yet slender evidence, predict winners and losers to narrow the field of eligibles who must be covered. Concentrating on the front-runners in public opinion polls makes newspeople's tasks more manageable, but it often forces trailing candidates out of the race prematurely. Early, highly speculative calculations become self-fulfilling prophecies because designated "winners" attract supporters whereas "losers" are abandoned. For example, in 2007—the "preseason" year for the 2008 presidential race—only Democrats who scored well in public opinion polls received more than scattered attention from television news. On the Democratic side, after the campaign had started in earnest, New York senator Hillary Clinton and Illinois senator Barack Obama received the lion's share of coverage, garnering 17 percent and 14 percent of the coverage, respectively. Republican hopefuls Rudy Giuliani, John McCain, and Mitt Romney trailed at 9 percent, 7 percent, and 5 percent. These imbalances persisted throughout the primary season, seriously handicapping the campaigns that remained in the shadows.[2]

Candidates who exceed expectations in garnering votes are declared winners; candidates who fall short are losers.[3] When journalist Pat Buchanan finished sixteen points behind George Bush in the 1992 New Hampshire Republican presidential primary, the media declared Buchanan the winner because he had exceeded their expectations. They did the same for Bill Clinton, who had trailed former senator Paul Tsongas in the Democratic primary in New Hampshire in 1992. The candidacy of Republican senator Bob Dole during the 1996 primaries was prematurely declared dead when he finished behind his competitors in a few early and insignificant contests.

Media coverage and public opinion polls tend to move in tandem in the early months of a campaign. Candidates who receive ample media coverage usually do well in the polls. Good poll ratings then bring more media coverage. Once the caucus and primary season has started in the spring of the presidential election year, the outcomes of these contests become more important predictors of media attention. One other pattern is common, though not universal. The substance of stories tends to be favorable for trailing candidates in the race and unfavorable for front-runners. During the 2004 primaries, for example, Howard Dean's favorable ratings plunged while he was the Democratic front-runner, only to soar again when he became the underdog.[4]

The media's role as kingmaker or killer of the dreams of would-be kings is often played over a long span of time. Image making for presidential elections now begins on a massive scale more than a year before the first primary. The "pre-pre-campaign," on a more limited scale, begins shortly after the previous election, with newspaper and magazine stories about potential presidential candidates. Senators and governors who have received favorable publicity over many years may gradually come to be thought of as likely presidential nominees. Losers in the previous campaign who were bruised but not badly beaten remain on the "possibilities" list.

Media coverage can be shaped to destroy candidacies. This happened to two Democratic candidates for the presidency in 1988. Sen. Joseph Biden of Delaware was forced out of the campaign by widely publicized charges that his speeches contained plagiarized quotations from other political leaders. Twenty years later, the stain had faded enough to permit Barack Obama to make him vice president. Media attention to this choice was negligible. The second media casualty in 1988 was Sen. Gary Hart of Colorado, who withdrew after charges of philandering. Recurrent media references to the Chappaquiddick incident, which linked Sen. Edward Kennedy, D-Mass., to the drowning of a young woman on his staff, also kept his supporters from drafting him as a presidential contender. However, adverse publicity can be overcome. In the 1992 campaign Bill Clinton was accused of adultery and draft dodging, charges that caused his poll ratings and positive media appraisals to plummet. Despite the bad publicity, Clinton managed to win major primaries and the presidency, earning the title "Comeback Kid."

Television images can be vastly important in making a candidate electable or unelectable. For instance, the televised Kennedy-Nixon debates of 1960, the Reagan-Mondale debates of 1984, and the Bush-Gore debates of 2000 helped to soften the public's impressions that John F. Kennedy, Ronald Reagan, and George W. Bush were unsuited for the presidency.[5] Kennedy was able to demonstrate that he was capable of coping with the presidency despite his youth and relative inexperience, and Reagan in 1984 conveyed the impression that he remained mentally fit for a second term. Bush's performance in the second debate counteracted charges that he lacked sufficient intellect and debating skills to become an effective president.[6]

When the media chose policy issues during crucial phases of the campaign, they sharply diminished the chances of presidents Jimmy Carter and George H.W. Bush to win second terms, and they ravaged John McCain's presidential aspirations. In Carter's case, just before the 1980 presidential election, the media chose to commemorate the anniversary of a major foreign policy failure—Carter's inability to win the release of U.S. hostages in Iran. Disapproval of Bush in the 1992 election was directed mainly at his highly publicized failure to solve major domestic economy problems during the last year of his term. In McCain's case, reminders about his support of the Iraq War and his admission that he knew little about economics reinforced voters' beliefs that it was time for a change to a Democratic administration.

Media-operated public opinion polls are yet another weapon in the arsenal for kingmaking. The major television networks, in collaboration with such newspapers as the *New York Times,* the *Washington Post,* and *USA Today,* all conduct popularity ratings and issue polls throughout presidential elections. The results are publicized extensively and then become benchmarks for voters, telling them who the winners and losers are and what issues are crucial to the campaign. Depending on the nature and format of the questions the pollsters ask and the political context in which the story becomes embedded, the responses spell fortune or misfortune for the candidates. Polls may determine which candidates enter the fray and which keep out. In the 1992 presidential campaign, major Democratic politicians shunned the race because they believed that President Bush's high approval ratings in national polls following the Persian Gulf War doomed their candidacies. That provided an opening for a little-known governor from Arkansas named Bill Clinton to propel himself into a two-term presidency.

Television-Age Recruits

Another important consequence of audiovisual campaigning is the change it has wrought in the types of candidates likely to be politically successful. Because broadcasts can bring the images of candidates for office directly into the homes of millions of voters, a candidate's ability to look impressive and perform well before the cameras has become crucial. People who are not telegenic have been eliminated from the pool of available recruits. Abraham Lincoln's rugged face probably would not have passed muster in the television age. President Truman's "Give 'em hell, Harry," homespun style would have backfired had it been presented on the nation's television screens rather than to small gatherings. The image of Franklin D. Roosevelt in a wheelchair would have spelled damaging weakness. Roosevelt, in fact, was keenly aware of the likely harmful effects of a picture of him in a wheelchair and never allowed photographs to be taken while he was being lifted to the speaker's rostrum.

During a campaign stop in Ohio in 2004, President George W. Bush hugs fifteen-year-old Ashley Faulkner after learning that her mother had died in the 2001 terrorist attacks on the World Trade Center.
Source: AP Photo/Family photo by Lynn Faulkner

Actors and other celebrities who are adept at performing before the public now have a much better chance than ever before to be recruited for political office. Ronald Reagan and Arnold Schwarzenegger, who were seasoned actors; John Edwards and Barack Obama, spellbinding orators; and Jesse Jackson, a charismatic preacher, are examples of typical television age recruits, whose chances for public office would have been much slighter in an earlier era. As columnist Marquis Child put it, candidates no longer "run" for office; they "pose" for office.[7]

In fact, good pictures can counterbalance the effects of unfavorable verbal comments. When CBS reporter Leslie Stahl verbally attacked President Reagan for posturing as a man of peace and compassion during the 1984 presidential campaign, a Reagan assistant promptly thanked her for showing four-and-a-half minutes of great pictures of the president. He was not in the least concerned about Stahl's scathing remarks. The pictures had shown the president

> basking in a sea of flag-waving supporters…sharing concerns with farmers in a field, picnicking with Mid-Americans, pumping iron…getting the Olympic torch from a runner…greeting senior citizens at their housing project, honoring veterans who landed on Normandy, honoring youths just back from Grenada, countering a heckler…wooing black inner-city kids.…[8]

During the 2004 campaign, an emotional ad showing President Bush hugging a fifteen-year-old orphan in Lebanon, Ohio, was credited with driving home the crucial message that Bush cared about people and would protect them. The ad, reproduced above, showed an obviously grieving president cradling the youngster, whose mother had died in the 2001 World Trade Center attack. Young Ashley Faulkner's voice could be heard saying, "He's the most powerful man in the world, and all he wants to do is make sure I'm safe, that I'm OK."[9]

Television advisers have become year-round members of presidential and gubernatorial staffs. These experts coach candidates about proper dress and demeanor for various occasions, create commercials for the candidates, and handle general news coverage of the campaign. Presidential contenders spend roughly two-thirds of their budgets on television. In 2008 candidates, political parties, and independent groups spent more than $2.6 billion on television ads. Most of it—$2 billion—went to local broadcast television, primarily in battleground states. Radio, cable, and national network advertising cost an additional $600 million. John McCain, the Republican standard-bearer, who accepted federal campaign funding in return for agreeing to spending limitations, spent a paltry $136 million on his campaign ads—less than half the $310 million spent by his opponent.[10] In election campaigns, such disparities usually are a grave handicap for the financial underdog, whose messages are drowned out by the opposition. Given the high cost of television commercials and of gaining news exposure, a candidate's personal wealth or ability to raise money remains an important consideration, even when federal funding is available and e-mail and social networks provide cheap, candidate-controlled access to potential voters. Candidates shun activities, statements, and policy proposals that are likely to alienate donors. The political consequences in recruitment and in postelection commitments that spring from such financial considerations are huge.

Media Campaigning Strategies

Twenty-first-century election campaigns are structured to garner the most favorable media exposure, reaching the largest number of prospective supporters, with the greatest degree of candidate control over the message. Candidates concentrate on photo opportunities, talk show appearances, or trips to interesting events and locations. Even when candidates meet voters personally at rallies, parades, or shopping centers, they generally time and orchestrate the events to attract favorable media coverage.

The New Venues. Appearances on entertainment shows, once considered "unpresidential," have become routine. Maverick candidate Ross Perot started the pattern during the 1992 presidential race by announcing his presidential aspirations on CNN's *Larry King Live* call-in television show. Other candidates flocked to the talk show trek, preferring the light banter and respectful questions of callers to the pointed inquisition in interviews by the national press. By 2000 it seemed almost obligatory for presidential contenders to appear on talk shows hosted by television personalities Larry King, Oprah Winfrey, Jay Leno, and David Letterman. McCain first announced his entry into the 2008 presidential contest on a Letterman show. In fact, voters under age thirty frequently claimed that late-night television comedians and shows like *Saturday Night Live* were their major sources of campaign information (see Box 8-1 for more on this trend).[11]

Candidates' escape from the highly critical national press to friendlier environments also takes the form of interviews on political satire shows like Comedy Central's *The Daily Show* and the *Colbert Report*. The *Daily Show* feature "Indecision 2008" covered the campaigns of Barack Obama, John McCain, and Joseph Biden, who had announced his own earlier presidential campaign on the show. Even network morning news shows now devote entire hours to conversations with the candidates and accept telephoned questions from viewers during the show. All in all, the trend seems to be toward more direct contact by candidates with voters and increased candidate control over campaign messages, all at the expense of message control by the major media.

The 2008 campaign also saw the debut of social Web sites as major outlets for candidates' messages.[12] In fact, many messages first aired on television were rebroadcast on the new venues and captured more viewers there than when they aired originally. Katie Couric's crucial interview of Republican vice presidential candidate Sarah Palin is a prime example. The interview, which undermined Palin's image as a knowledgeable politician prepared to be president if needed, was first aired on CBS television and seen by six million people. Subsequently, it garnered a substantially larger audience from broadcasts on Web sites such as MySpace, Facebook, and YouTube. Only one-third of the audience for Tina Fey's *Saturday Night Live* skit on the Palin campaign watched the live version of the show. The rest saw rebroadcasts elsewhere.

Candidate-sponsored Web sites are another addition to the venues that campaigners have used since 1996 to offer voters a carefully selected information diet. Most Web sites show videos about the candidates' issue positions and other topics, allowing the candidates to present their case at length in their own words and with carefully chosen pictures. The 2008 Obama campaign even launched a special Web site to defuse rumors and innuendo and nip their toxic effects in the bud. Many Web sites allow visitors to register to vote, to donate money to the campaign or volunteer to work for it, and to check campaign sites in their states. There may be special interest pages for groups like senior citizens, veterans, college students, or young children. Many Web sites provide e-mail connections that enable candidates to stay in regular contact with Web site visitors. E-mail lists have been exceedingly useful as a get-out-the-vote device during the final days of the campaign. The Obama campaign had more than thirteen million e-mail addresses and a million people who registered to receive text messages. Among other important sites that aired ample positive messages from and about Obama, the Huffington Post—HuffPo—was especially influential. It is a news Web site and aggregated weblog founded by Arianna Huffington, a syndicated liberal columnist. In addition to numerous other aggregated Web sites caught up in "Obamamania," millions of individual bloggers made themselves heard.

For the average voter, the consequences of the availability of these more candidate-centered approaches to campaigning are not entirely clear. Unquestionably, more people than ever before were exposed to them in 2008,

BOX 8-1 Political Humor in Campaigns

Humor has always been a potent political tool in society, from ancient times onward. In the Middle Ages, rulers employed court jesters to talk freely and frankly about flawed policies and politicians, at a time when it was a capital crime to mock the high and mighty. The inexcusable could be excused if, by definition, it was merely a "jest."

In modern times, truths told in jest, or satirized, and jokes about political leaders still are powerful weapons in political contests. They leap across the barriers of political correctness and chisel their message into human minds. Satire attracts huge audiences, especially among the best-informed segments of the public, who know enough about the political scene to understand the full meaning of veiled messages.

The 2008 presidential election was yet another exhibition of the popularity and power of political humor. Humorous messages took many forms, ranging from political cartoons in newspapers and on the Web to newspaper comic strips like Doonesbury and televised satirical soap operas like *Family Guy* and *The Simpsons*. Popular political Web sites such as JibJab attracted millions of people with short, poignant videos about the campaign. Viewers then told others, in chain-letter fashion, that the lighthearted spoofs should not be missed. The Web site www.peteyandpetunia.com/VoteHere/VoteHere. htm, released during the 2008 presidential race, is just one example.

"Fake" news programs like *The Daily Show* with Jon Stewart, *The Colbert Report*, and *Saturday Night Live* and the satirical newspaper *The Onion* became household names. Their barbs circulated widely. The late-night talk shows, including *The Late Show* with David Letterman and *The Tonight Show* with Jay Leno, added to the feast of political jokes. They made fun of the candidates' intellect and skills, and occasionally their policies. Only people familiar with ongoing news developments could relish the humor and savor the glee that comes from feeling that one is "in the know" when others are not.

To begin with an example that pre-dates the 2008 campaign, in 2003 comic Stephen Colbert, barbed tongue in cheek, told guests, including President Bush, at the Washington press corps's annual dinner that he supported the president. The reason was that "he stands for things. Not only for things, he stands on things, things like aircraft carriers and rubble and recently flooded city squares. And that sends a strong message: that no matter what happens to America, she will always rebound--with the most powerfully staged photo ops in the world."

but the content of the messages was quite similar on all platforms. Even the brief tweets on Twitter were in harmony. When the votes were counted, Obama's margin of victory was within the customary range, which is 50 percent of the popular vote plus or minus 3 percent. Compared with the 2000 presidential election, use of the Internet as a mainstay of election information almost doubled (Table 8-1). Still, television remains the chief source of election news by far, with cable increasing its share of the audience and

Colbert's sophisticated audience laughed heartily because it knew that he was referring to a 2003 speech in which President Bush had prematurely declared an end of major fighting in Iraq. The Bush speech had been staged on an aircraft carrier, where the president had arrived minutes earlier in a small navy plane that he had copiloted. A huge sign behind Bush proclaimed "Mission Accomplished." Colbert's mention of rubble and floods alluded to another failure of the administration—insufficient resource allocations to the Gulf Coast to prevent the flooding following Hurricane Katrina and to alleviate the aftermath. News dropouts would have missed Colbert's subtleties.

As is common during elections, a large number of jokes during the 2008 campaign referred to alleged personal weaknesses of the candidates. Television host Conan O'Brien made fun of John McCain's age when he announced on his show that "Barack Obama said today that he is going to fight for votes in all fifty states. Yeah. That's what he said. Meanwhile, John McCain said he's going to fight for votes in all thirteen colonies." In a similar vein, Jay Leno mocked vice presidential candidate Sarah Palin's intelligence by reporting, "A woman at a John McCain rally said that Barack Obama is an Arab. And McCain quickly corrected her. It was really awkward, because McCain had to tell her, 'Look, Governor Palin, you are wrong.'"

Jon Stewart took a swipe at the news media's worship of Barack Obama in a story about the candidate's visit to the Middle East, reporting, "After a quick meet-and-greet with King Abdullah, Obama was off to Israel, where he made a quick stop at the manger in Bethlehem where he was born." David Letterman, in turn, panned the contents and conduct of the New Hampshire debates, asking his audience rhetorically: "Did you folks see the debates in New Hampshire over the weekend? Oh my god, dull. . . . . I mean, they were so dull that today, and it was official, I saw it in the paper, New Hampshire changed its state slogan from 'Live Free or Die' to 'Please Shoot Me.' "

Such jokes may seem pretty tame, but repeated over and over again, they become part of the candidate's image that voters internalize and carry to the voting booth. No wonder *Newsweek* featured Jon Stewart on its cover shortly before the 2004 presidential election, calling him one of the most powerful media figures in that contest. In the same year, Stewart's parody of an American government textbook, *America (The Book): A Citizen's Guide to Democracy Inaction*, placed fifteenth on the *New York Times* list of best-selling books.

network television losing substantial ground. The disparities reflect the fact that cable television devoted nearly 60 percent of its news hole to the election, compared with slightly over 30 percent for broadcast TV. Among cable channels, the political orientation arcs from conservative Fox News to liberal MSNBC, with CNN in the middle. It is unclear how such choices affect election outcomes, as people tend to choose news venues in tune with their existing political orientations.

Jeff Stahler: © Columbus Dispatch/Dist. by Newspaper Enterprise Association, Inc.

Although the Web remains a secondary source of campaign information for the general public, and although the candidates budgeted most money for over-the-air television, the Web was tremendously helpful. It became a major source of money from millions of citizens who responded to Web site appeals.[13] The Web also served as a virtual pied piper for all candidates, luring thousands of supporters to the campaign. Web appeals enlisted them in e-mail recruiting efforts and mobilized them to go to the polls and bring their friends and neighbors along. That feat would have been impossible to achieve through direct mail or phone calls.

The Web also served as a rallying tool for political activists and political action committees who would have found it difficult to be heard without it. MoveOn.org, for example, used its Web site and e-mail blitzes to raise millions of dollars and mobilize more than two million passionate liberals to the cause of driving Republicans from office. The traditional media picked up many of the messages circulated by activists on the Web and in e-mails, giving their often extreme views a huge national audience. In addition, hundreds of Web sites, including blogs, provided a rich menu of information to voters who wanted to explore election issues in depth.

Attracting Coverage. Candidates maximize their chances of receiving attention by planning their schedules around events that are known to attract reporters. They spend disproportionate amounts of time during the primary season campaigning in Iowa and New Hampshire, where media coverage of the earliest contests is usually heavy. In a typical presidential campaign, coverage of primary elections in each of these states dwarfed television news coverage of later primaries by a ratio of more than four to one.[14] To keep a favorable image of candidates in front of the public, campaign managers arrange newsworthy events to familiarize potential voters with their candidates' best aspects. Managers show candidates dressed informally, mixing with enthusiastic crowds of average people and looking relaxed and happy and confident. If vigor has to be demonstrated, the candidate performs expertly in some popular sport. John Kerry, for example, was shown duck hunting, but an aide carried the dead ducks lest animal lovers take offense.

Incumbents have a distinct advantage over challengers. Although they may attract about the same number of campaign stories, incumbents receive additional attention through coverage of their official duties. Incumbents may also be able to dictate the time and place of media encounters. When a president schedules a meeting for reporters in the White House Rose Garden, ample coverage is certain. Once promising challengers have attained wide recognition as front-runners, newspeople compete for their attention as well. These candidates' power to grant or withhold attention can be translated into influence over the quality and quantity of coverage.

Media judge the newsworthiness of campaign stories by general news criteria. Therefore, they pay little attention to minor candidates and newcomers whose chances for success are small. Lack of coverage, in turn, makes it extremely difficult for unknowns to become well known and increase their chances of winning elections. This is one of many examples of unintentional media bias that redounds to the benefit of established politicians.

MEDIA CONTENT

What kinds of newspaper and television coverage have recent elections received? Did the media sufficiently cover the issues likely to require the new president's attention? Did they supply adequate criteria to enable voters to decide which policy options would best suit their priorities and which candidate would be most likely to govern successfully? Following some general comments about the media mix, we will address these questions and assess the adequacy of the information supply for making sound voting choices.

Although the link between the media and election outcomes has been studied more thoroughly than other links between media and politics, many unanswered questions remain because the dynamics of the process are always in flux. Moreover, the evidence suggests that the media's role varies substantially, depending on the influence of such factors as incumbency, the candidates' personalities and histories, and major national crises such as wars or economic tsunamis. Obviously, the effects and effectiveness of the media will vary depending on the changing political scene, the type of coverage chosen by newspeople, and the fluctuating interests of voters.[15]

Unscrambling the Message Omelet

When Humpty-Dumpty, the egg, fell off the wall in the nursery rhyme, all the king's horses and all the king's men couldn't put him together again. The many components of the media message omelet have had a similar fate. Campaign commercials, for instance, have become a major ingredient of contemporary campaigns and often give them a distinctive flavor. But it is well-nigh impossible to isolate their contribution because all of the ingredients—print and electronic news stories, editorials, talk-show banter and punditry, Internet messages, advertisements, even political jokes and skits on entertainment shows—mix inextricably with one another and become transformed in the process. Ads generate and influence news stories and news stories induce and influence ads, which in turn lead to other ads and news stories and editorials. And so it goes, on and on.

That is why I discuss campaign information as a whole, usually without isolating the unique contributions of different media. Distinctions exist, of course. Studies show, for example, that cable television and brief video formats are superior to newspapers for conveying particular messages, and that the content of advertising messages is often discounted because they are regarded as self-serving propaganda, even though they provide more information about policy issues than most campaign news stories. A shortage of good data has prevented researchers from intensive analysis of the role that commercials play when they are carried by venues other than television. Therefore, we know all too little about the impact of messages displayed on bumper stickers or billboards, printed in newspaper advertisements, or disseminated through video. Unfortunately the relevant research findings, in the archives of commercial advertising firms, are usually beyond the reach of outsiders.

For the many candidates the media ignore, television commercials and candidate Web sites often provide the only chance to gain attention.[16] That includes the vast majority of also-rans for national office, who seem unelectable to the major media, as well as most candidates competing for local and even state offices. Locally, the impact of commercials and Web sites can be decisive. Indeed, wisely spent advertising funds can buy elections, even for congressional candidates who receive news story coverage.[17] To quote political scientist Michael Robinson, commercials for congressional candidates "can work relative wonders," especially when they are not challenged by the other side. "A well-crafted, heavily financed, and uncontested ad campaign does influence congressional elections."[18] This fact raises the chilling specter that wealthy candidates may be able to buy major public offices by investing their fortunes in expensive advertising campaigns. That fear escalated with the entry of such multimillionaires as Ross Perot and Steve Forbes into the presidential sweepstakes. Perot bought large blocks of television time for infomercials—data-packed commercials—in the

1992 presidential campaign. Forbes used personal funds to finance an expensive advertising blitz in the 1996 Republican primaries. Speculations that New York's billionaire mayor, Michael Bloomberg, might run for president in 2008 raised fears that money might be the trump card for winning the presidency. Since neither Perot nor Forbes became president, it is obvious that superior funding does not guarantee victory.

Patterns of Coverage

Any evaluation of how the media perform their tasks must also take into consideration the commercial pressures that journalists face. It is extremely difficult to mesh the public's preference for simple, dramatic stories with the need to present ample information for issue-based election choices. Information that may be crucial for voting decisions often is too complex and technical to appeal to much of the audience. Hence newspeople feel compelled to write breezy infotainment stories that stress the horse race and skim over policy details.

Prominence of Election Stories. In a typical presidential election year, election stories constitute roughly 13 percent of all newspaper political coverage and 15 percent of television political news. That puts these stories on a par with foreign affairs news or coverage of crime. Election news receives average attention in terms of headline size, front-page or first-story placement, and inclusion of pictures, but stories are slightly longer than average. Although election stories are quite prominent when primaries, conventions, and significant debates are held, they do not dominate the news. Normally it is quite possible to read the daily paper without noticing election news and to come away from a telecast with the impression that election stories are just a minor part of the day's political developments. But, given the prominence of race and gender issues in the 2008 contest, along with an unpopular president, an unpopular war, and an economic collapse, coverage patterns were decidedly abnormal. Overall, election news, which filled 11 percent of the news hole in 2007, jumped to 36 percent in 2008. Another 15 percent of the 2008 news hole went to economic failures, casting a pall over the incumbent party's competence to continue at the helm.

Uniformity of Coverage Patterns. Patterns of presidential election coverage are remarkably uniform, regardless of a venue's partisan orientation. The major difference generally is the breadth of coverage, measured by the number and length of stories, and the favorable ratings of candidates and issues.[19] Figure 8-1 illustrates the coverage variations among media sectors. Percentages do not reflect absolute coverage, of course, given the different formats of these venues. Compared to newspaper coverage, the usual one- or two-minute television story gives little chance for in-depth reporting and analysis. To conserve limited time, television newscasters create stereotypes of the candidates early in the campaign and then build their stories around these stereotypes by merely adding new details to the established image. Once established, stereotypes stubbornly resist change. There is a feeling that leopards never change their spots.

FIGURE 8-1 Focus on Elections in Media Sectors (percentage of news hole)

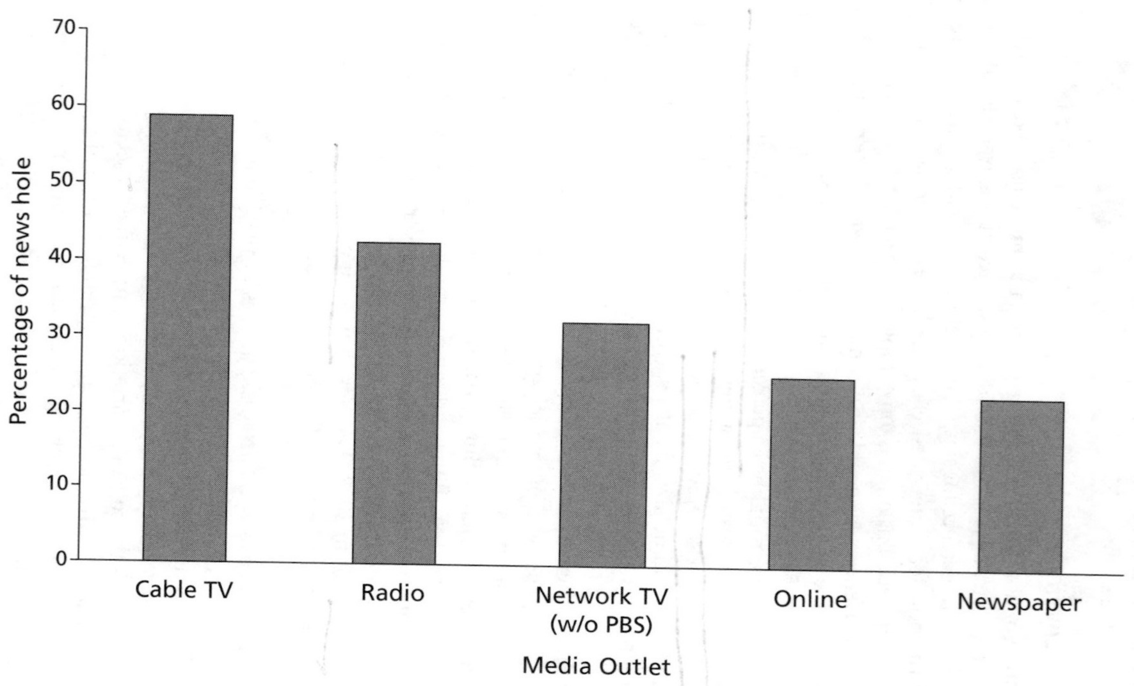

Source: Project for Excellence in Journalism, www.stateofthenewsmedia.com/2009/chartland.

Content analysis studies during congressional, state, and local campaigns show similar patterns. The political portraits that various media paint of each candidate match well in basic outline and in most details. But the time and space allotted to various aspects and the tone of evaluations can vary significantly. Generally, election news patterns are quite stable in successive elections, and all venues cover the major happenings. Thus Americans receive similar types of information on which to base their political decisions. Similarity in coverage of election campaigns has benefits as well as drawbacks. The large degree of homogeneity introduced into the electoral process is an advantage in a heterogeneous country such as the United States, where it can be difficult to develop political consensus. But it also means uniform neglect of many topics and criteria for judging candidates. Shared ignorance mars shared knowledge. A uniform information base obviously has not produced uniform political views throughout the country. Differences in political evaluations must be attributed to varying framing and interpretations of the same facts and to the different outlooks that audiences bring to the news. As the previous chapter pointed out, the impact of news usually is perceiver determined rather than stimulus determined.

Of the factors that encourage uniform coverage, journalists' professional socialization appears to be the most important. Newspeople share a sense of what is newsworthy and how it should be presented. Reporters cover identical beats in fashions that have become routine for election coverage. That means keeping score about who is winning and losing and reporting dramatic incidents and juicy personal gossip. It means avoiding dull facts as much as possible without totally ignoring essential, albeit unglamorous, information.

In the past, coverage has not followed the campaign model of reporting. In that model—the utopia of campaign managers—the rhythm of the campaign, as produced by the candidates and their staffs, determines what media cover. Reporters dutifully take their cues from the candidates. Instead, press coverage has largely conformed to an incentive model. Whenever exciting stories provided an incentive for coverage, the media published them, in a rhythm dictated by their needs and the tastes of their audiences. The needs and tastes of the candidates were ignored unless they managed to generate the kinds of stories and pictures that journalists find irresistible. The 2008 election was a mixture of both models. It is likely to be the prototype for future elections.

Substance of Coverage: Candidate Qualifications. The candidate qualifications that media highlight fall into two broad groups: those that are generally important in judging a person's character and those specifically related to the tasks of the office. Included in the first group are personality traits (integrity, reliability, compassion), style characteristics (forthrightness, folksiness), and image characteristics (confidence, levelheadedness). Professional qualifications at the presidential level include the capacity to develop and execute effective foreign and domestic policies, the ability to mobilize public support, and a flair for administration. The candidate's political philosophy is also a professional criterion. Presidential candidates over the years have most frequently been assessed in terms of their trustworthiness, strength of character, leadership capabilities, and compassion. Media have covered professional capacities—the very qualities that deserve the fullest discussion and analysis—only scantily and often vaguely even when an incumbent is running.[20]

The handful of professional qualifications that news stories mention from time to time include general appraisals of the capacity to handle foreign affairs, which has been deemed crucial in a global society, and the capacity to sustain an acceptable quality of life for all citizens by maintaining the economy on an even keel and by controlling crime and internal disorder. The same types of qualities reappear from election to election, but not necessarily in every candidate's profile. Disparate coverage then makes it very difficult for the electorate to compare and evaluate the candidates on important dimensions. Effective comparisons are also hindered by contradictions in remarks reported about the candidates. Bound by current codes of objective reporting and neutrality in electoral contests, the media rarely give guidance to the audience for judging conflicting claims. The exception is the trend toward "fact-checking," which involves analyzing candidates' claims and reporting the extent to which they are true or false.[21]

Verbal news commentary about the political candidates tends to be negative, so that voters' choices have seemed dismal in recent elections. The high praise that Barack Obama earned throughout his campaign was a notable exception. Overall, only 27 percent of the comments about him were negative. By contrast, McCain's negative score was 57 percent.[22] The typical downbeat mood of election coverage is epitomized by the lead paragraph in a *Time* magazine story at the end of the 1980 race between Reagan and Carter: "For more than a year, two flawed candidates have been floundering toward the final showdown, each unable to give any but his most unquestioning supporters much reason to vote for him except dislike of his opponent."[23] The negative characterizations, which have marred most presidential elections, are hardly fair to capable candidates, who often possess great personal strengths and skills that should be praised rather than debased.

Substance of Coverage: Issues and Events. Journalists' overriding consideration in reporting about particular issues, as in all political coverage, is newsworthiness rather than intrinsic importance. That is why happenings on the campaign trail, however trivial, receive extended coverage. Rather than exploring policy issues in depth, news stories emphasize rapidly paced, freshly breaking events. In fact, the amount of coverage for particular issues often seems to be in inverse proportion to their significance. For instance, during the 1992 primaries, one of every six campaign stories on the television networks referred to Governor Bill Clinton's personal life. Sexual foibles, reputed drug use during college days, slips of the tongue, and bad jokes all made headlines and were repeated endlessly on various entertainment programs. In the 2000 campaign, a story about George W. Bush's arrest on drunk-driving charges twenty-four years earlier received more coverage during the last three days of the campaign than all foreign policy issues had received after Labor Day.[24] When Hillary Clinton choked up a tiny bit in responding to questions during the New Hampshire primary campaign, it became a major media focus, as did an out-of-wedlock pregnancy in candidate Sarah Palin's family in 2008.

Three features stand out in coverage of issues and events: First and most significant, the media devote a large amount of attention to "horse race" aspects of campaigns. Figure 8-2, which shows the ten most-covered story topics, illustrates that point. In 2008 the Project for Excellence in Journalism examined nearly 25,000 campaign stories and found that 71 percent dealt with horse race issues.[25] That category encompasses stories about campaign strategies, polls, fund raising, and advertising. Only 13 percent of the coverage focused on policies. Seven percent covered candidate biographies, and 3 percent discussed the candidates' political records. The remaining 8 percent covered miscellaneous other matters. The horse race bias appears to be growing; these kinds of stories made up 55 percent of coverage in the 2004 election. The explosion of public opinion polling since 2004 accounts for much of the increase. Polls are welcome grist for the 24/7, cable news mill and for political Web sites, which need a constant stream of newly minted stories.

All this enlarges a particular media syndrome that might be best described as the "media echo effect." The expansion of polls and the media's fascination with seeing the race through their strategic lens create a repeating and reinforcing pattern in which the media reinforce and magnify the phenomena they observe. The press covers what the candidate does that day. The polls measure the political impact of that behavior. The media then analyze whether the latest campaign performance is helping in the polls. And that in turn influences the candidate's behavior. And winning in the polls begets winning coverage.[26]

Second, information about issues is patchy because the candidates and their surrogates try to concentrate on issues that help their campaigns and to avoid issues likely to alienate any portion of the huge and disparate electorate from which all are seeking support. Third, there is more issue coverage, albeit unsystematic, than scholars have acknowledged in the past. Audiences often overlook commentary about issues because it is embedded in many horse race stories and discussions of candidates' qualifications. For example, the claim that a candidate is compassionate may be linked to his or her concern about health care laws. When the design of content analyses focuses narrowly on recording only one issue per news story, multifaceted stories are forced into a single category and important facets become obscured.

In recent elections, some twenty-five issues, such as taxes, social security, or education, have usually surfaced intermittently in the press; for television the number hovers around twenty. Typically only half of these receive extensive and intensive attention. Many important policy questions likely to arise during a forthcoming presidential term are totally ignored. Although candidates like to talk about broad policy issues, such as war and peace or the health of the economy, newspeople prefer to concentrate on narrower, specific policy positions on which the candidates disagree.

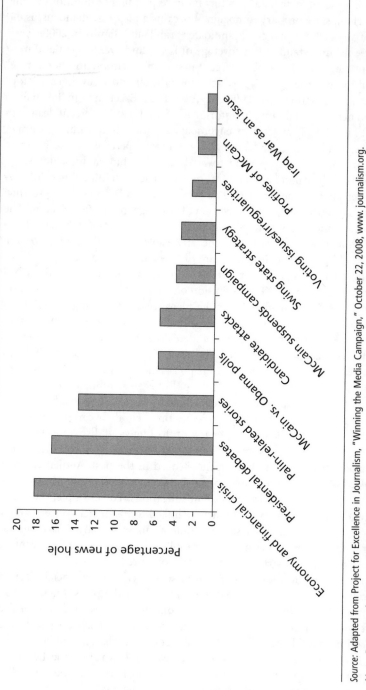

FIGURE 8-2 Top Ten Campaign Storylines, 2008 (percentage of news hole)

Source: Adapted from Project for Excellence in Journalism, "Winning the Media Campaign," October 22, 2008, www.journalism.org.

Note: Data come from 2,412 campaign stories from 48 news outlets, during six critical weeks of the general election phase, from the end of the conventions through the final presidential debate. That includes the three presidential debates on September 26, October 7, and October 15, as well as the vice presidential debate on October 2.

As is the case for coverage of presidential qualifications, issues discussed in connection with individual candidates vary. Voters thus receive little aid from the media in appraising and comparing the candidates on the issues. Compared with print media, television news usually displays more uniform patterns of issue coverage for all the candidates and involves a more limited range of issues. Television stories are briefer, touch on fewer aspects of each issue, and contribute to the stereotypic images developed for particular candidates. Events are often fragmented and barren of context, but what is left is dramatized to appeal to the audience. No wonder most people turn to television for news about the candidates and their campaigns.

We should assess media coverage not only in terms of the numbers of stories devoted to various topics but also in terms of political impact. There are times when election politics is particularly volatile and a few stories may carry extraordinary weight. Rapid diffusion of these stories throughout the major media enhances their impact. Michael Robinson calls such featured events *medialities*—"events, developments, or situations to which the media have given importance by emphasizing, expanding, or featuring them in such a way that their real significance has been modified, distorted, or obscured."[27] Medialities usually involve policy scandals, economic disasters, and personal foibles. Such key stories can have a far more profound impact on the campaign than thousands of routine stories and should be appraised accordingly. Examples during the 2008 election include the echo chamber coverage of Katie Couric's interview with Sarah Palin, the condemnation of the United States by Barack Obama's pastor, and John McCain's appraisal early in the campaign that the U.S. economy was basically sound.

Political and Structural Bias. Does election coverage give a fair and equal chance for all viewpoints to be expressed, so that media audiences can make informed decisions? Are the perennial charges of bias that disappointed candidates level evidence that newspeople always show favoritism? Or are they merely reactions to coverage that did not advance those candidates' causes? In general, journalists try to balance coverage for all major candidates for the same office. They aim for rough parity in the number of stories about each candidate and in the balance of favorable and unfavorable stories.

Nonetheless, imbalanced coverage occurs frequently. In the 2008 election, for example, coverage of Republicans was predominantly negative, while the reverse was true for Democrats. That raises the question whether political or structural bias is involved. Political bias reflects ideological judgments, whereas structural bias reflects the circumstances of news production. Balanced reporting may be impossible when candidates' newsworthiness and willingness to talk to reporters vary or when their campaigns are linked to different issues. Structural bias, even though it lacks partisan motivation, nonetheless may profoundly affect people's perceptions about campaigns.[28]

Editorials, of course, are intrinsically biased because their primary purpose is to express opinions. As part of the editorial function, many news media endorse candidates. That has little impact at the presidential level but does seem to matter for lower-level offices, particularly in elections in which voters have little information for making their own decisions.[29] Influential papers, such as the *Los Angeles Times,* the *Washington Post,* and the small but influential Manchester, New Hampshire, *Union Leader,* can be extraordinarily successful in promoting the election of candidates they have endorsed and in defeating unacceptable contenders. At the presidential level news coverage tends to be essentially evenhanded, regardless of the candidate endorsed. Below the presidential level, the media tend to give more coverage to their endorsed candidates than to those they have not endorsed.

The effort to keep coverage balanced does not extend to third-party candidates. Anyone who runs for president who is not a Republican or Democrat is out of the mainstream of newsworthiness and is slighted or ignored by the news profession. Especially newsworthy third-party candidates, such as Robert La Follette of the Progressive Party in 1924, George Wallace of the American Independent Party in 1968, John Anderson of the National Unity Campaign in 1980, independent Ross Perot in 1992, and the Green Party's Ralph Nader in 2000, were notable exceptions. Newsworthiness considerations also account for the sparse coverage of vice presidential candidates despite the importance of the office and the possibility that the vice president may have to replace a deceased incumbent. A total of 95 percent of the coverage in a typical presidential election goes to the presidential contenders and only 5 percent to their running mates. Again, the 2008 presidential contest was atypical in that respect.

Adequacy of Coverage

How adequate is current election coverage? Do the media help voters to make decisions according to commonly accepted democratic criteria? As discussed, the media do not make comparative appraisals of candidates and issues easy for voters. In presidential contests information is ample about the major, mainstream candidates and about day-to-day campaign events. It is sketchy and often confusing about the candidates' professional qualifications and about many important policy issues. Most primary contenders, candidates of minor parties, and vice presidential candidates are largely ignored. This is not surprising because the field of candidates usually is quite large, with several hundred individuals registering as formal candidates for the presidency. The prevalence of negative information about the candidates makes it seem that all of them are mediocre or even poor choices. This negative cast can be a major factor in many voters' decisions to stay home on election day. It also undermines the ability of newly elected officials to command support after the election, especially from members of the opposing party.

Nonetheless, voters give election news a passing grade, as Figure 8-3 shows. On average, there are slightly more D and F grades than A and B grades. Usually more voters think that Republican candidates, more than Democrats, are treated unfairly. That feeling grew sharply in 2008, when 44 percent of all voters charged unfair treatment of McCain, compared to 30 percent who believed that Obama had been treated unfairly. Nearly half

(46 percent) of the voters also told pollsters that the media had too much influence on the campaign.[30] In the 1996, 2000, and 2004 presidential campaigns, at least three out of four voters felt adequately informed. Many scholars and pundits would disagree with the good grades given for election news because citizens do not match the high standards of civic knowledge that democratic theory prescribes. The most serious deficiency in the news supply is inadequate analysis of policy issues, so that voters do not learn about the key points at stake, the scope and nature of various trade-offs, and the impact of their vote on the resolution of major political problems. The patterns of coverage force voters to make choices based more on the candidates' campaigning skills than on their governing skills and policy preferences. These are valid criticisms if one accepts the premise that policy issues, rather than leadership characteristics, should drive voting choices.

If the public's chief role is to choose a good leader, along with a general sense of the directions this leader will take, then judgments about the adequacy of the information supply become far more positive. The proliferation of news venues that has occurred in the Internet age allows average people easy access to a vast variety of information at diverse levels of depth and sophistication. Links on Internet election sites are an especially rich source for facts and interpretations that facilitate in-depth analyses, whenever voters feel the need—which they rarely do.[31]

The mainstream media do fall short when it comes to supplying the needs of political elites in ready fashion. Opinion leaders would benefit from more complete coverage of the candidates' stands on major and minor issues, more point-by-point comparisons of candidates and policies, and more ample evaluations of the political significance of differences in candidates and their programs. Stories covering important topics that candidates neglect would be useful, as would more coverage of third-party candidates and vice presidential contenders. In the end, though, no news consumer need hunger for information in the Internet age. With a little effort, a global cornucopia of facts and opinions is readily available to anyone with access to a computer and the Internet.

In presidential contests the deficiencies of media coverage are most noticeable during the primaries, when large slates of same-party candidates are competing in each. The media meet this challenge by giving uniformly skimpy treatment to all candidates except those designated as front-runners. It is not uncommon for two or three front-runners to attract 75 percent or more of the coverage, leaving a pack of trailing contenders with hardly any attention at all. As political scientist Thomas Patterson has noted, "Issue material is but a rivulet in the news flow during the primaries, and what is there is almost completely diluted by information about the race."[32] Whereas the quality of coverage during the primaries may be thin, the quantity is substantial, although it is unequally distributed so that the races in well-covered states become disproportionately influential. By the middle of the primary season, interest in these contests dwindles. Coverage shrivels. It perks up slightly during the conventions and when the final campaign starts following the Labor Day holiday in September.

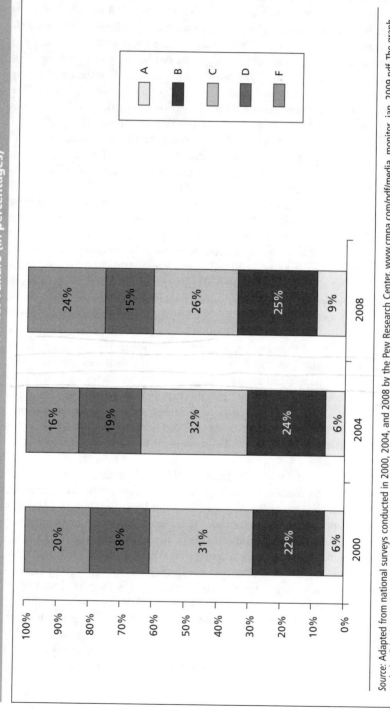

FIGURE 8-3 Grading Election News from A for Excellence to F for Failure (in percentages)

Legend:
A
B
C
D
F

2008
24%
15%
26%
25%
9%

2004
16%
19%
32%
24%
6%

2000
20%
18%
31%
22%
6%

Source: Adapted from national surveys conducted in 2000, 2004, and 2008 by the Pew Research Center, www.cmpa.com/pdf/media_monitor_jan_2009.pdf. The graph excludes "don't know" responses.

WHAT PEOPLE LEARN FROM CAMPAIGN COVERAGE

What do people learn from campaign coverage? The answer varies, of course, depending on their interest in the campaign, prior political knowledge, desire for certain information, and political sophistication. Good published research remains sparse, especially when it comes to the effects of advertising. Nonetheless several general trends emerge from national surveys, such as those conducted biannually by the Survey Research Center at the University of Michigan, and from intensive interviews of smaller panels of voters.

Learning about Candidates and Issues

A serious obstacle to understanding media influence on elections is the dearth of analyses of media content. Only rarely have researchers examined the content of election news, including commercials, and the context of general news in which it is embedded. That makes it impossible to test what impact, if any, diverse messages have on viewers' perceptions. In general researchers have also failed to ascertain media exposure accurately. They frequently assume that people have been exposed to all election stories in a particular news source without checking precisely which stories have come to the attention of which individuals and what the individuals learned.

The foremost impression from interviews with voters is that they can recall very little specific campaign information. That does not necessarily mean that they have not learned anything. As discussed in chapter 7, when people are confronted with factual information, such as news about a particular presidential candidate, they assess how it fits into their established view of that candidate. If it is consonant, the information strengthens that view and the person's feelings about the candidate. If it is dissonant, the person is likely to reject it outright or note it as a reasonable exception to their established schema. The least likely result is a major revision of their established beliefs about the candidate. Once people have processed the news they forget most of the details and store only their summary impression in memory. That approach is called "on-line processing." When people are later quizzed about details, they are likely to recall only what was frequently repeated in recent news stories. On-line processing thus creates the false impression that the average person has formed opinions about the candidate without having learned the appropriate facts.[33]

The issues that people typically mention as important during the campaign season generally do not match up with media emphases. Table 8-2 shows the top issues that attracted attention during the campaign and the percentage of the news hole devoted to them during the week when interest was measured. People commonly express much more concern about economic and social issues than do the media. This is not surprising because these issues affect people personally. Ordinarily people put much less emphasis on the campaign hoopla that is covered so plentifully by the media. Audiences find these fleeting events entertaining but make little effort to remember them.

TABLE 8-2 **The Public's Interest in News versus Extent of News Coverage**

Issue	% Highly interested	% of News hole
Conditions of U.S. economy	70	40
Rising price of gasoline	66	4
Debate over Wall Street bailout	62	45
2008 presidential election	61	51
Major drop in U.S. stock market	59	36
Falling price of gasoline	53	1
Hurricane Ike	50	14
Wall Street financial crisis	49	37
Obama transition	49	23
2008 primary election	44	40

Source: Project for Excellence in Journalism, "The State of the News Media, 2009," www.stateofthe-media.org/2009/narrative_yearinthenews_intro.php?media=2#1newsinterest.

Note: Highly interested respondents said they followed the story "very closely." News hole share for the topic was measured to match survey dates.

Voting Behavior

Do media-intensive campaigns change votes? The answer to this perennial question, so dear to the hearts of campaign managers, public relations experts, and social scientists, hinges on the interaction between audiences and messages. Crucial variables include the voters' receptivity to a message urging change, the potency of the message, the appropriateness of its form, and the setting in which it occurs. For most voters, the crucial attitudes that determine voting choices are already firmly in place at the start of the campaign, so that their final vote is a forgone conclusion. Vote changes are most likely when voters pay fairly close attention to the media and are ambivalent in their attitudes toward the candidates. Campaign messages are most potent if they concern a major and unpredicted event, such as a successful or disastrous foreign policy venture or corruption in high places, and when individuals find themselves in social settings where a change of attitude will not constitute deviant behavior. This combination of circumstances is fairly rare, which explains why changes of voting intention are comparatively uncommon. Fears that televised campaigns can easily sway voters and amount to "electronic ballot box stuffing" are therefore unrealistic.

However, even small numbers of media-induced vote changes might be important. Tiny percentages of votes, often less than 1 percent, decide many elections at all levels. That was demonstrated dramatically in the 2000 election, which was ultimately decided by fewer than a thousand votes. The media may also skew election outcomes when they can stimulate or depress voter turnout; a difference in turnout is more likely to occur than changes in voting choices. Do broadcasts that predict election results before voting has ended affect turnout? The answer remains moot despite several investigations of the problem. Current evidence indicates that the effects, if they do occur, have rarely changed election outcomes.[34]

Attempts to stop the media from projecting winners and losers while voting is still in progress have run afoul of First Amendment free speech guarantees. This may explain why the laws passed in more than half of the states to restrain exit polling are seldom enforced.[35] Congress has tried since 1986 to pass a Uniform Poll Closing Act. Although the measure has thus far failed to pass, prospects for ultimate success are good, especially after the presidential election of 2000, in which the issue of broadcasting election results while polling places remained open in parts of the United States became a huge political controversy. A smaller dispute arose in 2004 when media published exit polls that wrongly suggested a Kerry victory before the polls had closed. The concern about the impact of exit polls and early forecasts may be overdrawn. Voters are bombarded throughout the election year with information likely to determine their vote and turnout. Why should the media be squeamish on the campaign payoff day?

The most important influence of the media on the voter does not lie in changing votes once predispositions have been formed, but in shaping and reinforcing predispositions and influencing the initial selection of candidates. When newspeople sketched out the Clinton image and held him up as a potential winner during the 1992 primaries, ignoring most of his rivals, they morphed the obscure governor of a small southern state into a viable candidate. Millions of voters would never have cast their ballot for the unknown Arkansas politician had not the media thrust him into the limelight as a likely winner.

By focusing the voters' attention on selected individuals, their characteristics, and issue stands, the media also determine to a large extent the issues by which the public will gauge the competence of the candidates. Very early in the campaign, often long before formal campaigning starts, media interpretations of the significance of issues can shape the political and emotional context of the election. As Leon Sigal noted many years ago, the media "play less of an independent part in creating issues, sketching imagery, and coloring perceptions of the candidates than in getting attention for their candidacies. Newsmen do not write the score or play an instrument; they amplify the sounds of the music makers."[36]

A final, potentially crucial impact on election outcomes is the role that the media play in turnout, especially in close elections. The negative tone of news coverage obviously plays a part. So do personalized appeals to voters. E-mails by the millions sent by personal friends and celebrities, often stimulated by Web site appeals, may well be the most potent electioneering weapon of the twenty-first century.

Shoppers at the Mall of America in Bloomington, Minnesota, join millions of people worldwide to watch President Barack Obama's inauguration, January 20, 2009.

Source: AP Photo/Jim Mone

SUMMARY

The media's role, especially that of television, in recent campaigns has been powerful and pervasive. Campaigns have become battles for spreading favorable and unfavorable messages about candidates and issues through traditional and new media venues. The main quest is for a place in the limelight and a "winner" image. Candidates expect that public recognition and support—or opposition—are likely to follow, particularly at the presidential level.

In this chapter we have scrutinized newspaper, television, and Internet election coverage, considering general coverage patterns, the substance and slant of coverage, and the manner of presentation. The evidence shows that the media have placed heavy emphasis on the candidates' personal qualifications for office and on the ups and downs of the race. They often mention policy issues but rarely explore them in depth. Mainstream media stories are chosen primarily for their newsworthiness; Internet messages are more likely to caricature the contrasts between candidates' qualifications and policies with one side as veritable angels and the other as Satan's disciples or dunces. Structural biases abound and have important political consequences, but outright political bias is uncommon.

Although the public claims, off and on, to be very interested in learning about the election, it absorbs only a small portion of the considerable amount of available information. Nonetheless, the bits of information that people absorb create sufficient political understanding to permit sound voting choices based primarily on whether the chosen candidate seems trustworthy and capable of leading the country. Although news stories rarely change people's minds, they can influence undecided voters. Along with media impact on turnout, shaping the views of even small numbers of voters can determine the outcome in close elections and change the course of political life.

Before television, conventional wisdom as well as research suggested that news media impact on elections was minimal because election stories persuaded few people to change their votes. Television and Internet-age research has cast the net much wider to include the media's effects on all phases of the election campaign, from the recruitment and nomination stages to the strategies that produce the final outcome. In addition to studying the media's impact on the final choice of voters, social scientists now look at political learning during campaigns and at the information base that supports voting decisions. Television news stories and massive numbers of highly sophisticated commercials have changed the election game, especially at the presidential level. The Internet has made retail politicking possible again and has personalized appeals to individual voters. Personalization is taking place on a scale that was unimaginable before the Internet. One thing is certain: candidates and media remain inextricably intertwined. Those who aspire to elective office must play the media game by rules that continue to evolve.

NOTES

1. G.R. Boynton, "Ghosts of Campaigns Past and Campaigns Yet to Come," *Political Communication Report,* Winter 2008, www.politicalcommunication.org/PCR/1803_2008_winter/roundtable_boynton.html.

2. Project for Excellence in Journalism, "The Invisible Primary—Invisible No Longer: A First Look at Coverage of the 2008 Presidential Campaign: The Competition for Exposure," October 29, 2007, www.journalism.org/node/8193.

3. Larry M. Bartels, "Expectations and Preferences in Presidential Nominating Campaigns," *American Political Science Review* 79 (September 1985): 804–815. The importance of the winner image is discussed in Henry E. Brady and Richard Johnston, "What's the Primary Message: Horse Race or Issue Journalism?" in *Media and Momentum: The New Hampshire Primary and Nomination Politics,* ed. Gary R. Orren and Nelson W. Polsby (Chatham, N.J.: Chatham House, 1987), 127–186.

4. "Campaign 2004—The Primaries," *Media Monitor* 18, no. 1 (March–April 2004): 3. The Project for Excellence in Journalism has released several in-depth studies of press coverage of the 2008 primaries. For example, see "Character and the Primaries of 2008," www.journalism.org/node11266.

5. For analysis of the impact of debates, see David J. Lanoue and Peter Schrott, *The Joint Press Conference: The History, Impact, and Prospects of American Presidential Debates* (Westport, Conn.: Greenwood, 1991). Also see Judith S. Trent and Robert V. Friedenberg, *Political Campaign Communication: Principles and Practices,* 6th ed. (Lanham, Md.: Rowman and Littlefield, 2008); and Sidney Kraus, *Televised Presidential Debates and Public Policy,* 2nd ed. (Mahwah, N.J.: Erlbaum, 2000). Full texts of presidential debates can be found on the Web site of the Commission on Presidential Debates, www.debates.org.

6. The importance of looking "presidential" on the campaign trail, especially during debates, is discussed in Maria Elizabeth Grabe and Erik Page Bucy, *Image Bite Politics: News and the Visual Framing of Elections* (New York: Oxford University Press, 2009). Also see Kiku Adato, *Picture Perfect: Life in the Age of the Photo Op* (Princeton: Princeton University Press, 2008).

7. Quoted in Edwin Diamond, *Sign-off: The Last Days of Television* (Cambridge, Mass.: MIT Press, 1982), 175.

8. Martin Schram, *The Great American Video Game: Presidential Politics in the Television Age* (New York: Morrow, 1987), 26.

9. Clarence Page, "How 'The Hug' Helped," *Chicago Tribune*, December 8, 2004.

10. Katharine Q. Seelye, "About $2.6 Billion Spent on Political Ads in 2008," *New York Times*, December 2, 2008, http://thecaucus.blogs.nytimes.com.

11. "Campaign 2004 Final," *Media Monitor* 18 no. 6 (November–December 2004): 9; Leigh Holmwood, "Sarah Palin Helps Saturday Night Live to Best Ratings in 14 Years," www.guardian.co.uk/media/2008/oct/20/ustelevision-tvratings.

12. Greg Mitchell, *Why Obama Won* (Sinclair Books, 2008) online, reports the role of the new media from the perspective of a blogger at the Huffington Post and the DailyKos.

13. The Federal Election Commission reports precise numbers about campaign fund raising; http://query.nictusa.com/cgi-bin/cancomsrs/?_08+00+PR. It records roughly $533 million for Barack Obama and $379 million for John McCain. That amounts to $7.39 for each Obama vote and $5.78 for each McCain vote.

14. "Campaign 1996—The Primaries," *Media Monitor* (March–April 1996): 2.

15. Extensive election data are archived at the Annenberg School for Communication in Philadelphia, the Shorenstein Center at Harvard University's Kennedy School, at the Brookings Institution, and at the Pew Internet and American Life Projects. In addition, the Cooperative Campaign Analysis Project (CCAP) undertook a six-wave panel study of the 2008 campaign, conducting more than 100,000 on-line interviews. It is part of the YouGov/Polimetrix cooperative studies. For one of the first major attempts to study the full campaign cycle, covering multiple phases of the 1992 presidential campaign, see Marion R. Just, Ann N. Crigler, Dean E. Alger, Timothy E. Cook, Montague Kern, and Darrell M. West, *Crosstalk: Citizens, Candidates, and the Media in a Presidential Campaign* (Chicago: University of Chicago Press, 1996).

16. W. Russell Neuman, Marion Just, and Ann Crigler, *Common Knowledge: News and the Construction of Political Meaning* (Chicago: University of Chicago Press, 1992), 39–59; Just and others, *Crosstalk*, 62–66; Darrell M. West, *Air Wars: Television Advertising in Election Campaigns, 1952–2008*, 5th ed. (Washington, D.C.: CQ Press, 2009).

17. Bruce E. Gronbeck, "Mythic Portraiture in the 1988 Iowa Presidential Caucus Bio-Ads," *American Behavioral Scientist* 33 (1989): 351–364; J. Gregory Payne, John Marlier, and Robert A. Baucus, "Polispots in the 1988 Presidential Primaries," *American Behavioral Scientist* 33 (1989): 365–381.

18. Michael J. Robinson, "The Media in 1980: Was the Message the Message?" in *The American Elections of 1980*, ed. Austin Ranney (Washington, D.C.: American Enterprise Institute, 1981), 186.

19. For comparisons of coverage in Boston, Los Angeles, Fargo–Moorhead, N.D., and Winston-Salem, N.C., see Just and others, *Crosstalk*, 92–96; also see Project for Excellence in Journalism, "The State of the News Media, 2009," www.stateofthemedia.org/2009/index.htm.

20. Doris A. Graber and David Weaver, "Presidential Performance Criteria: The Missing Element in Election Coverage," *Harvard International Journal of Press/Politics* 1 (Winter 1996): 7–32. A companion analysis of the 2000 election yielded similar findings.

21. Tom Rosenstiel and Bill Kovach, "Lessons of the Election," www.stateofthenewsmedia.org/2009/printable_special_chapter.htm.

22. Project for Excellence in Journalism, "State of the News Media, 2009," www.stateofthemedia.org/2009/narrative_cabletv_intro.php?cat=0&media=7.

23. Quoted in Anthony King, "How Not to Select Presidential Candidates: A View from Europe," in Ranney, *The American Elections of 1980*, 305.

24. S. Robert Lichter, "A Plague on Both Parties: Substance and Fairness in TV Election News," *Press/Politics* 6, no. 3 (2001): 12.

25. Rosenstiel and Kovach, "Lessons of the Election."

26. Ibid., 12.

27. Robinson, "The Media in 1980," 191.

28. For an interesting discussion of the special concerns involved in covering African American candidates, see Jannette Lake Dates and Oscar H. Gandy Jr., "How Ideological Constraints Affected Coverage of the Jesse Jackson Campaign," *Journalism Quarterly* 62 (Autumn 1985): 595–600.

29. Byron St. Dizier, "The Effect of Newspaper Endorsements and Party Identification on Voting Choice," *Journalism Quarterly* 62 (Autumn 1985): 589–594.

30. Project for Excellence in Journalism, "The State of the News Media, 2009," www.stateofthemedia. org/2009/index.htm.

31. For a more detailed discussion of the quality of the information supply and its adequacy for informing voters, see Doris Graber, "The Media and Democracy: Beyond Myths and Stereotypes," *Annual Review of Political Science* 6 (2003): 139–160; and Doris Graber, "Mediated Politics and Citizenship in the Twenty-First Century," *Annual Review of Psychology* 55 (2004): 545–571.

32. Thomas Patterson, *The Mass Media Election: How Americans Choose Their President,* 3rd ed. (New York: Praeger, 1988), 250; also see Eric R.A.N. Smith, *The Unchanging American Voter* (Berkeley: University of California Press, 1989).

33. Doris A. Graber, *Processing the News: How People Tame the Information Tide,* 2nd ed. (New York: Longman, 1988); Milton Lodge and Patrick Stroh, "Inside the Mental Voting Booth: An Impression-Driven Process Model of Candidate Evaluation," in *Explorations in Political Psychology,* ed. Shanto Iyengar and William J. McGuire (Durham: Duke University Press, 1993).

34. For a wealth of detailed analyses of various aspects of the 2008 presidential election, especially outcome forecasts and the role played by gender and race, see *PS: Political Science and Politics* 41, no. 4: 679–802; also see Paul Wilson, "Election Night 1980 and the Controversy over Early Projections," in *Television Coverage of the 1980 Presidential Campaign,* ed. William C. Adams (Norwood, N.J.: Ablex, 1983), 152–153; Percy H. Tannenbaum and Leslie J. Kostrich, *Turned-on TV/Turned-off Voters: Policy Options for Election Projections* (Beverly Hills, Calif.: Sage, 1983); and Paul J. Lavrakas and Jack K. Holley, eds., *Polls and Presidential Election Campaign News Coverage: 1988* (Evanston: Northwestern University Press, 1988).

35. For a discussion of how state laws have fared in the courts, see Stephen Bates, "Lawful Exits: The Court Considers Election Day Polls," *Public Opinion* 8 (Summer 1986): 53–54.

36. Leon V. Sigal, "Newsmen and Campaigners: Organization Men Make the News," *Political Science Quarterly* 93 (Fall 1978): 465–470; also see D. Sunshine Hillygus and Todd G, Shields, *The Persuadable Voter: Wedge Issues in Presidential Campaigns,* Princeton: Princeton University Press, 2008.

READINGS

Adato, Kiku. *Picture Perfect: Life in the Age of the Photo Op.* Princeton: Princeton University Press, 2008.

Ceaser, James W. *Red over Blue: The 2004 Elections and American Politics.* Lanham, Md.: Rowman and Littlefield, 2005.

Davis, Richard. *Typing Politics: The Role of Blogs in American Politics.* New York: Oxford University Press, 2009.

Farnsworth, Stephen J., and S. Robert Lichter. *The Nightly News Nightmare: Network Television's Coverage of U.S. Presidential Elections, 1988–2004.* 2nd ed. Lanham, Md.: Rowman and Littlefield, 2007.

Hart, Roderick P. *Campaign Talk: Why Elections Are Good for Us.* Princeton: Princeton University Press, 2000.

Hollihan, Thomas A. *Uncivil Wars: Political Campaigns in a Media Age.* 2nd ed. Boston: Bedford/St. Martin's, 2009.

Just, Marion R., Ann N. Crigler, Dean E. Alger, Timothy E. Cook, Montague Kern, and Darrell M. West. *Crosstalk: Citizens, Candidates, and the Media in a Presidential Campaign.* Chicago: University of Chicago Press, 1996.

Stromback, Jesper, and Lynda Lee Kaid, eds. *The Handbook of Election News Coverage around the World.* New York: Routledge, 2008.

West, Darrell M. *Air Wars: Television Advertising in Election Campaigns, 1952–2004.* 5th ed. Washington, D.C.: CQ Press, 2009.

Winograd, Morley, and Michael D. Hais. *Millennial Makeover: MySpace, YouTube, and the Future of American Politics.* New Brunswick, N.J.: Rutgers University Press, 2008.

The Struggle for Control: News from the Presidency and Congress

"**B**oosting Obama" read a *Washington Post* headline, two months into President Barack Obama's presidency. That familiar pronouncement was followed by staff writer Howard Kurtz's report that "the networks have given President Obama more coverage than George W. Bush and Bill Clinton combined in their first months—and more positive assessments to boot." During the first fifty days of the Obama presidency, ABC, CBS, and NBC evening newscasts had spent half of their broadcast time discussing the new president. The most unusual thing about the coverage was its predominantly favorable tone. In the *New York Times* 73 percent of the assessments in front-page stories were positive. The *Times* had filled the equivalent of twenty-eight full pages of text documenting the president's activities. Fifty-eight percent of the Obama evaluations that the three networks aired also were positive. Comparable numbers for George W. Bush and Bill Clinton are 33 percent and 44 percent, respectively.

Normally the tone of coverage is heavily negative. That was largely true even for the evaluations of Obama's policy proposals, as distinguished from other aspects of coverage. Positive sound bites about Obama's policies amounted to 48 percent on ABC, but only 32 percent on CBS, 31 percent on NBC, and 8 percent on Fox. A bit of history will put these numbers into perspective. Personal attacks on presidents have been the rule more often than the exception since the birth of the nation. For example, the press smeared Andrew Jackson's reputation by calling his mother a prostitute; it routinely referred to President Rutherford B. Hayes as "his fraudulency" following a disputed election. Abraham Lincoln was called a horrid-looking wretch and a fourth-rate speaker who delivered hackneyed and illiterate speeches.[2]

When Katharine Graham was publisher of the *Washington Post*, she told her listeners during a speech that harsh appraisals were praiseworthy. The press must be independent, skeptical, and irreverent. Periods of truce between the press and presidents, in her opinion, were contrary to the spirit of the First Amendment, which ordains the press as the watchdog that alerts the public to government sins. The depression years, World War II, the Korean War, and the Cold War were exceptions to that hallowed tradition. Much of the Washington, D.C., press, in times of crisis, viewed itself as responsible adjuncts to the government's efforts to cope with the country's problems. There was criticism, of course, but it did not impugn the government's veracity and motivations, nor did it attack the substance of policies.

The tone of media evaluations of the president changed sharply after Vietnam and Watergate, which journalists saw as ventures based on false premises and involving government propaganda, lies, and cover-ups. From then on the press again became suspicious and adversarial, assuming flawed policies, bad motivations, and deceptive spinning of news most of the time, unless proven otherwise. Graham thought that there had been some softening over time as journalists became more sophisticated and realized the complexity of the contemporary political scene. But presidents Bill Clinton and George W. Bush would probably disagree with respect to the media coverage of their presidencies.[3]

Why do political leaders in democratic nations worldwide put so much energy into their media strategies when in the end the media may be their undoing? Why do they expose themselves to frequently hostile interrogations by journalists who routinely write stories attacking them and their policies? The answer is that politicians desperately need the media to achieve their goals. Conversely, journalists need politicians to get information for important stories. Because the two institutions have conflicting goals and missions and operate under different constraints, they cannot live comfortably with each other. Yet they dare not part company. Interdependence tempers their love-hate relationship.[4]

THE ADVERSARIAL RELATIONSHIP

To gain and retain public support and maintain power, executives and legislators strive to influence the information that media pass on to the public and to other officials. They seek to define situations and project images in their own way to further their objectives. Newspeople, however, have different goals. They want to monitor and appraise government performance, and they feel bound by the economics of the news business to present exciting stories that will attract large audiences in their markets. This often means prying into conflict, controversy, or ordinary wheeling and dealing—matters that government officials would like to keep quiet. Government wants its portrait taken from the most flattering angle; at the least it hopes to avoid an unflattering picture. The media, eager to find chinks in government's armor and to maximize audience size, prefer candid shots that show government at its worst.

In this chapter we will take a closer look at the interrelationship of the media and the executive and legislative branches of government at the national level, leaving the interface of the media and the court system and subnational levels of government for chapter 10. Casual as well as systematic observations readily establish that the media devote much attention to the affairs of national government, particularly the presidency. From April 2008 to March 2009 the early evening NBC news broadcasts ran an average of eighteen stories per month about some aspect of the presidency (Table 9-1). It was the most common story topic by far. The numbers for Congress and the Supreme Court were considerably lower, with a monthly average of seven congressional stories and

TABLE 9-1   **Evening News about the Three Branches of Government on NBC: April 2008–March 2009**

Month	President		Congress		Supreme Court	
	N	Time	N	Time	N	Time
2008						
April	23	0:46	5	0:18	2	0:04
May	10	0:29	4	0:09	3	0:07
June	11	0:30	2	0:50	3	0:08
July	21	0:50	10	0:26	1	0:03
August	15	0:50	1	0:30	1	0:02
September	19	1:31	7	0:46	0	0:00
October	17	1:09	6	0:23	8	0:23
November	15	0:42	14	0:32	1	0:01
December	20	0:52	25	1:07	4	0.07
2009						
January	36	1:28	7	0:19	0	0:00
February	15	0:38	4	0:13	0	0:00
March	12	0:31	3	0:11	0	0:00
Total	214	10:25	88	04:43	23	0:55
Monthly average	18	00:51	7	00:22	2	0:05

Source: Compiled by the author from the Vanderbilt Television News Archive.

Note: Time is listed in hours and minutes.

just two stories about the Court. The number of congressional stories would rise substantially if stories devoted to individual members were added. It is also important to keep the shifting news channel patterns in mind. In addition to coverage by legacy media, the president, Congress, and the Supreme Court are also pictured and dissected in the multiple news venues on the Internet. Most stories there are offshoots from mainstream channels and resemble their parents while adding fresh perspectives.

Changes in patterns of news coverage are quite common (Table 9-2). Emphasis on traditional political news wanes in times of relative political calm, only to rise again during crises like the Persian Gulf and Iraq wars or the 2001 terrorist attack on U.S. soil. Overall, the most consistent pattern depicted in Table 9-2 is a sharp decline in entertainment and weather news. The drop most likely reflects an adaptation to the abundance of such news on other channels. More significant trends include the increase of political news in newsmagazines, accompanied by a decrease in economic and social news, and the decline of political news in newspapers as the papers' resources shrink. Overall, the

TABLE 9-2 **Changing News Story Emphasis (in percentages)**

Media source	Traditional political 1997	2003	2008	Economic and social 1997	2003	2008	Entertainment and weather 1997	2003	2008
Network news	41	60	45	26	20	26	32	20	10
Newspapers	65	73	49	20	14	28	14	13	3
Newsmagazines	19	54	69	44	37	21	27	9	8

Source: Condensed from "The State of the News Media, 2004," and "The State of the News Media, 2008," www.stateofthenewsmedia.org; and Committee of Concerned Journalists, "Changing Definitions of News: Subject of News Stories by Medium," 1998, www.journalism.org.

Note: The "traditional political" category combines government, military, domestic affairs, foreign affairs, and for newsmagazines, "other." The "economic and social" category combines business/commerce, science, technology, arts, religion, personal health, and crime. The "entertainment and weather" category combines lifestyle, entertainment/celebrities, celebrity crime, sports, and weather/disaster. See the Web sites for coding details.

news holes of traditional media have shriveled at a time when Internet-based media are often struggling to fill their 24/7 news space.

The similarities between print and broadcast media in covering particular topics do not mean that stories project identical images. An example from the Reagan years is a case in point. When a local newspaper, an elite newspaper, and network television covered two items—a proposal by President Ronald Reagan to cut taxes and the president's 1984 trip to Europe—three different sets of images emerged from the stories.[5] The *Durham Morning Herald*, a local paper in North Carolina with limited resources for independent news analysis, presented accounts drawn largely from the wire services. The stories featured the themes, ideas, and perspectives provided by the White House and, as is typical for local media, cast the president and the events in a favorable light. The elite *New York Times* also reported the White House version of events but analyzed them critically. That created a much less rosy impression of the state of affairs. The *CBS Evening News* presented a more mixed picture. Verbal images were predominantly negative, but visual images, based as usual on controlled photo opportunities, were highly favorable. Audiences for these three news sources thus learned about the same events, but the tint of the interpretive lenses varied.

THE MEDIA AND THE EXECUTIVE BRANCH

The media perform four major functions for government executives.[6] First, they inform them about current events, including developments in other parts of the government. This information sets the scene for policy making. When the media highlight environmental hazards or growing home foreclosure sales, major or minor executive action often follows. Not infrequently, the media furnish daily news more quickly than bureaucratic channels. Stories about foreign affairs often reach presidents faster through the *New York Times,* on the Web, or on CNN than through State Department bulletins that first must be coded and then decoded.

Second, the media keep executive branch officials attuned to the public's major concerns. They do this directly by reporting on public opinion and indirectly by featuring the stories likely to shape public opinion. Public officials assume that newspeople keep in touch with popular concerns and report about them in their stories. Readers and viewers, in turn, take their cues about what is important from old and new media.

Third, the media enable executives to convey their messages to the general public as well as to political elites within and outside of government. Mushrooming news transmission channels, to which presidents have fairly ready access, provide unparalleled opportunities to explain administration policies. Political elites need these news transmission channels because there is no effective communication system that directly links government officials who are dispersed throughout the country. Political elites also use media channels to publicly attack opponents' positions.

Fourth, the media allow chief executives to remain in full public view on the political stage, keeping their human qualities and professional skills on almost constant display. Newspapers, television, radio, and the Internet supply a steady stream of commentary about a president's daily routines. Coverage of personal life may be extensive, even for the vice president. For instance, when Vice President Dick Cheney underwent minor heart surgery in 2001, extensive daily medical news briefings kept the public apprised of his progress. The media reported intimate details of the vice president's condition, including his energy level, his tolerance of medical procedures, and his daily diet. Beyond providing human-interest tidbits, such coverage reassures the public that it is fully informed about the disability and the patient's fitness to serve. Human-interest stories help to forge close personal ties between people and their leaders. They make it easier for them to trust leaders and therefore support their policies. But they may also diminish the stature of presidents by revealing their human flaws, which can seem even more pronounced when contrasted with the majesty of the office.

Media Impact

The political significance of the relationship between the media and the executive branch is much greater than the functions just described. Media coverage is the very lifeblood of politics because it shapes the perceptions that form the reality on which political action is based. Media do more than depict the political environment; they *are* the political environment. Because direct contact with political actors and situations is limited, media images define people and situations for nearly all participants in the political process. The richness of such images is rising thanks to new technologies.

As we saw in previous chapters, the age of live audiovisual politics that began in the 1950s has vastly enhanced the impact, and hence the power, of news media. In the past a story might have caused ripples on the political seas when thousands of people in one corner of the country read it in the paper or heard it on the radio. Today that same story can cause political tidal waves when millions worldwide see and hear it simultaneously on television and computer screens. Politicians feel compelled to react. They now can visit with millions of potential followers in their living rooms, creating the kinds of emotional ties that hitherto came only from personal contact. Electronic contacts may affect the political future of a member of Congress more than service on an important congressional committee.

Television tipped the political scales of power among the three branches of government in favor of the presidency, although increasing coverage of Congress and its members by local and Internet media combined has lessened the imbalance. Chapter 8 has already described how strongly the news media influence who becomes eligible for the presidency and how profoundly they affect the conduct and outcome of elections. After elections, the length, vigor, and effectiveness of a president's political life and the general level of support for the political system depend heavily on news media images. Making sure that the images are favorable therefore becomes a prime concern. Staffs of various presidents concur that "the national media play a very significant role in the White House decision-making process.... [I]n White House meetings, on the whole, more time is spent discussing the media than any other institution, including Congress.... [A]ll policies are developed and presented with media reaction in mind."[7]

The media frequently raise issues that presidents and other public officials would prefer to keep out of the limelight. Budget deficits, crumbling highways and bridges, and inefficient veterans' hospitals are just a few examples. Constant media prodding can keep damaging issues at the top of the public agenda. The list of major and minor scandals that the media have highlighted to the government's dismay is seemingly endless. The names of major scandals, like "Watergate" in the Nixon years and "Whitewater" during the Clinton era, are examples.

Media coverage can also increase public support for a president's policies and raise approval ratings. This is particularly important in national emergencies when backing by Congress and the public is vital. Following the 2001 terrorist attacks on the United States, President Bush's positive evaluations in the news jumped from 36 percent to 63 percent. Such steep gains may be short-lived because memories fade quickly. By 2002 Bush's positive media scores had slumped again to 38 percent. They rose to 56 percent during the initial stages of the Iraq War and plunged to 32 percent afterward.[8]

Sensational adverse publicity can kill the president's programs and abort new policies. For instance, welfare programs, such as financial aid for minority businesses or Head Start's prekindergarten training for underprivileged children, were sharply cut in the wake of news about inefficient management and corrupt handling of money in the programs. Media publicity can also be crucial in determining whether a presidential appointee will be confirmed by the

Senate. During the Clinton administration, negative publicity was instrumental in killing the nominations of Zoë Baird and Kimba Wood for attorney general. Media stories about unpaid taxes forced former Senate majority leader Tom Daschle to withdraw from consideration as secretary of Health and Human Services in the Obama administration, and fears of adverse publicity about a corruption scandal persuaded New Mexico's governor, Bill Richardson, to withdraw from an appointment as Secretary of Commerce. As television critic Tom Shales said about the failed Supreme Court nomination of Judge Robert Bork in 1987, "Television may not have cooked 'his goose' but it certainly did some gourmet basting."[9]

Direct and Mediated Transmission

News about the government reaches the public either directly or indirectly. Direct transmission allows government officials to convey their messages with a minimum of media shaping. President Harry S. Truman was the first to use the direct mode by broadcasting his entire State of the Union message in 1947 to a nationwide audience. In January 1961 President John F. Kennedy further expanded direct coverage by allowing news conferences to be broadcast live. Among public officials, presidents enjoy the greatest opportunities for uncontrolled access to the American people, although C-SPAN's gavel-to-gavel coverage of Congress has leveled the playing field. Other political leaders competing with the president for power and public support have tried for matching privileges with only moderate success.

Of course, even live television and radio broadcasts by the president are not totally devoid of media influence, because camera angles and other photographic techniques that journalists use slant all presentations somewhat. For example, in 1985, when President Reagan visited a military cemetery in Bitburg, Germany, to honor the war dead, CBS filmed the president against the backdrop of Nazi storm troopers' graves to suggest that the ceremony could be interpreted as support for the Hitler movement. The White House, disclaiming any intent to honor fallen Nazi soldiers, tried but failed to persuade the network to film the scene from a different angle.[10] When Barack Obama battled Hillary Clinton for nomination as the Democratic standard-bearer, he benefited from favorable camera angles. He was usually photographed from an upward camera angle that conveys deference, whereas the reverse was true for Clinton. Once the election is over, the presidential image benefits from photographs by the official White House photographer, whose job is to take photos that enhance the president's stature.

Indirect or mediated transmission—the framing of news presentations by media personnel—lies at the heart of the tensions between media and government because it permits journalists to pick and choose among the facts given to them. Lengthy official statements are routinely condensed into brief, one or two sentence quotations and then woven into an account constructed by journalists to match their goals. The president's pronouncements are often supplemented by information from hostile sources. Television sound bites featuring a speaking president averaged forty-five seconds in earlier decades; now they average less than nine seconds and rarely exceed twenty seconds. Journalists' comments take up the slack.

By judiciously selecting spokespeople for specific points of view and structuring questions to elicit answers that fit neatly into desired scripts, newspeople can counteract politicians' pro-government spin and shape the public's evaluations of public officials and policies. Their appraisals are frequently negative, especially when the popularity of an administration is low or falling. Newspeople are often accused of using mediated coverage deliberately, or at the least carelessly, to hurt public officials and their policies. They may give equal amounts of coverage to various viewpoints but favor one side with a preponderance of positive emphases. During the closing months of the 2008 election campaign, for example, network evening newscasts gave twice as much positive coverage to the Democratic Party and candidate Obama as it gave to the Republican counterparts. Figure 9-1 demonstrates the partisan aspects of such evaluations. Fox News, which is far more conservative than ABC, CBS, and NBC, showed the opposite pattern. McCain's positive comments soared from 27 percent on the liberal networks to 61 percent on Fox, and favorable comments for Obama dropped from 53 percent to 33 percent.

Media personnel deny that they deliberately show incumbent administrations in a bad light. They contend that they see themselves as guardians of the public interest who help to make government more honest and efficient. The politicians who produced the problematic situation featured in the news, not the newspeople who reported it, should be blamed, they argue. They point out that news focuses on nonroutine aspects of political life and therefore deals with isolated instances of socially undesirable behavior that, unfortunately, reflect badly on government. Journalists periodically generate political upheavals by blowing up minor sins as if they were major transgressions, particularly if politically influential opponents voice attacks. For example, during the 2004 presidential primaries, Howard Dean's campaign was badly hurt by reports that he uttered an unseemly scream when told about his disappointing third place finish in the Iowa caucus.

Managing a Rocky Marriage

All presidents profess to believe in a free press and to run an open government, but they rapidly develop a distaste for many of the reports about their administration. As President Kennedy told a news conference midway into his term in 1962, "[I am] reading more and enjoying it less."[11]

Presidents' displeasure with media coverage is readily understandable. Media coverage not only embarrasses them regularly and deprives them, to varying degrees, of control over the definition of political situations, but it also forces them to talk in sound bites that reporters find attractive and, in the process, to put themselves on record in ways that may narrow their options for future action. Media disclosures of secret activities, such as an impending military intervention or a planned tax hike, may actually force the president's hand.

FIGURE 9-1   **Positive Evaluations of Candidates' Policies by Nonpartisan Sources, August 24–November 3, 2008 (in percentages)**

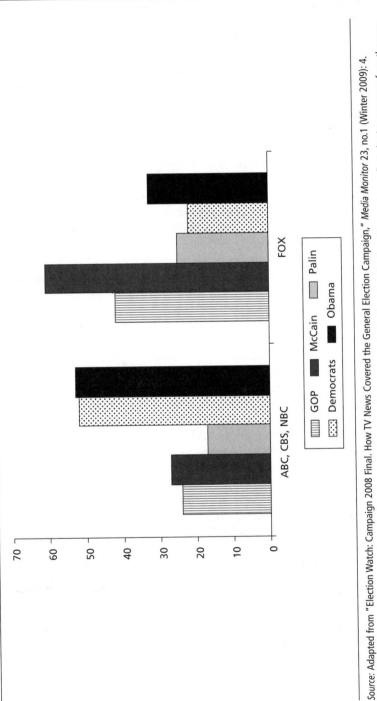

Source: Adapted from "Election Watch: Campaign 2008 Final. How TV News Covered the General Election Campaign," *Media Monitor* 23, no.1 (Winter 2009): 4.

Note: Senator Biden has been omitted from the table because he received fewer than 10 policy-based evaluations. The numbers reflect election coverage from the nominating conventions to election eve. ABC, CBS, and NBC combined had 682 stories with a *combined* airtime of 26 hours and 46 minutes. Fox's *Special Report with Brit Hume* had 524 campaign stories with an airtime of 14 hours and 33 minutes.

Bargaining advantages may be lost through premature publication of news; trivia, conflict, and public wrongdoing may receive undue emphasis.

In the rocky marriage between the press and the president, open battles are comparatively rare. Despite traded accusations that the government manipulates and lies and that the press distorts and entraps, each side is fully aware that it depends on the other. If presidents refuse to talk to hostile reporters, as happened periodically during the Nixon, Reagan, and Obama years, or if they instruct their staff and departments and agencies to refuse interviews, important stories cannot be covered firsthand. Alienating the prime news maker and source of government news is a serious loss for any news organization. Reporters' eagerness to get the news firsthand gives the president a tremendous advantage in influencing the substance and spin of news stories.

The media, for their part, can withhold publicity that the president needs or damage his administration through unwanted publicity. Journalists can stress the positive or accent the negative. They can give instantaneous, live coverage to an event or delay broadcasts until a time of their choosing. In 1993, for example, NBC broadcast only thirty minutes of President Clinton's first evening news conference. ABC and CBS, despite presidential pleading, refused to carry the event. All of the networks refused to broadcast President George H. W. Bush's last prime-time news conference in June 1992.[12] In 2000 and 2004 network news slighted the presidential election debates and the nominating conventions.

The upshot of the interdependence of the press and the government is a good deal of fraternizing and cronyism between these two "enemies," often to the dismay of those who favor an adversarial relationship. Each side works hard to cultivate the other's friendship. They often collaborate in examining political issues and problems. Such coziness may sap journalists' zeal to investigate government's misdeeds. Indeed, charges of collusion arise, particularly when media suppress news at the request of government departments or the White House. Many of these instances have concerned national security. In 1980, for example, the press delayed publicizing plans for a U.S. invasion of Iran to rescue U.S. hostages. In 1987 it suppressed technical data about eavesdropping devices designed to intercept information from Soviet marine cables. Similarly, television executives agreed in 2001 not to broadcast messages from Al Qaeda leader Osama bin Laden.[13]

The relationship between the media and the chief executive generally goes through three distinct phases.[14] There is an initial honeymoon period, a time of cooperation when the media convey the president's messages about organization of the new administration, appointments of new officials, and plans and proposals for new policies. At this early stage few policies and proposals have been implemented, minimizing opportunities for adverse criticism. Presidents and their advisers, eager to get their stories across, make themselves readily available to the media and supply them with ample information.

Once the administration embarks on controversial programs, it becomes vulnerable to criticism of its record and the honeymoon ends. That is happening earlier and more abruptly now than in the past.[15] For example, President George W. Bush received far less favorable attention from newspapers, newsmagazines, and network television news during his early days in office than either Clinton or the elder Bush.[16] President Obama's honeymoon was short as well, even though he began his presidency with high approval ratings across party lines. Controversial measures designed to halt and reverse a major economic recession tarnished his image.

Piqued by adverse publicity, the White House may retaliate by withholding news, by restricting presidential contacts with the press, and by increasing public relations activities. If the rifts between media and the executive branch become exceptionally wide, there may be a third phase in which both sides retreat from their mutually hostile behavior to take a more moderate stance. This phase frequently coincides with a reelection campaign, when newspeople try harder to provide impartial coverage and presidents are more eager to keep newspeople happy. The president may also arrange trips abroad to switch the focus of coverage to diplomatic ventures, which ordinarily is the area least likely to generate hostile coverage. There is political magic in scenes of U.S. presidents meeting with world leaders in foreign capitals. While presidents are abroad, domestic criticism abates because the president's foes do not want to be accused of undermining U.S. foreign policy.

The ability of administrations to get along with the media differs considerably. The president's interpersonal skills, as well as the nature of the political problems that an administration faces, account for much of the variation. In recent history the Kennedy and Reagan administrations were particularly good at press relations, whereas the Nixon administration was especially bad. Nixon's Watergate problems might never have developed into a major scandal had he been able to charm the press. The Clinton years featured a mercurial relationship, fluctuating between passionate love and passionate hate on both sides.

The relationship between the chief executive and the media varies not only from one administration to the next but also from one part of the country to another. Frictions are greatest between the White House and the Washington, D.C., press corps because they are most interdependent. Familiarity breeds a certain amount of contempt, and dependence breeds resentment. The northeastern seaboard press has a reputation of being more caustic than the press in the rest of the country. This is why recent presidents have often scheduled news conferences in other parts of the country and made major policy announcements away from the East Coast. For instance, President George W. Bush undertook a "Social Security reform tour" to friendly locations in 2005. As expected, it yielded a lush crop of favorable publicity for the reforms. Administrations have also made concerted efforts to schedule media interviews for cabinet members and other high-level officials away from the Washington, D.C., area.

All recent presidents have visited small communities throughout the country to bask in the adulation of local audiences and local media for the benefit of nationwide television viewers. Taking advantage of satellite technology, they can grant interviews to local television and radio stations throughout the country directly from the White House television studio. Presidents can tailor unedited, unfiltered messages for specific demographic groups and transmit them to local anchors in selected locations, pleading for their support. All recent presidents have broadcast weekly radio addresses, hoping to bring their unfiltered messages to the public.

Presidential Communication Strategies

Besides circumventing the eastern press, presidents use an array of strategies to control the substance and tenor of news. Four approaches are particularly common. First and most important, presidents try to win reporters' favor. This is not difficult because presidents are constantly surrounded by people who must have fresh news to earn their pay. Second, presidents try to shape the flow of news to make good publicity more likely and bad publicity less likely. Third, they pace and arrange their work schedules to produce opportunities for favorable media coverage. Fourth—and this is a recent trend—they try to evade the hurdles of news media gatekeeping by publishing their news on government Web sites, through video news releases, or through the social network sites on the Internet. We will discuss each of these strategies in turn.

Winning Favor. To woo reporters, presidents offer good story material as well as occasional scoops that may bring distinction to individual reporters. They cultivate reporters' friendship by being accessible, treating them with respect, and arranging for their creature comforts. To keep reporters in line, presidents may threaten them directly or obliquely with withdrawal of privileges. Privileges include accommodations on the presidential plane, special interviews, or answers to their questions during news conferences. Presidents may also publicly condemn individual reporters or their organizations for undesirable reporting.

Shaping the News Flow. Presidents try to guide the flow of news by the thrust of their commentary and by controlling contacts with the press. To avoid questions about embarrassing failures, presidents may even periodically restrict their contacts with the media to picture sessions. Presidents also may space out news releases to create a steady, manageable flow of news. If they want emphasis on a particular story, they may withhold competing news that breaks simultaneously. Sometimes administrations release a barrage of news or even create news to distract attention from sensitive developments. Administrations have averted criticism by the eastern press by withholding advance copies of speeches or by timing them late enough in the evening to preclude adequate coverage in the morning papers.

Shrinking financial resources have forced mainstream media to reduce hard news reporting and turn to more soft news and commentary. For the presidency, that has meant more "gotcha," negative stories, countered by White House official efforts to broadcast their own messages, including rebuttals, via the new media.[17] The new media sites, including e-mail, blogs, social Web sites, and various talk and comedy shows, have been receptive to covering presidents and their policies, albeit sometimes inaccurately and sensationally. The Internet has become an echo chamber where negative messages can rebound over and over. For example, an op-ed by *New York Times* columnist Thomas Friedman that decried President Bush's energy policy was immediately widely circulated via e-mail. The op-ed accused the president of fostering public addiction to oil and hindering the development of feasible alternatives. It sparked heated discussions on television talk shows, on talk radio, and on blogs, which then reverberated through the same communication networks.[18] For many types of messages, social networks are more credible than the legacy media because people trust their peers more than outsiders.[19] The fact that President Obama's MySpace Web site had millions of "friends," as he began his administration, turned out to be a major asset.

Orchestrating Coverage. The many tactics available for generating favorable publicity include creating newsworthy events, heightening suspense through news blackouts before major pronouncements, and staging public ceremonies as media spectacles at times when there are few competing events. Political successes may be coupled with political failures in hopes that publicity for the success will draw attention away from the failure. The Carter administration reportedly timed its announcement of the opening of formal relations with the People's Republic of China late in 1978 to buffer negative publicity in case its attempts to clinch a peace settlement between Israel and Egypt failed. Occasionally administrations may even intentionally deceive the press in hopes that false messages will accomplish important political goals. The Bush administration was accused of duping Congress, the press, and the public in 2003 by falsely claiming that war against Iraq was necessary because that country was poised to unleash weapons of mass destruction. At the time, the press reported these claims as reliable news. No such weapons were ever discovered despite extensive searches.

Presidential Web Sites. The White House maintains its own Web site at www.whitehouse.gov. It is an electronic portal to the president, his family, and the official mansion, and to messages prepared for public display by the incumbent and the presidential staff. It is also the gateway to www.usa.gov, which contains electronic links to the entire national government. From there visitors have access to the Web sites of all three branches of the national government as well as state government, local government, and international sites. Visitors can search for specific agencies or for such policy areas as consumer services, education, or veterans' benefits. Many sites are interactive, so that people can ask questions as well as request forms that can then be submitted electronically. The main sites, their links, and links to the links form a fantastic treasure trove of information.

What sorts of information do these links contain? They contain only what the site owners—the government and its agencies—wish to include, in the manner in which they wish to frame it. Site owners can add or delete information at will, depending on their appraisals of the political scene. The White House Web site was redesigned in 2007 to highlight the president's daily activities and his policies and speeches.[20] Aside from being unfailingly supportive of the president's policies, the government sites vary tremendously in the completeness and timeliness of their offerings. Some are little more than public relations portals, while others genuinely try to meet citizens' needs and to be transparent about their activities.

A great deal of research is still needed to assess how useful these sites are for the president's communication within the executive branch, with Congress, with interest groups, and with the citizenry at large. By and large we do not know who visits and for what purposes. We do know that the sites are widely used, and that suggests that they may be quite influential. On average, two million people access the White House Web site monthly; the number has risen to six million on special occasions. We also know that service-oriented sites have more visits than policy-oriented sites.[21] Finally, we know that the executive branch considers these sites important enough to allocate ample resources to them. This translates into attractive, user-friendly sites that present the government's story in words and pictures that reflect the president's, rather than journalists', preferences.

Institutional Settings

Relations between the president and the media are so important and so complex that they require the involvement of established as well as specially created institutions.

On the President's Side. A president can shape the news indirectly through appointments to the Federal Communications Commission (FCC) and other public agencies concerned with media regulation and through informal contacts with personnel in those agencies. Presidents can control financial lifelines through the Office of Management and Budget (OMB), which screens the budgetary requests of all federal agencies, including those dealing with the mass media. An administration can also wield control through the Justice Department. For instance, the Antitrust Division can challenge the FCC's approval of mergers and can carry appeals through the courts and ultimately to the Supreme Court.

Presidents involve themselves directly in media policy making through White House organizations, study commissions, and task forces. In 1970 President Nixon created the Office of Telecommunications Policy—the first permanent agency within the White House to plan communications policy. Since then every president has tinkered with institutional arrangements. Changes have generally revolved around four standing offices: the Press Office, the Office of Communication, the Office of Media Affairs, and Speechwriting—to use the post-Clinton nomenclature.[22] Staffs for these offices usually total fewer than fifty people, but communications experts in other offices in the executive branch perform much additional work.

The Press Office supplies Washington, D.C.–based reporters with news about the White House. By custom, the press secretary meets almost daily with the White House press corps to make announcements and take questions. These briefings supply reporters with the president's interpretation of events. Reporters then cast their stories into perspectives of their own choice.[23]

The Office of Communications is concerned with long-range public relations management of the presidency. In consultation with the president, it determines the images that the administration needs to convey to gain and retain the approval of important constituencies in the public and private sectors and to win support for desired policies. The office also coordinates the public relations activities of executive branch departments and agencies to make sure that the chorus of public voices is harmonious. If the president's approval ratings plunge, the communications director is likely to get the ax. As George Stephanopoulos, a victim of the communications wars during the Clinton administration, explained, "By definition, if the President isn't doing well, it's a communication problem. That's always going to be a natural place to make a change."[24]

The Office of Media Affairs serves the regional and local press and various ethnic news organizations in Washington, D.C. It also handles publicity during the president's travels. The office lets the president know how well his messages are faring with audiences. It also handles the president's Web site.

Officials in the Speechwriting Office keep busy by composing remarks for some 650 annual public events featuring the president.[25] Following the 2001 terrorist strike on the United States, President Bush added a unit to counter hostile messages emanating from the Middle East. The unit, called Coalition Information Centers, was based in London so that its operations matched Middle Eastern news cycles more readily. A more broadly oriented Office of Global Communication was established in January 2003. It is incorporated directly into the White House Office, unlike the other offices. The placement indicates that its operations are high political priorities.

Modern public relations activities involve many different techniques. "Focus groups and polling data are used to fashion presidential messages; sound-bites are written into the public pronouncements of the president and his underlings to articulate those messages; public appearances are choreographed so that the messages are reinforced by visual images."[26] To spread messages throughout the country, the administration sends cabinet officers and others on speaking tours and arranges satellite interviews in local markets.

It is, of course, essential for presidents to "sell" their policies by soliciting wide support for them and by presenting a united front within their administration. However, in the process democracy may be imperiled because "style is substituted for substance. Complicated issues are transformed into simple slogans and slick sound-bites.... [T]imid, self-interested policy makers...shy away from responsibility for their actions and delude themselves and their constituents with their own symbolic spectacle."[27] Ethical issues arise when the president or executive agencies commission propaganda messages from public relations firms and then distribute them as official news releases. In 2005, for example, Congress's Government Accountability Office (GAO) criticized the Office of National Drug Control Policy for distributing what it called "covert propaganda."[28] The GAO had admonished the Department of Education earlier for paying $240,000 to a syndicated columnist for promoting the president's education reforms.[29]

On the Media's Side. Close to 8,000 print and broadcast reporters are accredited to attend White House press operations, though only a small fraction—generally fewer than fifty—actually attend press conferences. Given the small quarters in which presidential news conferences are held, attendees are usually selected to represent a balanced pool of news venues, including wire services. Many reporters who serve routinely in the White House press corps have considerable experience and notable reputations. As a group, they are older and better educated and trained than the average U.S. journalist.[30] The *New York Times, Washington Post, Los Angeles Times, Chicago Tribune, Philadelphia Inquirer,* and other major newspapers have full-time reporters assigned exclusively to the president. So do a number of newspaper chains, such as the Scripps-Howard papers, the Hearst press, and the Newhouse papers. Smaller papers may send their Washington, D.C., bureau chiefs to the White House whenever there is news of special interest to their region.

Each of the major broadcast networks, as well as CNN, has several reporters at the White House on a regular basis; smaller networks have one. C-SPAN provides twenty-four-hour White House cable coverage as well as complete coverage of sessions of the House of Representatives. The White House is also covered by several all-news cable services, Internet news operations like the Huffington Post, weekly newsmagazines, and periodicals, as well as photographers and their supporting staffs. Hard economic times have forced cutbacks in personnel and increased pooling of resources among media organizations. Even big events such as presidential trips abroad or the national party conventions are covered by a smaller corps of journalists, and many reporters now work for several news organizations.

Most of the country's dailies and television and radio stations do not have a regular Washington, D.C., correspondent or part-time "stringer" to cover the White House. Inexpensive satellite time, however, has lowered news transmission costs and boosted the number of stations that can afford direct coverage of the Washington scene, often through the prism of local interests.

Forms of Contact

Press Releases and News Briefings. The release of news by chief executives or their aides takes several routine forms. Most of these represent a concerted effort to control the news output. The most common is the press release, a story prepared by government officials and handed to members of the press, usually without an opportunity for questions. In a news briefing, reporters have an opportunity to ask the press secretary about the news releases. But because executive officials furnish the news for the briefing, they control the substance and tone of the discussion.

News Conferences. Although a news conference may appear to be a wide-open question period, the official being questioned usually tries to control it tightly. Seemingly spontaneous answers usually have been carefully prepared by experts on the executive's staff and rehearsed during extensive briefings. Before Kennedy's presidency, press conferences were not covered live, permitting the White House to make corrections before conference records were published. Kennedy, who was a gifted extemporaneous speaker, stripped away this cloak of protection by allowing live filming of

President George W. Bush ducks shoes hurled as a gesture of extreme disrespect by an Iraqi journalist during a press conference in Baghdad, December 15, 2008.

Source: AP Photo/APTN

conferences. At the time, press critics called it "goofy" and likened it to "making love in Carnegie Hall."[31]

The live format remains controversial because it leads to posturing by the president as well as by members of the press. It also causes embarrassment for presidents who misspeak or suffer memory lapses. Presidents can often control the subject and tone of a news conference by recognizing friendly reporters for questions and avoiding follow-up questions. But no president has been able to squelch embarrassing questions entirely or to deny reporters the chance to use their questions as opportunities to express their own views about controversial issues.[32] By posing leading questions, reporters may force the president or press secretary to comment on matters that these officials may not wish to discuss. The questions listed in Box 9-1 give a taste of the sorts of interrogation that presidents face.

Backgrounders. Some news conferences are off-the-record "backgrounders." High officials call such events to give newspeople important background information that they are honor bound to keep entirely secret or to publish only without revealing the source. Forms of vague attribution are usually permitted, such as "Government sources say," "It has been reported by reliable sources," or even more specifically, "The White House discloses" or the "Defense Department indicates."

BOX 9-1   **Quizzing the President**

On March 24, 2009, President Barack Obama held a routine press conference at the White House. It began with the president's spirited, lengthy defense of his unprecedented economic recovery measures. Here is a slightly abbreviated version of the reporters' questions. The answers have been omitted.

◄ Your Treasury secretary and the Fed chair have been—were on Capitol Hill today, asking for this new authority that you want to regulate big, complex financial institutions. But given the problems that the financial bailout program has had so far—banks not wanting to talk about how they're spending the money, the AIG bonuses that you mentioned—why do you think the public should sign on for another new, sweeping authority for the government to take over companies, essentially?...Why should the public trust the government to handle that authority well?

◄ Some have compared this financial crisis to a war, and in times of war, past presidents have called for some form of sacrifice. Some of your programs, whether for Main Street or Wall Street, have actually cushioned the blow for those that were irresponsible during this—during this economic period of prosperity or supposed prosperity that you were talking about. Why, given this new era of responsibility that you're asking for, why haven't you asked for something specific that the public should be sacrificing to participate in this economic recovery?...

◄ Right now on Capitol Hill, Senate Democrats are writing a budget, and according to press accounts and their own statements, they're not including the middle-class tax cut that you include in the stimulus. They're talking about phasing that out. They're not including the cap-and-trade that you have in your budget, and they're not including other measures. I know when you outlined your four priorities over the weekend, a number of these things were not in there. Will you sign a budget if it does not contain a middle-class tax cut, does not contain cap-and-trade?...

◄ At both of your town hall meetings in California last week, you said, quote, "I didn't run for president to pass on our problems to the next generation." But under your budget, the debt will increase $7 trillion over the next 10 years. The Congressional Budget Office says $9.3 trillion. And today on Capitol Hill, some Republicans called your budget, with all the spending on health care, education and environment, the most irresponsible budget in American history. Isn't that kind of debt exactly what you were talking about when you said passing on our problems to the next generation?...

◄ Today your administration presented a plan to help curb the violence in Mexico and also to control any or prevent any spillover of the violence into the United States. Do you consider the situation now a national security threat? And do you believe that it could require sending national troops to the border? Governor Perry of Texas has said that you still need more troops and more agents. How do you respond to that?

◄ Mr. President, where do you plan to find savings in the Defense and Veterans Administration's budgets when so many items that seem destined for the chopping block are politically untenable,...from major weapons systems—as you mentioned, procurement—to wounded warrior care costs, or increased operations on Afghanistan, or the size of the military itself?

◀ You spoke again at the top about your anger about AIG. You've been saying that for days now. But why is it that it seems Andrew Cuomo seems to be, in New York, getting more actual action on it? And when you and Secretary Geithner first learned about this, ten days, two weeks ago, you didn't go public immediately with that outrage. You waited a few days, and then you went public after you realized Secretary Geithner really had no legal avenue to stop it. And more broadly—I just want to follow up on Chip and Jake—you've been very critical of President Bush doubling the national debt. And to be fair, it's not just Republicans hitting you. Democrat Kent Conrad, as you know, said, quote, "When I look at this budget, I see the debt doubling again." You keep saying that you've inherited a big fiscal mess. Do you worry, though, that your daughters, not to mention the next president, will be inheriting an even bigger fiscal mess if the spending goes out of control?...

◀ Taking this economic debate a bit globally, senior Chinese officials have publicly expressed an interest in an international currency. This is described by Chinese specialists as a sign that they are less confident than they used to be in the value and the reliability of the U.S. dollar. European countries have resisted your calls to spend more on economic stimulus. I wonder, Sir, as a candidate who ran concerned about the image of the United States globally, how comfortable you are with the Chinese government, run by communists, less confident than they used to be in the U.S. dollar, and European governments, some of them center-left, some of them socialist, who say you're asking them to spend too much?

◀ Are you reconsidering your plan to cut the interest rate deduction for mortgages and for charities? And do you regret having proposed that in the first place?...Are you confident that charities are wrong when they contend that this would discourage giving?

◀ A recent report found that as a result of the economic downturn, one in fifty children are now homeless in America. With shelters at full capacity, tent cities are sprouting up across the country. In passing your stimulus package, you said that help was on the way, but what would you say to these families, especially children, who are sleeping under bridges and in tents across the country?

◀ Yours is a rather historic presidency, and I'm just wondering whether in any of the policy debates that you've had within the White House, the issue of race has come up, or whether it has in the way you feel you've been perceived by other leaders or by the American people. Or have the last sixty-four days been a relatively color-blind time?

◀ In your remarks on stem-cell research earlier this month, you talked about a majority consensus in determining whether or not this is the right thing to do, to federally fund embryonic stem-cell research. I'm just wondering, though, how much you personally wrestled with the morality or ethics of federally funding this kind of research, especially given the fact that science so far has shown a lot of progress with adult stem cells but not a lot with embryonic?

◀ Mr. President, you came to office pledging to work for peace between Israel and the Palestinians. How realistic do you think those hopes are now, given the likelihood of a prime minister who's not fully signed up to a two-state solution and a foreign minister who's been accused of insulting Arabs?

Source: Excerpted from President Obama's news conference, March 24, 2009, www.nytimes
.com/2009/03/24/us/politics/24text-obama.html.

Government officials like backgrounders because they are a relatively safe way to test the waters. They permit officials to bring a variety of policy ideas before their colleagues and the public without openly identifying with them. Unlike government officials, reporters are ambivalent about backgrounders. They like having access to news that might otherwise be unavailable, but they dislike being prevented from publishing all aspects of the story or identifying the source of the information so that the story can be placed in its proper perspective. In addition to formal encounters, reporters and the president or White House staff meet informally in work or social settings.

Top government officials, and occasionally the president, give interviews on daytime news programs; nighttime serious, satirical, and humorous offerings; and during town hall meetings where the president meets with ordinary citizens in various locations. Questioning on these occasions can resemble a no-holds-barred cross-examination. More likely, they are friendly exchanges. Because they are broadcast by large media enterprises, they provide excellent opportunities to present the administration's position to an interested worldwide audience.

Leaks. An even less formal release of news occurs through "leaks," the surreptitious release of information by high- and low-level government sources who wish to remain anonymous or who do not want to release the information formally. Many leaks are sanctioned at the highest levels. But some officials may also leak information that they are not authorized to release. Sometimes low-level officials leak information to gain attention from top officials.

Leaks are a mixed blessing. They can destroy the timing of negotiations, alienate the parties whose secrets have been exposed, and cause great harm by disclosing politically sensitive matters. They also allow scrutiny of important suppressed issues, serve as trial balloons, and permit government officials to release information anonymously. Although presidents frequently leak confidential stories, they passionately hate news leaked by others. All recent presidents have therefore used federal investigative agencies, such as the Federal Bureau of Investigation and the Central Intelligence Agency, to find the sources of news leaks.

A typical leak occurred in 1991 during the Senate battle over confirmation of Judge Clarence Thomas as a justice of the U.S. Supreme Court. It involved confidential allegations about sexual harassment by the nominee. The leaks led to a second round of lengthy, acrimonious hearings before Thomas was confirmed. The episode seriously harmed Judge Thomas's reputation and undermined faith in the integrity of the confirmation process.

The harm that leaks cause must be weighed against their benefits. In a system in which the executive maintains tight control over the formal channels of news, leaks provide a valuable counterbalance. Take President Reagan's controversial budget proposals in 1983. Administration insiders, eager to bring their concerns to the public and to Congress, resorted to almost daily leaks of economic appraisals that contradicted the president's pronouncements. An irate Reagan proclaimed, "I've had it up to my keister with these leaks," but he modified his budget plans nonetheless.[33]

YOUR TAX DOLLARS AT WORK: CONGRESS STARTS THE DAY WITH THE PLEDGE.

THE MEDIA AND CONGRESS

According to political folklore, the television age has permanently altered the balance of political power. The presidency basks in the limelight of publicity at all times while Congress waits in the shadows, making the president dominant and the legislature inferior. As Sen. J. William Fulbright, D-Ark., told Congress in 1970, "Television has done as much to expand the powers of the president as would a constitutional amendment formally abolishing the co-equality of the three branches of government."[34]

Image versus Reality

If one probes beyond the impression that Congress is a media stepchild, the situation appears less clear. When coverage of legislative concerns is added to coverage that mentions Congress explicitly, Congress and the presidency receive roughly the same amount of national news attention. Moreover, the bulk of coverage of Congress comes through stories about individual members that are published in their home states. Although local coverage does not generally attract national attention, it is politically crucial for each member.

Table 9-3 presents a comparison of ten issues that emerged in television coverage of President Bush and Congress from July 2003 to June 2004. The scores represent a combination of offerings by ABC, CBS, and NBC. Besides showing the number of stories in each category and the length of broadcast time devoted to them, the table also records whether the story appeared in the first, second, or last ten-minute segment of the broadcast because story impact decreases with later placement. Four issues were covered prominently for both institutions, and six issues were unique to each. The three networks chose almost identical types of issues for stories about the presidency and Congress and placed them in similar order within broadcast segments. However, the networks differed in the total amounts of time allotted to particular stories. Stories about Congress generally were fewer, shorter, and less prominently placed than news linked to the presidency, confirming that "435 members of the House and 100 members of the Senate compete for the crumbs of network time left after the president has got his share."[35]

Why does Congress fare worse than the presidency? There are several reasons. Most important, the presidency makes a better media target because it is an institution with a single head, readily personified and filmed in the visible person of the chief executive. This gives media audiences a familiar, easily dramatized focus of attention. A president is like a superstar surrounded by a cast of supporting actors. Even stories originating from congressional sources frequently feature the president as the main actor. As the personification of the nation, the president can usually command national television or radio time, often at prime time and on a growing number of news venues. In the past the press was more likely to refuse than grant Congress members' requests for coverage. That has changed dramatically, starting with the Clinton presidency, most likely because respect for the president as a person has declined in the wake of numerous well-publicized scandals. Still, the president retains the lead in coverage, but the gap is narrowing.[36]

There are many reasons why Congress is unable to attract as much media coverage as the president. Unlike the chief executive, Congress is a many-headed Hydra with no single, widely familiar personal focus. It conducts its activities simultaneously in more than one hundred locations on Capitol Hill. No individual member can command nationwide media coverage at will because no one is regarded as a spokesperson for the entire Congress. Consequently, most stories about Congress deal with individual members or legislative activity on specific issues rather than with the body as a whole.

Another reason why stories about Congress escape wide attention lies in the nature of its work. The legislative branch drafts laws, makes compromises among conflicting interests, forges shifting coalitions, and works out legal details. Stories about the executive branch that describe *what* is actually done are far more memorable than reports about *how* the laborious process of hammering out legislation works. Besides, the most interesting aspect of the legislative process, the shaping of broad guidelines for policy, has become the preserve of the president rather than Congress.

Congressional coverage is frequently useless for the public because it tends to be sparse in the early stages of the legislative process, when there is still time for citizens to influence a bill. Coverage usually focuses on final action after the shape of the legislation is already firm.[37] Citizens then learn what the

Issue	Story rank (%)[a] 1	2	3	Time	Number of stories	Percentage of total stories
President						
U.S. elections	69	20	10	6:07	124	23.1
Iraq War	90	7	3	7:40	87	16.2
Economy	81	19	0	1:11	31	5.7
Middle East policy	71	21	7	0:22	14	2.6
CIA leak	64	14	21	0:33	14	2.6
September 11 Commission hearing	92	8	0	0:40	13	2.4
Environment	60	20	20	0:12	10	1.8
President's military record	78	22	0	0:27	9	1.6
Judicial appointments	50	50	0	0:09	8	1.4
Abortion	71	29	0	0:09	7	1.3
Average (Totals)	73	22	6	(17:30)	(317)	(58.7)
Congress						
Iraq War	97	3	0	4:37	72	16.9
Health care	33	49	17	2:43	63	14.7
September 11 Commission hearing	86	11	3	1:30	28	6.6
Economy	68	28	4	1:00	25	5.8
U.S. elections	36	36	28	0:39	14	3.3
Energy legislation	45	36	18	0:24	11	2.6
Gas prices	54	45	0	0:32	11	2.6
Airline security	70	0	30	0:26	10	2.3
Abortion	56	44	0	0:19	9	2.1
Gun legislation	33	56	11	0:17	9	2.1
Average (Totals)	58	31	11	(12:27)	(252)	(59.0)

Source: Compiled by the author from the Vanderbilt Television News Archives.

Note: N for president = 317 for top ten and 537 for all stories; N for Congress = 252 for top ten and 426 for all stories. The numbers are combined scores for ABC, CBS, and NBC early evening newscasts. Stories are rank ordered by time, in hours and minutes. Some percentages have been rounded.

[a] Position of story in first, second, or third ten-minute segment of broadcast.

new policies are, without being exposed to the pros and cons and the political interplay that led to the ultimate compromise.[38] Live television coverage of congressional sessions on C-SPAN is changing this tradition; it is making Congress more vulnerable to pressures from constituents and interest groups.

Fearing that legislative floor sessions would present an unedifying, boring spectacle, Congress resisted live radio and television coverage of most sessions until the late 1970s. Before 1979 only selected committee hearings were televised, primarily those involving spicy topics such as labor racketeering, communists in government, or high-level corruption. In 1979 the House of Representatives lifted the prohibition on televising its floor sessions. The action was prompted in part by the desire to counterbalance the political advantages the executive branch was reaping from heavy media attention. The rules for coverage by the House-run closed circuit system are strict: Only the member speaking may be filmed, not the listeners, unless the speaker of the House decrees otherwise. This stipulation bars the public from seeing the typically near-empty House chamber and inattentive members during routine sessions. Commercial, cable, and public television systems have access to House broadcasts but rarely cover them, except for the live coverage by C-SPAN. In 1986 the Senate finally followed suit and permitted live coverage of its proceedings. It was prodded by Sen. Robert Byrd, D-W.Va., who was concerned that the Senate was "fast becoming the invisible half of Congress," compared to the White House and the House of Representatives.[39]

Unlike the presidency, Congress has rarely become a first-rate "show" for the U.S. public, although its media coverage is vital for inside-the-beltway Washington politics. Representatives themselves are among the most avid watchers of House coverage because the television cameras permit them to keep up with floor action and issues reported by committees other than their own. Members of Congress try to use their appearances to create favorable images for themselves and their pet political projects among congressional and executive branch constituencies and the elite media. Some members claim that recent sharp increases in the time spent to pass legislation are largely due to television coverage. More members want to be heard, and they are likely to take more extreme positions because the media tend to focus on such confrontations.[40] Broadcasting may make it more difficult for congressional leaders to muffle dissident members and reach legislative compromises after representatives have publicly committed themselves to definite positions. However, there is little solid proof thus far that television coverage has harmed consensus building in the chamber or that the added publicity is making incumbents even more unbeatable at the polls than they are now.

Congress on the Web

Congress entered the Internet scene in earnest in 1995 with a formal House Web site that features all texts of bills, resolutions, and amendments introduced in the House of Representatives, along with brief, nontechnical descriptions of their content.[41] The Web site also provides a minute-by-minute summary of floor action. The actual debates can be monitored via an on-line version of the *Congressional Record*. The Senate now has a similar Web site. In addition, members of Congress have long had their own Web sites. Besides featuring the member's biographical data and major accomplishments—but not failures—most also link to the Web sites of committees on which the member serves and describe committee actions and the current status of specific bills. The most comprehensive information about ongoing congressional activities is available at the Library of Congress's THOMAS site (http://thomas. loc.gov/), named for Thomas Jefferson.

Detailed coverage of congressional activities is extremely useful for lobby groups and other Congress watchers. It has enhanced their ability to make their views known at key junctures in the legislative process. The Web site and its links are also a gold mine of information for reporters who want to incorporate detailed current information into their stories. In fact, three out of four Web sites provide "on-line newsrooms" to serve the special needs of the press.[42] There also are a few sites—such as the Legislative Information System, which offers research material on legislation, and sites operated by each party and its subdivisions—that are purely for internal use by members of Congress.

E-mail has become the most prolific Internet message system linking Congress with its various publics. But like the multiplying buckets in Paul Dukat's *Sorcerer's Apprentice,* the flood tide of e-mails threatens to overwhelm congressional navigation resources. Given their limited staffs, members of Congress find it impossible to cope promptly and adequately with e-mail from constituents, not to mention e-mailings from outsiders, including spammers, and from computer hackers who generate mail to clog communication arteries. Efficient electronic sorting and automatic response protocols ameliorate the problem but are far from resolving it.

Writing Stories about Congress

Journalists assigned to the congressional beat use normal criteria of newsworthiness and gatekeeping to decide who and what to cover and who and what to ignore. They prefer exciting, novel, or controversial topics that can be made personally relevant to the public and be simply presented, over recurrent complex and mundane problems, such as congressional reorganizations or the annual farm bill. Orderly, dispassionate debate usually is passed over in favor of pompous rhetoric and wild accusations that can produce catchy headlines. Heated confrontations are more likely to occur in the more intimate committee hearings than in full sessions. Accordingly, committee hearings attract most extensive coverage, particularly on television.

Because Congress is a regular beat, the leaders of each chamber conduct daily press briefings. Major media organizations, such as the *Washington Post* and the *New York Times,* the big newspaper chains, and the television networks and wire services have full-time reporters covering Congress. Specialized news services such as *Congressional Quarterly* and two highly competitive newspapers—*Roll Call* and the *Hill*—cover the congressional beat in detail. THOMAS provides much information that is sparse on the Web sites of individual representatives; most congressional Web sites link to it. For example, THOMAS contains information about bill sponsorship and the texts of otherwise unrecorded speeches. In all, more than 7,000 correspondents are accredited to the press galleries in the House and Senate. The ratio of journalists to senators thus is seventy-one to one; for representatives it is sixteen to one.[43]

Congressional press releases and written reports provide news to media sources that lack regular reporters on Capitol Hill. These documents are prepared and distributed via Web sites and by congressional press secretaries because reporters accredited to Congress are unable to attend the many hearings occurring simultaneously. Press releases enable members of Congress to tell their stories in their own words. They often use the opportunity to highlight problem areas, hoping that news media publicity will shame Congress into action.[44] Although all representatives now assign staff to serve the needs of the press, fewer than 10 percent of House members receive weekly coverage on national television. Newspaper coverage is somewhat more ample, especially in nationally circulating papers.[45]

Senators generally receive considerably more press coverage than representatives, even though an equal number of reporters cover both houses. On network television, stories about senators outnumber those about representatives almost seven to one. The reasons include senators' greater prominence, prestige, and publicity resources. Their larger constituencies hold the promise of larger audiences. In general, high media visibility for senators as well as representatives depends on their seniority and whether they serve in important leadership positions. By contrast, sponsoring legislation or regular committee service matters little. Who one is obviously counts for more than what one does. In practice, this means that more than half of the congressional membership receives no national television exposure at all. A mere twenty members of the Senate garner the lion's share of attention.[46] Such spotty coverage deprives the public of a chance to evaluate the contributions of the most representative branch of government. It also may explain why public approval of Congress ranged from a low of 12 percent to a quite modest high of 43 percent between 2005 and 2009. Most poll results were in the 20 percent to 30 percent range.[47]

The effects of neglect at the national level are mitigated by local coverage. Many members of Congress receive regular local coverage through their own news columns or radio or television programs.[48] They usually find their relations with the local media far more congenial than relations with a national press corps, whose members care little about the problems of particular congressional districts. Local media depend on senators and representatives for local angles to national stories because local slants make these stories more attractive to the target audience. Because Washington, D.C.–based senators and representatives are ideal sources, local newspeople are loath to criticize them. The Washington press corps lacks such qualms. During the first year and a half of the 103rd Congress, during the Clinton presidency, 64 percent of all congressional stories broadcast on national news were negative. Senate scores were a bit worse than House scores, whereas the president's press was a shade better than both houses during this time.[49]

Functions of Media

The functions that the *national* media perform for Congress and those that Congress performs for the *national* media parallel press-presidency relations. However, there are major qualitative differences. Neither Congress nor the media need the services of the other as much as the presidency needs the press. The national media can afford to alienate some legislators without losing direct access to congressional news. Similarly, except when the passage of important, controversial laws is involved, legislators can ignore national publicity and rely instead on publicity in their own districts. News items about national events and national public opinion are also somewhat less important to most members of Congress than to the president. The home media, discussed in the next chapter, rather than national news providers, are particularly important to legislators as sources of news relevant for their own constituents and as channels for transmitting messages to the home district while they are in Washington, D.C.

Publicity is especially important for minority party leaders, who may need the media to pressure an unresponsive majority to consider their concerns. However, most members cannot use "outsider strategies," as publicity efforts by the out-of-power party are called, because Congress members rarely receive enough coverage. Once members achieve visibility, their fame often grows by its own momentum. They become regulars on interview shows, and their opinions are solicited on national issues. For most members, however, media attention carries few benefits and has several drawbacks; for example, elected officials become more visible targets for lobby groups, and their exposure provides ammunition for rival candidates during the next election campaign. For members of Congress who do not need nationwide attention to achieve their legislative goals, favorable coverage by traditional media in their districts is the key objective. Local newspaper, radio, and television coverage lets their constituents know what they are doing and paves their way for reelection. Many members also communicate through Web sites, newsletters, and individual correspondence sent to selected constituents. Some prepare cable television programs for their district or transmit carefully chosen video excerpts from committee meetings to their Web sites and to the media in their home districts. Still others, eager to push their legislative agendas, write op-ed pieces for the local and national media.

A Cautious Relationship

Just as the functions that media perform are similar for the executive and legislative branches, so is the love-hate relationship. But it, too, is less ardent for Congress, even though mutual recriminations are plentiful. Senators and representatives compete with peers for media attention and bemoan the lack of coverage for their pet projects and pronouncements. They complain that reporters treat them like scoundrels conspiring to defraud the public and resent the cross-examinations that reporters love to conduct with an air of infallibility. Legislators charge, and can prove, that the media emphasize trivia, scandals, internal dissent, and official misconduct but generally ignore congressional consensus and the passage of significant legislation. They blame the media for the low approval ratings of Congress. Still, despite ample negative coverage, the media generally treat congressional leaders and Congress with a fair amount of deference and respect. Individual presidents have been more bloodied by adverse publicity than have individual members of the House. As Michael Robinson concluded from a detailed analysis of the impact of media coverage on Congress, the media have fostered a stronger presidency but weaker presidents, and a weaker Congress but more durable representatives.[50]

Journalists, in turn, complain with justification about legislators' efforts to manage the news through their professional publicity staffs. They point to members' lack of candor and grumble about being excluded from many congressional meetings and executive sessions. Broadcasters also resent the strict controls placed on their coverage of congressional sessions. They are barred from taping their own stories and are limited in the subjects they can photograph.

The realization of interdependence smooths the ruffled feathers. Senators and representatives realize that they need the media for information and for the publicity that is crucial to pass or defeat legislation. They know that the media will discreetly ignore their personal foibles so long as no official wrongdoing is involved. Newspeople, in turn, understand that they need individual legislators for information about congressional activities and as a counterfoil and source of leaks to check the executive branch. Members are valuable for inside comments that can personalize otherwise dull stories. Congress often creates story topics for the media by investigating dramatic ongoing problems like auto or aircraft safety. A congressional inquiry may be the catalyst that turns an everyday event into a newsworthy item. The story then may ride the crest of publicity for quite some time, creating its own fresh and reportable events until it recedes into limbo once more. Newspeople do not want to dry up these sources; nor do media enterprises want to forgo the financial rewards generated by paid campaign commercials.

Congress and Communications Policy

Journalists, particularly those who work in radio and television, appreciate the power that Congress has over regulatory legislation. In the past, Congress used its power to legislate communications policy sparingly, viewing it as a hornet's nest of political conflict best left alone. The major exceptions were passage of the Communications Act of 1934 and its 1996 sequel and the supplementary laws dealing with technical innovations and other changes in the mass communication scene. Whenever strong, unified pressures from industry or consumer groups develop and overcome the strong resistance to change in this controversial policy field, which also has multiple powerful stakeholders, Congress's power to legislate communications policy becomes extremely important. As the sixty-two-year time gap between major communications laws demonstrates, there usually is a vacuum in both policy formulation and oversight that neither the president nor the FCC has been eager to fill.[51]

The communications subcommittees of the Commerce, Science, and Transportation Committee in the Senate and of the Energy and Commerce Committee in the House also influence communications policy, primarily through the power of investigation. They have investigated the FCC more frequently than most regulatory bodies. In fact, since 1970 more than fifty different congressional committees and subcommittees have reviewed FCC activities, with few dramatic results. Investigations have included reviews of specific FCC actions, studies of corruption in television game shows, and examinations of such broad policy issues as the impact of television's portrayal of the aged or of alcohol and drug abuse. The appropriations committees have occasionally denied funds for FCC operations or explicitly directed which particular programs should be funded.[52] However, monetary control became stricter when Congress changed the FCC in 1982 from the status of a permanently authorized agency to one requiring biennial renewal.

Although the Senate has seldom used confirmation hearings to impress its views on new FCC commissioners, this does not mean that agency staff have ignored the views of powerful senators. Prospective commissioners are likely to study past confirmation hearings carefully and take their cues from them. Most presidential nominees have been confirmed. Appointments usually reward the politically faithful. Although congressional control over the FCC has generally been light, there is always the possibility of stricter control. All the parties interested in communications policy, including the White House and the courts, pay deference to that possibility.

Congressional control over the media includes such matters as postal rates and subsidies and legislation on permissible mergers and chain control of papers. Copyright laws, which affect print and electronic media productions, are involved, along with policies and regulations about telecommunication satellites, broadcast spectrum allocations, and cable television. The vast, congressionally guided changes in the telephone industry are yet another area of major concern to media interests.

Laws regulating media procedures occasionally have a strong impact on media content and policies. For instance, FCC encouragement of the diversification of radio programs was largely responsible for the development of a sizable number of FM rock music stations that provide alternatives to more conventional programs. Congressional scrutiny of documentaries may chill investigative reporting, as may have happened when Congress probed the circumstances surrounding a documentary on drug use at a major university to assess whether the events had been staged. Congress has also investigated charges of illicit public relations activity by the Pentagon. Congressional failure to act may have far-reaching consequences for news media. Congress has barely regulated cable television since 1996, leaving this medium mostly under control of the courts and state and local governments.

SUMMARY

In this chapter we examined the relationship between the media and the presidency and Congress—a rocky one because the goals of these institutions differ. Officials want favorable stories that mirror their sense of what is important and unimportant. Newspeople want stories that please their publics. Newspeople believe that their audiences are more interested in exciting events and human-interest tales than in academic discussions of public policies. Newspeople also feel a special mission, like Shakespeare's Mark Antony, "to bury Caesar, not to praise him." And like Brutus, they claim that their criticism is not disloyalty. They do not love the government less; they only love the nation and its people more.

Each side in this tug of war uses wiles and ruses as well as clout to have its own way. The outcome is a seesaw contest in which both sides score victories and suffer defeats, but each side is more attuned to its own failures than to its victories. The public interest is served in equally uneven fashion. If we equate the public interest with a maximum of intelligible information about important issues and events, media presentations fall short. But coverage also is good because it is continuous, often well informed, with sufficient attention to audience appeal to make dry information palatable. Investigative reporting has brought to light many shortcomings and scandals that otherwise might have remained hidden. Additionally, fear of exposure by the media has undoubtedly kept government officials from straying into many questionable ventures, although this effect is hard to document. On the negative side, fear of media coverage and publicity has probably inhibited many desirable actions.

Because the contacts between officials of the national government and the media are so constant, a formal institutional structure has been established to handle their interactions. This chapter describes the fairly elaborate setup at the presidential level and the simpler arrangements for Congress. It also explores some of the problems that newspeople face in covering a flood tide of complex news expeditiously, accurately, and with a modicum of critical detachment and analysis.

Problems in communications policy making remain. All three branches of government shape communications policy, but there is little coordination among them. Even within the executive and legislative branches, so many different committees and agencies share control that the outcome tends to be a compromise that pleases nobody. Few major policy decisions have been made except during crises. Even then the weaknesses of government structures have made it easy for industry spokespersons to dominate decision making.

The government's weakness in this area may be a blessing in disguise and in the spirit of the First Amendment. Because the Constitution commands that Congress shall make no law abridging the freedom of the press, it may be well to keep all communications policy making to the barest minimum. As Chief Justice John Marshall warned early in the nation's history, the power to regulate is the power to destroy.[53] Policy making and regulation overlap. A uniform, well-articulated communications policy, however beneficial it may seem to many people, still puts the government imprint indelibly on the flow of information.

NOTES

1. Howard Kurtz, "At These Dinners, Candor Is the Entrée," *Washington Post*, April 27, 2009. The article was based on a research report released by the Center for Media and Public Affairs and Chapman University.

2. Paul F. Boller Jr., *Presidential Campaigns: From George Washington to George W. Bush* (New York: Oxford University Press, 2004).

3. "George Bush's Postwar Blues," *Media Monitor* 17, no. 4 (November/December 2003): 4–5; Katharine Graham, "The Presidency and the Press," *Miller Center Report* 16, no. 1 (2000): 4–8.

4. Joe S. Foote, *Television Access and Political Power: The Networks, the Presidency, and the "Loyal Opposition"* (New York: Praeger, 1990), reports that just before President Carter publicly announced that he would recognize the People's Republic of China, he invited the anchors of the three major networks to Washington, D.C., to break the news to them first. "This incident was tacit recognition that network anchors had assumed a status comparable to congressional leaders for whom this special type of briefing was usually reserved. The media stars had become a powerful force who deserved special handling" (135).

5. David L. Paletz and K. Kendall Guthrie, "The Three Faces of Ronald Reagan," *Journal of Communication* 37 (Fall 1987): 7–23.

6. Presidential communication in general is discussed by John Tebbel and Sarah Miles Watts, *The Press and the Presidency* (New York: Oxford University Press, 1985); and Barbara Hinckley, *The Symbolic Presidency: How Presidents Portray Themselves* (New York: Routledge, 1990); also see Samuel Kernell, *Going Public: New Strategies of Presidential Leadership*, 4th ed. (Washington, D.C.: CQ Press, 2007). Martha Joynt Kumar, "The White House 2001 Project," reports 31–34, and *Managing the President's Message: The White House Communications Operation* (Baltimore: Johns Hopkins University Press, 2007) provide excellent observation-based accounts of White House press operations, http://whitehouse2001.org. Books about the relations of individual presidents with the press include Fredric T. Smoller, *The Six O'Clock Presidency: A Theory of Presidential Press Relations in the Age of Television* (New York: Praeger, 1990); and Carolyn Smith, *Presidential Press Conferences: A Critical Approach* (New York: Praeger, 1990). Also see Mark J. Rozell, *The Press and the Ford Presidency* (Ann Arbor: University of Michigan Press, 1992).

7. Quoted in Timothy E. Cook, *Governing with the News: The News Media as a Political Institution* (Chicago: University of Chicago Press, 1998), 131.

8. "George Bush's Postwar Blues," 5.

9. Quoted in S. Robert Lichter and Linda S. Lichter, eds., "Bork: Decline and Fall," *Media Monitor* 1 (October 1987): 5.

10. Martin Linsky, *Impact: How the Press Affects Federal Policymaking* (New York: Norton, 1986), 37–38.

11. *Kennedy and the Press: The News Conferences* (New York: Crowell, 1965), 239.

12. Refusal problems are discussed in Matthew A. Baum and Samuel Kernell, "Has Cable Ended the Golden Age of Presidential Television?" *American Political Science Review* 93, no. 1 (1999): 99–114.

13. Doris A. Graber, "Terrorism, Censorship and the First Amendment: In Search of Policy Guidelines," in *Framing Terrorism: The News Media, the Government, and the Public*, ed. Pippa Norris, Montague Kern, and Marion Just (New York: Routledge, 2003), 27–42.

14. Michael Baruch Grossman and Martha Joynt Kumar, *Portraying the President: The White House and the News Media* (Baltimore: Johns Hopkins University Press, 1981); Martha Joynt Kumar and Alex Jones, "Government and the Press: Issues and Trends," in *The Institutions of American Democracy: The Press*, ed. Geneva Overholser and Kathleen Hall Jamieson (New York: Oxford University Press, 2005); Martha Joynt Kumar, "The Importance and Evolution of Presidential Press Conferences," *Presidential Studies Quarterly* 35, no. 1 (2005): 166–192.

15. Smoller, *The Six O'Clock Presidency*, 61–77.

16. "The Disappearing Honeymoon: TV News Coverage of President George W. Bush's First 100 Days," *Media Monitor* 15, no. 3 (May/June 2001): 1–5; Committee of Concerned Journalists, "The First 100 Days: How Bush Versus Clinton Fared in the Press," www.journalism.org/publ_research/100days1.html, May 2001.

17. Jeffrey E. Cohen, *The Presidency in the Era of 24-hour News* (Princeton: Princeton University Press, 2008).

18. Diana Owen and Richard Davis, "Presidential Communication in the Internet Era," *Presidential Studies Quarterly* 38, no. 4 (2008): 658–672.

19. Joseph Graf, "New Media: The Cutting Edge of Campaign Communications," in *Campaigns on the Cutting Edge*, ed. Richard J. Semiatin (Washington, D.C.: CQ Press, 2008), 48–68.

20. David Almacy, "David Almacy Hosts 'Ask the White House,' March 1, 2007," www.whitehouse.gov/ask/print/20070301.html.

21. Michael Margolis and David Resnick, *Politics as Usual: The Cyberspace "Revolution"* (Thousand Oaks, Calif.: Sage, 2000); Kumar, *Managing the President's Message*.

22. John Anthony Maltese, *Spin Control: The White House Office of Communications and the Management of Presidential News*, 2nd ed. (Chapel Hill: University of North Carolina Press, 1994); also see Martha Joynt Kumar, "The Office of the Press Secretary," report 31, and "The Office of Communications," report 33, in "White House 2001 Project," http://whitehouse2001.org.

23. Woody Klein, *All the Presidents' Spokesmen: Spinning the News, White House Press Secretaries from Franklin D. Roosevelt to George W. Bush*. Westport, Conn.: Praeger, 2008.

24. Quoted in Kumar, "The Office of Communications," 5.

25. Martha Joynt Kumar, "Communications Operation in the White House of President George W. Bush: Making News on His Terms," *Presidential Studies Quarterly* 33, no. 2 (2003): 366–393; Martha Joynt Kumar, "The White House and the Press: News Organizations as a Presidential Resource and as a Source of Pressure," *Presidential Studies Quarterly* 33, no. 3 (2003): 669–683; Kumar and Jones, "Government and the Press."

26. Maltese, *Spin Control*, 253.

27. Ibid., 6.

28. Mark Silva, "Is It Public Relations or Propaganda?" *Chicago Tribune*, March 14, 2005.

29. David Barstow and Robin Stein, "Under Bush, a New Age of Prepackaged TV News," *New York Times*, March 13, 2005.

30. Kumar and Jones, "Government and the Press"; Kumar, "The Importance and Evolution of Presidential Press Conferences"; also see Stephen Hess, "A New Survey of the White House Press Corps," *Presidential Studies Quarterly* 22, no. 2 (Spring 1992): 311–321.

31. Smith, *Presidential Press Conferences*, 41.

32. For a thorough analysis of presidential press conferences, see Smith, *Presidential Press Conferences*; and Frank Cormier, James Deakin, and Helen Thomas, *The White House Press on the Presidency: News Management and Co-Option* (Lanham, Md.: University Press of America, 1983); and Kumar, "The Importance and Evolution of Presidential Press Conferences."

33. Steven R. Weisman, "Reagan, Annoyed by News Leaks, Tells Staff to Limit Press Relations," *New York Times*, January 11, 1983. For a list of measures taken by the Reagan administration to stop leaks, see Ronald Berkman and Laura W. Kitch, *Politics in the Media Age* (New York:

McGraw-Hill, 1986). The Bush administration tried equally unsuccessfully to stop further leaks following the Thomas affair.

34. Robert O. Blanchard, ed., *Congress and the News Media* (New York: Hastings House, 1974), 105.

35. Kathleen Hall Jamieson, *Eloquence in an Electronic Age: The Transformation of Political Speechmaking* (New York: Oxford University Press, 1988),14.

36. Stephen Hess, *The Washington Reporters* (Washington, D.C.: Brookings Institution Press, 1981), 99. The figures are based on 921 newspaper and 87 television stories.

37. Ronald D. Elving, "Making News, Making Law," *Media Studies Journal* 10 (Winter 1996): 50; Brian J. Fogarty, "The Strategy of the Story: Media Monitoring Legislative Activity," *Legislative Studies Quarterly* 33, no. 3 (2008): 445–469.

38. Hess, *The Washington Reporters*, 104–105; and Karen M. Kedrowski, *Media Entrepreneurs and the Media Enterprise in the U.S. Congress* (Cresskill, N.J.: Hampton Press, 1996) 5.

39. Quoted in Steven V. Roberts, "Senators Squint into a Future under TV's Gaze," *New York Times*, February 4, 1986.

40. Timothy E. Cook, *Making Laws and Making News: Media Strategies in the U.S. House of Representatives* (Washington, D.C.: Brookings Institution Press, 1989); and Kedrowski, *Media Entrepreneurs*, provide detailed analyses of congressional news making. Also see R. Douglas Arnold, *Congress, the Press, and Political Accountability* (Princeton: Princeton University Press, 2004).

41. Diana Owen, Richard Davis, and Vincent James Strickler, "Congress and the Internet," *Press/Politics* 4, no. 2 (1999): 10–29.

42. Daniel Lipinski and Gregory Neddenriep, "Using 'New' Media to Get 'Old' Media Coverage: How Members of Congress Use Their Web Sites," *Press/Politics* 9, no. 1 (2004): 7–21.

43. "Media and Congress," *Media Studies Journal* 10, no. 1 (Winter 1996); and Stephen Hess, *Live from Capitol Hill: Studies of Congress and the Media* (Washington, D.C.: Brookings Institution Press, 1991), 117; also see Kedrowski, *Media Entrepreneurs*; and Arnold, *Congress, the Press and Political Accountability*. For an excellent discussion of congressional press galleries, see Melissa Merson, "Big Picture and Local Angle," *Media Studies Journal* 10, no. 1 (winter 1996): 55–66.

44. Patrick J. Sellers, "Congress and the News Media: Manipulating the Message in the U.S. Congress," *Press/Politics* 5, no. 1 (2000): 22–31.

45. "How TV News Has Covered the 103rd Congress," *Media Monitor* 8, no. 5 (September/October 1994): 2.

46. Ibid.; Timothy E. Cook, "House Members as National Newsmakers: The Effects of Televising Congress," *Legislative Studies Quarterly* 11 (Summer 1986): 203–226; and Stephen Hess, *The Ultimate Insiders: U.S. Senators and the National Media* (Washington, D.C.: Brookings Institution Press, 1986); also see Hess, *Live from Capitol Hill*, 55–58; and Kedrowski, *Media Entrepreneurs*, chaps. 5, 8.

47. 2009 Polling Report.com, www.pollingreport.com/CongJob.htm.

48. Girish J. Gulati, "Members of Congress and Presentation of Self on the World Wide Web," *Press/Politics* 9, no. 1 (2004): 22–40; Fogarty, "The Strategy of the Story."

49. "How TV News Has Covered the 103rd Congress," 2.

50. Michael J. Robinson, "Three Faces of Congressional Media," in *The New Congress*, ed. Thomas E. Mann and Norman J. Ornstein (Washington, D.C.: American Enterprise Institute, 1981).

51. For a history on the politics of communications policy formulation, see Erwin G. Krasnow, Lawrence D. Longley, and Herbert A. Terry, *The Politics of Broadcast Regulation*, 3rd ed. (New York: St. Martin's, 1982), 87–132; and Robert Britt, *The Irony of Regulatory Reform: The Deregulation of American Telecommunications* (New York: Oxford University Press, 1989); also Patricia Aufderheide, *Communications Policy and the Public Interest* (New York: Guilford Press, 1999).

52. Krasnow, Longley, and Terry, *The Politics of Broadcast Regulation*.

53. *McCulloch v. Maryland*, 17 U.S. (4 Wheat.) 316 (1819).

READINGS

Arnold, R. Douglas. *Congress, the Press, and Political Accountability.* Princeton: Princeton University Press, 2004.

Cohen, Jeffrey E. *The Presidency in the Era of 24-Hour News.* Princeton: Princeton University Press, 2008.

Fleischer, Ari. *Taking Heat: The President, the Press, and My Years in the White House.* New York: William Morrow, 2005.

Fritz, Ben, Bryan Keefer, and Brendan Nyhan. *All the President's Spin: George W. Bush, the Media, and the Truth.* New York: Simon and Schuster, 2004.

Kedrowski, Karen M. *Media Entrepreneurs and the Media Enterprise in the U.S. Congress.* Cresskill, N.J.: Hampton Press, 1996.

Kerbel, Matthew R. *Netroots: Online Progressives and the Transformation of American Politics.* Boulder: Paradigm, 2009.

Kernell, Samuel. *Going Public: New Strategies of Presidential Leadership.* 4th ed. Washington, D.C.: CQ Press, 2007.

Klein, Woody. *All the Presidents' Spokesmen: Spinning the News; White House Press Secretaries from Franklin D. Roosevelt to George W. Bush.* Westport, Conn: Praeger, 2008.

Kumar, Martha Joynt. *Managing the President's Message: The White House Communications Operation.* Baltimore: Johns Hopkins University Press, 2007.

Pole, Antoinette. *Blogging the Political: Political Participation in a Networked Society.* New York: Routledge, 2009.

10

Covering the Justice System and State and Local News

I n a classic study of media and public opinion, the renowned U.S. journalist Walter Lippmann likened the performance of the media to "the beam of a searchlight that moves restlessly about, bringing one episode and then another out of darkness into vision." The media were not a "mirror on the world," as others had claimed. Lippmann concluded, "Men cannot do the work of the world by this light alone. They cannot govern society by episodes, incidents, and eruptions."[1]

What Lippmann observed in 1922 is still true today. The media provide spotty coverage, leaving much of the political landscape obscured. Unfortunately, the institutions covered in this chapter—the courts, state governments, and local governments—have been in the shadows of media coverage even though citizens' personal lives are affected far more directly by these institutions than by the White House and Congress, which are media darlings. Citizens' chances for influencing local government and local policies are also much greater than their chances on the national scene. Moreover, local news is for most citizens their primary political information source. They have told pollsters that loss of local news would hurt the civic life of the community and they would miss it a lot. That is a surprising judgment, given the generally poor quality of news about the justice system and state and local matters.[2]

THE MEDIA AND THE COURTS

Of the three branches of the national government, only the judiciary has been sparsely covered. This is the case even for the highest court in the nation (see Table 9-1). Over the span of one year, ending in March 2009, it received less than one hour of network evening news stories on NBC. That amounted to a mere 6 percent of the time allotted to all three branches of the national government. The presidency received 66 percent and Congress 28 percent. The pattern of sparse coverage is similar in major newspapers.

Federal-level judges are rarely in the limelight. They grant interviews infrequently, almost never hold news conferences, and generally do not seek or welcome media attention, lest their impartiality and mystique be compromised. Remoteness enhances the impression that judges are a breed apart, doling out justice to lesser mortals. At the state and local levels, where many judges are elected rather than appointed to office, media coverage is more common, especially during judicial elections. The aura of judicial majesty recedes accordingly.[3] On the rare occasions when the Supreme Court has been widely accused of unduly meddling in politics, its luster also dulls for many Court watchers. That happened in 2000 when its decision on the legality of vote counts in Florida decided the outcome of the presidential election.[4]

The immunity from personal media scrutiny that U.S. Supreme Court justices generally enjoy does not extend to the hearings conducted before their appointment to the Court is confirmed. These hearings, and the public debate they engender, can be highly acrimonious. Examples include the 1987 political battle that scuttled the nomination of conservative judge Robert Bork and the soap operatic hearings about alleged sexual improprieties committed by judge Clarence Thomas, whose appointment was ultimately approved in 1991. Because dramatic hearings have great audience appeal, they are often extensively reported on television programs and special Web sites like CNN's crime site and *truTv.*

Hearings also demonstrate how pressure groups use the media to influence judicial politics. For instance, during the confirmation hearings for Bork and Thomas, liberal as well as conservative groups mounted a massive media campaign to publicize their perceptions of the merits of the appointment. Spokespersons for such groups as the American Civil Liberties Union, the National Association for the Advancement of Colored People, the National Organization for Women, and the American Federation of Labor and Congress of Industrial Organizations spoke for the liberal camp, and conservatives lobbied through Pat Robertson's Christian Coalition and the Conservative Victory Committee. Tactics included television and radio advertisements, talk show appearances, essays in the editorial opinion sections of newspapers, wining and dining of media personnel, and careful research and coordination work.

The institutional aspects of the federal courts also receive comparatively little coverage. There are exceptions, of course. The courts' difficulties in coping with the flood of legal actions, the problems of disparate sentencing policies, and the flaws in the correction system have all been the subject of sporadic media investigations. Supreme Court justices' public speeches have been telecast and reported nationwide. Chief Justice Warren E. Burger even consented to regular questioning about his annual State of the Judiciary speech. The news conference before the speech remained off the record, however, and the media could not quote the chief justice directly.

Although federal judges and court systems are not very newsworthy by prevailing news selection standards because they generally do not become embroiled in open battles about policies, their work—judicial decisions—does make the news. This is particularly true of U.S. Supreme Court decisions, which frequently have major consequences for the political system. For example, *Brown v. Board of Education* (1954) was widely publicized because it declared the separate schooling of children of different races unconstitutional. *Roe v. Wade* (1973) and *Planned Parenthood v. Casey* (1992) received ample media attention because they involved the emotional issue of a woman's right to have an abortion.[5] *Ledbetter v. Goodyear Tire and Rubber Co.* (2007), an employment discrimination case, led to the passage of the 2009 Lilly Ledbetter Fair Pay Act, which expanded civil rights protections to equal-pay issues. In general the news media give disproportionately heavy attention to civil rights and First Amendment cases; they slight cases involving economic and business matters. Overall, the media cover only a fraction of the Court's decisions. The focus of news stories is limited to the formal decision; the Court's decision-making process remains largely shrouded in secrecy.[6]

Impact of Coverage

Publicity about Supreme Court decisions is very important because it informs public officials at all government levels, as well as the general public, about the law of the land governing important, controversial issues. A small corps of reporters is responsible for singling out the decisions that will receive abundant media attention. Some fifty reporters cover the Supreme Court, and of those only a dozen correspondents for major wire services and newspapers are full-time.[7] In 1998, for example, six reporters filed 88 percent of the 211 news stories about Court decisions. They represented just five news organizations: the Associated Press, *Los Angeles Times, New York Times, Washington Post,* and *USA Today.*[8]

Supreme Court coverage is difficult for reporters. The justices usually announce multiple decisions on a single day, forcing reporters to digest voluminous and often contradictory opinions rapidly. This must be done without help from the justices who wrote the opinions. Reporters' deadlines may be only minutes away, and the news may be stale after more than twenty-four hours have elapsed. Advice from outside commentators, including legal experts, is usually unavailable initially because experts are not allowed to preview the opinions and advance leaks are rare. The Supreme Court does have a press office, which provides some reference materials and bare-bones records of the Court's activities. But it refuses to interpret the justices' decisions in laypersons' terms, fearing entanglement in legal controversies. However, publications sponsored by the legal profession make brief analyses of important pending cases available to the media. In addition, universities and leading newspapers have Web sites featuring archived decisions and even audio files of arguments the Court has heard.[9]

Because of the shortage of skilled legal reporters, much reporting on the courts—even the Supreme Court—is imprecise and sometimes outright wrong. Justice Felix Frankfurter once complained that editors who would never consider covering a baseball game through a reporter unfamiliar with the sport regularly assigned reporters unfamiliar with the law to cover the Supreme Court. The situation has improved considerably in recent years, but it is far from cured. Many editors do not want to assign reporters with legal expertise, fearing their stories would be too technical and dull.

Two landmark decisions—*Engel v. Vitale* (1962), which outlawed school prayer, and *Baker v. Carr* (1962), which invalidated many electoral district boundaries—provide examples of faulty reporting.[10] Stories about these two decisions in sixty-three metropolitan daily papers featured misleading head-lines and serious errors.[11] Ill-informed statements by well-known people who opposed the Court's decisions made up the major part of the stories. For instance, the decision outlawing classroom prayer in public schools was attrib-uted to the wrong clause of the Constitution. Arguments made in lower courts were erroneously ascribed to Supreme Court justices. Moreover, the media covered the prayer decision more heavily because it presented an easy-to-grasp, emotionally stirring story, even though the duller reapportionment decision was far more significant. At times coverage is excellent, including commentary on legal issues and the long-range implications of cases.[12] For example, a study of network coverage of the 1978 *Bakke* racial discrimination case and the 1989 *Webster* abortion rights case revealed that three out of four TV news stories about these prominent cases featured valuable interpretations along with the factual account.[13]

The thrust of complaints about sketchy, inaccurate, and out-of-context judicial reporting is the same as for coverage of the presidency and Congress. But complaints are more justified. Reporting of Court activities has been more superficial and flawed than its presidential and congressional counter-parts.[14] The reasons are not difficult to understand. The volume of decisions clusters near the end of the annual term. The subject matter is often highly technical and is hard for reporters to understand and make understandable. With notable exceptions, stories about judicial decisions lack the potential to become exciting, front-page news. They are hard to boil down into catchy phrases and clichés. They rarely lend themselves to exciting visual coverage. The Supreme Court beat tends to be understaffed. All of these factors make it difficult for the assigned reporters to prepare interesting, well-researched accounts.

The information supplied to the public, though inadequate for providing important insights into the law and the judicial process, usually sustains respect for the judiciary and compliance with its rulings. The majority of the public hold its work in high esteem.[15] Seven in ten Americans have confidence in its rulings.[16] This is crucial because the Court lacks the power and institu-tional structure to enforce its decisions. Occasionally Court publicity has the opposite effect, however. For instance, Justice Tom Clark, one of the partici-pants in the 1962 prayer decision, complained that misunderstanding of *Engel v. Vitale* made this ruling unpopular. He blamed inadequate reporting for fail-ures to comply with the decision, and an abortive movement to nullify it through a constitutional amendment.

Public reactions to Supreme Court decisions may affect future decisions of the Court because justices are influenced in their work by what they read and hear from the media. Media reports of crime waves, or price gouging by busi-ness, or public opposition to aid for parochial schools are likely to set boundar-ies to judicial policy making.[17] This makes it tragic that much of the reporting leaves the public unprepared to make sound assessments of the Court's rulings.

" LADIES AND GENTLEMEN OF THE PRESS —
WHAT IS YOUR VERDICT..?"

Recent research provides evidence that news stories can influence court personnel. For example, the amount of publicity given to a crime influences prosecutors. When there is little publicity, prosecutors are less likely to press for a trial of the case and more likely to agree to a plea-bargain settlement. In federal murder trials, longer sentences tend to follow more pretrial publicity for defendants.[18] The effects of media coverage tend to persist for subsequent similar cases. News stories also have lasting effects on the public's perception of who is likely to be a perpetrator or victim of crime. For instance, television news often shows young black males as criminal offenders. Viewers then associate that demographic group with reported incidents of violent crime.[19]

News about Crime and the Justice System

Publications of decisions by the Supreme Court and lower courts are by no means the only significant news about the judiciary. General news about crime and the work of the justice system is also important in creating images of the quality of public justice. Here a plentiful media diet is available, especially on local television news, where nearly 32 percent of the coverage is devoted to the topic. Business and consumer news issues receive less than one-third as much attention.[20] Crime and justice news receives more than triple the news share allotted to any other topic. Like stories about other government activities, crime and justice system stories tend to focus on sensational events, often at the expense of significant trends and problems in the legal system that might benefit from greater public attention.[21]

TABLE 10-1 **Police versus Newspaper Crime Reports, Chicago (in numbers and percentages)**

Crime[a]	Police reports		Tribune reports	
Murder	651	0.3%	74	48.6%
Sexual assault	2,024	1.0%	26	17.1%
Assault	22,905	11.8%	32	21.1%
Theft/robbery/burglary/arson	167,725	86.8%	20	13.2%
Total	193,305		152	

Source: Compiled from police crime reports and *Chicago Tribune* index 2002.

[a] Murder includes manslaughter, assassination, mass murders, and serial murders. Assault includes aggravated assault and aggravated battery. Theft includes motor vehicle theft.

The nature of crime news coverage and its prevalence in the media, particularly on television, has long been a matter of concern to public officials and the public. It is widely believed that current coverage practices deflect attention from the social causes of crime and the policies needed to curb it. Sensational stories lead to exaggerated fear of crime because the focus is on the most violent incidents, which in real life constitute only a tiny portion of crime. Nearly 66 percent of the crime stories in the *Chicago Tribune* in 2002 dealt with murder or sexual assaults, in a year when these crimes constituted slightly under 2 percent of the actual crimes in the city (see Table 10-1). By contrast, white-collar crime, which is widely prevalent and often threatens public safety, receives little coverage, and that conceals its seriousness as a social problem. These figures are typical for crime coverage by local news media.[22] Many experts on criminal behavior contend that extensive, graphic coverage of crime can glamorize it and thereby encourage imitation. News stories that focus selectively on sensational aspects of a case can also mislead the public—and possibly jurors—about who is guilty and who is innocent. When that happens, guilty defendants may escape justice and innocent ones may be convicted.[23]

Probably the most graphic aspect of the "tabloidization" of crime news is the overemphasis of crimes involving celebrities or crimes that seem particularly heinous (Box 10-1). The total amount of coverage is disproportionate, especially since much of it is little more than a repeated spinning out of insignificant, often irrelevant details. Coverage is also disproportionate compared to other important stories that need attention. For example, there were 22,610 stories in sixty-five major newspapers about the murder case involving football legend O. J. Simpson between 1994 and 1997, including 1,471 front-page stories.[24] During the same period, the three national networks aired 1,225 Simpson stories, roughly four times the number of stories given to Medicare and welfare policies combined. The Simpson celebrity crime story was topped

BOX 10-1 **The *CSI* Effect**

Most Americans who watch the ample dramatic television stories about celebrities accused of heinous crimes are familiar with the details of the charges. But they know very little about the painstaking, detailed forensic work that goes into constructing a viable court case. The news media don't dwell on such tedious matters. By contrast, crime shows like *CSI: Crime Scene Investigations and Forensic Files* do so dramatically. Viewers learn from them and form opinions about how criminal cases should be handled, including the work that forensic laboratories should and can do. Prosecutors call such distorted knowledge the "*CSI* effect" and complain that it makes it difficult to get convictions in criminal cases. Jurors apply the hyped forensic science observed in fictional shows to the real trials that they are asked to judge.

In the case of actor Robert Blake, who was tried in 2005 on charges of murdering his wife, jurors refused to render a "guilty" verdict because the evidence lacked the absolute certainty that crime shows produce when they solve capital crimes during one evening's program. The Blake case jurors decided that there was not enough conclusive proof that Blake had shot his wife; they dismissed circumstantial evidence that should have been sufficient to yield a conviction. One juror stated outright that her high expectations about the quality of evidence were based on what she had learned from crime shows. She expected the kind of powerful evidence that she had seen in *CSI* cases.[1] Like 70 percent of the jurors who answered a recent survey, she was among the 60 million Americans who tune in weekly to *CSI* shows.[2]

The *CSI* effect—drawing on fictional events to form opinions about unfamiliar scenarios in real life—occurs quite often. What most people know about courtroom behavior comes from watching *Judge Judy* (more than 10 million people watched daily in 2009), the *People's Court,* and the dozens of shows like them.[3] Surveys show that jurors who watch crime shows often believe that trial judges usually reveal their own opinions about the case to all parties and that the judge's facial expressions and sarcastic remarks guide the jury's deliberations about the defendant's guilt or innocence. They are unaware that verdicts rarely are instantly executed because they are followed by various motions and appeals that delay the final outcome.

Applying false standards to reality is obviously harmful. What can be done about it when millions of Americans absorb a mixture of truth and fiction from their daily television exposure? When journalists report about criminal trials, they could include more details about the procedures involved in resolving criminal cases. They also could explode *CSI*–generated myths. For example, audiences can be told that DNA tests cannot be completed in minutes and that it is impossible to match fingerprints instantly to a national crime database. Given media norms, such a focus on public education is unlikely to emerge. The more likely solution is to demand higher standards of accuracy from fictional shows. Television producers routinely take great pains to produce accurate historical dramas and political shows. They should strive for the same standards of accuracy in fictional crime stories that are cast as quasi-reality and, in the process, become reality for millions of citizens.

1. Andrew Blankstein and Jean Guccione, "The Blake Verdict and the 'CSI Effect,'" *Chicago Tribune,* March 22, 2005.
2. Richard Willing, "'CSI Effect' Has Juries Wanting More Evidence," *USA Today,* August 5, 2004.
3. AbsoluteAstronomy.com, 2009

only by reports about the investigation of President Bill Clinton's relations with intern Monica Lewinsky, which totaled 25,975 stories in the sixty-five papers in just one year (1998), including 1,959 front-page stories. There is no record to show how many more significant stories news sources omitted to make room for these celebrity crime accounts.

Such stories are bonanzas for media enterprises because they sharply increase audience size and with it rates that can be charged for advertising. CNN, for example, more than tripled its average ratings at the height of the Simpson trial and more than quadrupled them during the peak phases of the Lewinsky affair.[25] A Web browser search in November 1998 found 498,932 Web pages on Netscape mentioning the Simpson trial and 622,079 mentioning either Monica Lewinsky or Paula Jones, two principals in the Clinton saga. No wonder, then, that 97 percent of the public were familiar with these cases, compared with 12 percent who could identify the chief justice of the United States.

If there is widespread agreement that current patterns of crime news coverage are excessive and undesirable, why do they continue in daily newspapers and on national and local television throughout the country? There are several reasons. Most important, despite their complaints, audiences flock to crime news, partly because it involves personal security but mostly to satisfy a hunger for excitement. This has been the case since the birth of tabloid newspapers more than 150 years ago. When crime news makes huge, front-page headlines, paper sales rise sharply and audience ratings for television news channels skyrocket. The local television news, with its heavy crime component, has eclipsed national news, which carries more serious political stories and less crime, in the battle for high audience ratings. In the entertainment world, crime shows are highly popular. Besides audience appeal, crime news has the advantage of ease of coverage. The police beat can supply a steady diet of new crimes for hungry reporters who prefer to mine a news-rich source rather than working leaner beats.

Judicial Censorship

There are several significant systematic omissions in media coverage of the U.S. crime and justice system. The Supreme Court bars reporters from all of its deliberations before the announcement of decisions. On the few occasions when forthcoming decisions were leaked ahead of time, justices have reacted with great anger and have curtailed contacts between newspeople and Court personnel. Television cameras are barred most of the time from federal courts, and proceedings may not be broadcast live. Federal district and appellate courts allowed cameras in the courtroom as a three-year experiment in 1991. They ended coverage in 1994 on the grounds that the cameras were distracting to the jurors and witnesses even though appraisals of the experiment had found little or no impact on the administration of justice.

For years many state courts prohibited radio and television reporters from covering trials and other proceedings. They feared that recording

devices might produce a carnival atmosphere that would intimidate participants, endanger witnesses, and harm the fairness of the proceedings. To allow
citizens to watch how their courts operate, all states now allow cameras to
record court proceedings subject to rules that protect the parties in the judicial drama from undue invasion of their privacy.[26] The debate about the
wisdom of televising court proceedings surged in the wake of the massive
media attention to the O. J. Simpson murder trial, which drowned out much
other news for nearly a year. Critics of televised sessions claim that the
judges' and lawyers' showboating distorted and delayed the verdict and
diminished the public's regard for the legal system. Televised trials tend to
focus on courtroom drama at the expense of explaining legal issues. Others
argue that the public is entitled to monitor the courts' performance via television in a public trial.[27]

Restraints on live audio and video coverage are not the only limitations on
judicial publicity. In the interest of ensuring fair trials, courts also limit the
information that may be printed while court proceedings are in progress.
These types of restrictions were discussed in chapter 3.

COVERING STATE AND LOCAL AFFAIRS

It is an axiom of U.S. politics that "all politics is local." Decentralized politics is
essential and invigorating in a nation that spans a continent and embodies
diverse political cultures and contexts. Because national politics is glamorous
and important, it is easy to ignore the grass roots that nourish and shape it. It
is therefore not surprising that most research has focused on the national level,
despite the significant impact that coverage of local politics and local perspectives has on national politics.[28]

The Changing Media Grid

Mirroring the nation's political geography and culture, U.S. newspapers and
radio and television stations have been primarily structured to serve a multi-
tude of local markets. At the start of the twentieth century, every large and
medium-sized city and even many small towns had at least one newspaper, and
often more, geared to local political needs. Most cities are now served by a
single newspaper, and many no longer have their own paper. Nearly every city
also used to have its own electronic media, to serve local audiences. Technological
changes and large-scale migration of former inner-city dwellers to the suburbs
have eroded this local focus, so that electronic media now are serving ever-
larger regions. It is not uncommon for television stations and metropolitan
dailies to reach people in fifty counties, making comprehensive local coverage
impossible. Reporting, of necessity, becomes highly selective and superficial.
Coverage areas typically include some 1,300 government units, whose policies
should be reported because they involve important public issues, including the
power to tax. Numerous state legislators, as well as several national legislators,

are elected within these counties. Media critic Ben Bagdikian describes the consequences:

> News distribution is no longer designed for individual towns and cities. American politics is organized on the basis of the 20,000 urban and rural places in the country, which is the way citizens vote. But the media have organized on the basis of 210 television "markets," which is the way merchandisers and media corporations sell ads. As a result, the fit between the country's information needs and its information media has become disastrously disjointed.[29]

The Vanishing Metropolitan Focus. Because market areas and political communities no longer coincide, reporting has turned away from strictly local problems to more generalized topics of interest to the entire market area. That has meant more focus on soft news and less information about important local problems that face citizens.[30] This is happening despite the fact that nationwide polls show that interest in local news is growing. In 2008, 52 percent of respondents to a nationwide poll said that they watched local news regularly. Only 29 percent expressed similar interest in nightly national newscasts.[31]

The problem of insufficient local news may be easing because some news suppliers, like the *Chicago Tribune*, besides launching more suburban versions are also branching out through Web sites dedicated to local news in specific nearby towns and villages. Another boost for access to local news comes from community access cable channels that allow citizens to watch local government in action. City council meetings, committee hearings, and court procedures have become directly accessible to the public without the intervention of journalists. The suburbs, where such channels have been scarce in the past, are joining the parade, thereby providing more competition for suburban newspapers. However, audiences for live broadcasts of local government activities are generally quite small.

Umbrella Competition Patterns. In response to large population shifts from inner cities to sprawling suburbs, print media have developed a structure of "umbrella competition," in which smaller units operate within the area covered simultaneously by the larger units.[32] The umbrella pattern consists of four layers. In the first layer, large metropolitan dailies provide substantial amounts of international, national, and regional coverage. In the second layer, smaller satellite dailies resemble their larger cousins but carry more local news. The third layer contains suburban dailies. They emphasize local news, much of it nonpolitical, and are a rapidly growing sector. Though their circulation is still below the metropolitan circulation figures, suburban papers have been profitable because they offer an attractive advertising opportunity to the many businesses whose customers now cluster in suburban areas. The fourth layer consists of weekly newspapers and "shoppers" that are distributed free of charge because they contain mostly advertising and only a sprinkling of news and feature stories.

The emphasis on local news increases as one moves through these layers. This has happened because newspapers with a narrower reach try to distinguish themselves from the metropolitan papers and thereby make themselves more attractive to their clientele. But because of the lack of fit between media markets and political units, most of the local news avoids detailed discussion and in-depth analysis of local public issues, so that it does not provide the information that citizens need to monitor local politics effectively. The audiovisual media follow similar patterns. Television stations in smaller markets feature more local and less national and international news than their larger cousins.[33] Citizens rely heavily on these broadcasts, which tend to be shallow because of time constraints.[34] Most local radio news stations devote more than half of their airtime to local news. Stations in smaller radio markets usually present fewer stories simply because the pool of local news is tiny.[35]

The Alternative Press. In addition to the four layers discussed, there is also an alternative national and local press. It tends to focus narrowly on issues of interest to people representing minority political cultures or people with distinctive lifestyles and cultural and political tastes. Many specialized media are targeted to ethnic, racial, linguistic, and religious groups, as well as to groups with alternative lifestyles, such as gays and lesbians. Examples of popular alternative papers include Boston's weekly *Dig,* San Francisco's *Bay Guardian,* and the *Isthmus* in Madison, Wisconsin. Some specialized media are published in foreign languages to meet the needs of immigrants. Although these media provide in-depth coverage of local, national, and international news of interest to their clientele, they omit news covering broader concerns. Their readers may therefore live in narrow communications ghettos that keep them from fully understanding their surroundings.

From time to time, specialized media try to generate support for issues favored by their audiences. They may influence local elections. Media serving African American and Hispanic communities are good examples. Besides having their own print media, large subcultural groups in the United States are also served by electronic news media tailored to their special concerns. Over-the-air and cable television and radio stations geared to the needs of subcultures, especially Spanish speakers, are multiplying and flourishing throughout the country. There are more than 400 Hispanic newspapers and two major television networks—Univision and Telemundo. In Los Angeles, Univision has become the leading supplier of television news.[36] Ethnic networks serve relatively youthful populations who are hungrier for televised news than the general population. They are a growing media force bound to carry increasing weight in U.S. politics, especially in urban areas. In New York City, for example, a dozen ethnic press ventures, out of fifty, claim circulations of more than 100,000. The five largest among them serve Jewish, Chinese, Hispanic, black, and Korean populations.[37]

Government-Press Relations at Subnational Levels

Subnational news is important for setting the public policy agenda at the state and local levels. It helps or hinders politicians in achieving their goals. It influences the election and appointment of public officials. It informs the public and officialdom about political affairs and politicians' wrongdoings. However, there are differences in emphasis between national and subnational political coverage, largely because subnational politics operates on a much smaller scale and in a much clubbier environment. Scholars have largely neglected the subnational media, despite unmistakable signs of their importance.[38]

How Officials Use the Press. At the subnational level, public officials find it much easier to stay in touch with each other without relying on news stories. They also remain in closer direct contact with a comparatively tiny corps of reporters, so that formal press conferences are less necessary. Moreover, their news is rarely so exciting that they can count on decent attendance if they do schedule a news conference.

Fewer subnational officials are experts in media relations. The public information and public relations materials they present to the media are often so poorly done that they do more harm than good. Many tasks that mayors and city managers perform are highly technical and difficult to condense into brief news stories suitable for lay publics. When officials do make the effort to tell their stories, reporters generally lack technical expertise to judge the accuracy of the account. Consequently, when the story relates to a policy decision involving important technical issues—for example, whether to start, continue, or stop a sewer project; how to finance it; and similar matters—the official views are likely to define the situation with little media scrutiny.

Media scholar Phyllis Kaniss identified six media styles that are especially common among public figures at the subnational level.[39] The *paranoid media-avoider* fears the press and tries to avoid it as much as possible. Information-hungry journalists are likely to retaliate with unfavorable publicity at every opportunity. The *naïve professional* supplies the media with information and talks freely with journalists without realizing that uncontrolled release of information empowers reporters to determine which topics will be highlighted and how they will be framed. The *ribbon cutter* is a media junkie heavily concerned with arranging events, however trivial, that are likely to attract journalists. The ensuing publicity may have few political payoffs. *Dancing marionettes* take their cues from media editorials and take action in areas suggested by newspeople, rather than initiating policies independently. The reward is likely to be favorable coverage, although the policy agenda that newspeople favor may be undesirable from the official's perspective. *Colorful quotables* excel in creating cool sound bites and making sure that these come to the attention of reporters. Like ribbon cutters, their political rewards are apt to be small. Finally, *liars* conceal or slant information or distort it outright to put themselves in a favorable light.

The era of informal, inexpert handling of the press by subnational officials seems to be ending. Currently, all governors and most big-city mayors have press secretaries or public information offices. Like their counterparts at the national level, public figures try to use these offices to push their programs through recalcitrant legislative bodies and to disseminate news about their activities to various political elites and interested citizens. However, as on the national level, such efforts often fail. Fearing to be hoodwinked by clever professionals, the media have become suspicious, cynical commentators rather than trusting friends.

Elected officials are not alone in craving good media coverage. Appointed officials, too, need favorable images to help them win funding and support for the policies their agencies pursue. A poll of high-level federal officials showed that 79 percent thought that positive coverage increased their chances of achieving major policy goals.[40] Legislatures rarely deny support to popular agencies. By the same token, bad publicity hurts. When media frame stories in ways that subvert official goals, public officials may have to reset their own sights. For example, city sanitation departments have been forced to concentrate on cleaning minor waste sites and neglecting more serious ones when publicity has highlighted a particular pollution hazard.

As on the national scene, local strategies designed to win media attention include press conferences, press releases, staging newsworthy events, writing op-ed pieces, and writing letters to the editor. Contacting media personnel directly seems to be the best approach, and apparently it is quite successful. Press releases are least productive. Estimates are that more than half of the content of the print and electronic media originates with publicity seekers rather than journalists.[41] Government officials at all levels provide a large share of these so-called news subsidies.[42]

In the past, most efforts to gain media coverage at the subnational level were directed at the print media, which governors, lieutenant governors, attorneys general, secretaries of state, and various legislative leaders deemed to be the most effective transmitters of state and local political news. That is changing. More local officials realize that television and the Web are most important for mobilizing public opinion. Therefore, they try harder to get television and Web site coverage for themselves and their agencies.[43]

How Reporters Operate at Subnational Levels. Reporters are also somewhat different at the subnational level. Taken as a group, they have less formal education and considerably less job experience. Still, the officials' level of education may rank considerably below reporters'. Turnover rates are high among reporters. They are often forced to move to a different market when they switch jobs because clauses in their contracts forbid them to work for a competitor in the same area. Reporters' unfamiliarity with local politics in their new surroundings may strain relations between reporters and officials when they disagree in their analyses of political events. However, most of the time, personal relations between reporters and officials tend to be more cordial at the subnational level because these people interact more. In fact, ties of friendship have been blamed for the dearth of press criticism of local officials and local businesses.[44]

Aside from media outlets under the wing of metropolitan newspapers, news organizations at the subnational level are usually considerably smaller than their national counterparts. Consequently, reporters have to cover many beats rather than becoming specialists. Roving reporters must depend more heavily on routine sources, such as daily inquiries at the police and fire departments, local newspapers, assorted press releases, tips from viewers, wire service stories, and the wire service "day books" that list significant local events.[45] Because most government business stops in the early evening hours, late evening local news broadcasts depend heavily on the staples supplied by police and fire department records.[46] Serious political news featured on early evening national newscasts is deemed "stale" by nine or ten at night. Stories with the best pictures and best sound bites tend to become leads, even when they are not necessarily the most important stories. Because many state and local stories are technical and undramatic, journalists strive mightily to make them entertaining. That means bypassing opportunities for detailed exposition of problems because that might bore the audience. In the process of tabloidizing news, the importance of events and their broader and long-term consequences are easily lost.

Why do journalists who work in large metropolitan areas ignore the politics of nearby suburban communities? There are several reasons for "city myopia" among metropolitan media.[47] Among them is the fact that metropolitan newspaper offices usually are closer to the central city hall than to the suburbs. That makes inner-city officials and other news sources located in the inner city easier to reach. City officials are more likely to visit newspaper offices and radio and television studios that are located nearby than are their geographically distant suburban colleagues. Inner cities are also more likely to generate the kind of news that political reporters ordinarily cover, such as political wheeling and dealing, ample doses of corruption, and heavy slices of crime. Stories of spectacular fires are more common in inner-city neighborhoods, as are stories about ethnic and racial strife and protest demonstrations.[48] Most journalists find the city more exciting and relate its problems to events in the suburbs rather than the other way around. When reporters are assigned to suburban stories on a regular basis, they view it as akin to exile in Siberia. The shrinking size of the press corps, including the loss of highly experienced journalists, also accounts for the lack of coverage for many important subnational stories and for more pack journalism. The overall quality of news has eroded.

THE CONTENT OF SUBNATIONAL NEWS

All of the news media slight news about state politics. News media situated in state capitals were the only exceptions until they were joined by state-oriented Web sites, including news and analysis providers like the Pew Center on the States. Among stories about government and politics in major newspapers and national and local television news, the share of state news is less than 10 percent. It averages around 6 percent. The share allotted to local news is better. It

Level of news	New York Times	Chicago Tribune	National ABC	National CBS	National NBC	Local ABC	Local CBS	Local NBC
National	43	38	32	41	39	24	26	29
International	38	32	56	49	50	16	8	9
State	6	5	6	6	6	9	9	9
Local	13	25	6	3	5	50	60	53
N	232	233	188	196	217	465	160	254

TABLE 10-2 **Government/Politics News Distribution (in percentages, Nov. 1–Dec. 15, 2004)**

Source: Author's research. National television news based on data obtained from the Vanderbilt Television News Archive. ABC local news obtained from the Museum of Broadcast Communication. CBS and NBC local news were recorded by the author.

Note: Newspaper and national television data and ABC local news are for 45 days, November 1–December 15, 2004. CBS and NBC local news are for 23 days because they were recorded on an alternate-day schedule, November 15–December 30. During that period, CBS news was preempted repeatedly for football or movies. Presidential election news was excluded. Totals may not equal 100% because of rounding.

garners one-quarter to close to half of the stories in newspapers like the *New York Times* and *Chicago Tribune* as well as local newscasts (Table 10-2).

State News: A Neglected Stepchild

Why does state news receive the least attention, when states play such important roles in politics? Some media, such as the national television networks, specialize in national news, and others specialize in local news, for example, many network affiliates. But few daily publications, aside from those located in state capitals, specialize in state news.

The Local Emphasis. Within states, the media enterprises with enough resources to cover news at all levels of government are usually located in the state's most populous cities, where local news abounds, rather than state capitals. Moreover, most state coverage has traditionally focused on the legislature rather than the governor. Because many state legislatures have relatively brief annual sessions, the flow of news about legislative activities is sparse and intermittent. Most daily papers do not make political activities at the state capital a regular full-time beat. In some cases—New Hampshire is an example—the state's media markets overlap state boundaries, so that news must appeal to residents of more than one state. That also puts a damper on state news.[49]

The National Emphasis. State news is a double loser on the national scene. It is extremely sparse and spotty. National television normally highlights a small number of states and neglects the rest. Some regions of the country receive more coverage than one might expect from the size of their populations, whereas others receive considerably less. Table 10-3 presents the data using electoral votes as a surrogate for population size. Compared to previous years, the discrepancies

TABLE 10-3 Regional Focus of Network News Coverage, September 2007–August 2008

Region	Percentage of mentions	Percentage of electoral votes	Discrepancy
Northeast (D.C., Del., Md., N.J., N.Y., Pa.)	16.9	15.4	+1.5
New England (Conn., Maine, Mass., N.H., R.I., Vt.)	7.9	6.3	+1.5
Southwest (Ark., La., Okla., Texas)	11.9	10.4	+1.5
Middle Atlantic (N.C., S.C., Va., W. Va.)	8.4	7.6	+0.8
Midwest (Ill., Ind., Iowa, Mich., Minn., Mo., Ohio, Wis.)	20.1	19.9	+0.2
Mountain (Ariz., Colo., Idaho, Mont., Nev., N.M., Utah, Wyo.)	7.9	8.2	−0.3
Plains (Kan., Neb., N.D., S.D.)	2.1	3.2	−1.1
South (Ala., Fla., Ga., Ky., Miss., Tenn.)	12.1	14.1	−2.0
Pacific (Alaska, Calif., Hawaii, Ore., Wash.)	12.7	14.9	−2.2

Source: Author's research based on the Vanderbilt Television News Archive.

Note: Data come from 4,629 mentions in news stories. Figures for the three major networks (ABC, CBS, and NBC) have been combined. The distribution of 538 electoral votes is based on the Federal Election Commission's 2004 and 2008 election results. Regions have been arranged from the most advantaged to least advantaged by network news coverage. Figures are rounded.

between population size and media attention are flatter. Five of the country's regions are still overcovered and four receive less than their share of media attention. But the gaps are small. It is too early to tell whether this is a fluke or a trend.

Table 10-4 provides a closer look at individual states. It shows the ten most covered and the ten least covered states and the degree of overcoverage or undercoverage judged by percentage of the electoral vote. As usual, Iowa and New Hampshire rank high among overcovered states, largely because they are lead-off states in the presidential campaign. The prominence of Texas and Florida is also election related. Journalistic criteria, rather than consideration related to the state's political significance, largely explain the placement of the other states. The states that offered the best story materials at a place and time that were most convenient for the media received the most ample coverage. States lacking in unusually stirring events suffered from neglect. Prolonged invisibility on the national scene is a serious problem that can damage the state's economic and political welfare. Compounding neglect, state news coverage on the national networks also is short on political substance,

TABLE 10-4 **State Distribution of Network News Attention, Ten Leaders and Trailers, September 2007–August 2008**

| State | Overcovered states | | |
	Percentage of mentions	Percentage of electoral votes	Discrepancy
Iowa	5.6	1.3	+4.3
New Hampshire	4.4	0.7	+3.7
Texas	8.3	6.3	+1.9
Florida	6.5	5.0	+1.5
Nevada	2.2	0.9	+1.3
New York	6.7	5.8	+0.9
Virginia	3.2	2.4	+0.8
Maryland	2.6	1.9	+0.7
South Carolina	2.0	1.5	+0.5
New Mexico	1.4	0.09	+0.5

| State | Undercovered states | | |
	Percentage of mentions	Percentage of electoral votes	Discrepancy
Connecticut	0.7	1.3	−0.6
Arizona	1.1	1.9	−0.7
Minnesota	1.0	1.9	−0.8
Ohio	2.7	3.7	−0.9
Alabama	0.7	1.7	−0.9
Tennessee	1.0	2.0	−1.0
Illinois	2.7	3.9	−1.2
Pennsylvania	2.6	3.9	−1.3
Georgia	1.3	2.8	−1.5
Washington	0.3	2.0	−1.7

Source: Author's research based on the Vanderbilt Television News Archive.

Note: Data come from 4,629 mentions in news stories. Figures for the three major networks (ABC, CBS, and NBC) have been combined. The distribution of 538 electoral votes is based on the Federal Election Commission's 2004 and 2008 election results. States have been arranged from the most advantaged to least advantaged by network news coverage. Figures are rounded.

focusing primarily on disaster, crime, and trivia stories. State economic, political, and social conditions and policies usually are ignored even when they have major national ramifications. Print media coverage of state news was more ample and considerably better in the past, but that changed when economic woes weakened or killed scores of print media, starting in 2007.[50]

Complaints about inadequate coverage must always be evaluated in light of the fact that media space and time are limited. What kinds of stories should the networks have omitted to make room for significant news about the states?

There is no good answer. Nonetheless, the growing importance of state politics has made the scarcity and thinness of state news ever more damaging.

Local News Characteristics

Local television news has become the biggest game in town. When audiences are asked which news topics they follow "very closely," crime news, which is a local news staple, is number two, named by 28 percent, preceded by weather news, named by 48 percent. News about people and events in the respondent's own community ranks in fourth place (22 percent), and local government news is seventh (20 percent).[51] These preferences are typical among the majority of news consumers, irrespective of their demographic characteristics or news consumption habits.

Live, local, late breaking

Primary Concerns. What do eager news audiences get when they turn to the nightly local news broadcasts? A massive, five-year research project by the Project for Excellence in Journalism tells the story. From 1998 to 2002 the project commissioned researchers to study 2,400 local newscasts presented by 154 randomly selected U.S. television stations. The stations varied in size and geographic location as well as in the kind of news they presented. Nonetheless, the investigators were able to draw some general conclusions: Local news tends to be "live, local, and late breaking," with a heavy dose of crime reports. News also tends to be formulaic, reactive, and short.[52] These findings were corroborated by a reanalysis of the 2002 data after a follow-up survey in 2005 and subsequent yearly surveys.[53]

The five-year content analysis of more than 33,000 news stories in fifty markets revealed that three-quarters of all stories featured on local broadcasts involve local events. Because of the heavy emphasis on crimes and accidents, roughly a third feature local law enforcement and fire-fighting personnel and crime suspects and victims. Another 14 percent feature local government officials or the local community's representatives in Congress. One in five stories is a live report of a locally breaking event. Many of these involve common accidents or crimes, which are plentiful in most communities, especially when one considers that most local broadcasts cover multiple urban and suburban communities.

News is formulaic because it features similar types of stories in similar fashion night after night. In general, 40 percent of all stories encompass fairly typical, everyday events. Stories tend to be brief. Roughly 70 percent are less than one minute, and 42 percent are less than thirty seconds long. Such brevity does not permit deep analysis and turns local newscasts largely into a headline service that provides a nibble for everyone but satisfies no one's hunger. The Project for Excellence in Journalism researchers complained that the presentation of controversial stories was predominantly one-sided, depriving audiences of the chance to fully assess the merits of different positions. Sixty percent of the stories involving a controversy reported it from just one perspective. The researchers also faulted local broadcasts for avoiding original investigative stories. On most stations only 7 percent of the stories originated from reporters' efforts to cover important issues on their own initiative, rather than relying on press releases or merely recording ongoing events.

As part of its mandate to ensure that the electronic media serve the public interest, the Federal Communications Commission (FCC) has urged local television and radio stations to gear their programming to local needs, including reporting about local politics. Obviously, that mandate is honored more by lip service than by actual performance. Local stations do carry some local political news, but it constitutes only 10 percent of the average broadcast. This is hardly what the FCC has in mind when it calls for an emphasis on "local" programming.

Although these figures show that local news is light on politics, one must keep in mind that there are generally multiple nightly local newscasts. The proportion of serious political news available to citizens may therefore be fairly substantial. Several studies of the consequences associated with watching local newscasts indicate that most viewers feel better informed about the local scene, trust and appreciate newscasts more, and are more prone to fear crime and develop false stereotypes about the perpetrators and their victims. Readers of local print media are also more likely to participate in local politics.[54] Whether reading stimulates participation or participation stimulates reading remains an open question.

Just as one cannot lump all national media together for purposes of analysis, so one must differentiate local media along a number of dimensions. Size is one of them. Stations in the largest markets offer considerably more political news than stations in smaller markets.[55] They devote a slightly smaller percentage of news space to local news, contrary to the FCC's "localism doctrine." [56] In fact, the doctrine has become little more than a pious wish, which may be abandoned in a global society.

National News on Local Media. One reason for growing attention to national and world news by local stations is greater ease of access. New technologies permit local stations to tap into the pool of national news at will and report it from a local angle. In addition, local stations are increasingly entering into cooperative news-gathering arrangements that allow member stations to send their stories to other members in the system via satellite. Local stations consequently have become less dependent on network coverage for national and world events.

As we saw in chapter 9, national news makers are eager to reach the hinterlands, where coverage tends to be gentler and more in tune with the news makers' agendas. Presidents tour the country in search of positive news about their policies. Their success rates are high but by no means perfect.[57] Members of Congress rely heavily on publicity in their home states. They strive to supply local media with ready-to-use stories posted on Web sites, blogs, Twitter, or any other platform likely to generate good publicity.[58] Lacking insider knowledge, local reporters are less likely to subject national political leaders to tough questioning. They tend to pay more attention—and more favorable attention—to their senators and representatives than the national media.[59] National issues viewed from a local perspective can move audiences more profoundly than stories without a local angle. The impact is heightened because audiences trust their local news providers more than outsiders.[60]

Election Coverage at the Local Level

The entire U.S. electoral system is organized to reflect local and statewide politics. All national officials—the president, senators, and representatives—are selected from state-based electoral districts, as are state officials and the half-million local officials who occupy legislative, executive, judicial, and administrative positions throughout the states. Candidates for most of these offices, including scores of positions on local government boards and committees, are of prime interest to geographically limited constituencies. They rarely attract the attention of nationwide broadcasts or the few newspapers that have a nationwide circulation. Their political fate—and that of the areas they serve—therefore depends largely on coverage by local media.

News about the Candidates. The role of the local media in promoting candidates in state and local campaigns is similar to what was described in chapter 8 for national campaigns.[61] It is a growing role because state officials are spending more money on their media campaigns now. Because they deal with friendly reporters, they try to obtain news story coverage rather than counting primarily on advertisements. In the past subnational officials relied heavily on radio advertisements because of the high costs of television. The new media have changed that pattern. Local officials use them extensively, along with advertisements on local radio stations and old-fashioned flyers and door-to-door campaigning.

Although data remain scarce, some evidence suggests that, compared to national television news, local stations generally provide citizens with less information about the comparative merits of the candidates. A study of thirty-one stations in fourteen television markets, during the last month of the 2000 presidential election campaign, found that local election news broadcasts were much briefer, on average, taking up only a 10 percent slice of the newscast in a presidential election year.[62] Studies of gubernatorial races in Ohio and Michigan yielded similar conclusions. These studies also show the characteristic local pattern of one-sided coverage, with incumbents usually receiving the lion's share of favorable attention.[63]

Newspaper endorsements are more important below the national level because most candidates for state and local offices are less familiar to the voters, who therefore turn more to the news media for guidance.[64] When viewers were asked to compare debates among presidential contenders at the national level with debates among candidates for state and local offices, they reported that they found the presidential debates more important and interesting, but learned more and were influenced more by the state and local debates.[65] Before watching the debates, 70 percent of the viewers of the local debate were undecided about their voting choices, compared with 40 percent of viewers in the presidential debate. If lack of information is a disease that plagues national elections, it apparently is far more virulent at state and local levels.

News about Referenda. Elections involving local politics often are completely issue centered. Referenda on prospective policies are examples. Although these political contests have low visibility, their impact on the average citizen can dwarf that of the more publicized contests. After studying seventy-two referenda in California, Massachusetts, Michigan, and Oregon between 1976 and 1982, political scientist Betty Zisk concluded that their coverage was impartial. Despite the liberal stance of the papers under investigation (the *Boston Globe,* the *Detroit Free Press,* the *Portland Oregonian,* the *Los Angeles Times,* and the *San Francisco Chronicle*), issues were amply discussed from a variety of perspectives.[66] However, Zisk faulted newspeople for merely reporting charges and countercharges rather than analyzing the merits of proposals and unmasking misleading rhetoric and advertisements. When ballots were tallied, voters had agreed with newspaper recommendations about 68 percent of the time. It is impossible to know with certainty whether this indicates media influence or merely an independently occurring concurrence of views. The side spending the most money, much of it to gain media coverage, won in three out of four cases (fifty-six of the seventy-two campaigns—78 percent). Zisk argues that money purchased victory, rather than good causes' attracting the most money.

Radio and television, the main sources of political information for average voters, carried little news and few editorials about the referenda. Thirty- and sixty-second television spot advertisements were inadequate to cover the important points of most of these complex issues. However, some radio talk shows gave extensive coverage to referenda, albeit often generating more heat than light. Unlike television, major regional newspapers provided comprehensive coverage of referendum issues. They carried extensive background features, pro and con articles and editorials, and news about campaign activities in the urban centers, though not elsewhere in the jurisdiction covered by the referenda.[67]

The Quality of Local News

Maintaining high-quality coverage is often more difficult for local than for national media. As mentioned, compared to most national television networks, local television has a far greater need for a steady stream of news because it usually has multiple daily newscasts. That puts a premium on broadcasting the latest news, rather than repeating more important stories that were featured earlier in the day. To maintain profitability through a wide audience reach, local television usually pitches its programs to a moderately educated audience that presumably is uninterested in sophisticated political analysis. It is also more difficult for local newscasters to find interesting political stories and solicit high-quality commentary for them. Lack of economic resources is also a problem for local stations and local newspapers. It forces them to use the most readily available stories, including press releases from government and the business community, and explains why they seldom feature original, in-depth investigations. Reporters rarely question estimates of costs and benefits of local development projects. They tend to be upbeat in reporting about local business leaders and economic trends. In the words of Phyllis Kaniss, "While there is much in the news and editorial columns that is critical of local officials, this criticism is limited when compared with the amount of information that is taken directly, and almost unquestioningly, from official bureaucratic sources."[68] As Ben Bagdikian has put it in his inimitable style, journalism is "a daily battle between God and Mammon. Too much of the time, it's Mammon 100 and God 5."[69] Larger local stations and newspapers with greater financial resources do somewhat better in seeking out important news, providing context for their stories, and resisting pressures from advertisers. Smaller news outlets cannot afford to antagonize the advertising hand that feeds them.

The difficulties of maintaining high-quality news have serious consequences because local news is the main political information source for many Americans. There are few competing sources of information about local politics, so that the local media may be the sole source of information available to interested citizens as well as government officials. It therefore matters if news content is too narrowly focused and reporters are soft on local politicians, or spare local projects and policies from criticism out of a sense of local boosterism.

The detailed content analysis of television news stories and the stations that broadcast them came to a bombshell conclusion: The excuses made for many low-quality local program features rest on mostly false assumptions about media audiences' likes and dislikes. Audiences do not like a surfeit of crime and disaster news at the expense of other salient topics. They prefer longer stories presented in context to isolated snippets of news that say little beyond the factual announcement. They like investigative stories, validated by expert testimony. The proof comes from a comparison of the offerings of stations that are deemed either successful or unsuccessful in their markets, judged by a variety of criteria. The successful stations—roughly one-third—provide a solid, well-balanced news diet; their unsuccessful peers do not. Hurrah for "Doing well by doing good"—the idealists' brave slogan. Documenting it in a landmark study provides a thrilling and hopeful note for ending our fairly dismal story about local news and justice system coverage.

SUMMARY

The media spotlight falls unevenly on the body politic. In this chapter, we examined institutions that do not receive sufficient light for the U.S. public to adequately assess them and the roles they play in the nation's political life. At the national level, the judicial branch suffers from inadequate news coverage. We have explained the reasons for neglect and some of the political consequences, given the federal courts' importance in shaping U.S. politics. We have also noted problems that arise in reporting about the crime and justice system, especially when the media focus on sensational events rather than political substance.

Local news is sparse and unevenly distributed at the national level and is chosen by news value rather than political significance criteria. At the subnational level, news about state politics is neglected nearly everywhere in the United States. It is drowned out by national and local news. Hence, most citizens remain uninformed about state politics in their own as well as sister states. Still, politicians seek it out because reporters at the subnational level rarely criticize politicians' performance and policies. News tends to be descriptive, rather than analytical and judgmental.

News about local politics is far more ample than state news. Many regions within metropolitan areas, as well as suburbs and outlying communities, have local newspapers. Regrettably, the quality of coverage of politics has deteriorated since the beginning of the twentieth century. Fewer cities now have their own daily newspapers, and intra-city competition among major dailies has almost vanished. Local television features an average of four hours of news daily, but nearly half of that is an unending tale of weather, crime, and disasters. The political dialogue has suffered. It may be too early, however, to mourn the death of solid local politics coverage. The new technologies that make it affordable to tailor broadcasts to the needs of niche audiences, and the realization that good programming is economically profitable may restore the vigorous publicity that is essential at all political levels in a democracy.

NOTES

1. Walter Lippmann, *Public Opinion* (1922; repr. New York: Free Press, 1965), 229.
2. Pew Research Center for the People and the Press, "Many Would Shrug if Their Local Newspaper Closed," March 12, 2009, http://people-press.org/report/497.
3. James Gibson, "New Style Judicial Campaigns and the Legitimacy of State High Courts," *Journal of Politics* 71, no. 4 (forthcoming November 2009).
4. Herbert M. Kritzer, "The Impact of *Bush v. Gore* on Public Perceptions and Knowledge of the Supreme Court," in *Judicial Politics: Readings from Judicature*, 3rd ed., ed. Elliot E. Slotnick (Washington, D.C.: CQ Press, 2005), 500–506.
5. *Brown v. Board of Education*, 347 U.S. 483 (1954); *Roe v. Wade*, 410 U.S. 113 (1973); *Planned Parenthood v. Casey*, 112 S. Ct. 2791 (1992).
6. Richard Davis, "Lifting the Shroud: News Media Portrayal of the U.S. Supreme Court," *Communications and the Law* 9 (October 1987): 46; and Bob Woodward and Scott Armstrong, *The Brethren* (New York: Simon and Schuster, 1979), claim to present an insider's view of Court proceedings.
7. Richard Davis, *Decisions and Images: The Supreme Court and the Press* (Englewood Cliffs, N.J.: Prentice Hall, 1994).
8. Rorie L. Spill and Zoe M. Oxley, "Philosopher Kings or Political Actors? How the Media Portray the Supreme Court," in *Judicial Politics*, ed. Slotnick, 462–470.
9. Davis, *Decisions and Images.*
10. *Engel v. Vitale*, 370 U.S. 421 (1962); *Baker v. Carr*, 369 U.S. 186 (1962).
11. Chester A. Newland, "Press Coverage of the United States Supreme Court," *Western Political Quarterly* 17 (1964): 15–36. Also see Kenneth S. Devol, *Mass Media and the Supreme Court*, 4th ed. (New York: Hastings House, 1990).

12. Stephanie Greco Larson, "How the *New York Times* Covered Discrimination Cases," *Journalism Quarterly* 62 (Winter 1985): 894–896; also see Stephanie Greco Larson, "Supreme Court Coverage and Consequences" (paper presented at the annual meeting of the Midwest Political Science Association, Chicago, April 1989).

13. *Regents of the University of California v. Bakke*, 438 U.S. 265 (1978); *Webster v. Reproductive Health Services*, 109 S. Ct. 3040 (1989); Elliot E. Slotnick and Jennifer A. Segal, *Television News and the Supreme Court* (New York: Cambridge University Press, 1998).

14. Davis, *Decisions and Images*, chaps. 4–6; also see Frank J. Sorauf, "Campaign Money and the Press: Three Soundings," *Political Science Quarterly* 102 (Spring 1987): 25–42.

15. Gregory Caldeira, "Neither the Purse nor the Sword: Dynamics of Public Confidence in the Supreme Court," *American Political Science Review* 80 (December 1986): 1209–1228; John M. Scheb II and William Lyons, "Public Perception of the Supreme Court in the 1990s," in *Judicial Politics*, ed. Slotnick, 496–499.

16. Gallup News Service, 2007, www.gallup.com/poll/28861.

17. Robert E. Drechsel, *News Making in the Trial Courts* (New York: Longman, 1983), 19–22; Thomas R. Marshall and Joseph Ignagni, "Supreme Court and Public Support for Rights Claims," *Judicial Politics*, ed. Slotnick, 487–495.

18. David Pritchard, "Homicide and Bargained Justice: The Agenda-Setting Effect of Crime News on Prosecutors," *Public Opinion Quarterly* 50 (Spring 1986): 143–159; Jon Bruschke and William E. Loges, "Relationship between Pretrial Publicity and Trial Outcomes," *Journal of Communication* 49, no. 4 (Fall 1999): 104–120; Dorothy Imrich, Charles Mullin, and Daniel Linz, "Measuring the Extent of Prejudicial Pretrial Publicity in American Newspapers: A Content Analysis," *Journal of Communication* 45, no. 3 (Summer 1995): 94–117.

19. Travis L. Dixon and Cristina L. Azocar, "Priming Crime and Activating Blackness: Understanding the Psychological Impact of the Overrepresentation of Blacks as Lawbreakers on Television News," *Journal of Communication* 57 (2007): 229–253; also see Paul M. Kellstedt, *The Mass Media and the Dynamics of American Racial Attitudes* (New York: Cambridge University Press, 2003).

20. Tom Rosenstiel, Marion Just, Todd Belt, Atiba Pertilla, Walter Dean, and Dante Chinni, *We Interrupt This Newscast: How to Improve Local News and Win Ratings, Too* (New York: Cambridge University Press, 2007); C. Danielle Vinson and John S. Ertter, "Entertainment or Education: How the Media Cover the Courts," *Press/Politics* 7, no. 4 (2002): 80–89.

21. A detailed account of coverage of crime and justice system news is presented in Ray Surette, *Media, Crime, and Criminal Justice: Images and Realities*, 3rd ed. (Belmont, Calif.: Wadsworth, 2007); David Malden Trend, *The Myth of Media Violence: A Critical Introduction* (Malden, Mass.: Blackwell, 2007); William Haltom and Michael McCann, *Distorting the Law : Politics, Media, and the Litigation Crisis* (Chicago: University of Chicago Press, 2004); also see Doris A. Graber, *Crime News and the Public* (New York: Praeger, 1980).

22. Vinson and Ertter, "Entertainment or Education"; also see Daniel Romer, Kathleen Hall Jamieson, and Sean Aday, "Television News and the Cultivation of Fear of Crime," *Journal of Communication* 53, no. 1 (2003): 88–104.

23. Mira Sotirovic, "How Individuals Explain Social Problems: The Influence of Media Use," *Journal of Communication* 53, no. 1 (2003): 122–137.

24. Richard L. Fox and Robert van Sickel, *Tabloid Justice: Criminal Justice in an Age of Media Frenzy* (Boulder: Lynne Rienner, 2001), chap. 2.

25. Ibid., chap. 3.

26. Susanna Barber, *News Cameras in the Courtroom: A Free Press–Fair Trial Debate* (Norwood, N.J.: Ablex, 1987); also see Vinson and Ertter, "Entertainment or Education."

27. Fox and van Sickel, *Tabloid Justice*; Fred Graham, "Doing Justice with Cameras in the Courts," *Media Studies Journal* 12, no. 1 (Winter 1998): 32–37; also see Patrick Lee Plaisance and Joan A. Deppa, "Perceptions and Manifestations of Autonomy, Transparency and Harm among U.S. Newspaper Journalists," *Journalism Communication Monographs* 10, no. 4 (Winter 2009): 327–386.

28. John J. Pauly and Melissa Eckert, "The Myth of 'The Local' in American Journalism," *Journalism and Mass Communication Quarterly* 79, no. 2 (2002): 310–326 explains why Americans venerate local news. Also see Pew Research Center for the People and the Press, "Many Would Shrug if Their Local Newspaper Closed."

29. Ben H. Bagdikian, *The Media Monopoly*, 3rd ed. (Boston: Beacon Press, 1990), 174. Also see Richard Campbell, Christopher R. Martin, and Bettina Fabos, *Media and Culture: An Introduction to Mass Communication*, 6th ed. (Boston: Bedford/St. Martin's, 2008).

30. Frederick Fico and Stan Soffin, "Fairness and Balance of Selected Newspaper Coverage of Controversial National, State, and Local Issues," *Journalism and Mass Communication Quarterly* 72, no. 3 (Fall 1995): 621–633; Janet A. Bridges and Lamar W. Bridges, "Changes in News Use on the Front Pages of the American Daily Newspaper, 1986–1993," *Journalism and Mass Communication Quarterly* 73, no. 4 (Winter 1997): 826–838; also see Project for Excellence in Journalism, "State of the News Media, 2004," www.stateofthenewsmedia.org.

31. Pew Research Center for the People and the Press, "Key News Audiences Now Blend Online and Traditional Sources: Audience Segments in a Changing News Environment," August 17, 2008, www.people-press.org.

32. James N. Rosse coined the term. See James M. Bernstein, Stephen Lacy, Catherine Cassara, and Tuen-yu Lau, "Geographic Coverage by Local Television News," *Journalism Quarterly* 57 (Winter 1990): 664, note 4.

33. See ibid.; Project for Excellence in Journalism, "State of the News Media, 2009," www.stateofthe-newsmedia.org/2009.

34. William R. Davie and Jung-Sook Lee, "Sex, Violence, and Consonance/Differentiation: An Analysis of Local TV News Values," *Journalism and Mass Communication Quarterly* 72, no. 1 (Spring 1995): 128–138; also see David C. Coulson, Daniel Riffe, Stephen Lacy, and Charles R. St. Cyr, "Erosion of Television Coverage of City Hall? Perceptions of TV Reporters on the Beat," *Journalism and Mass Communication Quarterly* 78, no. 1 (Spring 2001): 81–92.

35. Daniel Riffe and Eugene F. Shaw, "Ownership, Operating, Staffing, and Content Characteristics of 'News Radio' Stations," *Journalism Quarterly* 67 (Winter 1990): 684–691; Project for Excellence in Journalism, "State of the News Media, 2009."

36. Project for Excellence in Journalism, "State of the News Media, 2009."

37. Ibid.

38. Daniel M. Shea, "All Scandal Politics Is Local: Ethical Lapses, the Media, and Congressional Elections," *Press/Politics* 4, no. 2 (Spring 1999): 45–62.

39. Phyllis Kaniss, *Making Local News* (Chicago: University of Chicago Press, 1991), 175–179.

40. Martin Linsky, *How the Press Affects Federal Policymaking* (New York: Norton, 1986), 236.

41. Dan Berkowitz and Douglas B. Adams, "Information Subsidy and Agenda-Building in Local Television News," *Journalism Quarterly* 67 (Winter 1990): 725.

42. Judy Van Slyke Turk and Bob Franklin, "Information Subsidies: Agenda-Setting Traditions," *Public Relations Review* 13 (1987): 29–41; Dan Berkowitz, "TV News Sources and News Channels: A Study in Agenda-Building," *Journalism Quarterly* 64 (Autumn 1987): 508–513.

43. Roza Tsagarousianou, Damian Tambini, and Cathy Brian, eds., *Cyberdemocracy: Technology, Cities, and Civic Networks* (London: Routledge, 1998); Mordecai Lee, ed., *Government Public Relations: A Reader* (Boca Raton, Fla.: CRC Press, 2008); also see Mark J. Rozell, ed., *Media Power, Media Politics* (Lanham, Md.: Rowman and Littlefield, 2003).

44. Claire E. Taylor, Jung-Sook Lee, and William R. Davie, "Local Press Coverage of Environmental Conflict," *Journalism and Mass Communication Quarterly* 77, no. 1 (Spring 2000): 175–192.

45. Kaniss, *Making Local News,* 107.

46. News selection criteria are discussed in Camilla Gant and John Dimmick, "Making Local News: A Holistic Analysis of Sources, Selection Criteria, and Topics," *Journalism and Mass Communication Quarterly* 77, no. 3 (Fall 2000): 628–638; Rosenstiel et al., "We Interrupt This Newscast."

47. The term is used in Kaniss, *Making Local News,* 126.

48. Ibid., 76.

49. This discussion is based on Stephen Hess, "Levels of the Game: Federalism and the American News System" (paper presented at the Hofstra University Conference, Hempstead, N.Y., April 1992).

50. For a discussion of state news in the *New York Times,* see Doris Graber, "Flashlight Coverage: State News on National Broadcasts," *American Politics Quarterly* 17 (July 1989): 277–290.

51. Pew Research Center for the People and the Press, "Key News Audiences Now Blend Online and Traditional News."

52. Project for Excellence in Journalism, "State of the News Media, 2004"; "State of the News Media, 2009."

53. Rosenstiel et al., "We Interrupt This Newscast."

54. Patricia Moy, Michael R. McCluskey, Kelley McCoy, and Margaret A. Spratt, "Political Correlates of Local News Media Use," *Journal of Communication* 54, no. 3 (2004): 532–546; Franklin D. Gilliam Jr. and Shanto Iyengar, "Prime Suspects: The Influence of Local Television News on the Viewing Public," *American Journal of Political Science* 44, no. 3 (2000): 560–573; Dietram A. Scheufele, James Shanahan, and Sei-Hill Kim, "Who Cares about Local Politics? Media Influences on Local Political Involvement, Issue Awareness, and Attitude Strength," *Journalism and Mass Communication Quarterly* 79, no. 2 (2002): 427–444.

55. Stephen Hess, *Live from Capitol Hill! Studies of Congress and the Media* (Washington, D.C.: Brookings Institution Press, 1991), 49; also see Taylor, Lee, and Davie, "Local Press Coverage of Environmental Conflict," 175–192.

56. Bernstein and others, "Geographic Coverage by Local Television News," 668, 670; for similar results, also see Stephen Lacy and James M. Bernstein, "Daily Newspaper Content's Relationship to Publication Cycle and Circulation Size," *Newspaper Research Journal,* Spring 1988, 49–57.

57. Matthew Eshbaugh-Soha and Jeffrey S. Peake, "The Presidency and Local Media: Local Newspaper Coverage of President George W. Bush," *Presidential Studies Quarterly* 38, no. 4 (2008): 609–630; and Matthew Eshbaugh-Soha, "Local Newspaper Coverage of the Presidency," *Press/Politics* 13 (2008): 103–119.

58. C. Danielle Vinson, *Local Media Coverage of Congress and Its Members: Through Local Eyes* (Creskill, N.J.: Hampton Press, 2003); Brian J. Fogarty, "The Strategy of the Story: Media Monitoring Legislative Activity," *Legislative Studies Quarterly* 33, no. 3 (2008): 445–469; Brian F. Schaffner, "Local Coverage and the Incumbency Advantage in the U.S. House," *Legislative Studies Quarterly* 31 (2006): 491–512.

59. Hess, *Live from Capitol Hill!;* Vinson, *Local Media Coverage of Congress and Its Members.*

60. Scott Sigmund Gartner, "Making the International Local: The Terrorist Attack on the USS *Cole,* Local Casualties, and Media Coverage," *Political Communication* 21, no. 2 (2004): 139–159.

61. Schaffner, "Local Coverage and the Incumbency Advantage."

62. Stephen J. Farnsworth and S. Robert Lichter, "Increasing Candidate-Centered Television Discourse: Evaluating Local News Coverage of Campaign 2000," *Press/Politics* 9, no. 2 (2004): 76–93.

63. Frederick Fico, Geri Alumit Zeldes, and Arvind Diddi, "Partisan and Structural Balance of Local Television Election Coverage of Incumbent and Open Gubernatorial Elections," *Journalism and Mass Communication Quarterly* 81, no. 4 (2004): 897–910.

64. Byron St. Dizier, "The Effects of Newspaper Endorsements and Party Identification on Voting Choice," *Journalism Quarterly* 62 (Autumn 1985): 589–594.

65. A. Lichtenstein, "Differences in Impact between Local and National Televised Political Candidates' Debates," *Western Journal of Speech Communication* 46 (1982): 291–298; also see Dianne Bystrom, Cindy Roper, Robert Gobetz, Tom Massey, and Carol Beall, "The Effects of a Televised Gubernatorial Debate," *Political Communication Review* 16 (1991): 57–80.

66. Betty H. Zisk, *Money, Media, and the Grassroots: State Ballot Issues and the Electoral Process* (Newbury Park, Calif.: Sage, 1987).

67. For an excellent overview of the referendum process, see Claes H. de Vreese and Holli Semetko, *Political Campaigning in Referendums* (London: Routledge, 2004).

68. Kaniss, *Making Local News*, 90–91.

69. Quoted in John McManus, "How Local Television Learns What Is News," *Journalism Quarterly* 67 (Winter 1990): 672.

READINGS

Chiasson, Lloyd, Jr. *Illusive Shadows: Justice, Media, and Socially Significant American Trials.* Westport, Conn.: Praeger, 2003.

Entman, Robert M., and Andrew Rojecki. *The Black Image in the White Mind: Media and Race in America.* Chicago: University of Chicago Press, 2000.

Fox, Richard L., Robert van Sickel, and Thomas L. Steiger. *Tabloid Justice: Criminal Justice in an Age of Media Frenzy.* Boulder: Lynne Rienner, 2007.

Haltom, William, and Michael McCann. *Distorting the Law: Politics, Media, and the Litigation Crisis.* Chicago: University of Chicago Press, 2004.

Kaniss, Phyllis. *The Media and the Mayor's Race: The Failure of Urban Political Reporting.* Indianapolis: Indiana University Press, 1995.

Lipschultz, Jeremy H., and Michael L. Hilt. *Crime and Local Television News: Dramatic, Breaking, and Live from the Scene.* Mahwah, N.J.: Erlbaum, 2002.

Rosenstiel, Tom, Marion Just, Todd Belt, Atiba Pertilla, Walter Dean, and Dante Chinni. *We Interrupt This Newscast: How to Improve Local News and Win Ratings, Too.* New York: Cambridge University Press, 2007.

Surette, Ray. *Media, Crime, and Criminal Justice: Images and Realities.* 3rd ed. Belmont, Calif.: Wadsworth, 2007.

Trend, David. *The Myth of Media Violence: A Critical Introduction.* Malden, Mass.: Blackwell, 2007.

Vermeer, Jan P. *The View from the States: National Politics in Local Newspaper Editorials.* Lanham, Md.: Rowman and Littlefield, 2002.

Foreign Affairs Coverage

W hen fighting erupted between Israel and Hamas in December 2008, it was no surprise to Middle East observers. Military attacks by Israel on its Arab neighbors, and vice versa, are a dreaded staple on the international scene. The 2008 combat began with a massive bombing attack on the Gaza Strip, followed by ground operations. Israel blocked journalists, including Western media, from entering the combat zone, but reporters from Al Jazeera were already stationed there and therefore could not be kept out. The network's executives believed that it was vital to expose American publics and their leaders to eyewitness stories of the suffering inflicted on civilians in the Gaza Strip, where human casualty figures ran into the thousands and tens of thousands were left homeless. Al Jazeera went to great trouble to air its stories to large American audiences, including tweeting brief excerpts, posting videos on its dedicated YouTube channel, and making the network's reports available to other media free of charge.[1]

Are such heroic, unprofitable efforts really worthwhile? Do they change opinions in any meaningful and lasting way? What, if any, are the links between the mass media and the process of creating foreign policies and producing policy outputs? How do governments use the media to further their policy objectives around the world? Do the media perform their watchdog role appropriately in times of war? In this chapter we will try to answer such provocative questions about how the mass media influence U.S. foreign policy.

We will first focus on the overall significance that U.S. media and U.S. citizens assign to news about foreign countries. Then we will point out the main differences between the production of foreign and domestic news. We will consider the unique problems newspeople face in collecting news and shaping it to meet newsworthiness criteria while heeding the canons of journalistic ethics and independence. Producing high-quality foreign news in times of peace and times of war is an extraordinarily difficult task. We shall note how well it is currently carried out and point to accomplishments and failures.

THE FOREIGN NEWS NICHE

Newspeople commonly assume that the U.S. public is interested primarily in what goes on in the United States. Reports about the public's ignorance about foreign countries and foreign affairs lend credence to these assumptions.

Focus	AOL News	CNN.com	Google News	MSNBC.com	Yahoo News
U.S. domestic	62	52	36	56	35
U.S. foreign	39	48	63	43	65

TABLE 11-1 **News Focus of Major Web Sites: Domestic versus Foreign**

Source: Adapted from Pew Project for Excellence in Journalism, "State of News Media, 2008," www.stateofthemedia.org/2008/.

Americans profess modest interest in foreign news, but when given a choice, they do not seek it out. When survey researchers asked a randomly selected national sample of people in 2008 about the types of news that they watched routinely, or watched only when the story seemed especially important or interesting, less than half (44 percent) of the respondents claimed to watch international news routinely, whereas 56 percent said they watched only selectively. These numbers tend to fluctuate by ten percentage points or more, depending on the overall thrust of the news. How interest in foreign affairs waxes and wanes depends on the visibility of U.S. foreign involvements.[2]

Even when interest rises, it is rarely profound. Most news consumers do not follow stories about international events very closely. Very few are inclined to take actions to foster their beliefs, and if they do, their enthusiasm tends to be short-lived. Interest in news about the weather, crime, education, the local community, the environment, the nation, local government, health, sports, and religion, in that order, surpasses interest in news from abroad.[3]

Although most Americans do not make foreign news a prime focus of attention, print and electronic media give it considerable coverage. In 2007, which was a peak year for interest in foreign news because people were concerned about terrorism and fighting the Iraq War, 15 percent of newspaper coverage dealt with U.S. foreign relations and another 13 percent covered stories from abroad that were not directly related to the United States. Compared to newspapers, network and cable television allotted a slightly larger share of their news hole to foreign relations and a slightly smaller share to general coverage of events beyond the U.S. borders. Table 11-1 shows the balance between foreign and domestic news. News hole share for foreign news was largest in on-line offerings, which devoted 22 percent of their news hole to foreign relations plus almost 25 percent to more general global news. Differences in attention to foreign news are significant because the various platforms attract different clienteles and vary in overall credibility. It is important to keep in mind that news hole percentage figures tell nothing about actual amounts of news. Ten percent of the *New York Times* news hole can accommodate much more information than 10 percent of the news hole of a fifteen-minute radio show. Furthermore, the *New York Times* remains

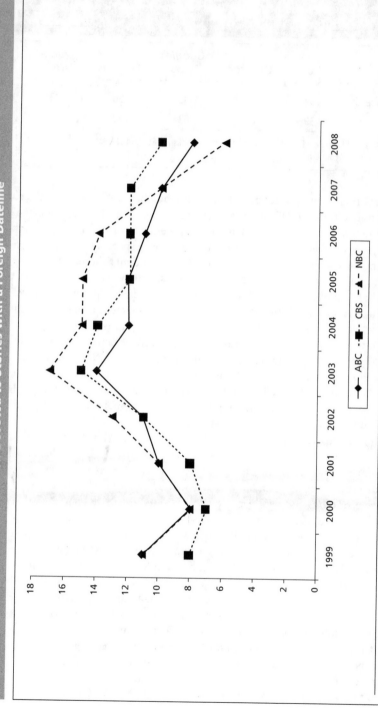

FIGURE 11-1 **Hours of Network Television Devoted to Stories with a Foreign Dateline**

ABC — ◆ — CBS ┄■┄ NBC – ▲ –

Source: Adapted from Pew Project for Excellence in Journalism, "State of News Media, 2009," www.stateofthemedia.org/2009/.

the preferred information source for "official" Washington. Figure 11.1 gives a sense of actual time, measured in hours, given to foreign news in the ten years between 1999 and 2008. It shows the range of variation as well as the similarities among ABC, NBC, and CBS.

Compared with attention to domestic affairs, foreign news is a neglected stepchild in terms of space, time, and prominence of display. News selection criteria are far more rigorous. To be published in the mainstream media, foreign news must have a more profound impact on the political, economic, or cultural concerns of the United States than domestic news. It must involve people of more exalted status and entail more violence or disaster.[4] As the analysis of 2007 news demonstrates, during crises, particularly prolonged ones that endanger U.S. lives, foreign coverage may double or even triple; it may even drown out most other news. Conversely, the number of stories and their length shrink when times seem unusually calm, as happened right after the Cold War ended with the collapse of the Soviet Union.[5] There is as yet no sign that the American public has accepted the proposition that there is no truly "foreign" news anymore because important happenings anywhere in a global world affect all of its people.

MAKING FOREIGN NEWS

Although news making for domestic stories and that for foreign stories differ substantially, there are many similarities. To make comparisons easier, we will follow the organization of domestic news making and reporting described in chapter 4. First we will consider the gatekeepers—the corps of foreign correspondents who are the frontline echelon among gatherers of foreign affairs news for the legacy media. Then we will discuss the setting for news selection, the criteria for choosing stories and the means of gathering them, the constraints on news production, and finally the effects of gatekeeping on foreign affairs coverage.

Gatekeepers: The Vanishing News Bureaus

A combination of advancing technology, globalization of news, and efforts to cut costs is changing gatekeeping for foreign news. Most news about events happening throughout the world used to be collected and sold by four major news agencies: the U.S.–owned Associated Press (AP), which leads the pack; Britain's Reuters, now merged with the Thomson Corporation; France's Agence France-Presse, the world's oldest news agency, dating back to 1835; and ITAR-Tass, which superseded the Soviet news agency, Tass, in 1992.[6] Among these world-class wire services, AP has always been by far the largest. It has now become the dominant international news agency.[7] All of these agencies have had financial difficulties, and their survival has hinged on government subsidies.

In 2007 the Associated Press maintained 243 bureaus worldwide with more than 4,000 employees.[8] It provided print and broadcast news in multiple languages to clients in 97 countries. AP reporters are initial gatekeepers who ferret out the stories that make up the pool from which other gatekeepers select reports or find leads to pursue stories more fully. Because news agency reporters work for a variety of clients throughout the world, their news reports must be bland, so that they do not offend people whose views span a wide political spectrum. Wire service news therefore emphasizes fast and ample factual reports of ongoing events. It does not provide interpretations but leaves that to the users of its reports.

Besides the reports provided by the wire service bureaus, much foreign news once came from news bureaus maintained by various other news organizations. That has changed. Permanent international bureaus are no longer the model for handling most international coverage. There are a few notable exceptions, like the *New York Times,* which has actually expanded its foreign correspondent corps abroad. The *Times* can afford to operate its twenty-six bureaus because their cost is defrayed largely by income from selling syndicated stories to other media enterprises. On the broadcast side, CNN, the twenty-four-hour Cable News Network, has been a major player in the international news game since the 1980s. It has nearly 4,000 reporters, scattered in forty-seven bureaus throughout the world, who collect and report news in multiple languages for worldwide audiences. As is typical of live broadcast coverage, CNN reports reach viewers in 212 countries and therefore are a mixed bag of events and interviews ranging from the trivial to the significant. The reports give less time to analysis and expert commentary than is usual for network television news. They tape whatever is readily and inexpensively available, so that viewers are the first to see a breaking news event at close range. Table 11-2 shows the types of news that CNN offers to its global audiences on a typical day. It represents an impressive romp through the scenes of newsworthy events happening in diverse locations north and south of the equator.

Gatekeepers: The New Types of Foreign Correspondents

In the past specially trained, experienced American journalists supplied much of the foreign news in the U.S. press. These elite journalists have become a nearly extinct breed. New types of foreign correspondents are joining and replacing them. Who are these new reporters? Journalism scholars John Maxwell Hamilton and Eric Jenner identify several types.[9] In addition to the traditional U.S. correspondents stationed abroad, a large number of foreigners now supply U.S. media with news about their home countries and adjacent regions. Their stories may lack the traditional U.S. perspective, but they are gathered at a fraction of the roughly $250,000 that it costs to station a U.S. newspaper correspondent abroad. The price doubles for broadcast correspondents. Given these cost differentials, it should come as no surprise that fewer than a third of the correspondents reporting news from abroad to the United States were Americans.[10] The belief that only native Americans are capable of reporting news with an appropriate U.S. flavor has given way to the idea that foreign news reported by foreigners may have a different flavor, but that may actually be beneficial. It may tell Americans how people in other countries interpret the political scene.

TABLE 11-2 One Day of CNN World News Headlines, May 14, 2009

EUROPE	ASIA PACIFIC
Germany: Nazi war crimes trial "could be last of its kind"	**Myanmar:** Aung San Suu Kyi faces trial
Italy: Pope celebrates Mass for 40,000	**Pakistan:** UN urges "massive" aid effort
Spain: Spanish protesters demand protection for jobless	**Afghanistan:** Place of "miracle" for Afghanistan's amputees
AFRICA	MIDDLE EAST
Nigeria: Soldiers, militants clash	**Iraq:** War, recession blight job market for Iraqis
Zimbabwe: Men accused in Mugabe plot released	**Israel:** Pope visits Jerusalem's holiest sites
Libya: Al Qaeda figure who provided link to Iraq dies	**Iran:** Released journalist "doing fine," father says
AMERICAS	UNITED STATES
Mexico: Former Mexican president wants pot legalized	**New York:** Fatigue cited as possible factor in plane crash
Guatemala: Guatemala rejects allegations in lawyer's death	**Washington, D.C.:** Pelosi accuses CIA of misleading her
Honduras: Student fights poverty one campus at a time	**Michigan:** Chrysler closing 789 dealerships

Source: CNN.com, *World News,* May 14, 2009.

Encouraged by easy international travel and cheap airline fares, more and more U.S.–based print and broadcast media are sending correspondents abroad for short jaunts to report about a particular event. These "parachute" journalists travel from the United States or, less commonly, from overseas jumping-off points. *USA Today,* for example, uses its overseas bureaus as regional jumping-off points for parachuters. Parachute journalism has become almost routine for large news organizations and fairly common for smaller ones. The horde of U.S. parachute journalists dispatched to report about the death of Pope John Paul II in 2005 and the selection of his successor is a good example. The majority of the news organizations that sent more than 6,000 journalists to Rome were newcomers to gathering foreign news.[11] Their inexperience was painfully apparent but only to knowledgeable news consumers.

So-called premium service foreign correspondents are another innovation. Hamilton and Jenner cite the example of the Bloomberg subscription news service.[12] Besides its contingent of expert, U.S.–based print and broadcast reporters, who cover economic stories in the United States, Bloomberg has a large number of print and broadcast reporters stationed all over the globe. A single subscription to Bloomberg news pays for access to global financial news gathered by this international corps of correspondents. News from all over the world may not be a high priority for most Americans. But in the age of globalization, foreign news is essential for large corporations with customers or branches all over the world. Nearly all of these corporations also have their own reporters, who often are professional journalists, located abroad to dispatch salient news via computer to their U.S. bases. Much of this news is not confidential and spreads beyond the confines of the company to the news media.

GlobalPost is a comparatively recent addition to the roster of news services that supply worldwide news to their members. Its reporters live in various parts of the world, including many countries that have received little attention from traditional news agencies. In addition to the usual focus on particular countries or regions, GlobalPost also has specialists who cover particular institutions, such as NGOs, or unique perspectives, such as "World Views," or problems like the environment and health, or activities like commerce and sports. The GlobalPost business model may herald the emergence of new patterns for financing news supplies. It consists of a combination of member fees, sales of individual stories, and syndication and advertising fees. The service is designed especially to meet the needs of media companies, businesses, NGOs, and nonprofit organizations.[13]

Another stream of special interest news comes from public relations agencies hired by foreign countries to promote their images. Public relations campaigns commonly promote tourism and trade, especially special events like the Olympics, or in the wake of political crises. Many countries are contracting for professional image management. Citizens for a Free Kuwait, a front organization for the government of Kuwait, for example, spent nearly $11 million with just one public relations firm to burnish Kuwait's image in the months after it had been invaded by Iraq.[14] By either stimulating or suppressing media coverage, public relations agencies try to improve their clients' media image, hoping to turn the political climate in their favor.[15]

The largest group of foreign correspondents—if they indeed deserve that name—are nonprofessionals who use Web sites to report their observations from abroad or from U.S. locations. The more serious and successful of this breed may become bloggers, whose Web sites may be visited by hundreds of people. Visitors to blogs often distribute blog information—and the responses it has provoked—to people far and wide. In fact, Web sites have become an important information source for journalists throughout the globe who either relay blog stories through established news organizations or use them as the basis for creating their own news organization.

Finally, large numbers of Americans now draw their information about events beyond U.S. borders from Internet visits to foreign newspapers and foreign broadcasts. They can learn, for example, about the perennial turmoil in the Middle East from an Arab perspective by turning to Al Jazeera, or from a

French perspective by reading *Le Monde*. Or they can listen to news from Britain's BBC or turn to English-language news from China transmitted by CNN. International news can be scanned easily and inexpensively by anyone who has a computer linked to the Internet. How many people use foreign news sources and what the consequences are remain uncertain. The sheer numbers are not nearly as important as the news consumers' position and activities within policy-making networks.

Given that news reporting through diverse cultural lenses varies in perspective, the same story raw materials yield different end products. At times the versions vary so widely that they seem to cover totally different situations. For instance, faced with the same information about global warming before, during, and after a 1997 international conference in Kyoto, Japan, U.S. reporters focused on U.S. stances on the issue, with little mention of international views; German reporters stressed global views but slighted European opinions. The U.S. media split attention about evenly between the substance of the debates at Kyoto and the strategies used by negotiators; the German media dwelled more heavily on policy substance and barely touched on strategy.[16] Once established, story stereotypes become fixed. The initial impressions gatekeepers have conveyed about countries, leaders, and specific policies remain stable even when the reality changes fundamentally.

It has become impossible to profile the "typical" foreign correspondent because there are so many new types. Foreign correspondents used to be better educated than domestic journalists, more experienced, more worldly wise, and better paid. They were U.S. citizens, and like most journalists working for elite media, they were politically liberal, taking positions to the left of mainstream views. Nonetheless, they rarely challenged the U.S. government's stance on foreign policy issues, unless prominent leaders questioned the policy. That demographic profile no longer fits most of the women and men who report from abroad. One unfortunate persistent characteristic of U.S reporters is their inability to communicate in most of the world's languages. Local interviewing consequently is minimal.[17] That deprives them of many potentially fruitful contacts with average local people.

It is difficult to profile foreign journalists dispatched to the United States by foreign media institutions. A fair amount of information is available about the roughly 1,500 formally accredited correspondents who are stationed in Washington, D.C., or in New York, but little is known beyond these elites. Media scholars Lars Wilnat and David Weaver conducted a mail survey in 2000 that confirmed that accredited foreign reporters are an exceptionally well educated group.[18] Forty-five percent are college graduates, 36 percent hold masters degrees, and 9 percent have PhDs. Most are fluent English speakers, and a majority are fluent in a third language as well. Nevertheless, their contacts with Americans are limited. In an earlier survey, only 7 percent said that their best and closest contacts were Americans. In political orientation, foreign newspeople covering the United States tend to be further to the left than most U.S. reporters and quite critical about U.S. policies and lifestyles.[19]

Most news about the United States goes to the press in friendly countries.[20] The poorer regions of the world find it too costly to send correspondents to Washington, D.C. In the 2000 survey, half of the correspondents (51 percent) represented western European countries. The next-largest contingent (12 percent) came from East Asian nations, and 11 percent came from Latin America. Only 7 percent came from poor countries in Africa and the Middle East.[21]

Most foreign reporters are stationed in the nation's capital and find it difficult to cover the whole United States adequately. They rarely travel to other parts of the country except to cover special events, such as spacecraft launches or sports competitions. Thus the impressions that foreigners receive about U.S. politics largely reflect official Washington perspectives. Many foreign reporters complain that top-level U.S. officials rarely grant them interviews that would allow them to file original reports. The frustrations that such slights produce, coupled with the leftward orientation of most overseas reporters, generate a substantial amount of criticism of U.S. economic, military, and foreign aid policies. The damage done to the conduct of U.S. foreign relations by hostile news coverage abroad is only slightly balanced by U.S. government broadcasts designed to polish the country's image.

The Setting for News Selection

News cannot be gathered and produced in a vacuum. It always reflects the spirit of a particular historical period and the reporters' backgrounds and experiences.

Cultural Pressures. The journalists who gather news for mainstream U.S. media, like journalists who report domestic stories, must operate within the context of U.S. politics and political culture. Besides reflecting the U.S. value structure, stories also must conform to established U.S. stereotypes. Leaders widely characterized as either villainous or virtuous must be depicted true to their image in news stories. The ready availability of contrary images on the Internet may eventually make it more difficult to maintain stereotypes. Whereas older people are usually wedded for life to the perceptions learned as young adults, younger people are free from firmly established stereotypes and open to fresh views.

Because the major news services perform the initial gatekeeping tasks for most American newspapers and electronic media, topic selection tends to be quite uniform. In the United States elite papers then take the lead in framing the stories, and editors and reporters of old and new media throughout the country follow suit. The upshot is a foreign news menu that is far more limited in scope than the menu of domestic news. By contrast, diligent Internet roamers can choose their news from a nearly infinite number of sources. As illustrated in Figure 4-2, the Internet is the leader among news venues in the percentage of its news hole devoted to world news.

Political Pressures. Overt and covert political pressures to publish or suppress news stories play a greater role in foreign news production than on the domestic scene. Correspondents reporting from various regions of the world often must do their host country's bidding. Many host governments are politically unstable and fear for their survival if they receive unfavorable publicity. Hence they censor all news stories. If foreign correspondents want to remain in the country, they must write dispatches acceptable to the authorities or face severe penalties that include confiscation of their notes and pictures, closure of transmission facilities, and expulsion or criminal prosecution. These circumstances have produced a strange phenomenon: The most undemocratic countries often receive the least criticism, whereas more open societies are freely reproached.

When countries previously closed to foreign journalists suddenly open their borders, journalists may be unprepared to produce insightful coverage. The opening of the People's Republic of China in 1972 is an example. American reporters accompanied President Richard Nixon and Secretary of State Henry Kissinger to China. During their brief visit, Chinese officials spoon-fed them carefully selected information. The American journalists dutifully reported those stories, treating their U.S. audiences to a romanticized travelogue rather than solid political analysis.

Scores of countries have barred foreign reporters entirely from entering or have expelled them after entry. Albania, Cambodia, El Salvador, Iran, Nicaragua, North Korea, South Africa, the Soviet Union, and Vietnam provide vivid examples from recent decades. Britain kept foreign reporters away from the embattled Falkland Islands in 1983, and Israel routinely imposes tight censorship on its military ventures in the occupied West Bank and Gaza Strip. Large areas of Central America and of the former Soviet Union have been closed to reporters, making it almost impossible to cover their politics adequately. The United States has also used a variety of tactics to limit reporters' access to sites of ongoing U.S. military operations.[22] Bureaucratic hurdles imposed on journalists range from difficult visa requirements, to failure to provide transportation to outlying areas, to hurdles in transmitting the news to a reporter's home base.

In some countries reporters face physical danger. Not infrequently they have been jailed, assaulted, and sometimes murdered. In a seventeen-year span between 1992 and 2009, 734 journalists were killed while performing their duties. Among them, 79 percent were murdered, primarily by political groups and government officials. Most of the remainder were killed in crossfire incidents or violent street demonstrations.[23] The most lethal countries were Iraq, Algeria, and Russia. The Helsinki Accords of 1975, in which signatory countries promised free and safe access to one another's newspeople, have done little to improve the situation.

Media Diplomacy. The extreme measures that many political leaders take to silence individual reporters or entire media organizations are sad testimony to the pervasive belief that media can subvert public policies and topple governments.[24] That belief also fuels the many efforts by image-conscious governments around the world to plant favorable stories in the news or to suppress unfavorable ones. At times, political leaders use interviews with foreign journalists to circumvent normal diplomatic channels and instead send messages to other leaders via the published interviews. Alternatively, leaders may send their messages directly to a news channel. For example, Al Qaeda leader Osama bin Laden has repeatedly communicated with the United States and other countries by sending taped messages to Al Jazeera. That channel has obliged him by broadcasting his words directly rather than merely reporting about them.

Scholars now talk about an "Al Jazeera Effect," referring to the demise of the Western media's virtual monopoly on creating the political images that shape world affairs. New broadcasters and narrowcasters of world news have mushroomed in all regions of the globe to report the news from non-Western perspectives.[25] The Internet has even made it possible to create virtual political enclaves beyond the control of established political powers. For example, the nations of the world have not recognized Al Qaeda as a full-fledged transnational organization. Nonetheless, the Internet enables scattered cells to communicate and act as a transnational organization. Similarly, no internationally recognized Kurdish state existed during the first decade of the twenty-first century. Nevertheless, Kurds dispersed throughout the Middle East made the Internet the site of their virtual state, jointly planning its policies. The political consequences of these developments are potentially enormous because people, including political leaders, base their beliefs and actions on the images of the world that they choose to accept. The Internet provides them with a broad array of competing choices beyond the Western media's versions that have been the only options in the past.

Journalists may even take the initiative in serving as go-betweens for hostile governments. A celebrated incident involved CBS anchor Walter Cronkite, who became a peacemaker in 1977 when he used a television interview to draw a promise from Egypt's president Anwar al-Sadat to visit Jerusalem if it would further peace. In a separate interview, Cronkite secured a pledge from Israeli prime minister Menachem Begin that he would personally welcome Sadat at Ben Gurion Airport. With such mutual commitments, the scene was set for the historic meeting.[26] When Sadat arrived in Israel, flanked by anchors from the three U.S. networks, 2,000 journalists from all over the globe were part of the welcoming crowds. This was media diplomacy in the broadest sense. In the weeks that followed, more than thirty million people in the United States and millions more worldwide watched and judged the peacemaking process. Television alone devoted twenty-four hours of broadcasts to the spectacle, supplemented by radio and print news.

Even when diplomatic relations are carried out through normal channels, reporters often become part of the political process by choosing the issues to be aired during interviews with political leaders and by selecting activities to cover during negotiating sessions and when leaders travel abroad. Reporters cover these events as they see them.[27] In the long-standing conflict in Northern Ireland, reporters have given voice to formally excluded parties, like Sinn Fein, the political wing of the Irish Republican Army, by publicizing their views about ongoing negotiations.[28]

Although media diplomacy is often helpful, it also is fraught with disadvantages and dangers. Government officials, who have far more foreign policy expertise than journalists, may be maneuvered into untenable positions. They may have to react to unforeseen developments with undue haste, especially when twenty-four-hour newscasts may also arouse interest groups that see peaceful or disruptive protests in front of television cameras as a way to promote their causes worldwide. That has been a common occurrence at the annual economic summit meetings of world leaders.[29] Also, journalists may inadvertently provide a propaganda forum for foreign leaders. This is why many Americans harshly condemned CNN's Peter Arnett when he engaged Iraqi president Saddam Hussein in a long television interview during the Gulf War. The interview permitted the Iraqi leader to broadcast accusations against his antagonists to a worldwide audience.

Economic Pressures. Economic considerations, like cultural and political factors, also influence foreign news selection. When the economy sours and profits become a huge concern, American news media feel pressured to avoid complex political stories and concentrate instead on audience-pleasing soft news. This constraint is more burdensome for news beyond the nation's borders than for domestic stories because news from abroad must be exceptionally good to attract the large audiences that permit high advertising prices. There is also pressure to minimize production costs. Some stories may be excluded when they cannot be covered cheaply; others may be included merely because they are comparatively inexpensive and convenient to produce.

Gathering the News: The Beat

The international beat system is quite similar to local beats. Foreign news bureaus usually are located wherever journalists can expect an abundance of political news. From there correspondents cover entire countries rather than particular types of stories. For example, in 2009 ABC, CBS, and NBC all had news bureaus in London, Moscow, Havana, Baghdad, Beijing, Hong Kong, and Tokyo. Fifteen other cities were covered by just one or two of these networks. Some of these were one-person bureaus, staffed by a single journalist who performed all the functions needed for modern print and electronic journalism. Advocates of the one-person pattern argue that it works well, thanks to modern technologies like cell phones that can take excellent videos. That judgment remains highly controversial.[30] Many experts blame the softening of foreign news and the lack of coverage of many crucial events on short-handed, inexperienced staffs who are unfamiliar with the countries that they discuss in their reports.

Despite greater ease of travel to all parts of the world, the bulk of foreign affairs news that U.S. media report still originates in Washington, D.C., from various beats in the executive branch, especially the White House, the State Department, and the Pentagon. When journalists try to cover foreign policy–relevant news, they often face officials who are reluctant to talk because delicate negotiations or the prestige of the United States may be at stake. That makes it

An embedded cameraman took this action shot of U.S. troops during a major battle to recapture Falluja, Iraq, November 9, 2004.
Source: REUTERS

difficult for the media to construct cohesive stories about some of the most important political issues facing the nation.

Foreign news bestows unequal attention on regions and countries of the world, just as domestic news covers regions of the United States unequally. There is no correlation between size of population and amount of coverage. In general, stories cover the countries with which the United States has its most significant diplomatic contacts. In recent years that has usually meant England, France, Germany, Italy, and Russia in Europe; Egypt, Iran, Iraq, and Israel in the Middle East; and more recently, the People's Republic of China and Japan in East Asia. Aside from Canada and Mexico, the Western Hemisphere is covered lightly, except when Americans become concerned about production and export of illicit drugs, civil strife, international business issues, or major regime transitions like President Fidel Castro's retirement in Cuba. Asian coverage was light until the Vietnam War replaced stories from other parts of the world for several years. Overall, coverage has dropped off sharply in all types of media since the end of the Cold War. Similar to domestic news, traditional political content is fading, and social and economic news is becoming more plentiful.[31] The softer focus is particularly apparent on news Web sites.[32] There is a preference for covering predictable events like elections or international conferences because coverage can be planned in advance.

Table 11-3 provides data on network television coverage of major regions of the world from March 9 to April 24, 2009. The table illustrates how a heavy

TABLE 11-3 **Network Coverage of World Regions, March–April 2009 (comparison with 2004 data in parentheses)**

Region	Total number of stories		Stories with visuals	Stories with link to United States
Middle East	56	(180)	28	39
Western Europe	29	(14)	24	18
Asia	28	(8)	18	15
Africa	25	(2)	9	11
North America	20	(5)	8	13
Latin America	8	(4)	4	5
Eastern Europe	4	(4)	0	2
Caribbean	0	(0)	0	0
Australia	0	(0)	0	0

Source: Author's research compiled from Vanderbilt Television News Archive data.

Note: The data cover 166 stories in 2009 and 217 stories in 2004. ABC data are from March 9 to April 8, 2009. CBS and NBC data were extended to April 24, 2009 because news was preempted repeatedly for sports and movies; 2004 data are from October 1–November 5.

focus on one region in 2004 could eclipse news from the rest of the world almost totally. By 2009, coverage patterns had returned to normal. Clearly that does not mean equal coverage of major events in all parts of the world. Heaviest coverage goes to areas involved in bloody conflicts, including massive injuries to civilians. If it bleeds, it definitely leads, thanks to what has been called the news media's "pornographic barbarism."[33] Stories about the Middle East conflict are most abundant; Latin America and the Caribbean, the "back-yard of the United States," are typically slighted. So is post–Cold War Eastern Europe, compared to Western Europe.

In general, journalists favor stories with visuals because they are more attractive to viewers than stories that are purely verbal. Pictures are especially important for foreign news because they bring unfamiliar sights, which might be hard to imagine, directly into viewers' homes. Starvation in India or Somalia, the lifestyles of tribes in New Guinea or Australia, or street riots in Spain or China become much more comprehensible if audiences can experience them visually. Still, not even words and pictures combined can tell a whole story if the audience is unfamiliar with the setting in which the reported events are happening. Ugly street scenes of protesters attacking police, torching buildings, and looting stores may be misinterpreted if the audience does not know the even uglier events that might have provoked the protest.[34] Audiences are also more likely to pay attention to stories that are linked explicitly to U.S.

interests. In 2008, 62 percent of foreign news stories made a link to U.S. interests, compared to only 53 percent in 2004.

Criteria for Choosing Stories

Foreign news, like domestic news, is selected primarily for audience appeal rather than for political significance. This means that stories must have an angle that interests Americans. Sociologist Herbert Gans examined foreign affairs news in television newscasts and in newsmagazines and identified seven subjects that media favor.[35] First in order of frequency of coverage are U.S. activities in foreign countries, particularly when the United States faces war with them or presidents and secretaries of state visit. Second are events that affect Americans directly in a major way, such as oil embargoes and international economic problems. Third are relations of the United States with potentially hostile states, especially when they are facing internal political and military problems. Fourth, the media cover government upheavals and leadership changes in friendly states, along with the activities of European royalty. Fifth are stories about dramatic political conflicts. Most wars, coups d'état, and revolutions are reported; protests, as a rule, are covered only when they are violent. Sixth are disasters, if they involve great loss of life and destruction of property. There is a rough calculus by which media measure severity: "10,000 deaths in Nepal equals 100 deaths in Wales equals 10 deaths in West Virginia equals one death next door."[36] In general, the more distant a nation, the more frequently a newsworthy event must happen to be reported. Seventh are the excesses of foreign dictators, particularly when they involve brutality against political dissidents. Genocides in Rwanda and Bosnia are examples. Noticeably absent from U.S. broadcasts and newspapers are stories about ordinary people and ordinary events abroad. These would be news to Americans, but except for occasional special features, they are not "news" in the professional dictionary of journalists.

Foreign news stories also must be exciting and engaging. Emphasis on violence, conflict and disaster; timeliness or novelty; and familiarity of persons or situations are the major selection criteria. Stories from areas that are familiar because of ample prior coverage or because they are common travel destinations are more likely to be published than stories from more remote parts of the world. When news from countries with unfamiliar cultures is published, the rule of "uncertainty absorption" comes into play. Only plausible stories are acceptable, and they must be cast into a familiar framework, such as the battle against poverty and racism or the moral bankruptcy of military dictators.[37] Such biases make it exceedingly difficult to change images of culturally distant countries.

The media's preference for news about current happenings has led to concentration on rapidly breaking stories in accessible places. Telling such stories is easier and cheaper than ever because the new technologies have spawned ample crops of pictures. They come from bystanders' cell phone photographs and videos, like the Bombay bombing scene shown in chapter 5. More significant, long-range developments, such as programs to improve public health or reduce illiteracy or efforts to create new political parties, are more difficult to capture in pictures. When such developments are reported without analysis of the context that spawned them, they acquire an unwarranted air of suddenness and unpredictability. They have no past, and without appropriate follow-ups, they also have no future. They are merely a brief presence in the parade of current events.

Space and time limitations are particularly troubling for reporting foreign events, which are often unintelligible without adequate background information or interpretation. Complexity therefore becomes a major enemy, and avoidance or oversimplification the defensive strategy. Reporters must write stories simply and logically even if the situation defies logic. Usually a single theme must be selected to epitomize the entire complex story. That leads to gross oversimplification of multifaceted situations like China's policies in Tibet or Iraq's pursuit of nuclear power.

☞ WARS IN THE TELEVISION AGE

In the wake of the Vietnam War, many politicians and other political observers believed that fighting lengthy wars had become nearly impossible for democratic societies in the age of full-color, battlefront television. Viewing the reality of the horrors of battle presumably would sap public support for wars. To avoid images that could interfere with conducting wars, the United States, like other countries, has often restricted war coverage over journalists' strong and vocal objections. Journalists remind military brass that exclusion from battlefronts constitutes undue muzzling of the press at a time when its watchdog functions are especially crucial.[38] In response to these complaints the military has repeatedly revised its rules to permit journalists more access to ongoing military operations. It has proved difficult to devise a workable system because it is well-nigh impossible to reconcile journalists' demands for press freedom with the military's security concerns. Whenever such conflicts make it into the courts, judges usually side with the military and public opinion supports their decisions.[39] However, the balance of forces shifted moderately in the media's favor when U.S. civilian and military officials realized that the impending war in Iraq would receive detailed coverage from Al Jazeera and other potentially hostile Middle Eastern sources. U.S. media were likely to pick up this coverage in the absence of frontline news from U.S. sources.

A new approach announced in February 2003 therefore provided for a pool of approximately 600 print and broadcast war correspondents from the United States and other countries to accompany troops from all branches of the military. These "embedded" journalists would be screened and trained by the Pentagon so that they would fit smoothly into the units to which they were assigned. "Embeds" had to sign an agreement on ground rules of coverage and pledge that they would submit potentially sensitive stories to prepublication scrutiny by military censors. The Defense Department promised only light censorship. Journalists who remained outside the embedded group, the so-called unilaterals, were not subject to restrictive rules. But in line with history, their access to frontline operations was severely restricted. Roughly 40 percent of journalists ultimately chose to be unilaterals.‖

When the plan was announced, critics immediately questioned whether embedded journalists would be able to retain their objectivity when they shared their lives with the troops and were likely to become close friends with many of them. Embedding might simply be another form of government news management that amounted to journalists being "in bed" with the military. Judging from the reports of journalists and observers, that apparently happened only rarely, and the embedding process received a good deal of praise. One observer noted that "embedding allowed far greater access to the battlefield than the press has enjoyed in more than two decades and has dampened the long hostility between the Pentagon and the press."[40] But another report warned that collaboration with the military comes at a price. "The weakness is that the embeds' accounts necessarily become the story of the war as seen through the eyes of American soldiers. No reporter is going to be 'objective' about those who are protecting his or her life."[41]

It is unlikely that the time will ever arrive when the military and the press will be fully satisfied with each other's conduct. Their respective goals are much too antagonistic. War is a dirty business that will never be photogenic when pictured in all its brutality. As long as "just" wars for "good causes" (whatever they may be) are condoned and even celebrated by the world community, full coverage of the horrors of war remains a sensitive issue. Cries for formal or informal censorship under the banner of patriotism will overwhelm cries for press freedom.

Flaws in Gatekeeping

Foreign affairs coverage is dramatic and fills the limited interests of most Americans. Still, foreign news buffs rightly complain that it lacks depth and breadth. It stereotypes and oversimplifies, and it often distorts facts by failing to place them in a realistic context. Analysis of forty-six years of news coverage of the Soviet Union between 1945 and 1991 revealed that the lion's share went to military aspects of the Cold War, while economic and science issues were neglected. Table 11-4 records the topics covered by the *New York Times,* the prime source of international news in the United States, when the spotlight focused on the Soviet Union during press conferences and in the paper's editorials. It is no wonder that most Americans, including political leaders, were taken by surprise when economic deficiencies led to the disintegration and collapse of the Soviet Union in the 1990s.[42] Those deficiencies had failed to capture media attention. Similarly, a study of twelve years of international terrorism stories led to the conclusion that "the limitations of production and presentation, concerns over audience share, and the narrow focus of journalistic notions of professionalism result in coverage more notable for its erratic nature than for its systematic biases."[43] Could better news coverage have alerted the U.S. government to the plans of the terrorists who struck the country in 2001 in time to abort the attack? One must wonder.

TABLE 11-4 **Soviet News Story Topics in the U.S. Press, January 1945–January 1991 (in percentages)**

Topic	Press conference themes	Editorial themes
Soviet foreign relations	23	14
U.S. attitude about Soviets	21	33
Soviet military policy	18	9
U.S.–Soviet meetings	14	5
U.S. military policy	5	6
U.S.–Soviet comparisons	5	4
Soviet attitudes about United States	4	7
Human rights	3	11
Soviet leaders' quality	2	4
Communism as ideology	2	3
U.S. policy about Soviet Union	1	2
Soviet technology	1	1

Source: Author's research.

Note: Data encompass 2,636 press conference themes and 5,310 editorial themes.

Good Frames for Friends, Bad Frames for Foes. The fact that foreign news reported in the U.S. press is based heavily on U.S. sources, who tend to support government policies, explains why the legacy media tend to cast U.S. policies into a favorable light. Coverage of the downing of two planes, one by Soviet fire and the other by U.S. fire, is a good illustration. In 1983 a Soviet fighter plane shot down Korean Airlines Flight 007 with a loss of 269 lives. Five years later, in 1988, the *Vincennes,* a U.S. Navy ship, shot down Iran Air Flight 655 with a loss of 290 lives. The Soviets justified the shooting by saying that the Korean plane was a hostile target; the Americans made the same claim for their action. Though the cases differed in detail and in the context in which they occurred, they were sufficiently alike that one might expect roughly similar action. That did not happen, judging from reports in *Time, Newsweek,* the *New York Times,* the *Washington Post,* and the *CBS Evening News.* As the saying goes, outcomes are judged by whose ox is gored. The framing, language, and pictures used in the stories cast the Soviet action as a moral outrage and the U.S. action as a regrettable technological failure.[44]

There is no evidence that the distortions that spring from such chauvinistic framing are deliberate. Rather, the framing reflects the actual perspectives of the journalists, based on their choice of sources and the predispositions with which they approach stories involving countries identified as friend or foe.

Nonetheless, many scholars believe that this type of coverage has undesirable political consequences. Following the negative coverage of the downing of the Korean plane by the Soviet aircraft, anti-Soviet feelings escalated among members of Congress and the public. The change in mood was attributed to media coverage, as was sharply reduced momentum in the nuclear freeze movement that had been gaining ground.[45] In 1988, following the downing of the Iranian plane by the United States, exculpatory coverage defused potential pressure for withdrawal of U.S. forces from the Persian Gulf region.

Uncritical, Flashlight Coverage. Reporting of foreign news usually lacks a sense of history and a sense of the meaning of successive events. Therefore, it often confuses the public. The news does not provide sufficient information to permit most Americans to understand the rationale for major foreign policies. Some stories, even those directly involving U.S. security, are ignored until events reach crisis proportions or until there is a precipitating incident. *New York Times* correspondent James Reston put the problem this way:

> We are fascinated by events but not by the things that cause the events. We will send 500 correspondents to Vietnam after the war breaks out…meanwhile ignoring the rest of the world, but we will not send five reporters there when the danger of war is developing.[46]

When news about the aftermath of the 2003 Iraq War turned sour in 2004, the news media were chided for neglecting their watchdog role. The *New York Times* and *Washington Post* apologized for supporting President George W. Bush's policies too wholeheartedly, true to their usual stance in covering news about U.S. military ventures abroad.[47] They had featured a limited amount of dissent about war strategies, without questioning the overall goals and the need for war. The criticism and self-criticism regarding the adequacy of prewar debates reflect the fact that the media did not live up to political elites' expectations about their watchdog role in the foreign policy realm. Unfortunately, there are no satisfactory solutions to the dilemmas that journalists face during international crises, when their feelings of patriotism demand support for the government while their journalistic duty calls for raising red flags of caution.[48]

News Distortions. Just like domestic news, foreign news neglects major social and economic problems. The reasons are readily apparent. Such problems are difficult to discuss in brief stories, pictures are scarce, and changes come at a glacial pace. Some social problems are extremely complex; most reporters are ill-equipped to understand them, let alone report about them. When news stories address economic development issues, the focus is on dramatic negative aspects like famines, health crises, and conflicts. As Rafael Caldera, former president of Venezuela, told a press conference at the National Press Club in Washington, D.C., "The phrase 'no news is good news' has become 'good news is no news.'…Little or nothing is mentioned in American media about literary or scientific achievements" or "about social achievements and the defense against the dangers which threaten our peace and development." Instead, "only the most deplorable incidents, be they caused by nature or by man, receive prominent attention."[49] It is small consolation for such ruffled feelings that news selection criteria applied to events in developing nations are typical for news from everywhere.[50] The situation is aggravated by the fact that many developing countries depend for their international news on western news media, especially the Associated Press and CNN. These countries complain about "media imperialism."[51] Critics in developing nations also decry the corrupting effects of western news and entertainment programs that feature violence and sexually explicit episodes. Western programs allegedly damage the cultural identity of people in developing nations, drawing them away from their own heritage.[52]

Overemphasis on Conflict. Negative news, including news about violent conflicts, is more prevalent in the U.S. media than in the media of many other societies. Comparisons of news coverage in the United States and that in Canada, two societies that are culturally close, are revealing. The rate of violence on Canadian television news is half the U.S. rate.[53] When the people of Quebec voted in 1980 on the question of separating from Canada, the *Washington Post* warned that civil war might erupt. U.S. papers focused on serious rioting by separatists in English sectors of Montreal. By contrast, the *Toronto Globe and Mail* buried a small story about minor unrest in Quebec in the back pages. The prospect of civil war was never mentioned and was characterized as "ludicrous" by knowledgeable observers.[54] During the Iranian hostage crisis, *New York Times* coverage featured stereotypical portrayals of Muslims and tales of violence. Far more peaceful images emerged in the French paper *Le Monde.*[55]

By and large, news media in democracies feature more conflict than do media in authoritarian and totalitarian societies. In part this happens because government-controlled and supported news organizations can afford to forgo dramatic negative news, since their financial health is unrelated to audience size. U.S. news media draw attention to conflict rather than to peaceful settlement and make much of the world beyond U.S. borders seem chaotic. Routine foreign news languishes in the back pages or is condensed into news snippets. Usually the issues are oversimplified and instead of interpreting what the conflict means to the country and its people, the story focuses mainly on what, if anything, the conflict portends for U.S. politics.

Distortions in domestic news are not likely to mislead most U.S. audiences because past experiences and socialization provide corrective lenses.[56] The foreign scene, by contrast, must be viewed without correction for myopia and astigmatism. Americans may be skeptical about the accuracy of the images, but they lack the means to judge the nature and degree of distortion.

• The Impact of Foreign Affairs Coverage

Support of the Status Quo. Finally, the thrust of most foreign news stories supports government policies. The media usually accept official designations of who are friends and enemies of the United States and interpret these friends' and enemies' motives accordingly. Whenever relationships change, media coverage mirrors the change. Coverage of the Soviet Union's attack on Korean Airlines Flight 007 is a good example of the approach used for disfavored countries. In the same way, a comparison of *New York Times* coverage of strife in Cambodia and East Timor and of elections in Nicaragua and El Salvador showed that the paper judged "communist-tainted" Cambodia and Nicaragua unfavorably. By contrast, comparable events in East Timor and El Salvador, countries deemed friendly to the United States, were cast in a favorable light.[57] Because the president and executive branch are the prime sources of foreign affairs news, they can, most of the time, set the agenda of coverage with stories that are framed to reflect official perspectives.[58]

On the whole, despite some coverage that challenges the official version of international politics and U.S. foreign policies, the tenor of news stories in mainstream media and on the Internet supports prevailing stereotypes about the world. Preoccupation with the developed world reinforces many Americans' beliefs about the importance of these nations. In the same way, portrayal of less-developed countries as incapable of managing their own affairs makes it easy to believe that they do not deserve higher status and the media attention that accompanies it.

Newspeople usually are willing to withhold news and commentary when publicity would severely complicate the government's management of foreign policy. For example, the media suppressed information about the United States' breaking Japanese military message codes during World War II and refrained from sharply criticizing Iranian leaders during the 1979 hostage crisis to avoid angering them. Both are examples in which major political interests were at stake. Likewise, news of delicate negotiations among foreign countries may be temporarily withheld to avoid rocking the boat before agreements are reached. When an invasion of Haiti by U.S. troops was in the offing in 1994, CNN and the three major television networks pledged to refrain from showing any pictures that might put the troops at risk (see Box 11-1 for more discussion of the potential risks of releasing graphic photos).[59]

The Indexing Hypothesis. If the media are generally supportive of government policies, how can their adverse comments about the Vietnam War or the Gulf War be explained? The answer is that the media generally emphasize the government's positions until many respected sources voice strong dissent. To use a term popularized by political scientist Lance Bennett, the media "index" their coverage to the degree of disagreement by powerful political leaders with the government's position.[60] The media do not care to lead dissent in this minefield of uncertainties about facts, and they fear that irate audiences will accuse them of a lack of patriotism. Only when respected opposition forces publicly express their concern do the media couple their government accounts with coverage of the dissenting voices.[61]

Tests of the indexing hypothesis in the post–Cold War era suggest that it may apply only in situations when consequential national security interests are at stake.[62] It may also be true that the end of the Cold War marked a break with the past that led to the "cascade" model of foreign affairs coverage identified by Robert Entman. Entman contends that foreign policy consensus among elites has become the exception rather than the norm. That leaves the media free to choose among competing interpretations of events happening abroad. The president's framing still has the best chance to be reflected in the news. But other frames may trump it, depending on how they cascade through communications networks that reach the media. As always, journalistic news selection criteria are also a major selection factor.

The CNN Effect. The belief that graphic media coverage of events abroad on occasion forces the U.S. government to engage in unplanned and undesired interventions has been dubbed the "CNN effect." The name was coined by scholars who studied the U.S. intervention in Somalia that began in 1992, shortly after CNN had published gruesome pictures of atrocities against civilians in that country. Subsequent analyses suggest that CNN was given undue credit in that case. Officials had formulated plans for the humanitarian intervention well ahead of the airing of the CNN stories.[63]

Further investigations suggest that there is, indeed, evidence for a CNN effect in situations in which television pictures of human suffering inflicted by nature or by fellow humans have aroused sympathies for the victims among the U.S. public as well as U.S. officials. But the effect is less automatic than initially postulated, and it seems to be limited to situations involving humanitarian crises. For example, political scientist Piers Robinson studied U.S. intervention in the conflict in Bosnia that began in 1992 and ended in 1995. He concluded that media coverage did play a role in the initial humanitarian intervention but that it was not a factor in subsequent military activities designed to end the war.[64] Similarly, intervention in northern Iraq in 1991 to protect Kurdish civilians from atrocities committed by Saddam Hussein, refugee rescue missions sent to Rwanda in 1994, and the efforts to protect civilians in Somalia are examples of media-encouraged humanitarian missions. But they never progressed to efforts to use military force to stop the conflict.

However, media coverage can influence foreign affairs even when it does not lead to military intervention. Effects include shortening the time for choosing a policy, which in turn shrinks the pool of people regularly consulted prior to decisions and increases the chances for ill-considered policies.[65] Televised coverage of a crisis may pressure the president to react hastily to avoid appearing weak and vacillating. As Lloyd Cutler, White House counsel to presidents Jimmy Carter and Bill Clinton, put it, "If an ominous foreign event is featured on TV news, the President and his advisers feel bound to make a response in time for the next evening news program."[66] This may leave no time to investigate the news report or for officials of the foreign country to explain it. President John F. Kennedy waited eight days in 1961 before commenting on the construction of the Berlin Wall; President George H.W. Bush had to respond overnight to its destruction.[67]

Madeleine Albright, President Clinton's secretary of state, commented in 2001 that the twenty-four-hour news cycle had changed things, but she saw advantages along with the disadvantages. "Some of it is very good, because you know what's going on and there is a real-time sense about things....But, in other ways, it makes you have to respond to events much faster than it might be prudent....So it's a double-edged sword."[68]

BOX 11-1   **News from the Global Village**

To varying degrees throughout the world, the connectivity of new media is superseding the traditional political connections that have brought identity and structure to global politics. This rewiring of the world's neural system is proceeding at remarkable speed, and its reach keeps extending ever farther. It changes the way states and citizens interact with each other and it gives the individual a chance at a new kind of autonomy, at least on an intellectual level, because of the greater availability of infor-mation.... [A] huge universe of new communications and information providers...are changing the relationship between those who govern and those who are governed...assisting those with previously unachievable political agendas. The advent of television a half-century ago pales in comparison with new media's effects on global political life today.[1]

Fifty years ago, media guru Marshall McLuhan predicted that electronic technology would one day contract the world into a village where information would instantaneously reach all people. As the above quote from Philip Seib's book about Al Jazeera suggests, that day has arrived. The Internet allows people to live in on-line virtual communities—global villages—that share news topics but have different interests and concerns.

The world as a village where people are in constant touch and react quickly to each other's behaviors is well illustrated by the torture memo incident that made waves throughout the globe in 2009. The story began when President Barack Obama released previously secret U.S. government memoranda that detailed torture tactics authorized for extracting information from suspected terrorists. Debate raged about the possible impact of publication of these documents at home and, far more importantly, abroad. Methods of prisoner interrogation were still a domestic policy issue, but they had become an international issue as well. Policy makers and journalists had to consider that reality. For most social,

SUMMARY

The quality of U.S. foreign policy and the effectiveness of U.S. relations with other countries are crucial to the welfare of people throughout the world. Sound policy and relations require a solid information base. This chapter has shown that the foreign affairs information base on which Americans depend leaves much to be desired. The flow of information about our world has become enormous and overpowering, but most stories are shallow. They lead audiences into a jungle of diverse perspectives without a road map. Many guideposts are misleading, unintentionally or deliberately.

The reasons for these reporting flaws are complex. They include the economics of reporting news from all parts of the globe, the sociopolitical setting in which news gathering takes place, and the audiences to whose

economic, and political issues the question, How well will it play in the United States? had to be permanently amended by adding, How well will it play in the world?

The torture memo story also illustrates another crucial aspect of telling news stories in our global village world. Pictures are powerful, but their meanings hinge on the captions and the viewers' diverse cultural prisms. Pictures absorb the meanings that accompanying words ascribe to them. Villagers around the globe will attach their own captions; their interpretations will reflect their unique preconceptions. The image of a man lying on the ground can be described as a tired hiker or a murder victim. The hiker designation is calming; the murder designation is alarming and possibly arousing. A purely verbal description of the scene, even if it referred to murder, would be less inciting.

Concerns about the unique potency of pictures prompted President Obama to balk when asked to release pictures of the shocking torture episodes, even though he had previously released the verbal memos which described the torture methods in graphic detail. Military officials had warned him that the pictures—spread throughout the global village by the Internet—were likely to infuriate global villagers, who might then attack American soldiers and civilians who happened to be nearby. That scenario was frighteningly realistic in a world where, just a few years earlier, more than one hundred people had been killed as a consequence of rage over blasphemous cartoons depicting the prophet Muhammad. The cartoons initially appeared in 2005, in an obscure Danish newspaper. Hundreds of other media then reprinted them or reported about them. The Danish journalists claimed that their cartoon story was intended as a contribution to the debate about the freedom of a global press to discuss potentially sensitive topics. That debate has been settled for the foreseeable future. The political firestorm that followed the cartoon story resolved it decisively.

---

1. Philip Seib, *The Al Jazeera Effect: How the New Global Media Are Reshaping World Politics* (Dulles, Va.: Potomac Books), 175.

worldviews and tastes the news must cater. Foreign affairs news often must be gathered under trying conditions. Strange locations and inadequate technological facilities can make nightmares of the physical aspects of getting to the scene of the action, collecting information, and transmitting it. These technical difficulties are compounded by political difficulties. They include the reluctance of public officials everywhere to commit themselves publicly on foreign affairs matters and the harassment of correspondents venturing into places where they are unwanted. Expulsion, imprisonment, and physical harm are common. With so much territory to cover, professional reporters frequently avoid areas where news is hard to get. Local citizen reporters are also scarce in such regions because access to cell phones is rare. This effectively removes many regions of the world from media scrutiny and contributes to unevenness of news flow.

How good is the foreign affairs news presented by traditional U.S. news media? The picture is mixed and must be judged in light of the problems faced in foreign news production. News from around the globe must be at once timely, exciting, personalized, and brief, yet understandable for a U.S. audience that is barely interested in most events abroad. To satisfy these criteria with shrinking resources of time and money, journalists focus on sensational, mostly negative news. They write stories primarily from a U.S. perspective and usually follow the current administration's foreign policy rationales and the public's stereotyped views of the world. Despite these shortcomings, Americans can obtain a rich mixture of stories about political events abroad. The Web is a gold mine of information for those who can tell the real metal from the dross. Elite newspapers generally give fairly thorough exposure to U.S. foreign policies. However, U.S. newspapers rarely challenge the objectives of foreign policies unless they can cite support from respected political sources. They may, however, question how effectively the administration is executing these policies.

Occasionally, television commentators have become active diplomats through interviews that set the stage for subsequent political developments. Graphic accounts of human suffering abroad have from time to time spawned humanitarian interventions, but scholars have not yet fully delineated under what circumstances this "CNN effect" occurs. The impact of new media remains unclear as well. We know that the influx of news from all parts of the world is huge. It is dispatched by thousands of amateur journalists who are unrestrained by the legal and ethical shackles that bind professionals. The quality of their reporting ranges from excellent to dismal. But it is unknown how much of their work leaves a mark and who is affected. Do powerful people listen? Are opinions changed? Speculations abound but solid answers are lacking. Many questions remain as well about the circumstances that propel American news media to cover dissenting views about foreign policy that may force a change in the goals and strategies favored by incumbent presidents. One thing is clear: It is no longer heresy in times of foreign crises to criticize the administration's foreign policy rather than rallying around the flag. In fact, criticism at such times may ultimately be deemed a hallowed duty. Its potency will depend on its wisdom and the credibility of the source that dispenses it.

NOTES

1. Noam Cohen, "Few in U.S. see Jazeera's Coverage of Gaza War," *New York Times*, January 9, 2009.
2. Pew Research Center for the People and the Press, "News Interest and Knowledge, 2008," http://people-press.org/report/?pageid=1356.
3. Ibid.
4. Pamela J. Shoemaker, Lucig H. Danielian, and Nancy Brendlinger, "Deviant Acts, Risky Business, and U.S. Interests: The Newsworthiness of World Events," *Journalism Quarterly* 68 (Winter 1991): 781–795.
5. Pippa Norris, "The Restless Searchlight: Network News Framing of the Post Cold-War World," *Political Communication* 12, no. 4 (1995): 357–370.

6. William A. Hachten and James F. Scotton, *The World News Prism: Global Information in a Satellite Age*, 7th ed. (Malden, Mass.: Blackwell, 2007). Other important international news suppliers are Germany's Deutsche Press Agentur (DPA) and Japan's Kyodo News Service, as well as China's Xinhua News Agency and United Press International, once second only to the Associated Press among U.S. news agencies.

7. Fons Tuinstra, "Caught between the Cold War and the Internet," *Nieman Reports* 58, no. 3 (2004): 100–103.

8. Associated Press, www.ap.org.

9. John Maxwell Hamilton and Eric Jenner, "Foreign Correspondence: Evolution, Not Extinction," *Nieman Reports* 58, no. 3 (2004): 98–100; John Maxwell Hamilton and Eric Jenner, "Redefining Foreign Correspondence," *Journalism* 5, no. 3 (2004): 301–321.

10. Hamilton and Jenner, "Foreign Correspondence."

11. Catholic World News, www.cwnews.com. The figure covers all reporters, not only Americans.

12. Hamilton and Jenner, "Foreign Correspondence"; Hamilton and Jenner, "Redefining Foreign Correspondence."

13. See www.globalpost.com.

14. Jarol B. Manheim, "Strategic Public Diplomacy: Managing Kuwait's Image During the Gulf Conflict," in *Taken by Storm: The Media, Public Opinion, and U.S. Foreign Policy in the Gulf War*, ed. W. Lance Bennett and David L. Paletz (Chicago: University of Chicago Press, 1994), 131–148.

15. Jarol B. Manheim and Robert B. Albritton, "Changing National Images: International Public Relations and Media Agenda-Setting," *American Political Science Review* 78 (September 1984): 641–657; Robert B. Albritton and Jarol B. Manheim, "Public Relations Efforts for the Third World: Images in the News," *Journal of Communication* 35 (Spring 1985): 43–59; Jarol B. Manheim, *Strategic Public Diplomacy and American Foreign Policy: The Evolution of Influence* (New York: Oxford University Press, 1994).

16. Brigitte L. Nacos, Robert Y. Shapiro, and Pierangelo Isernia, "New Issues and the Media: American and German News Coverage of the Global-Warming Debate," in *Decisionmaking in a Glass House: Mass Media, Public Opinion, and American and European Foreign Policy in the 21st Century*, ed. Nacos, Shapiro, and Isernia (Lanham, Md.: Rowman and Littlefield, 2000), 41–59.

17. Leo Bogart, "The Overseas Newsman: A 1967 Profile Study," *Journalism Quarterly* 45 (Summer 1968): 293–306. Judging from more recent profile studies of American journalists in general, these early profiles are still reasonably accurate; see chapter 4. Lars Wilnat and David Weaver, "Through Their Eyes: The Work of Foreign Correspondents in the United States," *Journalism* 4, no. 4 (2003): 403–422.

18. Wilnat and Weaver, "Through Their Eyes."

19. Shailendra Ghorpade, "Foreign Correspondents Cover Washington for World," *Journalism Quarterly* 61 (Fall 1984): 667.

20. Ibid., 667–671; and *Editor and Publisher International Yearbook, 1991* (New York: Editor and Publisher, 1991). In the United States the needs of foreign correspondents are served by the United States Information Agency (USIA). It maintains foreign press centers in major U.S. cities and arranges high-level briefings by government officials and news-gathering tours on major economic, political, and cultural themes. It also provides extensive information services and even helps with arranging appointments and filing facilities at international summits. United States Information Agency, Washington, D.C., "Foreign Press Centers," January 1996; also, Lori Montgomery presents a brief, first-person account of the life of a foreign correspondent in "Foreign Correspondent's Notebook," www.freep.com/jobspage/academy/foreign.htm.

21. Wilnat and Weaver, "Through Their Eyes."

22. Hillel Nossek, "Terrorism and the Media: Does the Weapon Matter to the Coverage?" in *Media and Political Violence*, ed. Hillel Nossek, Annabelle Sreberry, and Prasun Sonwalkar (Cresskill, N.J.: Hampton Press, 2007), 269–303; Doris A. Graber, "Terrorism, Censorship and the First Amendment," in *Framing Terrorism: The News Media, the Government, and the Public*, ed. Pippa Norris, Montague Kern, and Marion Just (New York: Routledge, 2003), 27–42.

23. Committee to Protect Journalists, "Journalists Killed: January 1, 1992–April 3, 2009: 734," www.cpj.org/deadly/.

24. Eytan Gilboa, "Media Diplomacy: Conceptual Divergence and Applications," *Harvard International Journal of Press/Politics* 3, no. 3 (1998): 56–75.

25. Philip Seib, *The Al Jazeera Effect: How the New Global Media Are Reshaping World Politics* (Dulles, Va.: Potomac Books, 2008).

26. Ibid.

27. For a full discussion of reporting on the Middle East peace negotiations between Israel and the Palestinians, see Gadi Wolfsfeld, *Media and Political Conflict: News from the Middle East* (Cambridge, UK: Cambridge University Press, 1997).

28. Kirsten Sparre, "Megaphone Diplomacy in the Northern Irish Peace Process: Squaring the Circle by Talking to Terrorists through Journalists," *Harvard International Journal of Press/ Politics* 6, no. 1 (2001): 88–104.

29. Patrick O'Heffernan, "Mass Media and U.S. Foreign Policy: A Mutual Exploitation Model of Media Influence in U.S. Foreign Policy," in *Media and Public Policy*, ed. Robert J. Spitzer (Westport, Conn.: Praeger, 1993), 187–211.

30. See www.stateofthemedia.org/2009/narrative_networktv_intro.php?cat=0&media=6.

31. Garrick Utley, "The Shrinking of Foreign News: From Broadcast to Narrowcast," *Foreign Affairs* 76, no. 1 (1997): 2–10. Also see Brent Cunningham, "The AP Now," *Columbia Journalism Review*, November/December 2000, www.cjr.org/year/00/4/ap.asp.

32. Daniela V. Dimitrova, Lynda Lee Kaid, Andrew Paul Williams, and Kaye D. Trammell, "War on the Web: The Immediate News Framing of Gulf War II," *Press/Politics* 10, no. 1 (2005): 22–44.

33. Paul Taylor, "The Pornographic Barbarism of the Self-Reflecting Sign," in *Media and Political Violence*, ed. Nossek, Sreberry, and Sonwalkar, 355–372.

34. Richard Fox, "Visions of Terror: On the Use of Images in the Mass Mediated Representation of the Bali Bombing," in *Media and Political Violence*, ed. Nossek, Sreberry, and Sonwalkar, 211–245.

35. Herbert J. Gans, *Deciding What's News: A Study of* CBS Evening News, NBC Nightly News, Newsweek, *and* Time (New York: Pantheon, 1979). See also Wolfsfeld, *Media and Political Conflict*, and David D. Perlmutter and John Maxwell Hamilton, eds., *From Pigeons to News Portals: Foreign Reporting and the Challenge of New Technology* (Baton Rouge: Louisiana State University Press, 2007).

36. Edwin Diamond, *The Tin Kazoo: Television, Politics, and the News* (Cambridge, Mass.: MIT Press, 1975), 94.

37. Daniel C. Hallin, "Hegemony: The American News Media from Vietnam to El Salvador: A Study of Ideological Change and Its Limits," in *Political Communication Research: Approaches, Studies, Assessments*, ed. David L. Paletz (Norwood, N.J.: Ablex, 1987), 17; Robert M. Entman, "Hegemonic Socialization, Information Processing, and Presidential News Management: Framing the KAL and Iran Air Incidents," in *The Psychology of Political Communication*, ed. Ann Crigler (Ann Arbor: University of Michigan Press, 1996).

38. David R. Gergen, "Diplomacy in a Television Age: The Dangers of Teledemocracy," in *The Media and Foreign Policy*, ed. Simon Serfaty (New York: St. Martin's, 1991), 47–63.

39. Graber, "Terrorism, Censorship, and the First Amendment."

40. Nancy Bernhard, "Embedding Reporters on the Frontline," *Nieman Reports* 57, no. 2 (2003): 87–90.

41. Dan Kennedy, "Embedded Reporting: Is Objectivity an Acceptable Casualty of This Kind of Reporting?" *Nieman Reports* 57, no. 2 (2003): 87; Sean Aday, Steven Livingston, and Maeve Hebert, "Embedding the Truth: A Cross-Cultural Analysis of Objectivity and Television Coverage of the Iraq War," *Press/Politics* 10, no. 1 (2005): 3–21; Michael Pfau, Michel Haigh, Mitchell Gettle, Michael Donnelly, Gregory Scott, Dana Warr, and Elaine Wittenberg, "Embedding Journalists in Military Combat Units: Impact on Newspaper Story Frames and Tone," *Journalism and Mass Communication Quarterly* 81, no. 1 (2004): 74–88.

42. Author's research.

43. Michael X. Delli Carpini and Bruce A. Williams, "Television and Terrorism: Patterns of Presentation and Occurrence, 1969 to 1980," *Western Political Quarterly* 40 (March 1987): 45–64.

44. Robert M. Entman, "Framing U.S. Coverage of International News: Contrasts in Narratives of the KAL and Iran Air Incidents," *Journal of Communication* 41 (Fall 1991): 6–27.

45. Ibid., 22–23.

46. James Reston, *Sketches in the Sand* (New York: Knopf, 1967), 195; for supporting evidence in the Gulf War, see Gladys Engel Lang and Kurt Lang, "The Press as Prologue: Media Coverage of Saddam's Iraq, 1979–1990," in *Taken By Storm,* ed. Bennett and Paletz, 43–62.

47. *New York Times* Editors, "*New York Times* Reviews Its Own Coverage of Iraq War," *New York Times,* May 26, 2004; Howard Kurtz, "The *Post* on WMDs: An Inside Story," *Washington Post,* August 12, 2004.

48. Ingrid A. Lehmann, "Exploring the Transatlantic Media Divide over Iraq," *Press/Politics* 10, no. 1 (2005): 63–89; Robert Entman, *Projections of Power: Framing News, Public Opinion, and U.S. Foreign Policy* (Chicago: University of Chicago Press, 2004); Stephen Hess and Marvin Kalb, eds., *The Media and the War on Terrorism* (Washington, D.C.: Brookings Institution Press, 2003).

49. Quoted in Fernando Reyes Matta, "The Latin American Concept of News," *Journal of Communication* 29 (Spring 1979): 169.

50. Gary D. Gaddy and Enoch Tanjong, "Earthquake Coverage by the Western Press," *Journal of Communication* 36 (Spring 1986): 105–112. For a conflicting analysis, see William C. Adams, "Whose Lives Count? TV Coverage of Natural Disasters," *Journal of Communication* 36 (Spring 1986): 113–122.

51. For a discussion of media imperialism, see Herbert I. Schiller, *Culture, Inc.: The Corporate Takeover of Public Expression* (New York: Oxford University Press, 1989); and René Jean Ravault, "International Information: Bullet or Boomerang?" in *Political Communication Research,* ed. David L. Paletz, 245–265.

52. The impact of foreign television is assessed in Alexis S. Tan, Sarrina Li, and Charles Simpson, "American TV and Social Stereotypes of Americans in Taiwan and Mexico," *Journalism Quarterly* 63 (Winter 1986): 809–814.

53. Benjamin D. Singer, "Violence, Protest, and War in Television News: The U.S. and Canada Compared," *Public Opinion Quarterly* 34 (Winter 1970–1971): 611–616. For another comparative perspective on media coverage, see Richard Gunther and Anthony Mughan, *Democracy and the Media: A Comparative Perspective* (Cambridge, UK: Cambridge University Press, 2000).

54. James P. Winter, Pirouz Shoar Ghaffari, and Vernone M. Sparkes, "How Major U.S. Dailies Covered Quebec Separatism Referendum," *Journalism Quarterly* 59 (Winter 1982): 608.

55. Edward W. Said, *Covering Islam: How the Media and the Experts Determine How We See the Rest of the World,* rev. ed. (New York: Vintage, 1987); also see Gunther and Mughan, *Democracy and the Media.*

56. Hanna Adoni and S. Mane, "Media and the Social Construction of Reality: Toward an Integration of Theory and Research," *Communication Research* 11 (July 1984): 323–340; see

also Doris Graber, *Processing Politics: Learning from Television in the Internet Age* (Chicago: University of Chicago Press, 2001).

57. Edward S. Herman, "Diversity of News: 'Marginalizing' the Opposition," *Journal of Communication* 35 (Fall 1985): 135–146. See also W. Lance Bennett, "An Introduction to Journalism Norms and Representations of Politics," *Political Communication* 13, no. 4 (1996): 373–384.

58. John A. Lent, "Foreign News in American Media," *Journal of Communication* 27 (Winter 1977): 46–50. See also Jyotika Ramaprasad and Daniel Riffe, "Effect of U.S.–India Relations on *New York Times* Coverage," *Journalism Quarterly* 64 (Summer/Autumn 1987): 537–543; Hallin, "Hegemony"; and David Altheide, "Media Hegemony: A Failure of Perspective," *Public Opinion Quarterly* 48 (Summer 1984): 476–490.

59. "TV Networks Say Coverage Would Not Endanger Troops," *New York Times,* September 19, 1994.

60. Bennett, "An Introduction to Journalism Norms."

61. Daniel C. Hallin, "The Media, the War in Vietnam, and Political Support: A Critique of the Thesis of an Oppositional Media," *Journal of Politics* 46 (February 1984); also see Jonathan Mermin, *Debating War and Peace* (Princeton: Princeton University Press, 1999); and John Zaller and Dennis Chiu, "Government's Little Helper: U.S. Press Coverage of Foreign Policy Crises, 1946–1999," in *Decisionmaking in a Glass House,* ed. Nacos, Shapiro, and Isernia, 61–84, for many examples.

62. Zaller and Chiu, "Government's Little Helper," 74–81.

63. Steven Livingston, *Clarifying the CNN Effect: An Examination of Media Effects according to Type of Military Intervention* (Cambridge, Mass.: Harvard University Press, 1996).

64. Pierce Robinson, *The CNN Effect: The Myth of News, Foreign Policy, and Intervention* (New York: Routledge, 2002); also see Nik Gowing, "Real-Time Television Coverage of Armed Conflicts and Diplomatic Crises: Does It Pressure or Distort Foreign Policy Decisions?" in *Terrorism, War, and the Press,* ed. Nancy Palmer (Cambridge, Mass.: Harvard University Press, 2003), 139–222.

65. Eytan Gilboa, "Television News and U.S. Foreign Policy: Constraints of Real-Time Coverage," *Press/Politics* 8, no. 4 (2003): 97–113.

66. Quoted in ibid.

67. Ibid., 48; Nicholas O. Berry in *Foreign Policy and the Press: An Analysis of the New York Times' Coverage of U.S. Foreign Policy* (Westport, Conn.: Greenwood Press, 1990) makes the same argument.

68. Madeleine Albright, "Around-the-Clock News Cycle a Double-Edged Sword," *Harvard International Journal of Press/Politics* 6, no. 1 (2001): 105–108.

READINGS

Entman, Robert. *Projections of Power: Framing News, Public Opinion, and U.S. Foreign Policy.* Chicago: University of Chicago Press, 2004.

Gilboa, Eytan, ed. *Media and Conflict: Framing Issues, Making Policy, Shaping Opinions.* Ardsley, N.Y.: Transnational Publishers, 2002.

Manheim, Jarol B. *Strategic Public Diplomacy and American Foreign Policy: The Evolution of Influence.* New York: Oxford University Press, 1994.

Nacos, Brigitte L., Robert Y. Shapiro, and Pierangelo Isernia, eds. *Decisionmaking in a Glass House: Mass Media, Public Opinion, and American and European Foreign Policy in the 21st Century.* Lanham, Md.: Rowman and Littlefield, 2000.

Norris, Pippa, Montague Kern, and Marion Just, eds. *Framing Terrorism: The News Media, the Government, and the Public.* New York: Routledge, 2003.

Nossek, Hillel, Annabelle Sreberry, and Prasun Sonwalkar, eds. *Media and Political Violence.* Cresskill, N.J.: Hampton Press, 2007.

Perlmutter, David D., and John Maxwell Hamilton, eds. *From Pigeons to News Portals: Foreign Reporting and the Challenge of New Technology.* Baton Rouge: Louisiana State University Press, 2007.

Robinson, Piers. *The CNN Effect: The Myth of News, Foreign Policy, and Intervention.* New York: Routledge, 2002.

Seib, Philip. *The Al Jazeera Effect: How the New Global Media Are Reshaping World Politics.* Dulles, Va.: Potomac Books, 2008.

Sylvester, Judith, and Suzanne Hoffman. *Reporting from the Front: The Media and the Military.* Lanham, Md.: Rowman and Littlefield, 2004.

12

Current Trends and Future Directions in Media Policy

In May 2009 the Public Library of Science (PLoS) published a twenty-seven-page article with the formidable title "Complete Primate Skeleton from the Middle Eocene of Messel in Germany: Morphology and Paleobiology." The six scientists listed as its authors were affiliated with well-known European and American universities.[1] The article detailed the discovery and biological appraisal of the most complete fossil primate skeleton ever found, dating back some 47 million years. The remains made it possible to reconstruct the life history of the apelike creature. It suggested that *Darwinius masillae*, as she had been named, might be the ancestor of the current human race.

The discovery of the fossil became a major media event. New York City's American Museum of Natural History hosted a widely advertised public ceremony and press conference. A two-hour documentary and book followed, along with a television teaser campaign that compared the significance of the fossil's discovery to the original moon landing or the Kennedy assassination. The History Channel showed the documentary on Memorial Day 2009 as a prime time special; Britain's BBC and Germany's ZDF in Germany also featured it. It became an ABC news exclusive that appeared on *Good Morning America, Nightline,* and *World News.*[2] YouTube, Facebook, MySpace, and Twitter spread the story far and wide. The heroic efforts to gain audience attention for the message via a multiplicity of platforms that reach millions of people are typical for the current media scene. Journalism is changing. But how much?

How many people actually paid attention to the fossil story or watched the documentary? How many people stored the information in their long-term memories? We do not know. We do know that the news supply is growing geometrically. Much of it is variations on the same theme. But even keeping that in mind, it is clear that the supply of news, especially political news, far exceeds the demand, or even the ability of humans to consume it within the limits of an inelastic, 24-hour day. In 2008 audiences relying primarily on television news spent 54 minutes per day watching it. That time allotment dropped to 41 minutes for radio listeners, 39 minutes for newspaper fanciers, and 35 minutes for Internet aficionados. In that tiny time slot, people prefer an overview of the day's news, rather than stories of special interest to them.[3] As discussed in chapter 7, we also know that human beings select their news intake carefully, in line with their needs and interests. Therefore, the vast majority of political and nonpolitical messages in cyberspace, including important ones, will find few listeners and viewers. Narrowcasting cannot match the impact of broadcasting; its reach is narrow, as the name suggests. In the battle for audience attention, trusted sources have a distinct advantage, be they legacy media or old and new political organizations. Audiences do not want to be misled by unknown information providers.

Nonetheless, journalism is definitely changing, but probably less drastically than many news media watchers believe. Predictions of cosmic changes are not new. They surfaced when the telegraph was invented, when the transatlantic cable was laid, and when wire services acquired a global reach. All of these technological advances emerged in the same thirty-odd years in the mid-nineteenth century. It is not that there is nothing new under the sun. It is just that we are not in a very good position to see which of the social changes of the past five or ten or twenty-five years are likely to prove earth shattering several decades from now. And maybe these changes are not shattering the earth so much as reshaping it, keeping the basic principles and ground rules intact.[4]

Who is right in assessing the impact of the Internet in its Web 2.0 phase, which makes continuous interactions among people simple? Is it the prophets of revolution who predict an entirely new era, or the incrementalists, who predict far more modest changes? Why are current trends so confusing that experienced journalists can see them moving in vastly different directions? What conclusions can we draw from the developments this book has examined? Those are the questions that we will tackle in this final chapter. We will highlight the forces pushing for major changes in communications policies and practices and the obstacles that lie in the way. We will also explore some of the areas of disenchantment with mass media performance that have fueled demands for reform and the steps that dissatisfied communicators and audiences have taken to improve and supplement the existing information supply. The potential impact of major new technologies on politics and policy alternatives will be examined. Finally, we will try to discern whether the arrival of the Web 2.0 era heralds important advances in democratic governance.

DISSATISFACTION WITH THE MEDIA

The pace and direction of changes in the framing and distribution of news will hinge heavily on how satisfied journalists and their audiences are with the current product. Dissatisfaction with U.S. mass media runs deep and wide. Journalists have become increasingly disenchanted with their efforts, pundits have voiced their disapproval, and audiences have joined the chorus of complaints.

The Journalists' Perspective

According to a 2007 survey by the Pew Research Center for the People and the Press, a majority of news professionals working for print, television, radio, and Internet organizations complain about the steadily narrowing scope of news dictated by economic pressures. The ranks of legacy media have thinned markedly, and reporting staffs have been decimated. Fewer reporters with fewer resources equates to fewer news stories and a focus on simple stories, cheaply gathered close to home. That then leads to another complaint that most journalists voice—the lack of attention to complex stories that deal with matters that citizens ought to know. Journalists also complain that news is becoming less objective and more ideological, contrary to the beloved ideal that news should be as objective as possible and commentary should appear only on the editorial pages. Still another significant self-critical complaint that close to half of the poll respondents voiced was that they are out of touch with the public. In sum, journalists want more objective news—from broader perspectives and more in tune with audience demands. They blame dwindling audiences primarily on a wider range of news choices and the growth of specialized news outlets, and secondarily on an overemphasis on scandal, sensationalism, and uninteresting stories. Journalists also want fewer factual errors and less sloppy reporting—wishes that are unlikely to be fulfilled by an Internet geared to giving voice to nonprofessional citizen reporters and to comments by random members of the audience.[5]

The sample of 585 journalists tapped by the Pew Research Center survey was broad-based. It included individuals working at the top, middle, and bottom levels of national and local newspapers, magazines, wire services, news services, television, cable, radio, and Internet organizations. Table 12-1 presents their reactions to nine major criticisms leveled against the press.[6] Although the differences among national, local, and Internet professionals are relatively minor, it is noteworthy that each group is internally split about the validity of particular complaints. Slightly more than half of the journalists in each group do not believe that the twenty-four-hour news cycle hurts journalism, for example. Such split appraisals about the quality of news are common because the appropriate political role of journalism remains contested.

The Public's Perspective

The flaws in current news reporting, which journalists blame largely on bottom-line pressures, have undermined the public's trust in the news media and contributed to the shrinking of media audiences. The legacy media's precipitous loss of audiences enhances the perception that traditional journalism is in trouble. Most crucially, consumers find news less relevant and less believable. The percentage of people who deem news venues highly credible has dropped in the past four years for nearly every type of news (Table 12-2). Although the drop is not dramatic, it is nonetheless shocking because credibility was already low in prior years. Large portions of the audience also believe that stories are often inaccurate and that journalists do not care about the people whose stories they report. Furthermore, audiences regard the news media as politically biased.[7]

The sizable discrepancies in believability assessments by Democrats and Republicans are also alarming. Republicans distrust news venues more than Democrats thanks to the widespread belief that the news bears a liberal imprint. Poll numbers add fuel to the fire. When asked about their ideological

TABLE 12-1 **News Professionals' Agreement with Press Criticism (in percentages)**

Major criticism	National professionals	Local professionals	Internet
Scope of news coverage cut too much	82	73	85
Too little attention to complex issues	78	83	81
Blurring of reporting and commentary	64	54	60
24-hour news cycle hurting journalism	47	45	40
Journalists are out of touch with the public	41	49	47
Ideological views showing too often	38	33	36
Factual errors and sloppy reporting	31	43	38
The press is too cynical	27	31	27
Reporters too close to sources	23	18	30

Source: Pew Research Center for the People and the Press, "Financial Woes Now Overshadow All Other Concerns for Journalists," http://people-press.org/report/?pageid=1269.

Note: Based on a survey of 585 national and local reporters, producers, editors, and executives. Respondents were drawn from national and local media samples representing a cross-section of news organizations. The Internet component was drawn from both on-line-only news organizations and national and local news outlets with a significant Web presence. They were interviewed between September 17 and December 3, 2007. Percentages add up to more than 100 percent because respondents were able to answer "yes" to more than one question.

orientation, roughly six in ten journalists call themselves moderates, another three profess to be liberals, and just one in ten confesses to being a conservative.[8] Justified or not, these answers support the fears of conservatives and make them prone to criticize the press. Ideology also plays a growing part in choosing particular news outlets. For example, Republicans flock to the conservatively oriented Fox News channel, while Democrats avoid it. Differential use of media heightens partisan divisions and lessens the chances for democratic compromises. This, too, is a disturbing trend.

Citizen Media as Alternatives

If citizens had their choice, how would they reshape the news media? Answering that question is no longer a counterfactual exercise because news-ranking sites like Digg and Redditt keep track of the stories that their members favor. Moreover, numerous "netizens" have become amateur reporters, whose work has been published on their own Web sites or on host Web sites, including the sites of professional news providers. Systematic studies of the content of citizen-generated news offerings are scarce. One example, a five-day study of several

TABLE 12-2 **News Consumers Who Believe "All or Most" of News Venues' Offerings (in percentages)**

News venue	Survey 2000	2004	2008	Democrats 2008	Republicans 2008
CNN	39	32	30	35	22
Fox News	26	25	23	19	34
Local TV news	33	25	28	32	27
ABC	30	24	24	28	19
CBS	29	24	22	26	18
NBC	29	24	24	31	16
Wall Street Journal	41	24	25	24	29
New York Times	—	21	18	24	10
USA Today	23	19	16	15	16
Your daily paper	25	19	22	29	19

Source: Pew Research Center for the People and the Press, "Key News Audiences Now Blend Online and Traditional Sources," http://people-press.org/report/?pageid=1358.

Note: This study is based on telephone interviews conducted between April 30 and June 1, 2008, among a nationwide sample of 3,615 adults.

news-ranking sites conducted June 24–29, 2007, found that Digg users focused on the release of Apple's new iPhone, while the mainstream media focused on ongoing debates about immigration policies. The Iraq War accounted for 10 percent of the stories in the mainstream media during that period, compared to 1 percent of the stories that the users of ranking sites preferred.

This sliver of evidence suggests that the public's news choice principle seems to be news that people can use in daily life, rather than news that has broad political significance. Besides the difference in topic selection, citizen-generated news diverged from mainstream media in the choice of sources for stories. Citizen reporters selected sources offering citizen-generated content, such as YouTube or blogs by nonjournalists. Most excluded audience postings aside from featuring comments on their stories.[9] Their stories tended to concentrate on local news and social events in their neighborhoods. Professional journalists featured a much broader and weightier political news diet and relied more on government officials, expert witnesses, and their own research. One can disagree about the respective merits of professional and nonprofessional reporting, but if airing information about complex political issues is important in a democracy, citizen media apparently are a poor alternative to the legacy media.

On-line videos and social networking sites are other alternative news sources that are dominated by nonprofessionals. The most prominent ones attract huge audiences each month. The MySpace audience had 114 million unique monthly visitors in late 2007, Facebook had 52 million, and YouTube had 44 million. Along with Twitter, these sites offer citizen-generated news to their audiences. However, they also draw heavily on news from legacy media or provide links to them, along with viewers' comments.

The fastest growing Web 2.0 activity, which has been doubling every 320 days, is blogging.[10] A small portion of the millions of netizen blogs contain political news. But when Americans are asked about the sources they draw on for news, they rarely mention their fellow citizens' blogs.[11] Although netizens disdain most news from blogs, they frequently contact the blogs of legacy media reporters to comment about news or ask questions. In turn, the reporters may incorporate some of these exchanges into the stories they write for the mainstream press.

This brief survey of the citizen media alternative suggests that it is an intriguing supplement to the legacy media's offerings. It is not a substitute. The legacy media still search out and report the bulk of the information about ongoing political developments. Nonprofessional citizen reporters and members of their audiences generally only add eyewitness information, alternative perspectives, or evaluations of these events to the reports of legacy media professionals. Judged by their behavior, netizens share the belief that citizen media are insufficient news sources. That explains why most users of citizen news blend on-line offerings with news from traditional sources. They use the Web primarily for special interest information and entertainment and legacy sites for keeping track of politics and other breaking news events.[12] These patterns make it important to assess and clarify the weaknesses of legacy news.

Putting Criticism into Perspective

Most of the concerns voiced by critics of the news media have been echoed in the pages of this book. Nonetheless, the evidence does not support a blanket indictment of the media for failure to serve the public well and give audiences what they want, as well as what they need, as citizens.[13] First and foremost, the collective noun *news media* covers a broad range of institutions. It does not refer only to newspapers, newsmagazines, television, radio, and the Internet as news media types; it also refers to individual news suppliers within these broad categories. There is a wide gulf between the broad sweep of global news offered by the *New York Times*, on one hand, and the scores of tabloids and small-town newspapers that highlight local society news on the other. U.S. media contain much journalistic wheat along with generous portions of chaff, and the proportions vary widely in individual media. In fact, any citizen willing to make the effort can find essential current information more readily in the Internet age than ever before, especially in the legacy media's Internet versions.[14] Those versions even include the views of citizen pundits along with the commentary of professionals.

Any fair indictment of the news media must consider mitigating circumstances. This does not mean that the charges are invalid; it means that they must be put into context to assess the degree of guilt. Critics should consider the pressures under which journalists do their work under normal and crisis

---

BOX 12-1   Is This the Future of Social Network Sites?

"**F**acebook Users Go to War over Gaza," shouts a headline in *Time;* "Flash Activists Use Social Media to Drum Up Support," says another in *USA Today.* Do these headlines herald how political and social activism will develop in the future? Or do they merely record an insignificant, transient development that will have little impact? No one knows for sure, but it is easy to imagine the potential power of cyberactivism if it becomes widespread on social Web sites.

The characteristics of social Web sites are well suited to create the emotional arousals that foster social activism. Indeed a 2008 survey by the Center for the Digital Future at the University of Southern California revealed that 81 percent of the members of social network communities participate in social causes.[1] Social Web sites can stir their audiences by showing streaming videos of villages in flames and people torn from their families, all in vivid colors and sounds. They can display close-ups of expressions on the faces of victims and perpetrators. These agitating pictures can be downloaded so that social network users can browse them over and over again and etch them into their memories. The scenes of disturbing situations can be watched by millions of people. They may create viewer communities spanning the globe. Based on shared information, such communities learn to think alike, to trust each other, to undertake joint ventures.

Two recent examples of cyberactivism must suffice to illustrate the possibilities.

On December 27, 2008, two hours after Israel began military operations in the Gaza Strip, an Israel sympathizer created an open Facebook group called "I Support the Israel Defense Forces in Preventing Terror Attacks from Gaza." A young accountant from Jordan had previously created a pro-Palestinian Facebook group to protest Israel's blockade of Gaza. He named it "Let's Collect 500,000 Signatures to Support the Palestinians in Gaza." It had attracted roughly 500 members. Within two weeks following the start of military operations in Gaza in 2008, the pro-Israel group had attracted close to 80,000 members; the pro-Palestinian group had swelled to nearly 550,000.

The second case is based on a constitutional amendment that Californians adopted by a 52 percent to 48 percent vote in November 2008. The amendment extended the right to marry solely to heterosexual couples, excluding same-sex

---

conditions. Among them the necessity to produce profits for the parent organization is paramount. It accounts for excesses of negativism and voyeur journalism. Other stresses arise from journalistic values and the conventions of news production. For example, the zeal to rush to publication with breaking news fosters mistakes and misinterpretations; the beat system privileges newsworthy events occurring on regular beats over important happenings that occur beyond these beats; pack journalism homogenizes criteria for news selection, so that most media become rivals in conformity.

Economic developments have heightened pressures. The multiplication of readily accessible news channels in the United States and elsewhere has forced electronic as well as print media to compete more fiercely for audiences and

couples. Campaigns for and against the constitutional amendment were hotly fought before and after the election, with millions of people taking sides in California and elsewhere. Contributions set a new record for a social policy initiative. Except for the presidential race, spending on the California race trumped every other race in the country.

The protesters on both sides of the gay rights issue included cyberactivists. One of them told a *USA Today* reporter that she had used social network sites, including Facebook, MySpace, and Twitter, along with blogs to organize a one-million-strong protest movement to oppose the gay marriage ban through petitions and protest marches. She had contacted potential protesters in 300 cities in eleven countries. And she felt very confident that the protests would ultimately lead to repeal of the amendment.

These stories demonstrate that social network sites can serve as launching platforms for social activism. Whether the causes that cyberactivists support have merit or not, and whether their efforts play a major or minor part in the ultimate settlement of political and social problems, are not the main issues here. If cyberactivism thrives in the future on social network sites, what truly matters is that hitherto silent majorities will have left the spectator sideline to become vocal citizens. America's youth, who have been the mainstay of social network sites, will be taking their world's problems seriously. Like the Gaza and gay rights partisans, they will participate in political dialogs and spend many hours organizing social movements. They will roll up their sleeves and put on their marching boots when the situation requires it.

This optimistic scenario must be leavened with caution because most social network users have not hitherto considered those Web sites as political platforms. That could change, of course. In the Web 2.0 world it has become possible to dream and expect that many impossible dreams will come true, sooner or later.

1. Deena Guzder, "Facebook Users Go to War over Gaza," *Time in Partnership with CNN*, January 13, 2009, www.time.com/time/world/article/0,8599,1871302,00.html; Jon Swartz, "Flash Activists Use Social Media to Drum Up Support," *USA Today*, May 5, 2009, www .usatoday.com/tech/news/2009-05-05-flash-activists-protests_N.htm.

advertisers. Shrinking profit margins in individual enterprises have forced cutbacks in staff that put additional workloads on the remaining employees. Rich databases have grown exponentially and could be mined to enrich the context for stories. Sadly, the time available to individual reporters to search them has shrunk. The traditional media find their news turf eroded by the new media's ability to publish breaking stories instantly. Accordingly, print media must abandon the lure of featuring freshly breaking news and attract audiences in other ways. But when they turn to more analytical and interpretive reporting, they are accused of improperly straying into the terrain of editorial commentary. The upshot has been that the public increasingly perceives newspaper reporting as unduly biased.

Finally, judging complaints about the media requires a historical perspective. We have been living in a period when regard for most major institutions in the United States is at a low ebb. Nonetheless, when people were asked in 2008 how much they enjoyed keeping up with the news, only 15 percent confessed to little or no enjoyment.[15] History also shows that politicians and the general public are fickle and schizoid in their condemnations as well as in their praise. The Founders of our nation were the first to carp about its venal, lying press on the one hand and on the other the first to agree that, warts and all, it was the bedrock on which democratic freedoms rest.

Specialized Media

Hundreds of specialized media address information needs that are neglected or poorly served by the regular media. They are a partial antidote for the general mass media's failure to cover many important groups and issues. In chapter 10, we highlighted the expanding role of ethnic media, noting that they provide an abundance of detailed news about the many regions from which U.S. immigrants hail. Other types of specialized media flourish as well. For example, numerous professional and trade journals, newsletters, and Web sites concentrate on subjects like religion, sports, fine and popular arts, automobiles, health, and animal welfare. Some specialized media, such as the *Nation, Mother Jones,* or the *Weekly Standard,* or the *Huffington Post* and the *Drudge Report* on the Internet, are primarily devoted to political commentary inspired by diverse ideological perspectives. Others, like New York's *Village Voice* or Chicago's *Reader* specialize in sharp-tongued, lengthy essays covering local politics and the arts. Still others, like the *Onion,* parts of the *New Yorker,* and Comedy Central's the *Daily Show* on television excel in humorous or satirical analyses. The Internet has enabled many special interest groups to voice their views about controversial political issues. Thanks to the Web, they can reach widely dispersed audiences. Environmental groups are an example, as are fringe candidates for political office and their supporters.

The demand for targeted information has spawned more than 10,000 magazines in the United States. Cable channels are multiplying, and specialized Web sites are mushrooming. Specialized media also encompass the politically radical, iconoclastic, and counterculture media that flourish in times of social and political stress, such as the late 1960s and early 1970s. These media feature the flagrant opposition to government policy that is permitted in the United States but often forbidden in other countries. At the height of underground press popularity, during the Vietnam War era and its aftermath, readership was estimated at ten million. The rise of the underground print and electronic press during troubled times demonstrates that mass media can be started and operated with modest means. Like most alternative media, the counterculture media of the 1960s were financed through small-scale local advertising and through classified ads. Staffs were paid meager salaries or no salaries at all.[16] At one time there were nearly

1,000 underground newspapers and 400 counterculture radio stations. Such vitality attests to the vigor and flexibility of the mass media system.[17] The abrupt decline of underground media with the end of the Vietnam War also shows that the system is able to prune its unneeded branches when demand ends.

Waning public support rather than official censorship led to the steep decline in this genre of journalism. It has been revived with the advent of the Internet, where thousands of vitriolic antigovernment sites urge opposition to established authorities and their policies and often suggest ways to implement radical ideas. Mao Tse-tung's admonition to "let a thousand flowers bloom," ignored in China, has come to fruition on the U.S. alternative media scene. However, given the explosive growth of electronic soapboxes from which citizens can broadcast their views, the competition for attention has become extraordinarily fierce.

Public Broadcast Stations

Yet another issue brought to the fore by the age of media plenty and criticism of media services is the fate of public broadcasting. As discussed in chapter 2, public television was organized to provide an alternative to the typical programming available on the three commercial networks that were the sole providers of televised news at the time. Many political leaders would like to abandon it and save the costs of public subsidies. They point out that the number of networks has grown, and cable television and the Internet provide infinitely more variety of programming than existed at the midpoint of the twentieth century. Although a goodly portion of public broadcast programming is geared to the needs of minorities, the disadvantaged groups it addresses largely ignore it. Instead, public broadcasting audiences tend to be upscale and, aside from its children's programs, quite small.

Proponents of keeping the public broadcasting system alive argue that it still fills an important need that merits public support. Poor families need access to the rich cultural programs that are a hallmark of public television. They cannot afford to pay for access to the likes of the History, Discovery, Learning, and National Geographic channels, which cover important realms of information in depth. Because sophisticated cultural and educational programming attracts only small audiences, it is unlikely that the other free television channels will feature such fare in the future, even when digital technology increases the number of available channels.[18]

The difficulty of keeping the public broadcasting system solvent without government subsidy may sound its death knell. PBS has been dreaming about creating a huge endowment from the money it hopes to earn when it completes conversion to HDTV and sells the spectrum space that will be released. But it is unlikely that Congress will consent to letting PBS keep that money. The European practice of funding public broadcasting principally through consumer fees has never been considered a realistic option in the United States.[19]

Jeff Stahler: © Columbus Dispatch/Dist. by Newspaper Enterprise Association, Inc.

THE IMPACT OF NEW TECHNOLOGIES

The new age of personalized mass media has arrived. Political scientist W. Russell Neuman predicted this development at the start of the 1990s when he pointed out that we now "have the opportunity to design a new electronic and optical network that will blur the distinction between mass and interpersonal communications....A single high capacity digital network will combine computing, telephony, broadcasting, motion pictures and publishing."[20] But Neuman has also warned that the provocative predictions that are apt to follow new technologies generally are off the mark because they ignore the human context that determines if, how, and when new technologies will be used. As Neuman sees it, "Technology does not determine, but it can make a difference."[21] That difference is usually small because most new technologies are designed and used to perform familiar functions. However, it can also be huge, as for instance when deadly riots erupted in Afghanistan because a small number of people reacted to an unsubstantiated ~~blog message~~ *Newsweek* alleging that American soldiers had desecrated the Koran.

Six features of the new technologies have the potential for generating major political changes:

1. The advent of nonprofessional journalism that competes with traditional journalism

2.   The Web 2.0 interactivity tools that have created a new global public sphere
3.   The leveling of barriers to communication created by time, space, and political constraints
4.   The multiplication of communication channels that has created a hyper-competitive media world
5.   The modernization of legacy journalism
6.   The growth of new approaches for financing the creation and distribution of news

The Face of Nonprofessional Journalism

In Horatio Alger's America, every boy could become president if he was honest, hardworking, and persevering when faced with adversity. Of course, that scenario was too rosy. But it is true that in twenty-first-century America every boy—and girl—can become a published print and broadcast author with a potential audience of millions of people. And she or he need not even be honest, hardworking, persevering, or a talented writer. Is this the age of the American dream of open access for everyone to the peoples of the world? Or is this the age of the American nightmare of circulating unverified, sometimes vicious or pornographic information that leads to disgust, distrust, cynicism, and even violence? What are the facts?

Millions of Americans whose identities are unknown to blog visitors now post their views on Internet sites where other people can read them, comment about them, and pass them on to still others. Anyone, at little cost and with no training in news collection and verification, can become a blogger and post any message, true or false. Bloggers are not bound by journalistic criteria like accuracy, objectivity, fairness, and balance. There is practically no form of censorship, governmental or private, on the Internet, nor are there requirements for ensuring transparency or accountability.

The upshot is a flourishing marketplace of disparate views—far richer than ever before. Thanks to links, citizen news sites often provide more background information and more access to diverse points of view than other venues. However, a mere third of their stories are originals; the remainder comes from the pool of stories available from traditional news sources.[22]

Some blog messages have contributed to the public dialog and even spawned significant political action. Examples are the vivid, firsthand accounts in which bloggers described the horrors of Hurricane Katrina in 2005 and inspired audiences to help the victims. Many of their stories received wide attention because legacy media used them as part of their own reporting. Bloggers have unearthed important stories that the media increasingly miss because the ranks of professional journalists are thinner than ever. Other blogs have become megaphones for spreading dangerous falsehoods, often without the antidote of counterarguments that is common in legacy media.

Most blog messages, of course, fall by the wayside like so many dead leaves in autumn. Fifty-eight percent of all Internet users in 2008 had never actually read a blog message.[23] Obviously, the right and opportunity to share one's views with the world are limited by the right and opportunity of potential audiences to ignore most messages. When Americans turn to the Web for news, 80 percent of their visits are to brand-name newspaper, television, and search engine sites because they are deemed more trustworthy than other Web sites. Figure 12-1 makes that clear; it shows the audience numbers for the top ten news Web sites. MSNBC, Yahoo News, and CNN lead the pack. Netizens have characterized the Internet as the most up-to-date medium, the easiest to use, and the most enjoyable. Despite such high praise, legacy television has remained their first choice for news. For example, during the 2008 presidential contest, which aroused tremendous public interest, 72 percent of the audience relied primarily on television, and 30 percent named newspapers as their primary news source. Only 26 percent named the Internet.[24]

So is blogging a dream or a nightmare? The answer is that it is a bit of both for the public, for news media professionals, and for American democracy. Fortunately or unfortunately, effects that run simultaneously in opposite directions are common in the evolving media scene and account for widely divergent appraisals by experts and publics. When it comes to blogging, the public benefits from a richer marketplace of ideas, but it is harmed when messages are based on misinformation or deliberate deception, often fueled by hate. News professionals benefit from blogging when the pool of ideas from which they can select their stories is enriched, particularly when the new voices cover unique slices of reality from fresh, previously unheard sources. But journalists and citizens suffer when blog stories of questionable newsworthiness dominate the news agenda and force journalists to focus on them at the expense of covering more important news.

In response to questions in a 2007 survey, journalists expressed mixed feelings about the impact of the Internet on traditional news values. Roughly half thought that the Internet would strengthen these values, while half thought the opposite. The strengths mentioned included more transparency because more eyes are scrutinizing the political scene, and lengthier, more detailed coverage of specific events. The weaknesses mentioned were insufficient quality control, use of sources with unproven reliability records, and increased time pressures in the 24/7 cycle, leading to sloppy reporting. When journalists rate the overall quality of news sites, the highest rankings still go to national newspapers and the Web sites of national news organizations. Local television news and current events bloggers rank at the bottom. On-line-only news sites, like *Salon* and *Slate*, and news aggregating sites like Google and Yahoo are in the middle range of the rankings.[25]

The Fruits of Interactivity

Interactivity is an extremely important feature of the Web 2.0 world. The stream of information about ongoing events is no longer one-directional, with news media voices doing all the talking and the audience, like dutiful children, listening silently. The new technologies permit audiences to use Internet channels to

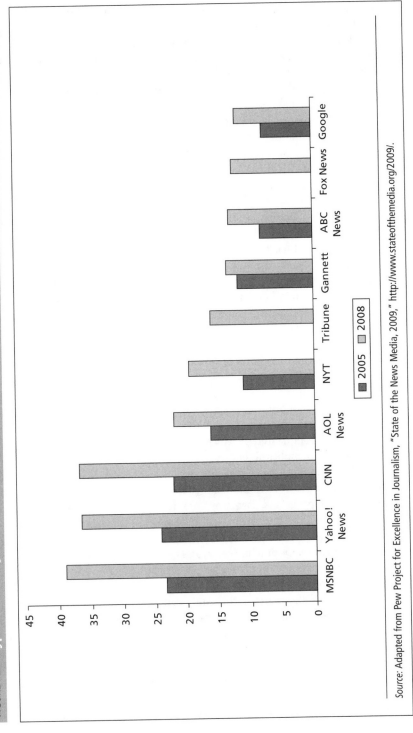

FIGURE 12-1 Typical Monthly Audiences for Top Ten News Web Sites (in millions)

Source: Adapted from Pew Project for Excellence in Journalism, "State of the News Media, 2009," http://www.stateofthemedia.org/2009/.

talk back to message senders, asking questions and providing new information and fresh comments. Nearly all news providers, including legacy media, encourage feedback. Millions of people have voiced their ideas, and a few of those ideas have aroused some public attention and dialog. But many more millions of citizens—the "silent majorities" of the Nixon era—have remained mute.

The Internet, as an open-access megaphone, has diminished the traditional news media's tight control over access to mass audiences. Individuals and groups who were virtually barred from access to legacy media platforms—labor unions, candidates for local political offices, and animal rights groups are examples—now have viable channels to target receptive audiences. Modest resources are no longer a barrier to individuals and groups that want to reach audiences widely dispersed throughout the United States and most other parts of the world. Moreover, they can shape their messages freely, deciding what is acceptable and credible and what is not, because the Internet, unlike most other news transmission venues, is largely free from censorship.

The Internet has turned out to be an excellent tool to rally supporters for specific causes and raise money. Environmentalists have used it to save deer from extermination in urban areas; students have used it to mobilize death penalty opponents when an execution was imminent. Politicians who have felt victimized by journalists who boiled their comments down to meaningless nuggets can now customize their messages and send them quickly, easily, and cheaply to specific populations. Additionally, e-mails and Web sites can be used to raise staggering amounts of money. During the 2008 presidential contest, candidate Barack Obama, with the help of a group of Boston geeks, used the Internet to raise $500 million, much of it in small donations.[26] Liberal Web sites like MoveOn.org and Meetup.org helped to recruit campaign workers, organize campaign rallies, and mobilize Democratic voters. Conservative Web sites like those sponsored by Move America Forward energized citizens on the other side of the political fence.

The new technologies make it possible for audiences watching talk shows on radio and television to interact instantaneously with others who are watching the same programs. Two-way communication technologies using radios, telephones, and the Internet have also been extraordinarily useful for connecting isolated areas in Alaska, northern Canada, and elsewhere with social service systems in more populated centers. These venues deliver educational and health services, as well as giving people a greater voice in government.[27]

The boom in interactive communication over long distances has been described as fulfillment of the American dream that promises that every American, regardless of expertise, can have a voice in the nation's political life. Undoubtedly the opportunity is there, but the reality remains far from the ideal. The people whose voices are heard in technology-enabled interactions predominantly are typical members of the upper crust: well educated, successful, confident, and economically secure. Most people who fall below these socioeconomic levels have never given public voice to their views and probably never will. Still, interactivity is a good thing because it has expanded the number of voices in the public sphere. Thus far, small interest groups that lack the resources to pay for public relations agents or lobbyists have probably been the main beneficiaries.

Do-It-Yourself News and On-Demand Consumption

Before the advent of the Internet, news professionals had full control over news dissemination, aside from the constraints imposed by the social, political, and economic environment. Journalists chose the news that would be reported, they framed it to suit their professional goals, and they disseminated it via print media and broadcasts run on schedules that they selected albeit with some considerations of audience preferences. News consumers had to adjust to these schedules and accept the news offerings that various providers had concocted. It was a take-it-or-leave-it situation.

That scenario has changed drastically, so that people now can consume news whenever they want it, around the clock and seven days and nights each week. There is as yet no way to gauge whether this flexibility amounts to little more than a nice convenience or is a major benefit because people whose schedules previously barred them from receiving news can now access it. More important, the greater flexibility of access to the news allows netizens to graze among a variety of news outlets, picking and choosing entire programs or specific stories as they wish. Netizens can even assemble their own news packages manually or arrange to have them assembled electronically. They can use RSS (Rich Site Summary) feeds that deliver regularly changing Web content to keep up with the latest developments in a particular field, like banking policy, or a specific topic, like rescue efforts after an aircraft disaster. They can use news-ranking sites like Reddit or Digg to check what news their peers are watching and then join them, becoming a shared-news community.

Cell phones, which have become an essential piece of equipment for most Americans, have further reduced barriers of space and time. One no longer must be physically present at a place with computer access to tune into the news. One can capture it via one's cell phone at any time and at any place. Again, the scope of opportunities to stay in touch with people and events and interact with them boggles the imagination. But the reality is disappointing. Only a small portion of the public actually uses these fantastic new opportunities to become more informed about public life and contribute to it.

The proliferation of news venues and the ability to customize news packages to suit news consumers' individual tastes have important downsides along with their benefits. Among them, the fragmentation issue looms large. Will the lack of a shared news supply fragment the nation's political consensus? When people rely primarily on specialized broadcasts, will their attention to politics diminish?[28] As discussed in chapter 7, in the past nationwide dissemination of similar news has fostered shared political socialization. When news becomes fragmented, people are more likely to be socialized in disparate ways. What will be the consequences?

If comprehensive political news is available only on channels dedicated to politics, will people choose to watch it? Will government leaders be able to convey their messages to the public? Will they be able to move the nation to agree with new policy directions, such as government-run health services, recycling requirements, or granting marriage privileges to gay and lesbian fellow citizens? A music fan, tuned in to an all-music station, may watch music programs only; an African American or Hispanic person may tune in only to stations concerned with African American and Hispanic affairs. Many citizens may become prisoners of their special interests and may miss out on happenings in the broader culture. The country may be carved up into mutually exclusive, often hostile political enclaves.[29]

Not everyone fears that fragmentation of the broadcast audience will lead to political balkanization.[30] Many people point out that the national consensus was not ruptured when alternative media were used in the past. They argue that fragmented interests create the demand for fragmented media, rather than the reverse. If there is political and social consensus, people will seek out information pertaining to the larger community. Others point out that commercially oriented media are unifiers because they will always try to attract large audiences by offering programs with wide appeal. That is why programming on cable television became uniform and similar to network television. Even if the new media increase political and social fragmentation, many people do not find that prospect objectionable, believing that pluralism is preferable to earlier melting-pot ideals.

Platform Multiplication

Most people can receive Internet messages and broadcast their own at relatively low cost. The Web, with its wide open, inexpensive, minimally regulated access features, has encouraged the creation of a multiplicity of different types of channels and services. They range from almost universally used channels like e-mail and cell phones, to less widely used channels like the Web sites of legacy media, low-activity individual or group sites, chat rooms, list serves, and RSS feeds.

The vast number of available channels expands the range of news that can be covered and instantaneously transmitted. For this reason, the Internet presents the stiffest competitive threat to traditional over-the-air and cable television. It duplicates many of their news and entertainment offerings and guides people to other information sources by listing links to other relevant Web sites that are just one mouse click away.

Some observers bemoan the fact that the role of professional journalists as selectors and framers of news has been undercut by lay news consumers' ability to perform these tasks themselves, albeit inexpertly. Others hail the weakening of the traditional media. News consumers, they say, have been relieved of the tyranny of the press, in which unelected journalists could determine what became news and frame it in ways that suit their own purposes better than the audience's goals. These critics claim that citizen-generated news is likely to yield a better fit between audience needs and the messages that reach them.

Government programs may operate more successfully when officials can use two-way channels and direct their messages to specific audiences.

Contrary to earlier forecasts, the multiplication of news providers has not as yet split off large chunks of the legacy media's audience or competed successfully with them in the battle for advertising revenues. The reason is twofold. Most important, the traditional media have become a major presence on the Web, using an assortment of Internet channels to transmit their news products. In the newspaper field, many major papers have more readers for their Web version than for the traditional hard copies. Second, in the battle for audiences, the traditional media have had the advantage of being known and trusted. The majority of Internet offerings, like the messages dispatched by millions of blogs, have failed to establish trust and have remained largely shunned. Nonetheless, a small minority of the Internet-birthed newcomers to the media scene have overcome the trust hurdle. High audience numbers and ratings have been their reward. Examples include Yahoo, Google, AOL, MSNBC, CNN, the *Huffington Post*, and the *Drudge Report*.

The political consequences of the multiplication of news providers have been substantial, although observers measure them with diverse scales and therefore disagree about their magnitude and significance. Most important, the store of information provided by news radio, television, cable, and Internet channels, by communication satellites, and by round-the-clock news programs offers an unrivaled diversity of news.[31] The addition of new information suppliers has diminished the danger that huge corporations might exercise monopoly or oligopoly control over the nation's news supply. Small communities with limited information sources can now readily escape from their communication ghettoes by turning to the Internet. They can supply an assortment of major newspapers to their citizens. Similarly, cable television systems now can offer broadcasts from hundreds of separate channels. That increases channel choices for consumers, although the news is essentially the same on most of them. Public access cable channels and government Web sites can keep citizens in closer touch with public institutions and political leaders. Local television stations and consumers with access to satellite dishes can tap into satellite news directly or via other carriers. Public and private groups can rent space from the satellites' owners and use it for electronic transmissions.

Media pluralism does herald more local programming. Most local governments eagerly use cable channels and Web sites to broadcast local political news. Many local school systems and police and fire departments air their concerns on their own channels. Because publicity means power, the new communications media tend to enhance the power of local institutions, frequently at the expense of national ones. The two-way capacity of the new media makes local programming more attractive for local audiences, even when it lacks the polish of professional programs.[32] Although the possibilities for strengthening local communities through increased publicity are good, the new narrowcasting technologies also can deflect interest away from the local scene and produce global villages of like-minded people.

A Muslim family in Calcutta and Palestinian Hamas militants watch President Barack Obama's speech of June 7, 2009. The shared experience is likely to produce clashing reactions.
Source: AP Photo/Sucheta Das (left); AP Photo/Eyad Baba (right)

However, the impression of a widely used, superrich menu of choices is more a mirage than reality because there is an informal concentration of control over the news supply. It springs from American news consumers' preference for news from brand-name media. When audiences turn to brand-name media for most of their news and Internet news organizations do the same, the pool from which the thousands of news channels feed is small indeed. What all of this means for individuals and organizations and political life in specific situations is still unclear. Besides, technology remains in flux and offers new products at an amazing pace. Some, like Twitter, become instantly popular, and others die on the vine or after a brief life. The changing mix of news providers, channels, and programs, therefore, makes most analyses of the full impact of new technologies stale by the time they have been completed, or even earlier.[33]

Transforming Journalism

Without a doubt, the Internet has reduced the power and influence of traditional media, which no longer enjoy a near-monopoly over news production and distribution. They share the control of news with nonprofessional providers. Their power to control the flow of news to and from various world regions has also eroded because the Internet empowers American news consumers to access news from all parts of the world. Moreover, the multiplication of news sources is a global phenomenon. The audiences shown above watching President Obama's speech delivered at Cairo University in Egypt, in June 2009, could have watched the event on dozens of Middle Eastern and Indian outlets that now have satellite transmission capacities.

The legacy media's diminished control over the audience pool is partly compensated by news improvements. Thanks to the new technologies, traditional news media have made noteworthy advances on three fronts: news gathering, news processing, and news dissemination. Access to computer databases and satellites has put an enormous store of usable information within reach of journalists wherever they may be. Even foreign countries kept off-limits by hostile rulers can be explored by satellite, as can remote areas of the globe and even the private retreats of powerful elites. The ability to search databases electronically for specific bits of information and to combine those data in a variety of ways opens up countless new possibilities for creating news stories and providing valuable contextual information for fast-moving current developments.

When it comes to the distribution of news gathered at far-flung locations, the array of channels for immediate or delayed transmission has multiplied far beyond the range deemed possible in the late twentieth century. Local stations can now import video footage from satellites and thereby eliminate their dependence on national network programming and vastly expand their programming options. Broadband technology has made Internet use far more attractive because it allows nearly instant, constant access without the delays and hassles of a modem. Information available on the Web reaches journalists faster, from more diverse sources, and in modes that allow reporters to question sources quickly with the expectation of a prompt response. The potential for producing excellent news therefore has grown by leaps and bounds, which is a welcome benefit for news consumers everywhere.

New broadcasting and narrowcasting technologies generate problems along with their benefits. There is, as yet, no widely available solution to the problem of finding one's way through the Internet's lush jungles of information, where search engines like Google and Yahoo provide only limited guidance.[34] Moreover, the stock of information that requires searching doubles every few months. For most news consumers, journalists therefore remain essential because they are trained to ferret out what seems "most important" within a particular cultural milieu and to present it in language that average people can understand. As mentioned before, news aggregating sites that list each day's most popular stories, as well as social networks and other Web sites that present summaries of the day's most important news, have become active competitors in determining what should be on the daily news agenda.

The process of switching from analog television to digital television illustrates the types of governmental problems that arise when new technologies make older ones obsolete. Digital technology, especially when combined with high definition technology (HDTV), improves picture quality and releases space for new commercial services and emergency-response networks. Besides requiring many consumers to buy adapters or new television sets to receive digital signals, the transition from analog to digital transmission required most television stations to spend millions of dollars for new equipment and transmission towers. In view of these massive and costly changes, the Federal Communications Commission conceived a multiyear transition plan in the early 1990s. Established broadcasters would receive a second channel free of charge so that they could duplicate their analog programs in digital versions on this second channel. In 2007 the broadcasters would return their original channels to the government, while retaining the digital channel as their sole outlet, free of charge. The plan immediately became embroiled in political battles.

Although the 1996 Telecommunications Act had embraced the principle of awarding digital channels free of charge, influential members of Congress wanted the channels auctioned off to the highest bidders, with the money going to the government rather than the channel owners. The telephone companies, which pay the government for the right to transmit information over the public airways, and who fear potential competition in data transmission from the broadcast industry, joined the lobby against free channels for broadcasters. Naturally, broadcast industry leaders strongly opposed any changes in the 1996 rules. They were eager to get digital broadcasting under way, as were the manufacturers of the new television sets. In fact, supporters of the plan wanted to shorten the transition period. PBS, ABC, NBC, CBS, and Fox actually began digital broadcasting in major television markets in 1998.[35] Other commercial stations, along with consumers, were dragging their feet. The 2007 transition date came and went. After numerous heated battles in Congress about extending the time, the conversion was finally completed in 2009.[36]

Another major problem exacerbated by the new technologies concerns the safeguarding of individual privacy. Ever-smaller cameras and microphones permit reporters to spy with little chance of detection. Professional and lay reporters can assemble scattered bits of historical and current information in seconds to derive a comprehensive, publishable portrait of any individual who has caught public attention or is likely to do so. Silly comments in high school yearbooks can doom a person's career fifty years later. Unless individual privacy becomes more fully protected, the Internet age could well turn into an Orwellian nightmare—with individuals living in glass cages, exposed to instant public scrutiny by all sorts of paparazzi reporters. Likewise, the new information-gathering techniques make it far more difficult to protect national security information from prying eyes. Congress and the courts have been unable to strike a sound balance between press freedom and national security.

New Ways to Pay for News

The decline in readers, viewers, and listeners brought about by audience defections to the Internet has plunged the legacy media into serious financial difficulties. This is particularly the case for the print media, where bankruptcies became common during the depression that started in 2007. Many newspapers went out of business entirely; others cut back on the number of publication days, and still others abandoned their hard copy operations and published Web versions only. Nearly all companies, including flagship enterprises like the *Christian Science Monitor* and the *Chicago Tribune,* cut staffs, reduced the scope of news gathering, and replaced hard news with cheaper, softer news in hopes of retaining their dwindling audiences. Still, profits continued to plunge. The financial shocks have led to reconsideration of the main financial underpinnings of the private sector press in the United States, based on the firm belief that the news values of old-style journalism must survive.

First a look at the traditional financial structures: The pillars of financing for a for-profit press have been advertiser support, audience payments, and government subsidies. Each has different policy consequences, which become blurred when they are used in combination, as is common. Print media, for example, have been financed by the price audiences pay for newspapers and, more important, by revenue from advertisers. They have also received government subsidies in the form of below-cost mailing rates.

The revenue system fell apart when earnings from advertising, which are pegged to audience size, plunged as audiences defected to the Internet. Some advertisers also defected to Internet outlets, but never in large enough numbers to make advertising a financial pillar for Internet information providers. In fact, outlets with small audiences, or audiences that are unattractive to advertisers because they represent small markets, may never be able to attract enough sponsors to pay for their operations. That then raises questions about who, in the long run, will pay for the expenses of Web site news operations, especially if they strive for excellence. Good journalism is expensive. What will happen if the alternative—reliance on unpaid, unskilled, and unaccountable amateurs—proves unacceptable in the long run?

To cope with reduced revenues, legacy media have tried to cut costs in various ways. They include news-sharing arrangements and combining multi-platform operations, like those arranged between NBC, MSNBC, the Washington Post Company, and *Newsweek*.[37] As mentioned, the legacy networks also expanded into their own Web enterprises so that the same news production operation can serve traditional and new media platforms. Journalism training has changed accordingly, forcing new graduates to become adept in handling traditional and emerging new formats.

Most new media broadcast facilities, along with cable television, rely heavily on audience payments. These have generally taken the form of monthly service charges for programs, plus installation or equipment charges. Additional programming may be available for a flat monthly rate or on a per-program basis. Service charge financing for broadcasting has become accepted abroad. In the United States, however, it initially met with resistance because good broadcast services were available everywhere free of charge. By the mid-1980s much of the initial resistance to paying for broadcasts had vanished. Many U.S. households were paying for special programs in addition to their standard monthly fees.

A major social drawback of service charges for broadcasts is that poor families who most need many of the specialized programs are least able to pay for them. Middle-income families, who already enjoy many social advantages, benefit most from the information resources available through new media platforms; low-income people who lack access fall further behind.[38] The problem can be reduced through government subsidies paid to cable and Internet companies or directly to the poor. Direct payment to citizens seems preferable. It avoids making media enterprises financially dependent on the government and thereby hampering their freedom of action.

The need for a new business model is clear when the I-beam of media financing—advertising money—no longer bears the load of expenses for news production and distribution and when people below middle-class economic status cannot afford service charges for news and entertainment. Newspapers have tried to stop the hemorrhaging in novel ways because a single hard copy reader is the financial equivalent of two or three dozen Web site readers.[39] Lures to retain hard copy readers have included launching tabloid sections aimed at specialized audiences or offering youth-oriented versions that are given away free of charge at public transportation stops.

Another possibility for financing hard copy newspapers is reversion to the nineteenth-century model of a partisan press. That means that political parties or other political sponsors would support news media operations, most likely as nonprofit enterprises. Judging by past history and by the experience of similar systems abroad, the approach leads to a high degree of political polarization. It also can lead to political paralysis because citizens living on incompatible information diets find it difficult to reach consensus.

Other models for financing old and new media operations are government financing or financing by privately controlled foundations like the Knight Foundation, help in news production from university centers like those at Columbia University or Northwestern University, or grants from individual philanthropists like billionaire George Soros. Another model that has been tried for investigative journalism involves the creation of freestanding research centers that employ professional reporters to cover particular types of news. Examples are the Center for Public Integrity in Washington, D.C., and New York–based ProPublica. Such centers can be run like a hoary predecessor, the Associated Press, which operates as a membership association. Payment of a membership fee entitles the member organization to use AP news reports. Instead of using membership fees, news-gathering associations, which usually are nonprofits, can also be run by private entrepreneurs or by foundations. Their products can be available for a fee, or they can be distributed free of charge. Such organizations can also produce particular stories on-demand for news organizations that lack the resources to do the necessary work on their own. Regardless of the source of financial support, the financial supporters are likely to influence the thrust of the news product to some degree. That becomes an important consideration in deciding which model for financing high-quality news is best for preserving the independence of the press—be it the control methods of the past, the Internet free-for-all model of citizen journalism, a government or nonprofit subsidized model, or a mixture of several of these.

REGULATION AS A BARRIER TO DEVELOPMENT

A number of psychological, political, and economic barriers commonly block the swift and full development of new mass communication technologies. Many new developments never get off the ground because most people are reluctant to change their media use habits, particularly when the changes are time-consuming and costly and require them to learn new techniques. Bureaucracies, often prodded by vested interests, impose too many regulations to guard against abuses. The regulations may impose unrealistically high standards that raise costs to unaffordable levels. State and local rules, piled on top of federal regulations, frequently complicate the picture even further. Not only do they add more requirements, but rules issued by various jurisdictions often conflict.

Many new communications technologies require large investments, so that their sudden obsolescence becomes a crushing financial blow. People whose knowledge and equipment will be made obsolete therefore vigorously fight against these changes. For example, large convention facilities and the many industries involved in hosting big professional meetings face serious harm or even extinction when convention sessions are broadcast live to the membership via the Internet. Similarly, teachers and their unions are unhappy when they fear job losses because long-distance learning programs transmit a master teacher's lessons to faraway classrooms. Adding insult to injury, televised programs featuring outstanding practitioners and facilities may establish standards for professional performance that ruin the reputations of average institutions that cannot match these standards.

Early entrants in a technological field frequently develop a squatter's mentality about rights they have acquired, such as the right to use certain broadcast frequencies or particular technologies. Newcomers, on the other hand, are eager to reallocate facilities in line with their special interests. They want to mandate the use of more advanced technologies, even before they can guarantee that a market for these technologies and services will develop. Yielding to their requests could destroy proven interests in favor of new claimants whose prospects for success are uncertain. Obstacles also arise because competing new technologies benefit groups unevenly. Power struggles, which may be prolonged, are fiercest before the status quo is determined. Meanwhile, technology continues its advance, raising problems that further delay the green light for implementing already-accepted new systems.

Cable television's rocky history in the United States illustrates many of the obstacles that technical innovations face. It also illustrates the controversial political decisions that must be made to fit a new information technology into existing legislative and administrative structures. When cable television first became available in 1949, established broadcasters viewed it as dangerous competition that would steal their audiences and pirate their programs. When satellite technology evolved, apprehension mounted. The television networks feared ruin if stations could pick up programs directly from satellites and broadcast them nationwide via cable television.

The FCC's initial response to cable technology was typical. To protect existing stakeholders, the commission passed rules that sharply limited the types of programs that cable television stations could broadcast whenever these offerings competed with established network services. Consequently, the growth of the cable industry was stunted. The regulations were eased some twenty years later when the FCC accepted the cable advocates' claim that cable technology was needed because it could reach people in locations inaccessible to regular television signals.

Most new communication technologies initially face very costly regulations designed to force them to serve hitherto unmet public needs. For example, the FCC asked the cable industry to offer a minimum of twenty channels, including outlets for the general public, educational institutions, and local governments. It was also required to carry signals of local broadcasters. It took a series of costly lawsuits to end these burdensome requirements.[40] The industry achieved its goal of breaking the regulation barriers with the passage of the Cable Communications Policy Act of 1984.[41] The act deregulated rates and made renewal of cable franchises nearly automatic in areas with ready access to over-the-air television—roughly 90 percent of the cabled areas.

Meanwhile, the resistance of the established industries to this new competition had softened. Heeding the old adage, "If you can't beat 'em, join 'em," a number of over-the-air broadcasters invested heavily in cable facilities once the FCC eased controls regarding cross-ownership and admitted the networks to the cable market. By 1993 broadcasters fully or partially controlled nearly half (47 percent) of the top fifty cable systems; newspaper and magazine publishers participated in one-third (34 percent).[42] Media conglomerates owned the three largest cable news outlets—CNN, Fox News, and MSNBC.

FCC rules and the opposition of the established industries were not the only hurdles that the cable industry faced during its development. There were numerous local political hurdles as well. Cable enterprises must obtain franchises to lay cables and serve consumers in each locality. The franchising process is always highly political both in the selection of a particular cable company and in the determination of the conditions of the franchise.[43] Franchisers and franchisees have to agree on the time to be allowed for constructing the system and the life of the franchise (usually fifteen years). They also must agree on how many customers they must accept in outlying, mostly rural or mountainous areas where costs often exceed revenues.

Despite all the obstacles, the cable television saga demonstrates that major innovations are possible in a government system built deliberately to slow down change and allow minorities to block unwanted developments. Technological advances and their political fallout will continue, but most major changes, much of the time, will develop at a very gradual pace.

Regulatory Options

How, if at all, should government regulate the news media to ensure that the liberty of the press does not become a license for socially harmful behaviors?

The explosive growth of unregulated information channels on the Internet makes it necessary to raise that perennial question once again. The wisdom of the current regulations that apply to legacy over-the-air broadcast systems also remains hotly disputed.

Governments have several broad policy options for dealing with broadcasting systems. First, they can adopt hands-off, laissez-faire policies, allowing market forces and private owners' preferences to dominate development.[44] The U.S. government has adopted the laissez-faire philosophy for print media but not for over-the-air television. The initial rationale for regulating television was the fact that transmission channels were scarce, so that government had to protect fairness of access to the channels. It also had to ensure that these prime sources of information conveyed essential messages to the public in politically correct formats.

If one believes that government should regulate information supply only when transmission channels are scarce, as happened with early radio and television, then it makes sense to leave the current rich crop of information transmission systems unregulated. When broadcast and narrowcast outlets are plentiful, market forces presumably come into play, so that necessary services will be supplied in a far more flexible way than is possible when government regulations intervene. The only restraints that may be needed are safeguards to protect national security and maintain social norms and privacy. Laissez-faire is the mantra of deregulation proponents.

Second, information transmission systems can be treated as common carriers, like the telephone or rail and bus lines. Common carrier status makes transmission facilities available to everyone on a first-come, first-served basis. Cable broadcast stations, and later the Internet, were classified as common carriers of information, rather than as creators of information whose messages had to be monitored to guarantee a rich information supply for all sectors of the American public. Owners of cable facilities presumably did not broadcast their own programs. Rather, they leased their channels to various broadcasters for fees regulated by government or by market forces. Under common carrier rules, they could not selectively exclude any programs.

The FCC and many local governments like the common carrier concept. Even though the U.S. Supreme Court decided in 1979 that cable systems could not be considered common carriers under federal laws, Congress and some state and local governments have treated the industry as a common carrier.[45] When Congress ordered cable systems to broadcast all local over-the-air programs, the industry brought suit. It won judgments in 1985 and again in 1987 that the "must carry rule" violated the First Amendment rights of cable companies.[46] The victory for cable systems was a defeat for champions of broad public access rights to the media. In sum, the application of common carrier rules has been confusing because the substance of the rules is disputed. Cable systems have become a poorly defined, mixed breed that resembles over-the-air television in some ways and traditional common carriers in others. By comparison, the Internet system is subject to very few rules, in part because it is deemed a common carrier and in part because its nature and structure make enforcement of regulations extremely difficult.

Third, the government can confer public trustee status on communication enterprises. Owners then have full responsibility for programming but are required to meet certain public service obligations. Examples are adherence to equal-time provisions, limitations on materials unsuitable for children or offensive to community standards of morality, and rules about access to broadcast facilities. Access rules are designed to ensure that there are channels available to governments and various publics to broadcast information about such public issues as education, public safety, and medical and social service programs. Over-the-air television in the United States has operated under trustee rules.

The rationale for conferring trustee status on broadcasters has been twofold. The scarcity argument, which was powerful in the past, has lost validity. The main surviving argument for trustee status is that television is a highly influential medium. There must be assurance that valuable programs are broadcast and harmful ones avoided and that canons of fairness are observed. That is a powerful argument with strong support in much of the world. It is the argument that underlies the rules set forth in the 1996 Telecommunications Act.

Periodically, trustee norms clash with the First Amendment. That is why free press purists are so alarmed about the increasingly strict enforcement of social and political correctness norms. They shudder when the majority of Americans applauds when journalists in the United States are fired for saying that some terrorist actions might be fueled by legitimate grievances, or when the FCC imposes heavy fines on a network because a female entertainer's breast was accidentally bared during a broadcast. Given majority approval of such restraints on the press, especially in times of crisis, it is difficult to predict how much freedom the trustee system will grant to the press in the future. The thrust of social pressures will decide that issue.[47]

Areas Most in Need of Reforms

The new communications technologies require a far more complete rethinking of the scope and purpose of federal regulation of broadcast media than has happened thus far. The Telecommunications Act of 1996 is inadequate for dealing with the revolutionary technological changes. There is a dire need for major policy innovations.

In the legacy media realm, the difference in treatment between the unregulated print media and the regulated electronic media has become highly questionable. It was based on the assumption that there would be numerous competing newspapers in the United States, while broadcast channels were scarce, so that the forces of competition could not work properly to make the airways an open market place of ideas. In reality, competition has been rising among broadcasters, especially with the proliferation of cable television and Internet sources. Meanwhile competition among daily newspapers has lessened.

There is no longer any merit in the argument that the scarcity of a particular type of news transmission, along with its importance to the public good, should be the litmus test for determining regulation policies. The distinctions made among publication formats are equally outdated. For example, many newspapers are now available in print and broadcast versions. Should the print version be free from controls, while the Web version is regulated, or vice versa? If the latter, the price of progress in electronic transmission of printed news could be the loss of freedom from government regulation.

Total deregulation of television broadcasts and reliance on traditional First Amendment values is not a realistic policy option in the United States for the foreseeable future. Opponents of deregulation contend that the impact of television on public life in the United States is so profound that the public interest requires controls. Even when competition is ample, it may be necessary to mandate access for neglected viewpoints and to provide programming for ignored audiences, such as children, who also need protection from unwholesome information. Insurmountable opposition to total deregulation makes it essential to think in terms of a complete overhaul of the policies adopted in the 1996 Telecommunications Act.

The outcome of such an overhaul is impossible to predict because the forces favoring regulation and the forces favoring deregulation are fairly evenly matched. It is even hazardous to predict that the regulatory system will be revised to deal with public needs in the Internet age. Remember, there was a sixty-two-year gap between the Communications Act of 1934 and the 1996 act! The only safe prediction is that piecemeal skirmishes and full-scale assaults on regulatory policies will continue apace in the years to come.[48]

It is also reasonably safe to predict that there will be some regulation to cope with unsavory developments on the Internet.[49] The battles for regulation have already begun in the courts with lawsuits involving property rights to information published on the Internet. Publishers of music videos, for example, have sued, claiming violations of copyrights and piracy of their offerings. The government has passed rules that allow legal action against individuals or groups accused of virus attacks on e-mail messages, spamming, and fraud committed with Internet tools. There is also a good chance that new rules may make Web site owners responsible for the information that they allow to appear on their sites. While the concept of a limited number of curbs on Internet freedom of information has become accepted, we can expect lengthy and heated battles over the nature and extent of appropriate curbs and the means for enforcing them. There has been a good bit of discussion about "net neutrality" principles that would require the government to abstain from intervention when various stakeholders lobby for rules that would serve their interests.[50] But what that ultimately means in the reality of the Web 2.0 world is hard to guess.

THE SHAPE OF THE FUTURE

The trends outlined thus far are not the only ones ahead. Many other issues will require decisions that go far beyond resolving technical issues. The direction of communications policy is at stake and with it the tone and possibly the direction of U.S. politics in general. John M. Eger, a former director of the White House Office of Telecommunications Policy, once remarked that the United States was "moving into a future rich in innovation and in social change." But this meant that the country was also moving into a storm center of new world problems. The new technologies are "a force for change throughout the world that simply will not be stopped, no matter how it is resisted." And then he asked, "Are we ready for the consequences of this change? Are we prepared to consider the profound social, legal, economic, and political effects of technology around the world?"[51]

Currently, the answer is no. In the communications field, the structure for policy making at all government levels is fragmented and ill-suited to deal with the existing problems, to say nothing of those that must be anticipated. Policies are improvised when pressures become strong, yielding in a crazy quilt pattern to various industry concerns, to public interest groups, to domestic or foreign policy considerations, to the pleas of engineers and lawyers, and to the suggestions of political scientists and economists. Narrow issues are addressed, but the full scope of the situation is ignored. As Neuman has noted, "The concept of a comprehensive industrial policy or even a broadly focused reformulation of communications policy for the information age is political anathema in the centers of power."[52] The decades-long struggle over the 1996 Telecommunications Act and over subsequent amendments proves that this assessment is unfortunately correct.

SUMMARY

Many people are dissatisfied with the performance of the mass media, including the Internet. Critics can and do air their dissatisfaction through formal and informal channels, but criticism usually has had limited success in bringing reforms. To fill the gaps left by the major legacy media, numerous alternative media have been created. These media either serve demographically distinct populations or cater to particular substantive concerns or political orientations. Two opposing trends have been simultaneously at work. One is a trend toward concentration of media power in the hands of a few huge corporations; the other is a trend toward multiplication of news suppliers and fragmentation of news audiences.

In this chapter we explored the social and political consequences of technological advances affecting mass media and outlined the areas in which new public policies are needed. We briefly sketched the political roles played by the medley of print media, over-the-air and cable television, and the Internet. We discussed the political and economic obstacles that media based on new technologies must overcome to compete against established competitors. We also outlined several looming problems and hailed the arrival of the age of broadcast plenty. The impact of these changes on life and politics in the United States could be enormous unless resistance to the pace of change slows progress. Fragmentation of the broadcast audience has raised fears of political balkanization and breakdown of the national political consensus that has been deemed essential for successful democratic governance. The reality has been far less grim. There has been increasing political polarization, but the news media's role in that development has been comparatively minor.

Changes in regulatory policy are in progress to integrate the new broadcast and narrowcast technologies into the existing mass media regulatory structure. But a total overhaul of the current policy regime is unlikely. The forces favoring greater government control of media content continue to be strong because the public is afraid that some news providers will abuse their powers and harm public interests. Whatever the outcome, the debate about media regulation and deregulation needs to safeguard First Amendment rights in the century that lies ahead. Freeing the electronic media from government supervision will undoubtedly lead to some misbehaviors and abuses. But that may be the lesser evil if more government regulation is the alternative. As Thomas Jefferson wrote to his colleague Edward Carrington in 1787, "Were it left to me to decide whether we should have a government without newspapers or newspapers without a government, I should not hesitate a moment to prefer the latter."[53]

NOTES

1. The authors were Jens L. Franzen, Philip D. Gingerich, Jörg Habersetzer, Jørn H. Hurum, Wighart von Koenigswald, and B. Holly Smith, "Complete Primate Skeleton from the Middle Eocene of Messel in Germany: Morphology and Paleobiology," *PLoS ONE* 4, no. 5: e5723, May 19, 2009, www.plosone.org/article/info:doi/10.1371/journal.pone.0005723. This is an open-access article distributed under the terms of the Creative Commons Attribution License, which permits unrestricted use, distribution, and reproduction in any medium, provided the original author and source are credited.

2. Tim Arango, "Seeking a Missing Link, and a Mass Audience," *New York Times*, May 19, 2009; Michael D. Lemonick, "Ida: Humankind's Earliest Ancestor! (Not Really)," *Time*, May 21, 2009, www.time.com/time/printout/0.8816.1900057.00.html.

3. Pew Research Center for the People and the Press, "The News and Daily Life," August 17, 2008, http://people-press.org/report/?pageid=1352.

4. Michael Schudson, "Orientations: The Press and Democracy in Time and Space," in *Institutions of American Democracy: The Press*, ed. Geneva Overholser and Kathleen Hall Jamieson (New York: Oxford University Press, 2005), 1–3.

5. Pew Research Center for the People and the Press, "Financial Woes Now Overshadow All Other Concerns for Journalists," March 17, 2008, http://people-press.org/report/?pageid=1269.

6. Ibid.; the survey was conducted September 17 to December 3, 2007.

7. Ibid.

8. Pew Research Center for the People and the Press, "The Web: Alarming, Appealing and a Challenge to Journalistic Values," March 17, 2008, www.stateofthemedia.org/2008/Journalist%20report%202008.pdf.

9. Project for Excellence in Journalism, "The State of the News Media, 2008," Citizen Media, www.stateofthemedia.org/2008/Journalist%20report%202008.pdf.

10. Ibid.

11. Amanda Lenhart and Susannah Fox, "Blogs," Internet and American Life Project, July 19, 2006, www.pewinternet.org/Commentary/2008/July/New-numbers-for-blogging-and-blog-readership.aspx?list=1&listtype=relatedresearch.

12. Pew Research Center for the People and the Press, "Key News Audiences Now Blend Online and Traditional Sources," August 17, 2008, http://people-press.org/report/444/news-media.

13. For an excellent comparative analysis of these issues, see Pippa Norris, *A Virtuous Circle: Political Communications in Postindustrial Societies* (Cambridge, UK: Cambridge University Press, 2000).

14. Robert M. Entman, "The Nature and Sources of News," in *Institutions of American Democracy: The Press*, ed. Overholser and Jamieson, 48–65. Entman identifies four types of journalism: traditional, advocacy, tabloid, and entertainment, each characterized by distinctive organizational values and missions.

15. Pew Research Center for the People and the Press, "Key News Audiences Now Blend Online and Traditional Sources," August 17, 2008, http://people-press.org/report/?pageid=1355.

16. John W. Johnstone, Edward J. Slawski, and William W. Bowman, *The Newspeople* (Urbana: University of Illinois Press, 1976), 157–179; and Project for Excellence in Journalism, "The State of the News Media: Ethnic/Alternative," http://stateofthenewsmedia.org/2005.

17. They are described more fully in Johnstone, Slawski, and Bowman, *The Newspeople*, 157–181; Laurence Leamer, *The Paper Revolutionaries: The Rise of the Underground Press* (New York: Simon and Schuster, 1972); and Jack A. Nelson, "The Underground Press," in *Readings in Mass Communication*, ed. Michael C. Emery and Ted Curtis Smythe (Dubuque, Iowa: W.C. Brown, 1972), 212–226.

18. The reasons for this situation are explained by David Waterman, "The Failure of Cultural Programming on Cable TV: An Economic Interpretation," *Journal of Communication* 36 (Summer 1986): 92–107. Also see Robert M. Entman and Steven S. Wildman, "Reconciling Economic and Non-Economic Perspectives in Media Policy: Transcending the 'Marketplace of Ideas,'" *Journal of Communication* 42 (Winter 1992).

19. John Tierney and Jacques Steinberg, "Conservatives and Rivals Press a Struggling PBS," *New York Times*, February 17, 2005.

20. W. Russell Neuman, *The Future of the Mass Audience* (New York: Cambridge University Press, 1991), ix–x.

21. W. Russell Neuman, "Globalization and the New Media," in *The Politics of News, the News of Politics*, 2nd ed., ed. Doris A. Graber (Washington, D.C.: CQ Press, 2008), 230–246, at 230.

22. Project for Excellence in Journalism, "The State of the News Media: Online: Conclusions," http://stateofthenewsmedia.org/2005; University of Southern California, "The Digital Future Report: Surveying the Digital Future, Year Four," 2004, www.digitalcenter.org. Like the studies produced by the Project for Excellence in Journalism, this study has been updated annually. The Poynter Institute and Stanford University have combined forces for a long-range study of Internet audiences. Reports are posted at www.poynterextra.org.

23. Pew Research Center for the People and the Press, "New Blog Readership Numbers from PEW Internet Study," June 23, 2008, www.labnol.org/internet/blogging/blog-readership-pew-internet-survey/3960/.

24. Pew Research Center for the People and the Press, "Internet's Broader Role in Campaign 2008: Social Networking and Online Videos Take Off," January 11, 2008, http://people-press.org/report/384/.

25. Pew Research Center for the People and the Press. "The Web: Alarming, Appealing and a Challenge."

26. David Talbot, "The Geeks behind Obama's Web Strategy," *Boston Globe*, January 8, 2009, www.boston.com/news/politics/2008/articles/2009/01/08/the_geeks_behind_obamas_web_strategy/?page=3.

27. Heather E. Hudson, "Implications for Development Communications," *Journal of Communication* 29 (Winter 1979): 179–186. Also see Bella Mody, Joseph D. Straubhaar, and Johannes M. Bauer, *Telecommunications Politics: Ownership and Control of the Information Highway in Developing Countries* (Hillsdale, N.J.: Erlbaum, 1995).

28. James G. Webster, "Audience Behavior in the New Media Environment," *Journal of Communication* 36 (Summer 1986): 77–91.

29. Lawrence K. Grossman, *The Electronic Republic: Reshaping Democracy in the Information Age* (New York: Viking, 1995).

30. W. Russell Neuman, *The Future of the Mass Audience* (New York: Cambridge University Press, 1991), 58–63; Pew Internet and American Life Project, "The Internet and Democratic Debate," October 27, 2004, www.pewinternet.org/~/media//Files/Reports/2004/PIP_Political_Info_Report.pdf.

31. W. Russell Neuman, Lee McKnight, and Richard Jay Solomon, *The Gordian Knot: Political Gridlock on the Information Highway* (Cambridge, Mass.: MIT Press, 1996); Helen Nissenbaum and Monroe Price, eds., *Academy and the Internet* (New York: Peter Lang, 2004); Lincoln Dahlberg, "Democracy via Cyberspace: Mapping the Rhetorics and Practices of Three Prominent Camps," *New Media and Society* 3, no. 2 (2004): 157–177.

32. Use of cable television is compared with use of other media in Gerald L. Grotta and Doug Newsom, "How Does Cable Television in the Home Relate to Other Media Use Patterns?" *Journalism Quarterly* 59 (Winter 1982): 588–591, 609. Also see "Cable TV," *Consumer Reports* 52 (September 1987): 547–554.

33. Doris A. Graber, Bruce Bimber, W. Lance Bennett, Richard Davis, and Pippa Norris, "The Internet and Politics: Emerging Perspectives," in *Academy and the Internet*, ed. Nissenbaum and Price, 35–70.

34. Richard Campbell, Christopher R. Martin, and Bettina Fabos, *Media and Culture*, 6th ed. (Boston: Bedford/St. Martin's, 2008). Google, for example, ranks its listings by their popularity, judged by how many other pages are linked to them. That puts small enterprises, featured well below the leaders, at a self-perpetuating disadvantage.

35. David Sharos, "HDTV Clearly Becoming the Standard to Watch," *Chicago Tribune*, July 31, 2004.

36. Hernan Galperin, *New Television, Old Politics: The Transition to Digital TV in the United States and Britain* (Cambridge, UK: Cambridge University Press, 2004); Joelle Tessler, "Congress Delays Digital TV Transfer to June," *ABC4.com*, June 8, 2009, www.abc4.com/content/about_4/dtv/story/UPDATE-Congress-delays-digital-TV-transfer-to-June/MTfMwYEnx0Cl1A863-6KUA.cspx .

37. Felicity Barringer, "Leading Media Companies Forming Joint Web Venture," *New York Times*, November 18, 1999.

38. Vincent Mosco, "Une Drôle de Guerre," *Media Studies Journal* 6 (Spring 1992): 56–60.

39. Thomas E. Patterson, "Creative Destruction: An Exploratory Look at News on the Internet," Joan Shorenstein Center on the Press, Politics, and Public Policy, John F. Kennedy School of Government, Harvard University, August 2007.

40. *Home Box Office, Inc. v. FCC*, 567 F.2d 9 (D.C. Cir.), *cert. denied*, 434 U.S. 829 (1977); and *FCC v. Midwest Video Corp.*, 440 U.S. 689 (1979).

41. Pay television had been freed from federal controls in 1977. Remaining federal controls were dropped by 1979. Benjamin M. Compaine and Douglas Gomery, *Who Owns the Media? Concentration and Ownership in the Mass Communications Industry*, 3rd ed., Mahwah, N.J.: Erlbaum, 2000; "Cable TV," *Consumer Reports*.

42. Edmund L. Andrews, "Hopes of Cable Industry Ride on Veto by Bush," *New York Times*, July 25, 1992. Also see Warren Communications News, *Television and Cable Factbook*, 2000, www.warren-news.com/factbook.htm, and subsequent annual versions.

43. FCC regulations prevail over conflicting state regulations; see *Capital Cities Cable v. Crisp,* 104 U.S. 2694 (1984). Federal law may preempt state laws; see William E. Hanks and Stephen E. Coran, "Federal Preemption of Obscenity Law Applied to Cable Television," *Journalism Quarterly* 63 (Spring 1986): 43–47.

44. Henry Geller, "Mass Communications Policy: Where We Are and Where We Should Be Going," in *Democracy and the Mass Media,* ed. Judith Lichtenberg (New York: Cambridge University Press, 1990), 290–329.

45. *FCC v. Midwest Video Corp.,* 440 U.S. 689 (1979).

46. "Cable TV," *Consumer Reports,* 555.

47. Doris A. Graber, "Terrorism, Censorship, and the First Amendment," in *Framing Terrorism: The News Media, the Government, and the Public,* ed. Pippa Norris, Montague Kern, and Marion Just (New York: Routledge, 2003), 27–42.

48. Jeff Chester, "Strict Scrutiny: Why Journalists Should Be Concerned about New Federal and Industry Deregulation Proposals," *Press/Politics* 7, no. 2 (2002): 105–115.

49. Nate Anderson, "The Future of the Internet is…Regulation?" *Ars Technica,* February 10, 2009, http://arstechnica.com/tech-policy/news/2009/02/the-future-of-the-internet-is-regulation.ars .

50. Matthew Lasar, "Senator to FCC: Time for Black-and-White Net Neutrality Rules," *Ars Technica,* May 6, 2009, http://arstechnica.com/tech-policy/news/2009/05/senator-pressures-fcc-on-net-neutrality.ars

51. John M. Eger, "A Time of Decision," *Journal of Communication* 29 (Winter 1979): 204–207.

52. Neuman, *The Future of the Mass Audience,* x.

53. Paul Leicester Ford, ed., *Writings of Thomas Jefferson,* vol. 5 (New York: Putnam's, 1894), 253.

READINGS

Anderson, Bonnie M. *News Flash: Infotainment and the Bottom-Line Business of Broadcast News.* San Francisco: Jossey-Bass, 2004.

Bimber, Bruce. *Information and American Democracy.* Cambridge, UK: Cambridge University Press, 2002.

Coleman, Stephen, and Jay G. Blumler. *The Internet and Democratic Citizenship: Theory, Practice and Policy.* New York: Cambridge University Press, 2009.

Davis, Richard, Diana Owen, David Taras, and Stephen Ward, eds. *Making a Difference: A Comparative View of the Role of the Internet in Election Politics.* Lanham, Md.: Rowman and Littlefield, 2008.

Ferguson, Charles. *The Broadband Problem: Anatomy of a Market Failure and a Policy Dilemma.* Washington, D.C.: Brookings Institution Press, 2004.

McChesney, Robert W. *The Political Economy of Media: Enduring Issues, Emerging Dilemmas.* New York: Monthly Review Press, 2008.

Mullen, Megan. *The Rise of Cable Programming in the United States: Revolution or Evolution?* Austin: University of Texas Press, 2003.

Norris, Pippa. *Digital Divide: Civic Engagement, Information Poverty, and the Internet in Democratic Societies.* Cambridge, UK: Cambridge University Press, 2002.

Ramey, Carl R. *How Washington Policymakers Shortchanged the American Public.* Lanham, Md.: Rowman and Littlefield, 2007.

Rettberg, Jill Walker. *Blogging.* Malden, Mass.: Polity Press, 2008.

Index

Boxes, figures, notes, and tables are indicated by b, f, n, and t after the page number.